The Palace Beautiful

Monographs in Baptist History

VOLUME 31

SERIES EDITOR
Michael A. G. Haykin, The Southern Baptist Theological Seminary

EDITORIAL BOARD
Matthew Barrett, Midwestern Baptist Theological Seminary
Peter Beck, Charleston Southern University
Anthony L. Chute, California Baptist University
Jason G. Duesing, Midwestern Baptist Theological Seminary
Nathan A. Finn, North Greenville University
Crawford Gribben, Queen's University, Belfast
Gordon L. Heath, McMaster Divinity College
Barry Howson, Heritage Theological Seminary
Jason K. Lee, Cedarville University
Thomas J. Nettles, The Southern Baptist Theological Seminary, retired
James A. Patterson, Union University
James M. Renihan, Institute of Reformed Baptist Studies
Jeffrey P. Straub, Independent Scholar
Brian R. Talbot, Broughty Ferry Baptist Church, Scotland
Malcolm B. Yarnell III, Southwestern Baptist Theological Seminary

Ours is a day in which not only the gaze of western culture but also increasingly that of Evangelicals is riveted to the present. The past seems to be nowhere in view and hence it is disparagingly dismissed as being of little value for our rapidly changing world. Such historical amnesia is fatal for any culture, but particularly so for Christian communities whose identity is profoundly bound up with their history. The goal of this new series of monographs, Studies in Baptist History, seeks to provide one of these Christian communities, that of evangelical Baptists, with reasons and resources for remembering the past. The editors are deeply convinced that Baptist history contains rich resources of theological reflection, praxis and spirituality that can help Baptists, as well as other Christians, live more Christianly in the present. The monographs in this series will therefore aim at illuminating various aspects of the Baptist tradition and in the process provide Baptists with a usable past.

The Palace Beautiful

The Evangelical Independent Ecclesiology of John Bunyan

Timothy M. Haupt

Foreword by Jason G. Duesing

☙PICKWICK *Publications* · Eugene, Oregon

THE PALACE BEAUTIFUL
The Evangelical Independent Ecclesiology of John Bunyan

Monographs in Baptist History 31

Copyright © 2025 Timothy M. Haupt. All rights reserved. Except for brief quotations in critical publications or reviews, no part of this book may be reproduced in any manner without prior written permission from the publisher. Write: Permissions, Wipf and Stock Publishers, 199 W. 8th Ave., Suite 3, Eugene, OR 97401.

Pickwick Publications
An Imprint of Wipf and Stock Publishers
199 W. 8th Ave., Suite 3
Eugene, OR 97401

www.wipfandstock.com

PAPERBACK ISBN: 979-8-3852-3669-5
HARDCOVER ISBN: 979-8-3852-3670-1
EBOOK ISBN: 979-8-3852-3671-8

Cataloguing-in-Publication data:

Names: Haupt, Timothy M., author. | Duesing, Jason G., foreword.

Title: The palace beautiful : the evangelical independent ecclesiology of John Bunyan / by Timothy M. Haupt ; foreword by Jason G. Duesing.

Description: Eugene, OR : Pickwick Publications, 2025 | Series: Monographs in Baptist History 31 | Includes bibliographical references and index(es).

Identifiers: ISBN 979-8-3852-3669-5 (paperback) | ISBN 979-8-3852-3670-1 (hardcover) | ISBN 979-8-3852-3671-8 (ebook)

Subjects: LCSH: Bunyan, John, 1628–1688. | Bunyan, John, 1628–1688—Criticism and interpretation. | Church.

Classification: PR3332 .H31 2025 (paperback) | PR3332 (ebook)

VERSION NUMBER 06/20/25

To my fellow pilgrims, the saints of First Baptist Nixa.

We have found the Wicket Gate,
We tread the King's Highway,
We are bound for the Celestial City,
Together.

He lift up his eyes, and behold there was a very stately Palace before him, the name whereof was *Beautiful*; . . .

Then said *Christian* to the *Porter*, Sir, What house is this? and may I lodge here to night? The *Porter* answered, This House was built by the Lord of the Hill: and he built it for the relief and security of Pilgrims.

Contents

Acknowledgments | ix
Foreword by Jason G. Duesing | xi

CHAPTER 1
Was Bunyan a Baptist? A Critical Question of Baptist Identity | 1

CHAPTER 2
Bunyan and the Bedford Church: The Origin of
   Bunyan's Ecclesiology | 43

CHAPTER 3
The Palace Beautiful: Bunyan's Evangelical Independent Ecclesiology | 71

CHAPTER 4
Bunyan vs. the Baptists: The Communion Controversy | 141

CHAPTER 5
Strict Communion and Seventeenth-Century Baptist Identity | 205

CHAPTER 6
Evangelical Independent: A Reevaluation of
   Bunyan's Ecclesiological Identity | 279

Bibliography | 301
Author Index | 319
Subject Index | 323

Acknowledgments

Just as Christian did not arrive at the Celestial City alone, but was aided and abetted by numerous figures along the King's Highway, neither have I brought this manuscript to publication on my own. Those who have strengthened and encouraged me throughout this project are too numerous to mention, but I will attempt to highlight a few.

I dedicate this study of Bunyan's ecclesiology to the saints of First Baptist Nixa, my fellow pilgrims and my Palace Beautiful, whom I have had the pleasure of pastoring for eleven years and counting. My gratitude to this church cannot be overstated. When I approached the congregation in 2018 about my desire to pursue a PhD, they not only graciously encouraged me in the endeavor, but generously paid my tuition. They have provided me with time for research and writing, and have indulged my love for Bunyan in a number of ways. One of our elders joked that no one is permitted to preach from our pulpit unless his sermon contains at least one Bunyan reference. While that may not be the official policy, Bunyan does cast a long shadow across our church, and we are the better for it.

I must also express my profound debt of gratitude to Dr. Jason Duesing, Provost of Midwestern Baptist Theological Seminary, who supervised my dissertation and guided me through my doctoral studies. Dr. Duesing refers to himself as a "blue-collar scholar," which is his self-effacing way of humbling himself before those scholars who publish best-selling, groundbreaking works of scholarship. While it is true that the majority of Dr. Duesing's career has been devoted to the work of education rather than publication, he is a first-rate church historian and one of the kindest men I

Acknowledgments

have ever known. I will be ever grateful for his influence upon my life, and for his steady hand at the helm of MBTS.

I also wish to thank Dr. Jason Lee, Professor of Theological Studies at Cedarville University, who served as the second reader of my dissertation. His vast knowledge of Baptist history and ecclesiology has shaped my thinking on these topics in immeasurable ways. I am grateful for his input and interaction with this project.

I am grateful to Dr. Charlie Collier and the team at Wipf & Stock, who guided me through the publication process and helped to bring this manuscript to print. Thank you as well to Dr. Michael Haykin for including this book in the Monographs in Baptist History series. I have benefited from many of the volumes in this series, and I am honored to have my work included among them.

In the first part of *The Pilgrim's Progress*, Christian's family functions as a hindrance to his pilgrimage. They do not understand his sense of conviction, nor the necessity of going on pilgrimage. I suspect that upon reflection, Bunyan regretted the aspersions this unintentionally cast upon his own wife and children. Thus, in the second part, Christiana plays the role of the faithful heroine, lovingly and loyally leading her children along the King's Highway. This was certainly a more accurate portrait of Bunyan's home life. My own experience resonates with this latter portrait as well. I have been blessed to share twenty years with my own Christiana. To Ashley, and our four beautiful children—Abby, Benjamin, Isaac, and Susanna—thank you for your faithful love and steadfast encouragement.

Above all, I am grateful to the Triune God from whom all blessings flow. May this book glorify Jesus and benefit his church. "To him be the glory in the church and in Christ Jesus throughout all generations, forever and ever. Amen" (Eph 3:21).

Timothy M. Haupt
New Year's Eve, 2024

Foreword

JUST A FEW MILES north of St. Paul's Cathedral in London there is a cemetery that dates to the fourteenth century. It lacks the grandeur of Christopher Wren's architectural masterpiece and, indeed, the precise location of many of those buried there have been lost in history via German bombing in World War II.

Originally called "Bonehill," this cemetery developed in the seventeenth century as a resting place for Nonconforming Dissenters from the Church of England. These Separatists, Independents, and Baptists, parted ways with the State Church bound by their consciences and, thus, were not privy to more formal spaces.

Eventually, the graveyard took on the name Bunhill Fields and close to 6,000 from this early era found it as their final place of rest. The funeral of the Separatist, Samuel Eaton, was one of the first recorded in August 1639 and is said to have brought the attendance of over 200 Separatists and Baptists. He was joined by the godfather of the English Particular Baptists, Henry Jessey, also with a large funeral of devoted friends in 1663.

The English Baptists who served to shape much of the foundational 1644 London Confession and the 1689 Second London Confession, William Kiffin and Hanserd Knollys are buried there though the precise location of their graves has long been lost.

Yet, John Bunyan lies at the center of the cemetery in a visible tomb for all pilgrims to see.

Charles Spurgeon, the famous nineteenth-century English Baptist pastor, loved John Bunyan. Acquainted with Bunyan's writings since his youth, Spurgeon read *Pilgrim's Progress* over one-hundred times. His devotion to

Foreword

Bunyan no doubt led him to Bunhill Fields, and on one occasion, Spurgeon mentioned Bunyan's tomb in a sermon:

> Go into Bunhill-fields, and stand by the memorial of John Bunyan, and you will say, "Ah! there lies the head that contained the brain which thought out that wondrous dream of the Pilgrim's Progress from the City of Destruction to the Better land. There lies the finger that wrote those wondrous lines which depict the story of him who came at last to the land Beulah, and waded through the flood, and entered into the celestial city. And there are the eyelids which he once spoke of, when he said, 'If I lie in prison until the moss grows on my eyelids, I will never make a promise to withhold from preaching.' And there is that bold eye that penetrated the judge, when he said, 'If you will let me out of prison to-day, I will preach again to-morrow, by the help of God.' And there lies that loving hand that was ever ready to receive into communion all them that loved the Lord Jesus Christ: I love the hand that wrote the book, *Water Baptism no Bar to Christian Communion*. I love him for that sake alone, and if he had written nothing else but that, I would say, 'John Bunyan, be honored for ever.' And there lies the foot that carried him up Snow Hill to go and make peace between a father and a son, in that cold day, which cost him his life. Peace to his ashes! Wait, O John Bunyan, till thy Master sends his angel to blow the trumpet; and methinks, when the archangel sounds it, he will almost think of thee, and this shall be a part of his joy, that honest John Bunyan, the greatest of all Englishmen, shall rise from his tomb at the blowing of that great trump."[1]

Despite the value Spurgeon saw in visiting Bunyan's tomb, any attempt to heed Spurgeon's advice is fraught with challenges. Even if one were to visit London, Bunhill Fields is not included in many city tours and, while able to be found, is still unknown to many. Nevertheless, Bunyan's life and ministry is worth memorializing whether one can stand at his tomb or not.

This is one of the many reasons I am grateful for the publication of Timothy Haupt's *The Palace Beautiful*. For in this book, you will see how Bunyan dedicated his life to the building of the household of God, built on the foundation of the apostles and prophets, with Christ Jesus himself being the cornerstone (Eph 2:20). As you read, I hope you will find yourself

---

1. Spurgeon, "Wicked Man's Life."

Foreword

joining with Spurgeon in giving thanks for this servant of Christ, John Bunyan.

Jason G. Duesing
Provost and Professor of Historical Theology
Midwestern Baptist Theological Seminary

January 2025

Chapter 1

Was Bunyan a Baptist? A Critical Question of Baptist Identity

Thus he went on his way, but while he was thus bewayling his unhappy miscarriage, he lift up his eyes, and behold there was a very stately Palace before him, the name whereof was *Beautiful*, and it stood just by the High-way side.... Then said *Christian* to the *Porter*, Sir, What house is this? and may I lodge here to night? The *Porter* answered, This House was built by the Lord of the Hill: and he built it for the relief and security of Pilgrims.[1]

---

1. Bunyan, *Pilgrim's Progress*, 1:45–47. This monograph employs the Oxford edition of Bunyan's works, including W. R. Owens's 2003 update of Roger Sharrock's original 1960 edition of *The Pilgrim's Progress* and John Stachniewski and Anita Pacheco's 1998 update of Roger Sharrock's original 1962 edition of *Grace Abounding to the Chief of Sinners*. All works of Bunyan will be cited by author, title, *Miscellaneous Works* volume (if applicable), and page number. Additionally, since Part One (1678) and Part Two (1684) of *The Pilgrim's Progress* were originally published six years apart yet are included in the same Oxford volume, it will be noted whether the citation is from Part One or Part Two. Thus, the citation above is rendered Bunyan, *Pilgrim's Progress*, 1:45–47. Spelling, punctuation, italicization, and capitalization of all primary sources have been left in the original form.

The Palace Beautiful

Statement of Thesis

JOHN BUNYAN WAS NOT the first to write allegorical theology, but he has without a doubt been the most influential.[2] For three and a half centuries, the vivid characters, locations, and events of *The Pilgrim's Progress* have shaped the way readers think about the Christian life. Few works outside of the Bible have so transcended generational, cultural, and denominational lines.[3] Christopher Hill famously wrote, "Just as Oliver Cromwell aimed to bring about the kingdom of God on earth and founded the British Empire, so Bunyan wanted the millennium and got the novel. The tinker's books lasted longer than anyone else's preaching: longer in fact, than

---

2. Roger Pooley argues that Protestants had a long history of allegory prior to Bunyan: "The line of Protestant allegory runs through high culture and popular culture alike. There is Edmund Spenser, whose *Faerie Queene* (1590-6) with its complex, layered allegory based on the Book of Revelation as much as Arthurian legend Bunyan was once thought to have read [Pooley later states that most of the supposed parallels 'can be ascribed to Bunyan's self-confessed reading in prose chivalric romances']. There is Richard Bernard, whose *The Isle of Man* was immensely popular from its first publication in 1626, and has affinities with some of the central allegorical devices of *The Holy War* (1680) as well as the journey motif of *The Pilgrim's Progress*; and there is the Leveller Richard Overton's *The Araignement of Mr Persecution* (1645), whose satiric portrait of a prejudiced jury may have suggested some of the names of the jury in Vanity Fair" (Pooley, "*Pilgrim's Progress* and the Line of Allegory," 83, 93n10). George Offor, in his lengthy introduction to *The Pilgrim's Progress*, surveyed over fifty works of allegory that preceded Bunyan's magnum opus, though his purpose was to demonstrate the originality and superiority of Bunyan's allegory (Offor, *Works of John Bunyan*, 3:29-55; see also Forrest, "Allegory as Sacred Sport," 93-112). Bunyan, of course, argued that allegorical theology originated in Scripture—e.g., The Song of Solomon, portions of Daniel and Revelation, and the parables of Jesus. In his prefatory apology to *The Pilgrim's Progress*, Bunyan appealed to the example of the prophets, as well as to Christ and his apostles, stating that *"holy Writ . . . Is every where so full of all these things, (Dark Figures, Allegories)"* (Bunyan, *Pilgrim's Progress*, 1:6).

3. For the reception history of *The Pilgrim's Progress*, see Keeble, "Of Him Thousands," 241-63; Owens, "Reception of *The Pilgrim's Progress*," 91-104; Alblas, "Reception of *The Pilgrim's Progress*," 121-32; Greaves, *Glimpses of Glory*, 610-34; Hofmeyr, *Portable Bunyan*, 11-41; Newey, "Bunyan's Afterlives," 25-48; Walker, "Bunyan's Reception in the Romantic Period," 49-67; Hammond, "*Pilgrim's Progress* and its Nineteenth-Century Publishers," 99-118; Sim, "Bunyan and His Fundamentalist Readers," 213-28; Wall, "Bunyan and the Early Novel," 521-36; Rivers, "*Pilgrim's Progress* in the Evangelical Revival," 537-54; Shears, "Bunyan and the Romantics," 555-72; Newey, "Bunyan and the Victorians," 573-89; Rasmussen, "Bunyan and America," 590-607; Brown, "Bunyan and Empire," 665-81.

the British Empire."[4] David Calhoun summarizes the worldwide impact of *The Pilgrim's Progress*:

> Twenty-two editions of *The Pilgrim's Progress* had been published by 1700, 70 by 1800, and more than 1,300 by 1938. Until recently the sales of no other book except the Bible have exceeded it. It has followed the Bible to almost every land and has been translated into over two hundred languages. Isabel Hofmeyr's *The Portable Bunyan: A Transnational History of the Pilgrim's Progress* describes how Bunyan's book was translated into eighty African languages during the nineteenth century. In 1986, 200,000 copies of *The Pilgrim's Progress* printed in Chinese by the government of the People's Republic of China as a sample of western literature and culture sold out in three days.[5]

While many know Bunyan for his famous allegories *The Pilgrim's Progress* and *The Holy War*, as well as his renowned autobiography *Grace Abounding to the Chief of Sinners*, comparatively few are familiar with his vast corpus of doctrinal treatises, polemical writings, and lengthy biblical expositions.[6] Although overshadowed by his more celebrated contempo-

---

4. Hill, *Tinker and a Poor Man*, 368.

5. Calhoun, *Grace Abounding*, 193. In his concluding chapter on the enduring legacy of Bunyan, Calhoun provides a number of quotations and anecdotes in praise of Bunyan from the pantheon of great British and American authors: Jonathan Swift, Samuel Johnson, Sir Walter Scott, Samuel Taylor Coleridge, Daniel Defoe, Charles Dickens, Herman Melville, William Makepeace Thackeray, Charlotte Brontë, George Eliot, Walt Whitman, Robert Browning, Rudyard Kipling, Robert Louis Stevenson, George Bernard Shaw, and C. S. Lewis. Shaw wrote an essay in which he argued that Bunyan was "Better than Shakespeare" (Shaw, "Better than Shakespeare," 143, cited in Calhoun, *Grace Abounding*, 191). Kipling's "The Holy War" paid homage to the Tinker:

A Tinker out of Bedford,
A vagrant oft in quod,
A private under Fairfax,
A minister of God ...
A pedlar from a hovel,
The lowest of the low—
The Father of the Novel,
Salvation's first Defoe.

(Kipling, "Holy War," 234–35, quoted in Calhoun, *Grace Abounding*, 191).

6. Michael Davies locates *Grace Abounding* in a long line of conversion narratives reaching back to Augustine's *Confessions*, and he writes that *Grace Abounding* "remains still the most engaging and affecting of all Puritan spiritual autobiographies" (Davies,

raries John Owen and Richard Baxter, Bunyan was one of the most prolific theologians of seventeenth-century England, publishing over sixty works, most of which are of a doctrinal, polemical, or experimental nature. Bunyan's was not a scholastic theology for the academy, formulated in the ivory towers of Oxford or Cambridge. His was an exegetical theology for the church, forged in the fires of Restoration-era Nonconformity. Bunyan's primary concern lay in the realm of soteriology; justification by grace through faith in the imputed righteousness of Christ was his constant refrain. Nevertheless, his most influential and lasting contribution may lie in the realm of ecclesiology.

During the 1670s, a heated debate erupted between Bunyan and a number of influential Baptists over the terms of communion.[7] The debate centered upon the question of whether a paedobaptist should be received into the membership of a visible church and admitted to the Lord's Supper. Bunyan argued strongly in the affirmative; the Baptists argued just as vehemently in the negative. Was this debate merely a quarrel among fellow Baptists about a secondary matter of church practice, or was this a dispute over fundamentally disparate ecclesiologies?

The communion controversy represents the eruption of tensions that had been building since the emergence of the Particular Baptist movement three decades earlier, and the issue has reemerged in every century of Baptist history since. What theological commitments and contextual factors drove each side to their respective ecclesiological conclusions? Was open communion a recognized seventeenth-century Baptist position? Should John Bunyan be considered a seventeenth-century Baptist? And if not, how should Bunyan be understood, both historically and ecclesiologically?

"Grace Abounding," 67–79). See also Sharrock, "Spiritual Autobiography," 97–104; Hindmarsh, *Evangelical Conversion Narrative*, 50–58, 309–10.

7. In this monograph, "communion" is used in the sense in which Bunyan and his opponents employed the term, that is, in reference to membership in the local church together with its privileges, including admission to the Lord's Supper. Bunyan wrote that "by the word Communion I mean fellowship *in the things of the kingdom of Christ*, or that which is commonly called Church communion, the Communion of Saints" (Bunyan, *Confession of My Faith*, 4:154). Matthew Ward notes that for Bunyan and Kiffin, "'Fellowship,' and by extension 'communion,' is the rough equivalent of what we mean by 'membership' today" (Ward, "Baptism as Worship," 18). This monograph also distinguishes between "credobaptist" and "Baptist." The former is the broader term referring to those who hold the conviction that believers are the only proper subjects of baptism; the latter is the more restrictive term referring to those who believe credobaptists are the only proper subjects for church membership and participation in the Lord's Supper.

This monograph offers a systematic analysis of Bunyan's ecclesiology and a reevaluation of his ecclesiological identity. It argues that the controlling principle of Bunyan's ecclesiology was an evangelical unity grounded in a common evangelical faith and holiness, and that this principle determined Bunyan's ecumenical, open-communion views and brought him into irreconcilable conflict with seventeenth-century Baptists, whose controlling principle was ecclesiological purity.[8] In addition, by analyzing seventeenth-century Baptist confessions and the works of representative seventeenth-century Baptist theologians, this monograph demonstrates that strict communion was a seventeenth-century Baptist distinctive. Therefore, Bunyan should not be classified as a seventeenth-century Baptist. Rather, Bunyan's evangelical, ecumenical ecclesiology represents a unique contribution to the seventeenth-century ecclesiological landscape. Neither Baptist nor Congregationalist, the most accurate ecclesiological label for Bunyan and the network of open-communion churches among which he was the most influential voice is Evangelical Independent.

Relevance of Thesis

This monograph makes a contribution to three distinct yet interrelated fields of study: Bunyan scholarship, Baptist history, and Baptist ecclesiology.

Relevance to Bunyan Scholarship

First, this monograph contributes to Bunyan scholarship by offering the first comprehensive, systematic analysis of Bunyan's ecclesiology. Bunyan's doctrine of the church has received little attention relative to other areas

---

8. The identification of ecclesiological purity as the controlling principle of seventeenth-century Baptists is similar to the thesis of Matthew Ward in his monograph *Pure Worship: The Early English Baptist Distinctive*. Ward convincingly argues that pure worship according to Scripture is more plausible as the early Baptist distinctive than other suggestions that have been offered, such as credobaptism (W. H. Whitsitt, James Leo Garrett Jr.), regenerate church membership (Jeremiah Jeter, Robert Middleditch), soul competency (E. Y. Mullins), biblical authority (R. Stanton Norman, John Hammett), or, more recently, apocalypticism (Mark Bell). For the aforementioned works, see Whitsitt, *Question of Baptist History*; Garrett, "Restitution and Dissent," 198–210; Jeter, *Baptist Principles Reset*; Middleditch, *Baptist Church*; Mullins, *Axioms of Religion*; Norman, *Baptist Way*; Hammett, *Biblical Foundations for Baptist Churches*; Bell, *Apocalypse How?* The preceding list is from Ward's discussion on "the winding quest for a Baptist distinctive" in Ward, *Pure Worship*, 2–8.

of scholarly interest. Literary-critical analysis of Bunyan's allegorical and autobiographical works abounds.[9] Literary critics have given deserved attention to Bunyan the allegorist and proto-novelist, yet they have largely ignored Bunyan the theologian. To borrow the language of Coleridge, they have attempted to extricate (and perhaps liberate) the Bunyan of Parnassus from the Bunyan of the Conventicle.[10] Recent scholarship has begun to correct this error, recognizing that the Bunyan of Parnassus cannot be understood apart from the Bunyan of the Conventicle, for they are one and the same.[11] Additionally, older literary-critical scholarship tended to view Bunyan as a harbinger of modernism, whose works emphasized the modern,

9. For example, Keeble, *John Bunyan*; Collmer, *Bunyan in Our Time*; Dunan-Page, *Cambridge Companion to Bunyan*; Davies and Owens, *Oxford Handbook of John Bunyan*. The preceding volumes are collections of essays by leading Bunyan scholars, many of which offer contemporary literary analyses of Bunyan's works. These volumes provide a representative sample of literary-critical Bunyan scholarship. Journal articles and dissertations on Bunyan written from the literary-critical perspective are too numerous to mention.

10. In 1818, Samuel Coleridge glossed in the margin of *The Pilgrim's Progress*, "His piety was baffled by his genius, and the Bunyan of Parnassus had the better of the Bunyan of the Conventicle" (Coleridge, *Marginalia*, 801). Coleridge imagined a battlefield on which Bunyan the theologian and Bunyan the author were locked in a combat for supremacy. Often, the theologian won out and the result was (in the eyes of Coleridge) a dry doctrinal treatise fit only for the conventicle. But sometimes, particularly in his magnum opus, the Bunyan of Parnassus (the mythical home of the Muses) gained the upper hand, and the result was a work of literary genius. Coleridge would later conclude that the theologian and the author were never really at odds. In 1830, Coleridge praised *The Pilgrim's Progress* as "incomparably the best SUMMA THEOLOGIAE *Evangelicae* ever produced by a writer not miraculously inspired" (Coleridge, *Marginalia*, 814). Both references cited in Keeble, "Of Him Thousands," 255–56.

11. Two recent examples are Davies, *Graceful Reading*; Johnson, *Prisoner of Conscience*. See also Johnson, "Be Not Extream," 447–64. Davies argues that one cannot understand the literature of Bunyan apart from the Calvinistic ("grace-ful") theology of Bunyan, which, contrary to scholarly opinion, is not "harsh and inhumane," but rather "essentially comforting and accommodating" (Davies, *Graceful Reading*, 5). Davies writes, "Far from denying that a variety of interpretations of Bunyan's works is possible or even welcome, I simply argue that non-doctrinal readings can sometimes be inappropriate (if not pernicious, on occasion) and often for distinct historical and polemical reasons. This study aims consciously to question the validity of those readings of Bunyan's works that effectively ignore Bunyan's own position as a Nonconformist writer whose subject always is the salvation of his reader's soul" (13). Johnson similarly concludes that the various critical theories ("New Critical, Marxist, psychoanalytical, feminist, poststructural, and reader-response") that have been employed in the reading of Bunyan "are each ultimately self-limiting when they do not sufficiently consider Bunyan's *theology* as both the inspiration and aspiration of his works" (Johnson, "Be Not Extream," 447–48, italics original).

individualistic, subjectivistic self.[12] In recent decades, however, a number of literary-critical scholars have demonstrated that Bunyan's view of the Christian pilgrimage was essentially communal.[13] Many historical-critical studies have been offered that examine Bunyan's life and thought within the context of the tumultuous seventeenth century.[14] Historical-theological studies have provided an overview of the whole of Bunyan's theology, leaving the treatment of Bunyan's ecclesiology necessarily brief, or else they have focused upon Bunyan's soteriology, in particular his idiosyncratic view of justification.[15] Nevertheless, though it is now widely accepted that

12. For example, Pooley, "*Grace Abounding*," 105–14; Harding, *Journey into Self*, 18; Furlong, *Puritan's Progress*, 179; Newey, "Bunyan and the Confines of the Mind," 24; Sharrock, "Bunyan Studies Today," 55. These examples (and others) are cited in Johnson, *Prisoner of Conscience*, 1–4. Johnson summarizes this perception of Bunyan as "the ultimate lonely individual wrestling with his private conscience" (4). Johnson challenges this consensus view: "I do not deny that Bunyan stood astride the premodern and modern eras; indeed, I have asserted as much in previous chapters. But I also believe that once *The Pilgrim's Progress*, Part II, is read in light of Bunyan's larger thought on conscience, individuality, and selfhood, it shows Bunyan retreating from a modern, subjectivistic interiority that undermined an objective view of Christ's person and work, toward a deeper submersion into the communal Christian life" (Johnson, *Prisoner of Conscience*, 164).

13. For example, Knott, "Bunyan and the Holy Community," 200–225; Johnson, *Prisoner of Conscience*, 141–61; Davies, "Spirit in the Letters," 323–60; Pfatteicher, "Walking Home Together," 90–104. Davies writes, "Literary criticism's stress on loneliness and alienation in Bunyan's writings might suggest that there is little more to his religious imagination than an awful doctrine: one that demands a never ending regime of self-examination, and which leaves its anxious followers navigating the mazy paths of predestination alone. Such an approach has little positive to say about Bunyan's theology or the pastoral purposes of his works. But a more obvious problem with reading Bunyan solely in terms of Calvinism's allegedly harsh individualism is that it elides, if not erases altogether, the significance of community from Bunyan's writings" (Davis, "Spirit in the Letters," 323–24).

14. For example, Brown, *John Bunyan*; Greaves, *Glimpses of Glory*; *John Bunyan and English Nonconformity*; Hill, *Tinker and a Poor Man*; Mullett, *John Bunyan in Context*; Sharrock, *John Bunyan*; Talon, *John Bunyan*; Tindall, *John Bunyan*; Wakefield, *Bunyan the Christian*. Greaves's *Glimpses of Glory* is without parallel and remains the foremost historical-critical study of Bunyan.

15. For an excellent and influential overview of Bunyan's theology, see Greaves, *John Bunyan*. The precise relationship between justification and faith in Bunyan's soteriology remains an open question. Early in his career, Richard Greaves asserted that a shift in Bunyan's *ordo salutis* may be detected in his later ministry (Greaves, *John Bunyan*, 81–82). Pieter de Vries argued that Greaves overstated his case, and that any shift was a change in accent and not in substance (Vries, *John Bunyan on the Order of Salvation*, 150–55). Greaves responded to Vries in his 2002 *Glimpses of Glory*, arguing once again that Bunyan indeed reversed the order of justification and faith, and thus displayed

The Palace Beautiful

Bunyan's literature is incomprehensible apart from his theology, and that ecclesiology was central to his life and doctrine, no comprehensive, systematic analysis of Bunyan's ecclesiology exists.[16]

Furthermore, this monograph offers a reassessment of Bunyan's ecclesiological identity, a question about which Bunyan scholars have failed to reach a consensus. A majority of scholars have classified Bunyan as an open-communion Baptist, and not without reason.[17] Bunyan was personally convinced of credobaptism by immersion, and a few isolated remarks in his writings may indicate that he considered himself a Baptist. For instance, in *The Heavenly Foot-Man*, written in 1667/1668 but published posthumously in 1698,[18] Bunyan wrote: "keep Company with the soundest Christians, that have most Experience of Christ, and be sure thou have a care of *Quakers, Ranters, Free-willers*: Also do not have too much

---

antinomian tendencies (Greaves, *Glimpses of Glory*, 532–33). Other works on Bunyan's doctrine of justification include Ahenakaa, "Justification and the Christian Life"; Beeke, "John Bunyan on Justification," 107–30; Urban, "John Bunyan's Experiential Exposition," 129–58. The last three authors argue that Bunyan's doctrine of justification is in harmony with Reformed orthodoxy.

16. Richard Greaves included a chapter on Bunyan's ecclesiology in his early monograph on John Bunyan's theology (Greaves, *John Bunyan*, 123–51). Robert Archer likewise provided a systematic survey of Bunyan's ecclesiology (Archer, "Like Flowers in the Garden," 280–93). While these works are helpful, both are brief, and neither gives sufficient attention to the communion controversy or the question of Bunyan's ecclesiological identity. Gordon Wakefield provided a short chapter on "Bunyan and the Church" (Wakefield, *Bunyan the Christian*, 66–71), but the entire chapter spans six pages and offers only a cursory survey of Bunyan's ecclesiology. The same is true of Michael Mullett's treatment of Bunyan's writings during the communion controversy (Mullett, *John Bunyan in Context*, 176–81). Dewey Wallace contributed an essay on Bunyan's theology to *The Oxford Handbook of John Bunyan* that contains a brief section on ecclesiology (Wallace, "Bunyan's Thought and Religious Context," 69–85). See also Dunan-Page, "Bunyan and the Bedford Congregation," 53–68; Simpson, "Desired Countrey," 220–40. This monograph offers a far more comprehensive and systematic treatment of Bunyan's ecclesiology than what has been offered to date.

17. Influential Bunyan scholars who have identified Bunyan as a Baptist include Brown, *John Bunyan*, 237–38; Tindall, *John Bunyan*, 3, 225n1; Talon, *John Bunyan*, 105n44; Sharrock, *John Bunyan*, 30; White, "Frontiers of Fellowship," 252–54. See also White, "Open and Closed Membership," 330–34; Wakefield, *Bunyan the Christian*, 70; Archer, "Like Flowers in the Garden," 283; Greaves, *Glimpses of Glory*, 275; Dunan-Page, "John Bunyan's A Confession of My Faith," 19–40; Davies, "Spirit in the Letters," 328.

18. Though published by Charles Doe in 1698, Richard Greaves locates the date of composition of *The Heavenly-Footman* from December 1667 to February 1668 (Greaves, *Glimpses of Glory*, 638).

Company with some *Anabaptists*, though I go under that name my self."[19] Furthermore, there is evidence that at least some of Bunyan's Baptist opponents numbered him among their ranks. Bunyan reported the following from Thomas Paul's second published reply during the 1670s communion controversy: "You ask me next, *How long 'tis since I was a Baptist?* and then add, *'Tis an ill Bird that bewrays his own Nest.*"[20] Though Bunyan's Baptist *bona fides* have been accepted by the majority of Bunyan scholars, such identifications have usually been quite tentative.[21] For, as this monograph

19. Bunyan, *Heavenly Foot-Man*, 5:153. It is not immediately clear whether by "Anabaptist" Bunyan meant Baptists in particular or credobaptists in general. The term was used derisively by seventeenth-century opponents of anyone holding credobaptist convictions. It was repudiated by Particular Baptists, who wished to distance themselves from the continental Anabaptists (see, for example, the title of the 1644 London Baptist Confession: *The Confession of Faith, of Those Churches Which Are Commonly [Though Falsly] Called Anabaptists*). In any case, Bunyan's use of the term here is intriguing.

20. Quoted in Bunyan, *Peaceable Principles and True*, 4:270. This reply from Thomas Paul to Bunyan's *Differences in Judgment about Water-Baptism* is no longer extant, but its contents can be pieced together from Bunyan's response in *Peaceable Principles and True*. After quoting Paul, Bunyan replied, "I must tell you (avoiding your *slovenly* Language) I know none to whom that Title [Baptist] is so proper as *to the Disciples of* John. And since you would know by what Name I would be distinguished from others; I tell you, I would be, and hope I am, a *Christian*; and chuse, if God shall count me worthy, *to be called a Christian, a Believer* or other such Name which is approved by the Holy Ghost. And as for those Factious Titles of *Anabaptists, Independents, Presbyterians*, or the like, I conclude, that they came neither from *Jerusalem*, nor *Antioch*, but rather from *Hell* and *Babylon; for they naturally tend to divisions, you may know them by their Fruits*" (Bunyan, *Peaceable Principles and True*, 4:270). Clearly, Bunyan was uncomfortable with the title of Baptist or any title other than "Christian."

21. For example, though in 2002 Richard Greaves plainly identifies Bunyan as "an open-communion, open-membership Baptist" (Greaves, *Glimpses of Glory*, 275), forty years earlier Greaves stated that it is "pointless to attempt to identify him as either a thorough-going Baptist or a staunch Congregationalist in the light of his liberal views on the subject of baptism and church membership" (Greaves, *John Bunyan*, 22). This hesitancy is also witnessed in B. R. White: "They could almost equally be represented as 'open' membership Particular Baptists or as Independents who tolerated diversity of view in their congregations about the right and proper subjects of baptism" (White, "Open and Closed Membership," 331). Likewise, Gordon Wakefield admits, "Whether Bunyan may be called a Baptist or not is still a matter of dispute," before stating, "It is most satisfactory to conclude that Bunyan was 'an open-membership Baptist'" (Wakefield, *Bunyan the Christian*, 70). Michael Mullett suggests that Bunyan grew less Baptist with time: "The growing insistence within Baptist churches on believers' baptism was a natural response to a post-Restoration need for tighter organization and membership standards and a developing sectarian consciousness. Bunyan was becoming marginalized by such developments. . . . Yet if Bunyan was becoming cut off from the Baptist centre, he was, the same time, reaching out to a wider audience. Works such as the

demonstrates, Bunyan's ecclesiological convictions differed from those of his Baptist contemporaries at a number of fundamental points.

A small minority of scholars have identified Bunyan as a Congregationalist, a claim that likewise has some merit.[22] When in 1672 Bunyan

---

forthcoming *The Pilgrim's Progress* reached far beyond Baptist churches, and Bunyan's ecumenical churchmanship matched this wide appeal" (Mullett, *John Bunyan in Context*, 181). An exception to the tentative identification of Bunyan as a Baptist represented in the works cited above is Dunan-Page, "John Bunyan's *A Confession of My Faith*," 19–40. Dunan-Page confidently argues that Bunyan's open-communion position, while certainly the minority view among seventeenth-century Particular Baptists, did not have the effect of isolating him from his majority brethren, as is commonly assumed. Rather, both during and after the communion controversy, Bunyan was classified as a Baptist by Baptists and Congregationalists alike.

22. This view is rather dated within Bunyan scholarship; most contemporary scholars who opt for a non-Baptist ecclesiological label for Bunyan prefer the more generic "Independent" over the more specific "Congregationalist." Joseph Ban notes, "John Bunyan, 1628–1688, is generally considered, especially in English-speaking North America, to have been a Baptist preacher. . . . British writers, both Baptist and Congregational, claim Bunyan as one of their own" (Ban, "Was John Bunyan a Baptist?," 367). Among those British writers who claim Bunyan for Congregationalism, Ban cites Waddington, *Congregational History*; Peel, *Hundred Eminent Congregationalists* (375n1). Geoffrey Nuttall appears to regard Henry Jessey's Southwark, London Church, Bunyan's Bedford Church, and the Broadmead Church in Bristol, the three most famous open-communion churches of the seventeenth century, as Congregational, for all three receive ample attention throughout his study. Yet Nuttall does not appear to consider Baptist churches (those insisting upon credobaptism for membership) as belonging to the Congregational Way. Although Nuttall writes, "By this date [the 1672 publication of Bunyan's *Differences in Judgment about Water-Baptism*] the churches which insisted on believers' baptism had become a separate and self-conscious community; but in 1652 Richard Baxter still recognized only '4 differing partyes (Episcopall, Presbyterian, Indepdent and Erastian)' and thought of 'Anabaptists' as differing solely 'in p^t of Worshipp.'" Yet Nuttall continues, "To Congregational men tolerance [on the issue of baptism] meant not indifference but the refusal of one willing mind to compel another" (Nuttall, *Visible Saints*, 120–21). Joseph Ban also notes, "Apparently, no biographer had questioned Bunyan as being a Baptist until the appearance of John Brown's work in 1885" (Ban, "Was John Bunyan a Baptist?," 368). Brown cast doubt upon the orthodox view when he discovered baptismal records indicating that three of Bunyan's children were baptized as infants, the youngest in November 1672, several months *after* Bunyan became pastor of the Bedford Church (Brown, *John Bunyan*, 237–38). Brown's assertion that the Joseph Bunyan baptized at St. Cuthbert's, Bedford, on November 16, 1672, was the son of John Bunyan was immediately refuted by Thomas Armitage in *A History of the Baptists* (1886), and touched off a transatlantic debate (Ban, "Was John Bunyan a Baptist?," 368–69). Richard Greaves, citing a 1910 article by W. T. Whitley, asserts that the Joseph Bunyan in question was John Bunyan's grandson (Greaves, *Glimpses of Glory*, 275n33). Michael Mullett, on the other hand, accepts John Brown's identification: "Even so, his relative openness to the Church of England can perhaps be seen in the baptism

applied for a license to preach for himself and twenty-five others under the Declaration of Indulgence, he applied as "Congregationall."[23] Bunyan's closest ministerial associates were Congregationalists, including the London pastors George Cokayne, George Griffith, Anthony Palmer, and John Owen.[24] *The Minutes of . . . Bunyan Meeting* demonstrate that the Bedford Church refused to transfer members to strict-communion Baptist churches. For example, at a church meeting "holden at Bedford on the 29th of the 3d. month [1674]," the Bedford Church, with Bunyan as pastor, "Ordered that a letter be sent to that church of whom brother Jesse once was pastor, to know whether it be their church principle still to hold communion with saints as saint[s] though differing in judgment about watter baptizm, that we may the better know what to doe as to our sister Martha Cumberland as to her joyning with them or not."[25] In fact, rather than permit Sister Cumberland to join any of the strict-communion Baptist churches of London, the Bedford Church recommended she join the Congregationalist churches of George Cokayne, John Owen, or Anthony Palmer.[26] Furthermore, the later history of the Bedford Church lends credence to the argument for Bunyan's Congregationalist identity. The pastor who succeeded Bunyan was a paedobaptist.[27] In time, the church became

---

of his son Joseph in the parish church in November 1672. For the Bunyans, this would have amounted to little more than the registration of a birth" (Mullett, *John Bunyan in Context*, 101). As there is no evidence of a softening of Bunyan's views toward the Church of England, Greaves's explanation is the most likely.

23. Brown, *John Bunyan*, 232–33.

24. Richard Greaves identifies these men as the Captains Boanerges, Conviction, Judgment, and Execution from Bunyan's *The Holy War* (Greaves, "John Bunyan's 'Holy War,'" 159). Greaves elsewhere writes, "Although Bunyan is rightly regarded as an open-membership Baptist, his closest relations in the Nonconformist community were with Congregationalists" (Greaves, *John Bunyan and English Nonconformity*, 64).

25. *Minutes*, 77; the letter itself is found on pp. 79–80. For similar letters, see pp. 65–66, 68–69, 71, 77, 79–80, 87. This monograph employs H. G. Tibbutt's transcription of the Bedford Church book throughout.

26. The Church was none too pleased that Sister Cumberland refused these recommendations: "We have heare to fore over and over offered to give hir up to that church walkeing with our honored brother Coken, brother Palmer or brother Owen, but non of these congregations would content hir, the which we have taken very ill, . . . neither would we ever git from hir a reason of hir so refuseing, but instead therof a discovery of a stoborne and selfe willed spirit signifying to us that if we should not consent to give hir up to walke with those whose principles touching the thinge in question we know not, she would take hir leave to doe it" (*Minutes*, 79–80).

27. "In an understanding reached by the congregation in 1691, its pastor Ebenezer

predominantly paedobaptist.²⁸ Joseph Ban provides a glimpse of the convoluted ecclesiological history of the Bedford Church:

> The effort to accommodate Baptists and paedobaptists in the same living fellowship has proven divisive at times. When a pastor was converted to Baptist views in 1773, for example, a part of its Congregational membership seceded. Similarly, twenty years later, nineteen Baptists left when a Congregational minister was appointed. Today the congregation retains the Gifford-Bunyan tradition. . . . The Church is a full member of the Baptist Union of Great Britain and Ireland and remains in full fellowship with the United Reformed Church, formed in 1972 by a Union of Congregationalists and Presbyterians.²⁹

Finally, a growing number of scholars claim that the question of Bunyan's ecclesiological identity is itself anachronistic, as strict denominational lines were not yet drawn in Bunyan's day. Typical of this view is the opinion of Joseph Ban in his influential 1984 essay, "Was John Bunyan a Baptist? A Case Study in Historiography": "In resolving the question of affiliation, it is necessary to remember that Bunyan's ministry took place before the Congregationalists and Baptists emerged as recognizable denominations. It is also significant to recognize that he pastored a church that in its polity and ecclesiology resisted the pressure to be denominated as either Congregational or Baptist."³⁰ Likewise, Harry Poe writes,

> If one classifies Bunyan a Baptist, one should not think in terms of a fully developed denominational orientation. Though he practiced believer's baptism, he distanced himself from the developing organization of Calvinistic Independent churches practicing believer's baptism that came to be called Particular Baptists. . . .
>
> As one who practiced believer's baptism, Bunyan took part in the debate that helped draw the parameters of institutional Particular Baptist life. At the end of the debate, Bunyan stood outside the camp of how Baptists came to be defined. In his own

---

Chandler was to be allowed liberty in baptizing infants, but without promoting the practice. Church members were to have similar freedom in following believers' baptism but were to forebear 'discourse and debates on it that may have a tendency to break the peace of the church'" (Underwood, *Miscellaneous Works of John Bunyan*, 4:xvii–xxviii).

28. Underwood, *History of English Baptists*, 104, cited in Ban, "Was John Bunyan a Baptist?," 373.

29. Ban, "Was John Bunyan a Baptist?," 373.

30. Ban, "Was John Bunyan a Baptist?," 375.

time, however, when "baptist" and "congregational" were still adjectives more than proper nouns, Bunyan could easily call himself an "Anabaptist."[31]

Each of these answers contains an element of truth, yet none is entirely satisfactory. This monograph argues that Bunyan cannot be identified as either a Baptist or a Congregationalist without qualifications so restrictive as to render both labels unhelpful. Furthermore, the denominational lines were not as blurred as some have suggested. The proliferation of confessions in the middle of the seventeenth century attests to an emerging sense of distinctive identity on the part of both Baptists and Congregationalists. Therefore, this monograph offers a new classification for Bunyan, the Bedford Church, and the network of churches of which it was a part that takes these factors into account.

Relevance to Baptist History

Second, this monograph has relevance to the field of Baptist history. The topic of Baptist origins and identity has received significant attention in recent decades, as scholars have reexamined the question of what distinguished and defined the Baptist movement in the seventeenth century. Two questions emerge from this scholarship. First, did seventeenth-century Baptists constitute a distinct, self-identified movement, or were they virtually indistinguishable from other mid-century Nonconformist groups, their distinctive identity only coming into focus at the end of the century? Second, if seventeenth-century Baptists did constitute a distinct, self-identified

---

31. Poe, "John Bunyan," 41–42. Elsewhere, Poe comments, "To an extent, Bunyan's debate with the Baptists helped to define the perimeter of the emerging Baptist denomination" (Poe, "John Bunyan's Controversy with the Baptists," 26). Christopher Hill echoes the same sentiment: "Bunyan himself rejected the label 'Baptist,' no doubt in part because of his unhappiness about the rigidity of 'closed-communion' Baptists.... When the Bedford church took out its license in 1672 it was as 'congregational'; not 'Baptist.' Other churches which historians pigeon-hole as Baptist did the same. Sectarian lines were not yet fully drawn. Many churches traditionally called 'congregationalist' sheltered under the name 'Presbyterian' in 1672. As late as 1766 the Bedford church still thought of itself as 'Independent'" (Hill, *Tinker and a Poor Man*, 293–94). In a later essay, Hill writes, "It is anachronistic to attempt to decide whether he [Bunyan] was a Baptist or a Congregationalist" (Hill, "Bunyan's Contemporary Reputation," 3). T. L. Underwood asserts, "The debate over Bunyan's denominational inclinations warns of the dangers of insufficiently recognizing the fluidity of thought and practice of the times and of drawing lines of division between seventeenth-century sects more sharply than they themselves have done" (Underwood, *Miscellaneous Works of John Bunyan*, 4:xxvi–xxvii).

movement within Nonconformity, what were its boundaries? Who qualified as a Baptist?

In his 2000 *Apocalypse How? Baptist Movements During the English Revolution*, Mark Bell argues that Baptists shared a "collective eschatology," a vibrant millenarianism that set them apart from other Nonconformists, and that a factor distinguishing one Baptist movement from another was the difference in the degree to which they held these convictions and the direction these convictions took them.[32] Bell acknowledges from the outset that

> denominational terminology can be dangerous. The distinctions between religious groups were amorphous in the seventeenth century. As long as there was a state church that persecuted those who stepped outside its bounds, many dissenters found common cause; often when persecution eased they found they had irreparable differences. . . . Therefore the greatest caution must be exercised to avoid associating modern connotations with denominational names. This story is concerned with how the denominational foundation came into existence. It is a story about beginnings, about the process of development from baptists to Baptists. The group of Christians whose origins are early in the seventeenth century were not called Baptists until the end of that century.[33]

Yet even though outsiders were not sure what to call the Baptists (and Bell suggests that "the early Baptists were equally uncertain of what to call themselves"), it was clear what they were and where their boundaries were set. They were "a gathered congregation of Christians who practiced believer's baptism."[34] Although it would seem that the Bedford Church would fall outside the scope of this definition, as its members did not all practice believer's baptism, nevertheless Bell includes such churches within the pale of seventeenth-century Baptist movements, denominating them as "Independent Baptists," which he defines as "'mixed communion' congregations, churches made up of both people who did and did not accept believer's baptism. The presence of these Independent Baptists forced the other Baptist movements to make a decision on the issue of open versus closed communion."[35]

32. Bell, *Apocalypse How?*, 5–6. "A sense of living in the final days and preparing for the establishment of God's Kingdom were prevalent in early modern England. What is notable about Baptist eschatology is its degree and direction" (5).

33. Bell, *Apocalypse How?*, 1–2.

34. Bell, *Apocalypse How?*, 3.

35. Bell, *Apocalypse How?*, 4. Bell later writes, "The most famous Independent Baptist

Was Bunyan a Baptist?

In his 2001 *Antipaedobaptism in the Thought of John Tombes*, Michael Renihan argues for a new ecclesiological identity for John Tombes, namely, that of "Anglican Antipaedobaptist."[36] Renihan contends that Tombes has been misclassified as a Baptist merely upon the basis of his credobaptistic convictions.

> Tombes will be shown to be reformational, Calvinistic, baptistic as regards baptism and his view of the Covenant of Grace, a "divine" in the sense of one who attained great proficiency in divinity. However, he was not a Baptist in the common use of the term, then, or in the present. A belief that states baptism is for believers exclusively is not enough to call someone a Baptist, just as this view alone was not enough to denominate one as an Anabaptist in the seventeenth century. . . . "Baptist" as a title entails more than a certain view of baptism.
>
> It is the Baptist historians who have muddied the waters surrounding John Tombes. They have perceived him as one of their own standing against the establishment for his ideals. In actuality, Tombes was trying to bring greater reform to the established church. This is a needed distinction in order to understand the tension between his sacramental theology and his ecclesiology.[37]

Renihan defines a "Baptist" as one who "(1) believed in baptism for believers alone by immersion, and who (2) organized themselves into particular societies as churches of believers and baptised men and women."[38] Nevertheless, Renihan later states that open-communionists like Bunyan and Henry Jessey were a minority opinion within the Particular Baptist camp, a qualification that undercuts his main thesis.[39] If Tombes cannot be classified as a

---

congregation was that of John Bunyan in Bedford," and that these Independent Baptist congregations "forced the General and Particular Baptists to make a decision concerning open versus closed communion" (67–68).

36. M. Renihan, *Antipaedobaptism*, 1. Renihan divides seventeenth-century Antipaedobaptists into four subsets: Anabaptists, Baptists, Abaptists, and Anglican Antipaedobaptists (19–31).

37. M. Renihan, *Antipaedobaptism*, 3–4.

38. M. Renihan, *Antipaedobaptism*, 22.

39. "Among the Particular Baptists there was a dispute between advocates of open communion (church membership) and closed communion. Open communion men like John Bunyan and Henry Jessey did not believe baptism was essential to church membership. They believed it essential to the good order of a Church. Others like William Kiffen and Hanserd Knollys argued that right baptism is essential to church membership. Closed communion became the majority practice by the end of the seventeenth century. Therefore, even the Particular Baptists of the era should be distinguished into

Baptist because he rejected the ecclesiological implications of credobaptism, why is Bunyan considered a Baptist when he rejected the same?

Peter Naylor's 2003 *Calvinism, Communion, and the Baptists* examines the communion controversies among Calvinistic Baptists during the seventeenth, eighteenth, and nineteenth centuries, arguing that (contrary to the claim of Strict Baptists) there was no necessary connection between high (or Hyper-) Calvinism and strict communion: "It is submitted that from the occasion of their appearance in England in the mid-1600s, 'Particular' and 'General' Baptists assumed what has come to be termed 'strict' communion to be the norm, and that there was no relation between this discipline and the more extreme interpretations of historic Calvinism embraced by some within the former community."[40] The present monograph stands in substantial agreement with Naylor's thesis, but seeks to clarify and extend it. It is true that strict communion is not a Hyper-Calvinistic Baptist distinctive; strict communion is simply a Baptist distinctive. Strict communion was not merely the "norm" among Baptists; strict communion was the position of *all* Baptists, provided "Baptist" is properly defined as not only entailing a conviction of credobaptism, but also the conviction that credobaptism is essential to the gathering of a rightly-ordered visible church. This monograph demonstrates this to have been the case throughout the seventeenth century. But even into the late-eighteenth century Abraham Booth asserted that "every Baptist *ought*

---

these two camps. The London Baptist Confession of 1677/aka 1689 does not address this phenomenon because mutual fellowship was extended beyond the boundaries of this particular debate" (M. Renihan, *Antipaedobaptism*, 28). This monograph disagrees with two assertions made in the preceding statement. First, it claims too much to say that Bunyan "believed it [credobaptism] essential to the good order of a Church." It is difficult to come to that conclusion from Bunyan's writings on the subject. Second, to say that closed communion "became the majority practice by the end of the seventeenth century" assumes that open communion was recognized as a viable Baptist position in the seventeenth century, an assumption this monograph rejects. It may be true that fellowship among Baptists widened towards the end of the century to include open-communion credobaptists, and that this widening of fellowship is indicated in the 1677/1689 London Baptist Confession's silence on the issue, but to say this is to admit that Baptist fellowship did not include open-communion credobaptists in the decades prior to the drafting of the Confession.

40. Naylor, *Calvinism, Communion*, 239. Naylor earlier asserts, "It seems that for many years it has been held, at least in Strict Baptist circles, that the association between restricted communion and high Calvinism was virtually indigenous, although this has not always been a universal perception" (8).

to be a *strict* one, or else to renounce the name."[41] Booth concluded his work with the following plea: "That is, be either consistent *Baptists*, or *Pedobaptists;* for, according to your present practice, all thinking and impartial men must pronounce you an *heterogenous mixture* of both."[42] The reason Naylor finds dissent on the terms of communion among Baptists in the first centuries of the Baptist tradition is that his definition of what it meant to be "Baptist" is too broad. Thus, he includes Bunyan among the Baptists, though he acknowledges the difficulty in doing so.[43] Naylor does, however, suggest that the omission of explicit language regarding strict communion in the 1689 London Baptist Confession

> was to a greater or lesser extent a needful political ploy, being introduced after the accession of William of Orange to demonstrate that the Particular Baptists did agree in most matters with other dissenters and to a considerable extent with the Thirty-Nine Articles of the Church of England. This may be one reason why the terms of communion held by the majority of Baptist churches represented at the 1689 Assembly were not mentioned explicitly. . . .
>
> It follows that what the Confession does *not* say about the relationship between baptism and the Lord's Table may be as significant as any of its declarations. If so, the 1689 formulary does not represent the fixed position of most English Calvinistic Baptists concerning terms of communion.[44]

---

41. Booth, *Apology for the Baptists*, 170, cited in Naylor, *Calvinism, Communion*, 237.

42. Booth, *Apology for the Baptists*, 176, cited in Naylor, *Calvinism, Communion*, 237–38.

43. "John Bunyan was usually most careful about wearing a denominational label. In Bedford, the church he pastored and which would become known as the 'Bunyan Meeting' contained some who queried the validity of infant baptism, yet was not explicitly a Baptist congregation. This was consistent with Bunyan's habitual reluctance to side openly with the Baptists, although in his *The Heavenly Footman* (1698) he does exhort his readers to 'have a care of Quakers, Ranters, Freewillers [Arminians]; also do not have much company with some Anabaptists, though I go under that name myself.' Yet, as has been sensibly noted, Bunyan's ministry took place before the Congregationalists emerged as a recognizable denomination, and that he pastored a church which resisted the pressure to be denominated as either Congregational or Baptist" (Naylor, *Calvinism, Communion*, 95, citing Ban, "Was John Bunyan a Baptist?," 375).

44. Naylor, *Calvinism, Communion*, 238–39. Likewise, regarding the 1677 London Baptist Confession, Naylor suggests that the silence regarding the terms of communion "might have been tactical rather than ideological" (87). This monograph argues the same in chapter 5.

The present monograph likewise suggests that the startling omission of strict communion from the 1677/1689 London Baptist Confession reflects a concern for political expediency rather than a change of conviction regarding the terms of communion.

Stephen Wright's influential 2006 monograph *The Early English Baptists*, offers a reconstruction of Baptist origins. Wright argues that Anabaptism exerted almost no influence on Baptist origins, which instead were firmly rooted in the Puritan-Separatist tradition.[45] Wright then asserts that there was no connection between the Helwys/Murton circle that returned to London from Holland in 1612 and the Baptist churches that emerged out of the Jessey circle in the 1640s.[46] Wright further contends that strict lines of division between General and Particular Baptists did not emerge until after 1644, and even then, the divide was frequently more political than theological.[47] For example, as the present monograph demonstrates, early General and Particular Baptists were unanimous on the ecclesiological question of strict communion.

In his 2008 *Edification and Beauty: The Practical Ecclesiology of the English Particular Baptists*, James Renihan argues that while inheriting much of their theology from their Puritan ancestors, English Particular Baptists nevertheless possessed a unique ecclesiology driven by a "keen primitivistic impulse," a relentless desire to pattern their churches' faith and practice upon the principles and precedents of the New Testament church, and that this "was the impetus behind the development of believer's baptism, the practice of immersion, the order and government of the church, the roles of officers, the various aspects of worship and the outworking of inter-church

---

45. "It would seem, therefore, that anabaptism left no mark on the puritan-separatists" (Wright, *Early English Baptists*, 6). Wright is not alone in this assertion; Bell likewise argues that while Anabaptism exercised profound influence upon the English Baptist movement: "This influence was largely negative as the subsequent Baptist movements tried to define themselves in contrast to the Continental Anabaptists" (Bell, *Apocalypse How?*, 3).

46. "It is unclear whether the pre-war Murton tradition survived in 1630s London" (Wright, *Early English Baptists*, 72). "There is little reason to connect (or identify) the London churches of Edward Barber and Thomas Lambe (both known later as General Baptists) with the pre-war tradition of Helwys and Murton" (76).

47. "'General' and 'Particular' Baptists have traditionally been presented as separate branches of the same genus, like horses and zebras, on the tree of denominational evolution. This palaeontology reflects a lack of scientific caution. The problem centres on those Baptists who emerged from the Jessey circle of churches during the Laudian ascendancy" (Wright, *Early English Baptists*, 11).

relationships."⁴⁸ This monograph stands in substantial agreement with Renihan's thesis, arguing that ecclesiological purity according to Scripture was the controlling principle of seventeenth-century Baptist ecclesiology. However, on the question of whether open communion was an accepted seventeenth-century Baptist position, Renihan states, "A careful reading of the [1677/1689 London Baptist] Confession will demonstrate that baptism is never explicitly tied with church membership. This was purposely done in order to comprehend churches of both kinds. At the London Assemblies, the majority of churches would have been closed membership, but open membership churches were present as well. The more strict churches were willing to unite with others whose views were slightly different from their own."⁴⁹ This monograph offers an alternative explanation for the omission of explicit strict communion language in the 1677/1689 London Baptist Confession. It is interesting to note that Renihan differentiates between open-membership churches that associated with strict-membership churches, and open-membership churches that refused to associate with strict-membership churches: "Some, such as Broadmead, Bristol, maintained intimate relations with the closed-membership churches, even to the point of participating in the General Assemblies. Others, such as John Bunyan's Bedford church were more closely akin to the Paedobaptist Independent churches, and maintained cool, and sometimes antagonistic relations

---

48. J. Renihan, *Edification and Beauty*, xxii–xxiii. A similar work examining late-seventeenth-century Particular Baptist identity is Copeland, *Benjamin Keach and the Development of Baptist Traditions*, which traces Keach's profound influence upon the Baptist tradition, particularly in the areas of religious liberty, baptismal theology (including closed communion), the laying on of hands, and congregational singing.

49. J. Renihan, *Edification and Beauty*, 47. Renihan adds, "The Universal church was not a Baptist body, but a Christian body, incorporating assemblies of various types, and even individuals within the confines of apostate communions. Various congregations, whatever their constituting principles may have been, were true churches when visible saints were called out of the world, and united together in obedience to Christ" (47–48). Chapter 5 of this monograph will demonstrate, however, that while seventeenth-century Baptists considered paedobaptist believers to be true Christians, they did not regard paedobaptist churches to be true churches; or, if they did consider them true churches, they did so in violation of the consistent reasoning of their confessions of faith. It should also be noted that Renihan sees continuity between the ecclesiology of later seventeenth-century Particular Baptists and the earlier generation. He writes, "There is no bifurcation between the earlier men and churches and the later, rather there is continuity. As a movement that only emerged self-consciously in the 1640s, there is a natural progression without significant differences" (xxii). This implies that what Renihan is claiming for late-seventeenth-century Baptists was likewise true of mid-seventeenth-century Baptists.

with the closed-membership Particular Baptists."[50] In other words, while including open-communion credobaptist churches among seventeenth-century Baptists, Renihan recognizes the difficulty of classifying Bunyan and the Bedford Church as "Baptist."

Matthew Ward's 2014 *Pure Worship: The Early English Baptist Distinctive* argues that the concern for "pure worship" was the foundational Baptist distinctive, and that this concern for purity created a distinctive Baptist ecclesiology.[51] In his chapter on this distinctive Baptist ecclesiology, Ward identifies the essential issue in the question of whether open communion was a valid seventeenth-century Baptist position, namely, whether baptism is of the essence (the form) of a church. That is, is a church that practices paedobaptism a true church? According to Ward, "Bunyan and Barbone, as well as Jessey and Tombes, all acknowledged the validity of believers' baptism, but none were willing by such a belief to declare all churches not in its practice false."[52] The Baptists did not agree. "At its heart this scandal was a debate about worship. A true church would worship truly because false worship was of the Antichrist. . . . Any church that violated any part of God's Word proved by its action not to be a true church at all."[53] Ward then asks the crucial question: "Could the Devonshire Square and Bedford churches recognize each other in communion?"[54] Ward does not provide a definite answer, but he does conclude that for the Baptists, "Every error in worship was potential grounds for separation."[55] The present work stands

---

50. J. Renihan, *Edification and Beauty*, 30n109. See also J. Renihan, *Edification and Beauty*, 23–24, where Renihan discusses the Bedford Church's censure of Nehemiah Coxe, likely over the issue of strict communion. There, Renihan specifically identifies the Bedford Church as "Independent." See also J. Renihan, *Edification and Beauty*, 109–10.

51. "It is one thing to argue that English Baptists had a distinct theology of worship; it is a much different thing to argue that their theology of worship was in fact *the* ultimate distinctive of this group. . . . I will argue that everything we find distinctive about this group, including their hermeneutic, their ecclesiology, and their soteriology, was driven by their fundamental desire to worship God purely" (Ward, *Pure Worship*, xii). In his third chapter ("Free Worship and a New Concept of the Church"), Ward argues that the distinctive Baptist ecclesiology arose out of the concern for "pure worship" (52–109).

52. Ward, *Pure Worship*, 97.

53. Ward, *Pure Worship*, 98.

54. Ward, *Pure Worship*, 104.

55. Ward, *Pure Worship*, 108. Ward's reluctance to provide a definite answer could be because, in his mind, these were unresolved tensions inherent within the seventeenth-century Baptist movement rather than disputes between Baptists and baptistic Independents. Viewing Barbone, Tombes, Jessey, and Bunyan as non-Baptists allows for an answer to some of the questions Ward leaves unanswered.

in substantial agreement with Ward's thesis as to the ultimate seventeenth-century Baptist distinctive, but applies it to the particular case of John Bunyan and the Bedford Church, making explicit what Ward merely implies.[56] Could the Devonshire Square and Bedford Churches recognize one another in communion? No, they could not; in fact, they did not. Seventeenth-century Baptists held baptism to be essential to pure worship, and pure worship to be of the essence of a true church.[57]

Also in 2014, Jason Duesing published a monograph on the life and work of Henry Jessey. As Jessey held to a similar ecclesiology to Bunyan, and even posthumously contributed to Bunyan's defense of open communion in *Differences in Judgment about Water-Baptism, No Bar to Communion* (1673), what Duesing concludes about Jessey's ecclesiological identity bears upon the question of Bunyan's identity as well. Was Henry Jessey a Baptist? Duesing answers in the affirmative, basing his conclusion upon two factors: Jessey seems to have considered himself a Baptist and strenuously defended believer's baptism in his *Storehouse of Provision* (1650), and secondary sources from the seventeenth century to the present have generally regarded Jessey as a Baptist.[58] However, while it is true that the majority of scholars throughout the centuries have regarded Jessey, Bunyan, and other open-communion credobaptists as Baptists, a significant and growing minority question this classification, as well as the propriety of assigning denominational labels at this juncture in the seventeenth century, as Duesing himself admits.[59] Duesing also gives extended attention to Jessey's

---

56. While Ward argues that liturgical purity ("pure worship") was the seventeenth-century Baptist distinctive, this monograph argues that the foundational Baptist distinctive was ecclesiological purity (a church purely formed and ordered according to the Word of God). The difference is subtle, but the latter is broader than the former.

57. It is possible that this strict view was tempered as the century wore on such that, as James Renihan's thesis asserts, late-seventeenth-century Particular Baptists were able to recognize paedobaptist and open-communion churches as true churches, but this does not seem consistent with the logical implications of their position nor the tenor of their writing.

58. Duesing, *Henry Jessey*, 44–46. Duesing later writes, "Concluding that because Jessey's personal convictions align most near that of the Baptists, as well as a consistent consensus throughout history that Jessey should receive a Baptist classification, it is therefore proper and fair to say that Jessey was a Baptist" (249).

59. Duesing affirms the judgment of Joseph Ban that the era of Jessey's ministry (and that of Bunyan) "took place before the Congregationalists and Baptists emerged as recognizable denominations" (Ban, "Was John Bunyan a Baptist?," 375). Duesing adds, "Indeed, when examining denominational progress prior to the Restoration in 1660 or even the Act of Toleration in 1689, historians must admit that they are dealing with an imprecise and fluid era" (Duesing, *Henry Jessey*, 250).

"mixed ecclesiology," its foundational influence upon John Bunyan and the Bedford Church, and the communion controversy into which Jessey was unwittingly thrust a decade after his death.[60]

In 2017, Ian Birch argued that "Christocratic" rule was the controlling principle of early English Calvinistic Baptist ecclesiology. Birch examines the "contours" of Calvinistic Baptist ecclesiology from its origins in the JLJ Church in London to the Restoration, finding that Calvinistic Baptist churches of this era were Christocratic, believing, baptized, gathered, visible, separatist congregations.[61] The question is whether one could reject one or more of these contours and still qualify as a Baptist, as Bunyan rejected the necessity of believer's baptism. Birch seems to accept that open-communion credobaptists like Jessey, Tombes, and Bunyan were Baptists, but he acknowledges that there were some Baptists who did not think so:

> This response shows that the early Baptist practice of closed communion, which required believer's baptism as necessary for church membership and the primary evidence of faith, though the majority view, was not universally maintained. Even John Tombes, who defended believer's baptism so strongly, did not press the necessity this far. He questioned "whether a Minister can justify it before God, if he reject such a *Christian* from the Lord's Supper, because not baptized." On the other hand, there were a number of Baptists who clearly believed that churches practicing open communion were not "true churches."[62]

The idea that a church practicing open communion was not a true church has roots going back to the very beginning of the Baptist movement. In 2017, Marvin Jones published a monograph in which he argues that Thomas Helwys's *A Short Declaration of the Mystery of Iniquity*, while rightly regarded as a seminal work in defense of religious liberty, is primarily a foundational text on Baptist ecclesiology.[63] Jones asserts that Helwys's rejection of royal supremacy and a national church was in part the result of his emerging views of local church autonomy and congregational polity.[64]

---

60. Duesing, *Henry Jessey*, 215–52.

61. Birch, *To Follow the Lambe*, 32–64. For the section dealing with "Baptism, Infant Baptism, and Church Membership," see pp. 39–48.

62. Birch, *To Follow the Lambe*, 47–48.

63. Jones, *Beginning of Baptist Ecclesiology*, 1.

64. For Helwys's critique of royal supremacy, see Jones, *Beginning of Baptist Ecclesiology*, 76–89. For Helwys's critique of the Roman Catholic Church (which he identified as

He further argues that Helwys rejected Puritanism because it attempted to reform a false church rather than restore the true church.⁶⁵ While Helwys approved of Separatism's renunciation of the Church of England and its concept of the gathered covenanted congregation, he thought the Separatists failed to understand the relationship between the eternal covenant and the local covenant, failed to understand who was included in these interrelated covenants, and therefore, failed to understand who was eligible for the covenant sign of baptism, which is the means of entering into the gathered covenant community.⁶⁶ According to Jones, "Helwys's words for a gathered community, which did baptize without a proper profession of faith, were harsh but effective: he said they 'had a false profession, and a false Christ.' The point is that Christ would not baptize a person unless a profession of faith was proclaimed. Helwys doubts that Christ could be part of the church that embraces such heresy."⁶⁷ According to Helwys's understanding, Bunyan would be a Separatist and not a Baptist, and the Bedford Church would be a false church.

In 2019, Matthew Bingham published a provocative monograph entitled, *Orthodox Radicals: Baptist Identity in the English Revolution*, which he considers "a major reinterpretation of Particular and Calvinistic Baptist self-identity during the English Revolution and Interregnum."⁶⁸ Bingham argues that the category "Baptist" is an anachronism imposed upon the mid-seventeenth century by denominational historians, and that the earliest Particular Baptists should be denominated "baptistic congregationalists," as their commitment to congregationalism preceded and superseded their commitment to credobaptism.⁶⁹ Those known

---

the first beast of Rev 13) and the Church of England (which he identified as the second beast of Rev 13), see Jones, *Beginning of Baptist Ecclesiology*, 38–54.

65. For Helwys's critique of Puritanism, see Jones, *Beginning of Baptist Ecclesiology*, 95–96, 104–11. "Helwys wrote that Puritans were false prophets, because they taught 'many false doctrines.' The rationale for Helwys labeling the Puritans as false prophets was that they would not leave the corrupt Church of England.... In Helwys's mind, the second beast [of Rev 13] was using the false prophets; for example the Puritans to deceive the people of England" (36–37).

66. For Helwys's critique of Separatism, see Jones, *Beginning of Baptist Ecclesiology*, 121–39.

67. Jones, *Beginning of Baptist Ecclesiology*, 138.

68. Bingham, *Orthodox Radicals*, 7–8.

69. "The very category 'Baptist' was an eighteenth-century development and to impose it upon the mid-seventeenth century is to think anachronistically about the past" (Bingham, *Orthodox Radicals*, 10). Bingham earlier argued that "despite the ubiquitous

today as "Baptists" were in reality the minority report within the emerging congregationalist movement alongside their majority paedobaptist counterparts. Bingham writes,

> I am arguing, then, that mid-century congregationalists and those commonly regarded as Calvinistic or Particular Baptists ought to be held closer together than historians have been wont to do. During their early, formative decades between 1638 and 1660, the men and women long labeled "Particular Baptists" can be better understood as baptistic congregationalists—a "Baptist" denominational identity would only begin to solidify after the Restoration. In their theological framework, their favored emphases, and even their personal associations, the Particular Baptist leaders and those who followed them were cut from congregational cloth.[70]

Furthermore, Bingham argues that credobaptism emerged out of congregational convictions by a resistless logic.[71] An underlying assumption of Bingham's argument is that the rejection of paedobaptism is not sufficient to qualify an individual or church as "Baptist" and distinguish it from other Nonconformist groups.[72] In other words, credobaptism is not a sufficient Baptist distinctive. Bingham further contends that during the Interregnum (if not before), "baptistic congregationalists were divided into two diverging streams: one was open, irenic, and ecumenical, the other narrow, combative, and sectarian; the first stream looked to solidify its connection to mainstream congregationalism, while the second began to seek distance from it."[73] Bingham, however, sees this divergence as due

---

assertion that the participants were clearly 'Baptists,' it is not at all clear that Kiffin, Knollys, and Coxe would have self-identified as being included within this category. Instead, the three men struggled to settle on a consistent, coherent self-designator.... I will argue that many of those presently described in the literature as 'Baptists' were actually far closer in their theological affinities and relational networks to the more mainstream paedobaptistic congregationalists or independents. The label 'Baptist,' as we shall see, is unhelpful and obscures rather than clarifies" (3–4).

70. Bingham, *Orthodox Radicals*, 40–41.

71. Bingham, *Orthodox Radicals*, 68.

72. Bingham refers to "the inadequacy of 'Baptist' as a generic label for any and all denying paedobaptism" (Bingham, *Orthodox Radicals*, 117).

73. Bingham, *Orthodox Radicals*, 120. Bingham later writes, "Some [baptistic congregationalists] moved further away from the mainstream of English religious life and toward a more well-defined sense of baptistic identity, one in which believer's baptism became ever more deeply entrenched as the *sine qua non* of fellowship. Simultaneously, others maintained a keen sense that the disagreement over baptism was an in-house debate among other like-minded congregationalists" (121).

to much more than the question of open or strict communion, with the result that he places William Kiffin in the former category (ecumenical) rather than the latter (sectarian).[74]

To date, the majority of Baptist historians still classify open-communion credobaptists like Bunyan as a subset of seventeenth-century Baptists, though most will acknowledge the historical difficulty and fluidity of such labels. Against this mainstream of Baptist historical scholarship, this monograph argues that Particular Baptists identified as a distinct movement by 1644, and that an integral element of this distinctive identity was strict communion. When the seven congregations of London published their confession in the attempt to distinguish their views from the Continental Anabaptists and thus from the specter of Münster, Pelagianism, and political anarchy, they established an inseparable connection between baptism and church membership.[75] The 1644 London Baptist Confession defines a visible church as "a company of visible Saints, called & separated from the world, by the word and the Spirit of God, to the visible profession of faith of the Gospel, being baptized into that faith, and joyned to the Lord, and each other, my mutuall agreement, in the practical injoyment of the Ordinances, commanded by Christ their head and King."[76] And though the 1644 London Baptist Confession did not explicitly connect baptism to the Lord's Supper, the 1646 revision remedied this oversight, stating that "Baptisme is an ordinance of the new Testament, given by Christ, to be dispensed upon persons professing faith, or that are Disciples; who upon a profession of faith, ought to be baptized, and after to partake of the Lord's Supper."[77] In fact, strict communion is explicitly enjoined in every subsequent General

---

74. Bingham, *Orthodox Radicals*, 127–28.

75. William Lumpkin, in his classic collection of Baptist confessions, writes, "By 1644, however, the rapid growth of Baptist views called forth serious opposition to the Baptists and their program. The most serious accusations levelled against them by their enemies were of Pelagianism and anarchy, both of which were associated in the popular mind with the radical wing of the Anabaptist movement of the Continent" (Lumpkin, *Baptist Confessions of Faith*, 144). Lumpkin lists three publications that provoked the confession: *A Short History of the Anabaptists of High and Low Germany* (1642), *A Warning for England Especially for London* (1642), and *A Confutation of the Anabaptists and of All Others Who Affect Not Civil Government* (1644). Lumpkin then writes, "In order to distinguish themselves from both the General Baptists and the Anabaptists, the Calvinistic Baptists of London determined to prepare and publish a statement of their views" (145).

76. *Confession of Faith* (1644) art. 33.

77. *Confession of Faith of Seven Congregations . . . in London* (1646) art. 39.

and Particular Baptist confession of the seventeenth century with the sole exception of the 1677/1689 London Baptist Confession.[78]

For seventeenth-century Baptists, strict communion was not a peripheral issue admitting of dissent; rather, they considered credobaptism essential to the constitution of a rightly-ordered church. Credobaptism was essential to ecclesiological purity, and ecclesiological purity was the *raison d'être* of the Baptist movement. Neither did Bunyan, the Bedford Church, or those within its sphere of influence tolerate dissent from its own professed principles, as evidenced by its refusal to dismiss members to strict-communion churches. Open communion was as much a distinctive of the Bunyan circle as strict communion was of the Baptists. Therefore, Bunyan, the Bedford Church, and the network of open-communion churches of which it formed the hub are best understood, not as open-communion Baptists, but as a separate entity within seventeenth-century English Nonconformity. For these churches, open communion was essential to evangelical unity, and evangelical unity was their preeminent ecclesiological distinctive.

Relevance to Baptist Ecclesiology

Finally, this monograph has relevance to contemporary Baptist ecclesiology. Debate over the terms of communion has reemerged in every century of Baptist life down to the present.[79] The 1770s saw debate between John Collett Ryland, Daniel Turner, and Robert Robinson arguing for open communion, and Abraham Booth advocating for strict communion.[80] Though strict communion remained the dominant view among English Particular Baptists, by the last decades of the eighteenth-century open communion emerged as a minority report within the Baptist denomination.[81] In *A*

---

78. These seventeenth-century confessions, including the glaring omission of strict communion in the 1677/1689 London Baptist Confession, are examined in chapter 5.

79. Although in the seventeenth century, the debate over "communion" referred to church membership and its privileges, including admission to the Lord's Supper, from the eighteenth century on, debate over "communion" has usually referred specifically to access to the Lord's Table. Contemporary discussion treats "open membership" and "open communion" as separate yet related issues.

80. Ryland, *Modest Plea for Free Communion*; Turner, *Modest Plea for Free Communion*; Robinson, *General Doctrine of Toleration*; Booth, *Apology for the Baptists*. An overview of this eighteenth-century debate may be found in Oliver, *History of the English Calvinistic Baptists*, 58–88; Naylor, *Calvinism, Communion*, 107–24.

81. Oliver, "John Collett Ryland," 77–79. Ryland and Turner refer to being "severely

Modest Plea for Free Communion at the Lord's Table (1772), Ryland and Turner made many of the same arguments in favor of open communion that Bunyan made a century earlier: the church must receive all whom Christ himself receives, Romans 14–15 instructs the church to welcome the weak in faith, there is neither precept nor precedent for excluding the unbaptized from communion, and the contrast between the evangelistic power of evangelical unity and the destructive effect of disunity.[82]

Likewise, Abraham Booth, in his *An Apology for the Baptists* (1778), echoed many of the arguments marshalled by Thomas Paul, William Kiffin, and the rest of Bunyan's Baptist opponents: strict communion is the universal practice of the historic Christian church, strict communion is established by dominical precept and apostolic precedent, the regulative principle of worship demands strict communion, Romans 14–15 addresses a church that is already baptized and does not mention the Lord's Supper, and loyalty to Christ is more important than charity to paedobaptist brethren.[83] Robert Robinson's response to Booth, *The General Doctrine of Toleration Applied to the Particular Case of Free Communion* (1781), again retread much of the same ground as Ryland, Turner, and Bunyan before them, as Robinson freely admitted.[84] Nevertheless, Robinson did offer some novel

---

censured by several of our stricter brethren of the Baptist denomination for admitting Paedobaptists to commune with us at the Lord's Table" (Ryland and Turner, *Modest Plea for Free Communion*, 3). This tract originally appeared as two identical tracts, published anonymously by "Candidus" and "Pacificus." Robert Oliver established in 1981 that "the tracts are really one and must be the result of collaboration between Ryland and Turner" (Oliver, "John Collett Ryland," 78). Therefore, this monograph treats *A Modest Plea for Free Communion at the Lord's Table* as the work of both Ryland and Turner.

82. The tract is comprised of three sections: pp. 3–8 contain eight arguments in favor of open communion, pp. 9–13 contain answers to four objections, and pp. 14–16 contain a concluding argument.

83. Booth's *Apology for the Baptists* was not merely addressed to open-communion credobaptists, but to paedobaptists as well: "It is entirely on the defensive that the author takes up his pen; for had not the principles and practice of those professors who are invidiously called, Strict Baptists, been severely censured, by many that maintain, and by some who deny, the divine authority of Infant Baptism, these pages would never have seen the light" (Booth, *Apology for the Baptists*, iii).

84. Robinson wrote in the preface, "So much, and so much to purpose, has been published on the doctrine of church-fellowship, that nothing but the repeated solicitations of friends, who would take no denial, could have induced me to add to the number of such publications. I do not pretend to say anything new on the subject, I have only endeavored to state the case, and arrange the arguments, leaving every reader to form his own judgment" (Robinson, *General Doctrine of Toleration*, 2). An example of a recycled argument is Robinson's assertion that baptism is not a church ordinance and therefore cannot be an initiating ordinance (30–31). Bunyan repeatedly made the same claim.

arguments, including repeatedly and forcefully advocating for the "right of private judgment" (similar to what would later be termed "soul competency"), which must be respected even *within* the church.[85] In fact, so novel were some of Robinson's arguments that Robert Hall Jr. refused to use them in his own treatise on open communion a few decades later because he thought Robinson's case "rests on principles more lax and latitudinarian, than it is in [the author's] power conscientiously to adopt."[86]

In addition to Ryland, Turner, Booth, and Robinson, John Brown (open communion) and William Buttfield (strict communion) also penned influential works during this time.[87] After this furious barrage of tracts, however, the attention of Particular Baptists turned to other matters, not least of which was the fallout from Andrew Fuller's challenge to Hyper-Calvinism in his *Gospel Worthy of All Acceptation* (1784) and the founding of the Particular Baptist Missionary Society in 1792.[88] Though the debate was not settled, Robert Oliver states, "Strict communion remained the practice of most of the churches until well into the nineteenth century."[89]

In the early decades of the nineteenth century, debate over the terms of communion reignited. The two most important works to emerge from this period were Robert Hall Jr.'s *On Terms of Communion* (1816) and Joseph Kinghorn's *Baptism, A Term of Communion at the Lord's Supper* (1816).[90] At the opening of *On Terms of Communion*, Hall asserted: "There is no position in the whole compass of theology, of the truth of which [the author] feels a stronger persuasion, than that no man, nor set of men, are entitled

---

85. "If any reply, We allow his right of private judgment, and he may join a church of his own sentiments; we answer, That does not alter the case, you are required to allow the exercise of private judgment *in* your own community, not out of it, where your allowance and disallowance operate nothing" (Robinson, *General Doctrine of Toleration*, 28).

86. Hall, *On Terms of Communion*, vii.

87. Brown, *House of God Opened*; Buttfield, *Free Communion an Innovation*. For a time, Brown pastored the Kettering church later pastored by Andrew Fuller (Naylor, *Calvinism, Communion*, 114–16), and Buttfield held a brief pastorate in Bedfordshire (116–19). Brown's arguments mirror those of Bunyan; Buttfield's arguments mirror those of Kiffin, Paul, Danvers, and Denne.

88. Oliver, *History of the English Calvinistic Baptists*, 86.

89. Oliver, *History of the English Calvinistic Baptists*, 87. Similarly, Philip Naylor writes, "In the latter half of the 1700s, most Baptists, both in London and the counties, maintained a closed-table system" (Naylor, *Calvinism, Communion*, 109).

90. Hall, *On Terms of Communion*; Kinghorn, *Baptism*. An overview of this nineteenth-century debate may be found in Oliver, *History of the English Calvinistic Baptists*, 231–59; Naylor, *Calvinism, Communion*, 124–63.

to prescribe, as an indispensable condition of communion, what the New Testament has not enjoined as a condition of salvation."[91] Hall's work is divided into two sections. In the first, he considered four arguments for strict communion, while in the second, Hall marshaled six arguments in favor of open communion. Among the novel arguments made by Hall against strict communion was that the claim that baptism was instituted before the Lord's Supper rests upon a falsehood, for John's baptism was distinct from Christian baptism, which was instituted in the Great Commission after the Lord's resurrection.[92] In fact, Hall asserted that the apostles never actually received Christian baptism: "It now appears that the original communicants at the Lord's table, at the time they partook of it, were with respect to the christian baptism, precisely in the same situation with persons they exclude."[93] Nevertheless, novel arguments and superior organization notwithstanding, many of Hall's arguments appeared a century and a half earlier in the writings of Bunyan: the disunity of the church hinders its effective witness; the problem of paedobaptism did not exist in the apostolic era, rendering the argument from apostolic precedent irrelevant; all Christians are entitled to all Christian privileges; it is improper to force baptism upon those whose conscience will not permit it; the command to brotherly love is preeminent; Romans 14–15 commands the church to receive those who are weak in faith; the exclusion of an otherwise-qualified paedobaptist from church communion is tantamount to excommunication; and paedobaptist churches are true churches despite their erroneous view of baptism.[94] In other words, Hall's work, which Robert Oliver calls the "ablest defence of open communion yet to appear in print," is not a departure from Bunyan's argument, but rather builds upon it.[95]

---

91. Hall, *On Terms of Communion*, iv. Hall continued, "To establish this position, is the principal object of the following work; and though it is immediately occupied in the discussion of a case which respects the Baptists and the Paedobaptists, that case is attempted to be decided entirely upon the principle now mentioned, and it is no more than the application of it to a particular instance" (iv).

92. Hall offered six proofs for this claim. See Hall, *On Terms of Communion*, 15–31.

93. Hall, *On Terms of Communion*, 31. Hall asserted that the apostles "were not converted to the Christian religion subsequently to their Lord's resurrection, nor did the avowal of their attachment to the Messiah, commence from that period, and therefore, they were not comprehended under the baptismal law, which was propounded for the regulation of the conduct of persons in essentially different circumstances" (30).

94. Hall, *On Terms of Communion*, 9–10, 43, 44, 46, 56–60, 60–71.

95. Oliver, *History of the English Calvinistic Baptists*, 244.

Joseph Kinghorn, who offered the most substantial response to Hall, likewise restated arguments previously made by Paul and Kiffin in the seventeenth century: dominical precept supported by apostolic precedent establishes the necessity of baptism to church communion; biblical fidelity must not be sacrificed upon the altar of charity and unity; Romans 14–15 is irrelevant to the question, as it deals with matters of Mosaic law rather than the ordinances of Christ; and strict communion has been the universal practice of the historic church.[96] For Kinghorn, there was simply no justification for disobedience to Christ: "That toleration and forbearance will justify us in allowing an omission of a law of Christ in his Church, operates as a repeal of that law."[97] Robert Hall Jr. replied to Kinghorn in 1818; Kinghorn responded again in 1820.[98] Others joined in the debate, including William Newman (strict communion), Andrew Fuller (strict communion), Francis Cox (open communion), and Joseph Ivimey (strict communion).[99] This time around, open communion held

---

96. "If a law, supported and explained by such precedents, ought not to be strictly followed, I shall be glad to know, what is the use, either of command, or example?" (Kinghorn, *Baptism*, 25–26). "I maintain farther, that brotherly love, as love to the image of Christ, will and ought to lead us to walk with others as far as we walk in common in the ways of Christ; but should never induce us to act contrary to the will of Christ, or to shew love to *men*, at the expense of obedience to the directions of the *Lord*" (39). "The peculiarities of the Jewish Christians at Rome, who were perplexed about meats and drinks, interfered with *no divine command*" (47). "Here I would respectfully ask, in what instances have the suffrages of the church, at any early period, been in favour of communion *without baptism?*" (143). Though Kinghorn restated arguments previously used in centuries past, in many instances he stated them with greater clarity and cogency. Indeed, Kinghorn's defense of strict communion was arguably the best to appear until the twenty-first century.

97. Kinghorn, *Baptism*, 53. Kinghorn responded forcefully to Hall's contention that to refuse communion to an otherwise qualified paedobaptist is tantamount to excommunication by asserting that it is impossible to excommunicate one who was never a member in the first place: "But which way the censure, or punishment of excommunication and expulsion, can take place on one who never was *in* a society, the strict Baptists have yet to learn" (60).

98. Hall, *Reply to the Rev Joseph Kinghorn*; Kinghorn, *Defence of "Baptism a Term of Communion."* Peter Naylor surveys these two works, concluding that "Hall's rejoinder contains no new arguments," and that Kinghorn "ventur[ed] solely to expand his previous arguments" (Naylor, *Calvinism, Communion*, 147–53).

99. Newman, *Baptism; Moral and Ritual Precepts*; Fuller, *Admission of Unbaptized Persons*; Cox, *Letter on Free Communion*; Ivimey, *Baptism*. See Oliver, *History of the English Calvinistic Baptists*, 233–34, 251–53. Fuller wrote at least four documents in defense of strict communion: *Strictures on the Rev. John Carter's "Thoughts on Baptism and Mixed Communion"*; *Thoughts on Open Communion*; *Strict Communion in the Mission*

its own and eventually won the day among credobaptists in England.[100] Baptist historian Gregory Wills writes, "By 1900, open Communion was the common practice among English Baptists."[101]

The middle of the nineteenth century also saw debate over the terms of communion emerge among Baptists in the United States. Up to that point, strict communion was the universal practice among Baptist churches in America, at least according to R. B. C. Howell, who wrote in the introduction to his influential 1846 work *The Terms of Communion at the Lord's Table*:

> The internal controversy in relation to strict and free communion, the American churches have, thus far, almost entirely, escaped. I cannot but congratulate them on an event so fortunate. Agitations of this character are always productive of consequences the most lamentable. On the other side of the Atlantic they have prevailed for more than a century, and are now shaking the English church to its very foundation. Individuals have been found in our country, who express doubt as to the propriety of strict communion. A few isolated instances exist of communities who practise upon the opposite principles. But no association, nor even a single church, respectable for either numbers or intelligence, has, within the compass of my information, seceded from the great body of the denomination upon this ground. Our whole

---

Church at Serampore; and the aforementioned *Admission of Unbaptized Persons to the Lord's Supper* (published posthumously by William Newman in response to Hall's *On Terms of Communion*). Fuller identified the essential point of departure between open and strict communion: "If baptism be *not* necessary to communion; or, though it be, yet if immersion on a profession of faith be *not* necessary to baptism; or, though it be, if the candidate for communion be the *only* part with whom it rests to judge what is baptism; then *the strict communion of the Baptists seems to be wrong*. But if baptism *be* necessary to church communion, and immersion on a profession of faith *be* necessary to baptism, and it *be* the duty of a church to judge of this as well as of every other prerequisite in its candidates, then *the strict communion of the Baptists seems to be right*" (Fuller, *Strictures*, 854). It is worth noting that Fuller regarded Bunyan and open-communion credobaptists as fellow Baptists: "The *first* [that baptism is necessary to communion at the Lord's table] was denied by John Bunyan; but, being generally admitted by Paedobaptists, they are not entitled to his arguments. Those who follow Bunyan are chiefly Baptists who admit of mixed communion; and Bunyan himself was of this denomination. Against these Mr. Booth's Apology is chiefly directed" (853).

100. Whether this was due to the force of the arguments for open communion or the influence of external factors is beyond the scope of this monograph.

101. Wills, "Sounds from Baptist History," 290. Nathan Finn adds: "During the course of the twentieth century, open membership became the dominant view among Baptists in the British Isles" (Finn, "Historical Analysis of Church Membership," 73).

mighty army, bearing the banner of undeviating obedience to the word of God, the *whole* word of God, and *nothing but* the word of God, upon the ample folds of which is inscribed—"ONE LORD, ONE FAITH, ONE BAPTISM," presents an unbroken front. The internal controversy, therefore, need be considered, only in so far as may be necessary to guard our churches against its evils, and to maintain ourselves in opposition to the arguments drawn from that source by Pedobaptists.[102]

Nevertheless, Howell reported a growing tide of interest in open communion, as evidenced by the immense popularity of Robert Hall Jr's *On Terms of Communion,* to which Howell devoted abundant space, as well as mounting pressure from society at large.[103] Howell wrote, "Here the popular breeze appears, for the moment, to favor our assailants, and the onset is universal in all quarters. The more grave of our neighbors read us solemn lectures on christian liberality, humility, brotherly affection, and the importance of spirituality above mere form in religion. The pedantic and flippant catch the theme of detraction, and shower around us the shafts of their ridicule. The vulgar crowd follow, with coarse epithets, and boisterous denunciations!"[104] In response to this "spirit of *liberalism* which hesitates not to sacrifice the commandments of God to the courtesies of religious intercourse," Howell offered the first substantial defense of strict communion among Baptists in America.[105] *The Terms of Communion* consists of five major sections. Howell first argued that the indispensable, nonnegotiable terms of communion instituted by the Lord Jesus Christ are repentance toward God, faith in the Lord Jesus Christ, baptism in the triune name,

---

102. Howell, *Terms of Communion,* 16.

103. "If any apology is necessary for replying, as much at large as our limits would permit, to the imposing theories of which he was the advocate, it may be found, not only in his great abilities as a writer, joined to the fascination of his glowing and brilliant style,—characteristics which must ever invest them with no small degree of popularity,—but in the additional consideration that, in all parts of our country, they have been procured in great numbers, and circulated with the utmost industry, as the strongest weapons that can be employed against us. It was thought necessary that the charm of his authority should be dispelled; the sophistry of his principal arguments exposed; and that our brethren who cannot find time, or facilities, for extensive reading, should have at command, in a small compass, the information requisite to meet and refute those who may employ his reasoning" (Howell, *Terms of Communion,* 13–14). Hall is Howell's primary interlocutor.

104. Howell, *Terms of Communion,* 19.

105. Howell, *Terms of Communion,* 20. The work is thorough, consisting of 17 chapters and 271 pages.

and a Christian character free from immorality or heresy (chapters 1–7). Next, Howell discussed three reasons why Baptists may not engage in sacramental communion with paedobaptists (chapters 8–13). Third, Howell warned of the "ruinous" consequences that would befall Baptists were they to adopt open communion (chapter 14). Fourth, Howell asserted that far from being full of selfishness and bigotry, Baptists are "palpably more free and liberal in our communion than any class of Pedobaptists whatever" (chapter 15). Finally, Howell contended that it is not Baptists who are guilty of schism, but it is paedobaptists who have departed from the truth. The way forward, then, is not for Baptists to depart from the truth to reconcile with paedobaptists, but for paedobaptists to turn from the error of their ways and return to "the path of holy and full obedience" (chapter 16).[106] The work ends with a summary of Howell's argument, and a bold declaration that, "No Baptist can permit such considerations [of free communion] to occupy a place in his heart."[107]

While Robert Hall Jr. continued to be the most influential nineteenth-century proponent of open communion on both sides of the Atlantic, John L. Dagg emerged as another significant mid-century voice among strict-communion American Baptists.[108] Dagg published *An Essay in Defense of Strict Communion* in 1845, followed by his magisterial *Treatise on Church Order* in 1858. The latter work dedicates significant space to refuting ten arguments in favor of open communion, many of which were first put in print by Bunyan two centuries prior.[109] Though Robert Hall Jr. was the favored interlocutor of nineteenth-century strict-communion advocates like Howell and Dagg, it was in many cases Bunyan whom they were actually debating.

---

106. Howell, *Terms of Communion*, 267, 268, 270.

107. Howell, *Terms of Communion*, 270.

108. Hall's position as the foremost proponent of open communion in nineteenth-century America is evidenced by the fact that the two most substantial nineteenth-century defenses of strict communion (Howell's *The Terms of Communion at the Lord's Table* and Dagg's *An Essay in Defense of Strict Communion*) were directed against Hall's *On Terms of Communion*.

109. Examples include: the widely divergent circumstances of the first-generation church to the contemporary church; the command to brotherly love and unity; the relation of the particular to the universal church and the membership thereof; exclusion from church communion amounts to preemptive excommunication; the command of Romans 14 to receive those whom God has received; the inconsistency of holding certain forms of communion with paedobaptists while refusing church communion. See Dagg's rebuttal in Dagg, *Treatise on Church Order*, 214–25.

And though their rebuttals were dressed in new guise, the echoes of William Kiffin, Thomas Paul, John Denne, and Henry Danvers could still be heard.

In the early decades of the twentieth century, controversy over the terms of communion provoked the secession of conservatives from the Northern Baptist Convention (NBC) to the Southern Baptist Convention (SBC), followed by controversy within the SBC itself.[110] Wills notes, "Baptist churches [in the United States] traditionally insisted on close Communion and until the 1890s disfellowshipped any pastors or churches that adopted open Communion. By 1900 Northern Baptists tolerated open Communion churches and the practice spread. Around 1950 Southern Baptists experienced a similar transformation."[111] In 1907, strict communionists within the Illinois State Convention (NBC) broke away and affiliated with the SBC. In 1910, a group of New Mexico Baptists followed suit. The same occurred in Arizona in 1928, California in 1940, and Oregon and Washington in 1948.[112] Soon, however, open communion began to spread even among SBC churches. Wills notes, "Open Communion views spread significantly after the 1940s. . . . By the 1970s many conservatives had acquiesced and no longer resisted open Communion. . . . By the late twentieth century, most conservative Southern Baptist pastors practiced open Communion."[113]

Debate over the terms of communion continues into the present day. In 2005, influential pastor and theologian John Piper unsuccessfully

---

110. Wills, "Sounds from Baptist History," 285. Wills highlights the link that existed in the twentieth century between open communion and theological liberalism: "The acceptance of open communion was an important step toward a more progressive religion among Baptists" (285); "Open communion appealed to those clergy who sympathized most with the emerging liberal theology" (301); "Open Communion represented the advance of a liberal and enlightened faith" (303); "For Baptists, the road to apostasy began at open Communion" (307). For a detailed account of the rise of open communion in the Northern Baptist Convention and its correspondence with the rise of theological liberalism, see Straub, *Making of a Battle Royal*. See especially the detailed list of publications surrounding John D. Rockefeller Jr.'s famous 1917 plea to the Baptist Social Union of New York for a new ecclesiology that "would do away with denominational markers such as immersion in favor of an undenominational body dedicated to social action," in Straub, *Making of a Battle Royal*, 10n30. See also Augustus H. Strong's vigorous, yet ultimately unsuccessful defense of strict communion directed particularly toward theological students in Northern Baptist seminaries in Strong, *Systematic Theology*, 969–80. Strong's *Systematic Theology* interacts with a number of contemporary defenses of open communion.

111. Wills, "Sounds from Baptist History," 285.

112. Wills, "Sounds from Baptist History," 306–7.

113. Wills, "Sounds from Baptist History," 309, 311.

attempted to move his congregation, Bethlehem Baptist Church in Minneapolis, to adopt a qualified open-communion, open-membership position. The proposed change would have amended the church constitution to allow for the membership of convictional paedobaptists. The stated rationale for this change was that, "We believe it is fitting that membership in the local church (distinct from *leadership* in the local church) should have prerequisites similar to the prerequisites for membership in the universal church. In other words, we believe it is unfitting to deny membership to a person who, by faith in Christ, gives evidence of regeneration."[114] The motion originally carried amongst the elders with only two dissenting votes; but when it was presented to the church, the response was not positive. As a result, a number of elders changed their position, and the eldership decided to withdraw the motion.[115]

Nevertheless, Piper's high-profile plea provoked renewed interest in an old debate over the terms of membership and communion. When in 2007 Wayne Grudem revised his view on the relationship between baptism and church membership (and therefore, between baptism and communion) for the second printing of his influential and best-selling *Systematic Theology*, moving from an open membership to a strict membership position, Piper responded in an article published on the Desiring God website, which also published Grudem's reply to Piper's objections.[116] Through this online dialogue, countless evangelicals were witness to a debate between two of evangelicalism's leading figures. As Piper and likeminded authors have continued to press their case for open membership on the Desiring God website and in other popular mediums, it is difficult

---

114. See Piper et al., "Baptism and Church Membership," 38, italics original. There were some important qualifications to the proposed open-communion position. First, the church would continue to teach and practice credobaptism as the only valid form of baptism, regarding all other forms as "misguided, defective, and illegitimate." Second, no unbaptized (paedobaptist) member would be qualified to serve as an elder of the church. Third, the prospective paedobaptist member would be required to give a "plausible, intelligible, Scripturally-based argument" for paedobaptism rather than adhering merely to "tradition or family expectations." Fourth, the church would not admit into membership "persons who refuse to practice any form of baptism at all, or who believe that their water baptism caused their regeneration."

115. Piper, "Can You Update Us?"

116. Piper, "Response to Grudem"; Grudem, "Wayne Grudem's Response to Piper." For the change in Grudem's position, see Grudem, *Systematic Theology* [1994], 982–83; cf. *Systematic Theology* [2007], 982–84.

to deny that Piper's visibility and influence among evangelicals is at least partially responsible for this revived interest.[117]

The twenty-first century has witnessed a resurgence of interest in Baptist ecclesiology, and a number of recent works have delved briefly into the relationship between baptism, church membership, and the Lord's Supper.[118] Most works, however, fail to offer a robust, comprehensive argument

---

117. This is not to suggest a causal link in all cases, but it is worth noting that Bobby Jamieson identifies Piper's plea as a stimulating factor in the renewed interest in the relationship between baptism and church communion and selects Piper as one of his primary interlocutors in his published defense of strict communion: "But this isn't just a historic debate; it's also an issue that's receiving renewed attention today. For example, John Piper made waves when he advocated the open membership position at Bethlehem Baptist Church in 2005. Because Piper argued his case with his usual verve, he'll be my primary dialogue partner. Piper is a hero in the faith to me and many others, so please don't confuse critique with condemnation. Anecdotally it also seems like this issue is receiving renewed attention among a variety of baptistic evangelicals in at least the US and the UK" (Jamieson, *Going Public*, 11–12). For articles in defense of open communion posted on the Desiring God website, see Desiring God, "Are Paedobaptists Unrepentant?"; Rigney, "Do Infant Baptisms Count?" See also the article written by Desiring God Executive Director David Mathis, posted on the Gospel Coalition website, Mathis, "Happy Baptist."

118. John Hammett notes in the preface to the second edition of his *Biblical Foundations for Baptist Churches*, "In the past ten years and more, there has been a welcome renaissance in writings on ecclesiology, especially from a Baptist perspective" (Hammett, *Biblical Foundations for Baptist Church*, 7). Recent works on ecclesiology that argue for strict membership or strict communion include Finn, "Baptism as a Prerequisite"; Allison, *Sojourners and Strangers*, 400–406; Hammett, "Regenerate Church Membership," 27–30; "Church Membership, Church Discipline," 18–20; *40 Questions about Baptism*, 259–72; *Biblical Foundations for Baptist Churches*, 175–79, 327–33; Vandiver, *Who Can Take the Lord's Supper?* Recent works on ecclesiology that argue for open communion or open membership include Tyler, *Baptism*, 113–46; Clarke, "Feast for All?," 92–116. For a substantive online discussion between two leading evangelicals, see Ortlund, "Can We Reject Paedobaptism?" (January 3, 2019); Leeman, "Church Membership and the Definition of Baptism" (January 4, 2019); Ortlund, "There Is One Baptism," (January 7, 2019); Leeman, "Baptist Sacramentology," (January 8, 2019). See also Watson, *In the Name of Our Lord*, which provides an explanatory framework for the various views on the relationship between baptism, catechesis, and the Lord's Supper, and discerns a theological catalyst for how a church arrives at its position. Watson finds that the theological catalyst is "the way in which the decisive confirmation of faith for entrance is connected to baptism" (204). In other words, does the decisive confirmation of faith take place *in* baptism, *after* baptism, or *separate from* baptism? Another recent work that is relevant to this discussion is Fowler, *More Than a Symbol*. Fowler argues that there is no inherent connection between British Baptist sacramentalism and open membership; quite the opposite: "However, even if some such approach [i.e., open membership on the basis of the higher priority of visible unity] may be possible, what seems impossible is to claim that open membership logically follows from a Baptist-sacramental understanding of baptism. It may be defensible *in spite of* such a baptismal theology, but the British practice of

for either position. One notable exception is Bobby Jamieson's 2015 volume entitled *Going Public: Why Baptism Is Required for Church Membership*, which provides perhaps the most theologically constructive and coherent argument for strict membership and strict communion to date.[119]

> The thesis of this book, then, is that baptism and the Lord's Supper are effective signs of church membership: they create the social, ecclesial reality to which they point. Precisely because of their complementary church-constituting roles, baptism must precede the Lord's Supper and the status of church membership which grants access to the Lord's Supper. Therefore, what this book offers is not merely an answer to the question of whether baptism should be required for membership. Instead it offers an integrated account of how baptism and the Lord's Supper transform a scattered group of Christians into a gathered local church.[120]

As the "initiating oath-sign" of the new covenant, baptism initiates the believer into the visible new covenant community, thus incorporating the one into the many.[121] As the "renewing oath-sign" of the new covenant, the Lord's Supper renews the church's covenantal existence as a church, thus making

---

open membership appears to be grounded in the complexities of the British ecclesiastical context and in other ecclesiological principles, not in a logical inference from Baptist sacramentalism" (232).

119. The constructive emphasis of the book is demonstrated in the following statement: "To reiterate, I'm trying to do only one thing in this book: argue that baptism is necessary for church membership and the Lord's Supper. Along the way I aim to rebuild a coherent, biblical understanding of the role both ordinances play in the formation of the church" (Jamieson, *Going Public*, 9). Jamieson further comments, "Simple proof texting won't settle the issue either way. Churches have no explicit biblical command to admit only baptized persons to membership; yet all Christians are commanded to be baptized, and the New Testament Epistles address all church members as having been baptized (e.g., Rom 6:1–4; Gal 3:27). So again, I think the way forward lies through a holistic theological account of the relationship between the ordinances and church membership" (18).

120. Jamieson, *Going Public*, 2.

121. This is the thesis of chapter 4 (55–80) in Jamieson, *Going Public*. In the fifth chapter (81–105), Jamieson explores baptism in light of the kingdom of God, arguing that baptism is the "passport of the kingdom." This metaphor allows Jamieson to avoid the trap into which earlier Baptists stumbled: if baptism is the means of entering into the particular church, then is baptism required each time a member moves to another particular church? Jamieson writes, "Baptism is the passport of the kingdom. We become kingdom citizens by faith in the king, but in baptism the church recognizes and affirms our citizenship. And baptism enables other embassies of the kingdom—that is, other local churches—to recognize us as kingdom citizens" (163).

the many one.[122] "Baptism and the Lord's Supper, therefore, are effective signs of church membership. For a new convert, baptism confers membership, and then the Lord's Supper ratifies and enacts membership."[123] By logical necessity, then, baptism must precede church membership, and church membership must precede the Lord's Supper.[124] To those who might argue (like Bunyan) that it is not the ordinances but the mutual covenant that constitutes the church (i.e., is the form of the church), Jamieson responds that "this is a false dichotomy. A church and church membership aren't constituted by a covenant as opposed to the two ordinances, or vice versa, but *by the two ordinances which ratify a covenant*. . . . Just as these ritual acts ratify the new covenant, so they also constitute the new covenant's corporate correlate on earth: the local church."[125] After constructing the positive case for strict membership and strict communion, Jamieson moves "from offense to defense," first responding to seven of the most common arguments for open communion, many of which were offered by Bunyan, and then making seven arguments against open membership.[126]

After four centuries of the Baptist tradition, the communion debate remains unsettled, and few arguments have been offered that were not first made in the 1670s.[127] Each iteration of the debate must deal with Bunyan.

---

122. This is the thesis of chapter 6 (107–35) in Jamieson, *Going Public*.

123. Jamieson, *Going Public*, 138. Jamieson later writes, "In other words, baptism and the Lord's Supper make the church visible. They are the hinge between the 'invisible' universal church and the 'visible' local church. They draw a line around the church by drawing the church together. They gather many into one: baptism by adding one to many, the Lord's Supper by making many one" (142).

124. Jamieson argues for a modified version of close communion in which baptized believers (for Jamieson this means credobaptized believers) who are members in good standing of another evangelical church are welcome to partake of the Lord's Supper (130).

125. Jamieson, *Going Public*, 150, italics original.

126. "Now it's time to switch from offense to defense" (Jamieson, *Going Public*, 168). Chapter 9 (169–91) answers seven arguments for open communion. Chapter 10 (193–207) offers seven arguments against open membership.

127. Peter Naylor writes, "It appears that everything that was worth saying about terms of communion was said [in the 1700s], boundaries being set for the future. One might even suppose that for this reason modern discussions, if any, about a link between believer's baptism and attendance at the Lord's Table cannot afford to ignore the word battles in which our predecessors engaged themselves. There is nothing new under the sun" (Naylor, *Calvinism, Communion*, 10). A little later, Naylor draws the boundary of novel arguments even earlier: "But a word of explanation is necessary: lest the reader suspects that the exposition is repetitious and tedious, it appears that after 1688 Baptists on both sides of the baptism-communion issue echoed their predecessors and anticipated

Those in favor of open communion marshal Bunyan for support. When Piper attempted to move his church to an open-communion stance, three times he referenced arguments made by John Bunyan, the only extrabiblical author Piper cites.[128] Those in favor of strict communion must engage and refute Bunyan. Jamieson, for instance, repeatedly engages with Bunyan's arguments in his monograph, as did Abraham Booth three centuries earlier.[129] As Bunyan continues to cast a long shadow over the communion debate, this monograph will contribute to contemporary Baptist ecclesiology by synthesizing and clarifying the fundamental issues at stake in Bunyan's original battle with the Baptists.[130]

---

their successors. Subject to the idiosyncrasies of personalities and backgrounds that intrude, no substantially fresh arguments appeared for or against restricted communion during the period under review. The litany perpetuated itself" (11).

128. Piper et al., "Baptism and Church Membership," 18, 21. Piper twice references *A Confession of My Faith* and once *Differences in Judgment about Water-Baptism*. Piper does claim the support of Wayne Grudem's *Systematic Theology* (1994); however, as noted above, Grudem changed his mind on open membership between his first and second edition.

129. Jamieson, *Going Public*, 3, 13, 16, 50–51, 55, 79, 98, 170, 174, 178, 184, 198, 201; Booth, *Apology for the Baptists*, 36, 54, 56, 59, 96, 103, 114, 119, 160. Booth castigated Bunyan and Henry Jessey for their "pretended theological knowledge" by which they "amused mankind, by crafting new light on the positive institutions of Jesus Christ, and by placing baptism amongst those things of little importance to the Christian religion; of which no ancient theologue had ever dreamed—none, we have reason to think, that ever loved the Lord Redeemer" (Booth, *Apology for the Baptists*, 36). Booth allowed that Bunyan "was an eminent servant of Jesus Christ, and patiently suffered in his Master's cause. Many of his writings have been greatly useful to the church of God, and some of them, it is probable, will transmit his name with honour, to future ages. But yet I cannot persuade myself, that either his judgment or his piety appeared in this bold innovation. The disciples of George Fox [the Quakers whom Bunyan opposed in *Some Gospel-Truths Opened* and *A Vindication of . . . Some Gospel-Truths Opened*], acted more consistently with their own principles, than did the justly celebrated Dreamer then, or our brethren who practice free communion now" (36).

130. In a 2016 article, Matthew Ward examined the origin, course, and significance of the communion controversy, arguing that at the heart of the debate was the question of whether baptism was an individual expression of worship (Bunyan) or a corporate act of worship (the Baptists) (Ward, "Baptism as Worship," 17–31). Ward argues that seeing this debate as essentially a debate over church worship reveals: (1) it was a debate over the nature of the church and the relationship between God and man; (2) it exposed differing hermeneutical principles, particularly the regulative principle; (3) it forces one to define the relationship between baptism and church membership. This monograph does not dispute Ward's thesis, but offers a far more comprehensive analysis of the communion controversy and suggests additional foundational differences between Bunyan and the Baptists in the 1670s, and therefore between open- and strict-communion advocates

Summary of Chapters

Was Bunyan a Baptist? This monograph argues that John Bunyan held to a fundamentally disparate ecclesiology than seventeenth-century Baptists, and therefore, Bunyan should not be considered a seventeenth-century Baptist. Rather, Bunyan is best described—historically, theologically, and ecclesiologically—as an Evangelical Independent.

Chapter 1 has introduced this thesis, and established that the answer has relevance to Bunyan scholarship, Baptist history, and Baptist ecclesiology.

Chapter 2 explores the origin of Bunyan's ecclesiology. It demonstrates that Bunyan's doctrine of the church was profoundly shaped by his experiences with the Bedford Church, a Nonconformist congregation founded upon explicitly evangelical and ecumenical principles. Bunyan's own conversion was occasioned by his interactions with the Bedford Church, and his ecclesiological convictions were nurtured and refined by his ministry in and to this congregation.

Chapter 3 provides a systematic overview of Bunyan's Evangelical Independent ecclesiology, examining the nature, unity, membership, purpose, polity, officers, worship, ordinances, and discipline of the church. It demonstrates that the driving concern of every aspect of Bunyan's ecclesiology was the promotion of evangelical faith and holiness. The theme of "faith and holiness," by which Bunyan meant justification by faith in the imputed righteousness of Christ and Spirit-wrought obedience to the "moral law gospelized," permeates his writings and colored his conception of the church.

Chapter 4 examines the communion controversy of the 1670s, a debate that brought to the fore the fundamental ecclesiological differences between Bunyan and his Baptist opponents. The controversy did not begin in the 1670s; rather, the debate was the eruption of tensions that were inherent within the Particular Baptist movement from its inception. From the beginning, differences of opinion existed among credobaptists over

---

today. It is worth noting, however, that Ward offers a way forward for Baptists struggling with the question of whether baptism belongs to the "form" of a church. Ward concludes that a covenant, and not baptism or a profession of faith, must be the form of a church, and that baptism is a corporate act of worship. Therefore, a church's covenant should include within it the proper mode, meaning, and subjects of baptism. And because each covenant is unique and binding only upon the local church that adopts it, this does not "unchristian" paedobaptist believers, nor "unchurch" paedobaptist churches, as Bunyan and open-communion advocates ever since have argued (30–31).

the ecclesiological significance of baptism, and consequently, what to do with paedobaptists who desired membership and communion within the particular/visible church. This chapter surveys the seven extant works that emerged from this debate. It then identifies seven significant points at which Bunyan diverged from the ecclesiology of his Baptist opponents.

Chapter 5 argues that strict communion was a seventeenth-century Baptist distinctive. It defends this thesis: first, by surveying the works of prominent and purported open-communion advocates in order to demonstrate that open communion was an isolated ecclesiological position, not sufficiently widespread or connected to the broader Baptist movement to qualify as a minority view within that movement; second, by examining every significant seventeenth-century Baptist confession and the writings of representative seventeenth-century Baptist theologians in order to demonstrate that strict communion was so dominant among seventeenth-century Baptists and so integrated into their ecclesiological framework as to be considered universal; third, by demonstrating that the omission of strict-communion language in the 1677/1689 London Baptist Confession was driven by changing historical circumstances rather than by shifting biblical convictions, and therefore does not represent a new openness to open communion as a valid Baptist position. Chapter 5 demonstrates that all but a small minority of seventeenth-century credobaptists held that credobaptism was essential to the constitution of a properly-ordered visible church. Therefore, it is best to consider Bunyan, the Bedford Church, and other seventeenth-century open-communionists as something other than Baptist.

Chapter 6 proposes an answer to the question of Bunyan's ecclesiological identity. It examines the four historical, theological, and ecclesiological labels that are most often applied to Bunyan in the secondary literature, then suggests a new label that more accurately describes his theological and ecclesiological convictions and differentiates him from his contemporaries who held to significantly different views. First, it argues that though Bunyan was a theological heir of Puritanism, yet because he was not a Puritan in the historical sense of the term, "Puritan" is not the most accurate label for Bunyan. Second, it argues that Bunyan possesses the four characteristics of Evangelicalism as defined by Bebbington's Quadrilateral; yet because he preceded Evangelicalism according to Bebbington's widely-accepted historical classification, "Evangelical" as a proper noun is not the most helpful label for Bunyan. Third, in light of the evidence presented in chapters 2 through 5, "Baptist" is not an accurate ecclesiological label for Bunyan. Neither is "Congregationalist" an accurate descriptor, for it carries the wrong baptismal connotation. Therefore, Bunyan is best described as an Evangelical Independent. "Independent" distinguishes Bunyan from both Baptists and Congregationalists, and "Evangelical" describes Bunyan's driving ecclesiological conviction—evangelical unity rooted in evangelical faith and holiness.

Chapter 2

Bunyan and the Bedford Church: The Origin of Bunyan's Ecclesiology

> And me thought they spake as if joy did make them speak: they spake with such pleasantness of Scripture language, and with such appearance of grace in all they said, that they were to me, as if they had found a new world, as if they were people that dwelt alone, and were not to be reckoned amongst their Neighbours.[1]

BUNYAN'S FAMOUS ENCOUNTER WITH the "three or four poor women sitting at a door in the Sun, and talking about the things of God," occurred in 1650 and began a nearly forty-year relationship with the Bedford Church.[2] Bunyan's life and thought cannot be understood apart from his interactions with the congregation that guided him to conversion, sent him out to preach, visited him in prison, ordained him as an elder, inspired him to write, benefited from his ministry, and mourned his death. As Michael Davies observes, Bunyan is far from the "lonely and tormented Calvinist" imagined by so many literary critics, who stress the "loneliness and

---

1. Bunyan, *Grace Abounding*, 14.
2. Bunyan, *Grace Abounding*, 14. The chronology of Bunyan's experiences between his discharge from the Parliamentary Army in 1647 and his imprisonment in November 1660 must be reconstructed from two sources, *Grace Abounding to the Chief of Sinners* and *The Minutes of . . . Bunyan Meeting*. Based upon these sources, Richard Greaves provides a rough chronology, which this monograph follows (Greaves, *Glimpses of Glory*, 33–34).

alienation in Bunyan's writings."[3] On the contrary, from the time of his 1650 awakening in Bedford, Bunyan was never far from his church. Even during his twelve-year imprisonment, Bunyan was intimately involved in the affairs of the congregation, as the *Minutes* amply testify. Bunyan was not a lonely pilgrim, making his solitary way to the Celestial City. His entire pilgrimage took place within the shadow of the Palace Beautiful, amidst fellow pilgrims whose fundamental principles were likewise evangelical faith and holiness. This chapter examines the origin of Bunyan's Evangelical Independent ecclesiology, which he inherited from the Bedford Church and from its founding pastor, John Gifford.

Bunyan's Early Religious Encounters

By the time John Bunyan encountered the Bedford Church, he was well-acquainted with the ecclesiological options available to a man living in Interregnum England. Born in November 1628 in Elstow, a small hamlet about a mile south of Bedford, Bunyan was baptized in the parish church the same month.[4] References to his parents are scant; Bunyan never so much as mentioned their names.[5] From his father, Bunyan inherited a rudimentary education, his profession as a tinker (or brazier), and a prodigious habit of cursing.[6] Bunyan wrote in *Grace Abounding* that as a young

---

3. Davies, "Spirit in the Letters," 323–24.

4. For extensive information on Bunyan's ancestry in Elstow, see Brown, *John Bunyan*, 17–38. A facsimile of Bunyan's baptismal entry on November 30, 1628 in the Elstow parish register may be found on p. 32 of Brown's work.

5. His father was Thomas Bunyan, and his mother was Thomas's second wife, Margaret. Thomas Bunyan's first wife died childless in 1627 (Brown, *John Bunyan*, 33).

6. Of his education, Bunyan wrote, "But yet notwithstanding the meanness and inconsiderableness of my Parents, it pleased God to put it into their heart, to put me to School, to learn both to Read and Write; the which I also attained, according to the rate of other poor mens children" (Bunyan, *Grace Abounding*, 6). Roger Sharrock speculated that Bunyan may have even attended grammar school for a time, which "enabled him from the start of his writing to construct grammatical and coherent sentences and paragraphs" (Sharrock, "When at the First," 74). Though acknowledging the possibility, Greaves writes, "If so, he distanced himself from its curriculum, preferring to link classical philosophy and its embodiment in medieval scholastic thought with the traditional divines in the Church of England" (Greaves, *Glimpses of Glory*, 5). Of Thomas Bunyan, who described himself in his will as a "braseyer," Brown wrote, "Working at his forge by the cottage in the fields, repairing the tools and utensils of his neighbours at Elstow or Harrowden, or wandering for the purposes of his trade from one lonely farmhouse to another, he would be neither better nor worse than the rest of the craftsmen of the hammer and the forge" (Brown, *John Bunyan*, 34).

adult experiencing the first pangs of conviction, "I wished with all my heart that I might be a little childe again, that my Father might learn me to speak without this wicked way of swearing."[7] What he does not seem to have inherited from his father was an evangelical upbringing.[8] Bunyan testified concerning his young soul, "It was my delight to be taken captive by the Devil *at his will*, being filled with all unrighteousness; the which did also so strongly work, and put forth it self, both in my heart and life, and that from a childe, that I had but few Equals, (especially considering my years, which were tender, being few) both for cursing, swearing, lying, and blaspheming the holy Name of God."[9] Nevertheless, he possessed a tender, and at times tormented, conscience, for when he was "but nine or ten years old," he was haunted by fearful dreams, visions, and thoughts of the day of judgment and eternal damnation.[10]

When Bunyan was just sixteen, he either enlisted or was conscripted into the Parliamentary Army.[11] During these military years (1644–1647)

7. Bunyan, *Grace Abounding*, 12.

8. In *Christian Behaviour* (1674), near the end of the section dealing with the duties of children to their parents, Bunyan wrote, "O! how happy a thing would it be, if God should use a Child to beget his Father to the Faith! Then indeed might the Father say, With the fruit of my own bowels hath God converted my soul. The Lord if it be his will, convert our poor Parents, that they, with us, may be the Children of God" (Bunyan, *Christian Behaviour*, 3:40). Whether this is autobiographical is speculation. At any rate, Bunyan's father appears to have had no influence upon Bunyan's faith. Bunyan's mother died before his sixteenth year (Brown, *John Bunyan*, 36).

9. Bunyan, *Grace Abounding*, 6–7.

10. That Bunyan's age was "but nine or ten years old" when the fearful dreams began appears in the third edition of *Grace Abounding* (Stachniewski and Pacheco, *Grace Abounding*, 231). He added, "In these days the thoughts of Religion were very grievous to me; I could neither endure it my self, nor that any other should: so that, when I have seen some read in those books that concerned Christian piety, it would be as it were a prison to me" (Bunyan, *Grace Abounding*, 8).

11. Greaves, *Glimpses of Glory*, 11. Bunyan did not mention his military service except in one brief passage in *Grace Abounding*: "When I was a Souldier, I with others were drawn out to go to such a place to besiege it, but when I was just ready to go, one of the company desired to go in my room, to which when I had consented he took my place, and coming to the siege, as he stood Sentinel, he was shot into the head with a Musket bullet and died" (Bunyan, *Grace Abounding*, 8). George Offor identified this as the siege at Leicester and on that basis contended that Bunyan served in the Royalist forces of Charles I (Offor, "Memoir of John Bunyan," 1:vi–vii). Most scholars disagree. Richard Greaves writes, "The evidence for his service in a parliamentary garrison is persuasive. The muster rolls for the garrison at Newport Pagnell, Buckinghamshire, list John Bunnion (or Bunion) as a member of Lieutenant-Colonel Richard Cokayne's company from 30 November 1644 through 8 March 1645. . . . Although the muster rolls for this

Bunyan encountered a cacophony of religious voices. On the one hand, there were the Presbyterian reformers who at that time enjoyed control of Parliament. One such influence was Sir Samuel Luke, governor of Newport Pagnell, where Bunyan was garrisoned, who sought to require all the men in his city to swear an oath to the Solemn League and Covenant.[12] Furthermore, Thomas Ford was chaplain of Bunyan's regiment in the winter of 1644/1645, before becoming a member of the Westminster Assembly. Under their influence, Bunyan would have been exposed to Westminster Presbyterianism.[13]

On the other hand, the Parliamentary forces, especially in the New Model Army, were a hotbed for religious radicalism, and Newport Pagnell saw its fair share, particularly after Samuel Luke was relieved of command in June 1645 under the Self-Denying Ordinance.[14] One figure in particular stands out as a potential source of influence upon Bunyan.[15] Captain

---

company terminate on 8 March 1645, Bunyan's name appears with sixty-six others on the rolls for the company of Major Robert Bolton between 21 April and 27 May of the same year" (Greaves, *Glimpses of Glory*, 11). Bunyan then reenlisted in June 1647 to go with Colonel O'Hara's company to Ireland, but the company was disbanded by Parliament on July 21, 1647, thus ending Bunyan's military career (19). Greaves suggests that "if there is any truth to the story about Bunyan's narrow escape when a compatriot took his place during a siege, it must have been at Oxford rather than Leicester" (18). See also Laurence, "Bunyan and the Parliamentary Army," 19–20.

12. Greaves, *Glimpses of Glory*, 21. Much of the information on military and religious matters in Newport Pagnell during the years 1644–1645 comes from Luke, *Letter Books*.

13. Greaves, *Glimpses of Glory*, 21–22. Greaves remarks that, "At the changing of the guard each morning Bunyan would also have heard prayers and the reading of a chapter from Scripture" (22).

14. For religious radicalism in the Parliamentary and New Model Army, see Hill, *Tinker and a Poor Man*, 45–55; Greaves, *Glimpses of Glory*, 21–29. Before his departure, Luke complained, "If I stay here, I must have liberty to free the town of [sectaries] lest God in his wrath deal with them as he did with Sodom and Gomorrah" (Luke, *Letter Books*, 192, cited in Hill, *Tinker and a Poor Man*, 49).

15. In addition to Paul Hobson, Greaves mentions William Erbery, John Gibbs, and Richard Carpenter as potential sources of influence (Greaves, *Glimpses of Glory*, 22–29). But the evidence of influence in each case is lacking. Erbery held unorthodox views repugnant to Bunyan, including a denial of the deity of Christ, a denial of the necessity of the gathered church, and an affirmation of universal redemption. Gibbs and Carpenter debated baptism in 1647, but there is no evidence that Bunyan witnessed it. Gibbs, about Bunyan's same age and hailing from Bedford, was known to Bunyan, and may have been the J. G. who wrote the introduction to *A Few Sighs from Hell* (1658). But this is no evidence that Bunyan was privy to his views in 1647. Greaves's suggestion, "Conceivably, Bunyan, perhaps having gone to school with Gibbs, wanted to hear him debate," is unconvincing (Greaves, *Glimpses of Glory*, 28).

Paul Hobson, a signatory of the 1644 London Baptist Confession, arrived in Newport Pagnell eleven days before Luke was relieved of duty, preaching to large crowds. Luke had Hobson and his companion, Captain Richard Beaumont, arrested, but they were soon acquitted by Thomas Fairfax, commander-in-chief of the New Model Army. Bunyan would have heard several points of emphasis from Hobson that would later feature in his own thought and writing, including the denial of formal education as a qualification to preach, the repudiation of a state church and parish membership, the true visible church as a voluntary gathering of visible saints, the devaluing of the ordinances, the severing of baptism from church membership, and the typological interpretation of the Old Testament. Like Bunyan, Hobson rejected paedobaptism, and reconciled predestination with the free offer of the gospel.[16] Hobson and others during Bunyan's stay in Newport Pagnell may have had a formative influence upon Bunyan's thought, but the evidence of such is circumstantial and pales in comparison with the obvious influence that would later come through the Bedford Church.

After his discharge from the Parliamentary Army, Bunyan returned to Elstow, took up the occupation of a tinker, and married. No record remains of the marriage, nor even his wife's name.[17] She brought no dowry into the union; what she did bring was the godly heritage of her Puritan father and two works of Puritan devotion her father left her upon his death.

> Presently after this, I changed my condition into a married state; and my mercy was, to light upon a Wife whose Father was counted godly: this Woman and I, though we came together as poor as poor might be, (not having so much as a Dish or Spoon betwixt us both) yet this she had for her part, *The Plain Mans Path-way to Heaven*, and *The Practice of Piety*, which her Father had left her

---

16. Greaves, *Glimpses of Glory*, 24–25. Greaves writes, "The affinity between so many of Bunyan's fundamental tenets and Hobson's views suggests influence" (25). Hill writes, "[Hobson] may or may not have influenced Bunyan at a susceptible time in the mid-1640s. But he is representative of the radical antinomian and ecumenical Particular Baptists whose thought always had its attraction for Bunyan: though he never fully identified himself with it" (Hill, *Tinker and a Poor Man*, 55). The ignominious and scandalous end of Hobson's career is detailed on the same page (55). See Greaves's account of Hobson's life in Greaves, *Saints and Rebels*, 133–56.

17. Brown, *John Bunyan*, 53. Greaves states, "Because their first child, the blind daughter Mary, was christened on 20 July 1650, the marriage probably occurred no later than October 1649. The Elstow parish register has no record of the event, suggesting that it may have been a private, informal ceremony or that it took place elsewhere, perhaps because his bride was not a local woman" (Greaves, *Glimpses of Glory*, 30).

when he died. In these two Books I should sometimes read with her, wherein I also found some things that were somewhat pleasing to me: (but all this while I met with no conviction.) She also would be often telling of me what a godly man her Father was, and how he would reprove and correct Vice, both in his house, and amongst his neighbours; what a strict and holy life he lived in his day, both in word and deed.[18]

The Plaine Mans Path-way to Heaven (1601) was written by Arthur Dent, a parish minister in Essex.[19] *The Practise of Pietie* (1611) was written by Lewis Bayly, a Welsh clergyman and eventual Bishop of Bangor.[20] These classic works of Puritan piety undoubtedly had some impact upon Bunyan, but once again their influence was not determinative, as Bunyan himself admitted. What later influence they had upon his theology and devotion was either filtered through or superseded by the theology and devotion Bunyan would later receive from Gifford and the Bedford Church.

Though these works did not "reach my heart to awaken it about my sad and sinful state, yet they did beget within me some desires to Religion: so that, because I knew no better, I fell in very eagerly with the Religion of the times."[21] Thus began Bunyan's brief sojourn within the established Church.[22] At first, Bunyan's relation to the Church was superstitious and superficial:

---

18. Bunyan, *Grace Abounding*, 8–9.

19. In Brown's opinion, *The Plaine Mans Path-Way to Heaven* is "long, and for the most part wearisomely heavy and theologically narrow." Nevertheless, its dialogue format may have influenced Bunyan's *The Life and Death of Mr. Badman* (Brown, *John Bunyan*, 55). The dialogue addresses such common Puritan topics as "the misery of man by nature, the corruption of the world, the marks of the children of God, the difficulty of entering into life, the ignorance of the world, and the sweet promises of the gospel . . . regeneration, pride, adultery, covetousness, contempt of the gospel, swearing, lying, drunkenness, idleness, oppression, effects of sin, predestination, hindrances to salvation, and Christ's second coming" (Beeke and Pederson, *Meet the Puritans*, 174–75).

20. Brown's opinion of this work was likewise less than flattering: "Reading the book now, it is difficult to account for its widespread popularity" (Brown, *John Bunyan*, 56). The book is concerned with inculcating classical Puritan piety ("prayer, Bible-reading, meditation, psalm-singing, Sabbath-keeping, stewardship, the commemoration of the Lord's Supper, and walking daily with God") in order that one may tread the narrow way leading to life rather than the broad road that leads to destruction, and thereby maintain readiness for the second advent of Christ (Beeke and Pederson, *Meet the Puritans*, 73–74).

21. Bunyan, *Grace Abounding*, 9.

22. If Bunyan was married in 1648/9 and his spiritual awakening in Bedford occurred

> To wit, to go to Church twice a day, and that too with the foremost, and there should very devoutly both say and sing as others did; yet retaining my wicked life: but withal, I was so over-run with a spirit of superstition, that I adored, and that with great devotion, even all things (both the High-place, Priest, Clerk, Vestments, Service, and what else) belonging to the Church; counting all things holy that were therein contained....
>
> This conceit grew so strong in little time upon my spirit, that had I but seen a Priest, (though never so sordid and debauched in his life) I should find my spirit fall under him, reverence him, and knit unto him; yea, I thought for the love I did bear unto them, (supposing they were the Ministers of my God) I could have layn down at their feet, and have been trampled upon by them; their Name, their Garb, and Work, did so intoxicate and bewitch me.[23]

Richard Greaves remarks, "Although Parliament had proscribed the Book of Common Prayer and imposed the Directory of Public Worship, the traditional liturgy was used in many churches, even in London. Bunyan's description suggests that Hall [Christopher Hall, Vicar of Elstow] continued to employ the Book of Common Prayer and wear the traditional vestments."[24] The lasting influence of Anglican worship upon Bunyan was entirely negative, however, as he would soon reject the Church and its liturgy as vain repetition devoid of the Spirit.

Although Christopher Hall seems to have continued in the traditional liturgy, he was not unaffected by Puritan piety. One Sunday, Hall preached upon "the Sabbath day, and of the evil of breaking that, either with labour, sports, or otherwise."[25] At this preaching of the law, Bunyan was struck to the heart and had his first encounter with conviction: "Wherefore I fell in my conscience under his Sermon, thinking and believing that he made that Sermon on purpose to shew me my evil-doing; and at that time I felt what

---

in 1650, Bunyan's Anglican phase could have lasted no more than two years. Indeed, Bunyan says his "outward Reformation" lasted "a twelve-month, or more" (Bunyan, *Grace Abounding*, 12–13).

23. Bunyan, *Grace Abounding*, 9.

24. Greaves, *Glimpses of Glory*, 32.

25. Bunyan, *Grace Abounding*, 10. George Offor wrote that during the Laudian era, "whether to promote Popery—to divert his subjects from political grievances—or to punish the Puritans," *The Book of Sports* was republished, and clergy were directed to read it from the pulpit, thus encouraging Sunday sports and entertainments (Offor, "Memoir of John Bunyan," 1:x). Had Hall been a traditional Laudian clergyman, he would not have preached against Sabbath-breaking with such vehemence.

guilt was, though never before, that I can remember."[26] Nevertheless, before he was finished with his midday meal, the conviction had evaporated and that Sunday afternoon found Bunyan on the Elstow lawn engaged in a game of tip cat.[27] But "a voice did suddenly dart from Heaven into my Soul, which said, *Wilt thou leave thy sins, and go to Heaven? or have thy sins, and go to Hell?*" Bunyan looked up to heaven, and "with the eyes of my understanding" saw the Lord Jesus "looking down upon me, as being very hotly displeased with me, and as if he did severely threaten me with some grievous punishment for these, and other my ungodly practices."[28] Despair fell upon Bunyan as he feared he had sinned beyond hope of forgiveness. Concluding that it was too late for mercy, he decided to throw himself headlong into sin: "for thought I, if the case be thus, my state is surely miserable; miserable, if I leave my sins; and but miserable, if I follow them: I can but be damned; and if I must be so, I had as good be damned for many sins, as to be damned for a few."[29]

Bunyan threw himself headlong into vice, "still studdying what sin was yet to be committed, that I might taste the sweetness of it."[30] This desperate pursuit of sin continued "about a moneth, or more," until suddenly, Bunyan's wanton pursuit was arrested by an unlikely source.

> But one day as I was standing at a Neighbours Shop-window, and there cursing and swearing, and playing the Mad-man, after my wonted manner, there sate within the woman of the house, and heard me; who though she also was a very loose and ungodly Wretch, yet protested that I swore and cursed at that most fearful rate, that she was made to tremble to hear me: And told me further, *That I was the ungodliest Fellow for swearing that ever she heard in all her life; and that I by thus doing, was able to spoile all the Youth in a whole Town, if they came but in my company.*[31]

26. Bunyan, *Grace Abounding*, 10.

27. "Wherefore when I had satisfied nature with my food, I shook the Sermon out of my mind, and to my old custom of sports and gaming I returned with great delight" (Bunyan, *Grace Abounding*, 10). Tip cat was a sport played with a cudgel and a "cat"—"a piece of wood, about six inches long and two thick, diminished from the middle to form a double cone." A player struck the cat with the cudgel, making it rise and rotate in the air, then hit it as far as he could (Offor, *Works of John Bunyan*, 1:8n22).

28. Bunyan, *Grace Abounding*, 10.

29. Bunyan, *Grace Abounding*, 11.

30. Bunyan, *Grace Abounding*, 11.

31. Bunyan, *Grace Abounding*, 11–12.

If this encounter brought Bunyan to shame, another encounter with a local villager sparked an interest in the Bible.

> But quickly after this, I fell in company with one poor man, that made profession of Religion; who, as I then thought, did talk pleasantly of the Scriptures, and of the matters of Religion: wherefore falling into some love and liking to what he said, I betook me to my Bible, and began to take great pleasure in reading, but especially with the historical part thereof: for, as for *Pauls* Epistles, and Scriptures of that nature, I could not away with them, being as yet but ignorant, either of the corruptions of my nature, or of the want and worth of Jesus Christ to save me.[32]

As a result of these two encounters, Bunyan embarked upon an "outward Reformation, both in my words and life, and did set the Commandments before me for my way to Heaven."[33] Bunyan was evidently successful in this moral transformation, which lasted about a year and during which time his "Neighbours did take me to be a very godly man, a new and religious man, and did marvel much to see such a great and famous alteration in my life and manners." But, he confessed, "I knew not Christ, nor Grace, nor Faith, nor Hope.... I was nothing but a poor painted Hypocrite."[34]

Bunyan's Conversion and the Bedford Church

Bunyan's first encounter with the saints of the Bedford Church occurred about the year 1650. His work as a tinker took him one day to Bedford, the county seat of Bedfordshire. It was there that he happened upon "three or four poor women sitting at a door in the Sun, and talking about the things of God."[35] Their conversation piqued Bunyan's interest, as he was now "a brisk talker ... in the matters of Religion."[36] But he soon realized that their topic was beyond both his knowledge and experience:

> But now I may say, *I heard, but I understood not*, for they were far above out of my reach, for their talk was about a new birth,

---

32. Bunyan, *Grace Abounding*, 12. This man eventually "turned a most devilish *Ranter*, and gave himself up to all manner of filthiness, especially Uncleanness; he would also deny that there was a God, Angel or Spirit" (16).

33. Bunyan, *Grace Abounding*, 12.

34. Bunyan, *Grace Abounding*, 13.

35. Bunyan, *Grace Abounding*, 14.

36. Bunyan, *Grace Abounding*, 14.

the work of God on their hearts, also how they were convinced of their miserable state by nature: they talked how God had visited their souls with his love in the Lord Jesus, and with what words and promises they had been refreshed, comforted, and supported against the temptations of the Devil. . . . They also discoursed of their own wretchedness of heart, of their unbelief, and did contemn, slight and abhor their own righteousness, as filthy, and insufficient to do them any good.[37]

Surely Bunyan had heard of the depravity of man, the necessity of regeneration, and the imputation of righteousness under the Puritan preaching of Thomas Ford and the Presbyterian reformers who ministered under the command of Sir Samuel Luke at Newport Pagnell. He had also encountered such doctrines in the works of Dent and Bayly. But there was something different about the way these untutored women spoke of their evangelical experience and convictions that affected Bunyan in a way the words of the learned Puritan divines had not. Bunyan's religious self-image was immediately shattered.

> At this I felt my own heart began to shake, as mistrusting my condition to be naught; for I saw that in all my thoughts about Religion and Salvation, the New birth did never enter into my mind, neither knew I the comfort of the Word and Promise, nor the deceitfulness and treachery of my own wicked heart. . . .
>
> Thus therefore, when I had heard and considered what they said, I left them, and went about my employment again: but their talk and discourse went with me, also my heart would tarry with them, for I was greatly affected with their words, both because by them I was convinced that I wanted the true tokens of a truly godly man, and also because by them I was convinced of the happy and blessed condition of him that was such a one.[38]

Though he was as yet unsettled about the state of his soul, Bunyan could not deny that something had changed that day in Bedford:

> And, as I still do remember, presently I found two things within me, at which I did sometimes marvel, (especially considering what a blind, ignorant, sordid, and ungodly Wretch but just before I was) the one was, a very great softness and tenderness of heart, which caused me to fall under the conviction of what by Scripture they asserted; and the other was, a great bending in my mind to a

---

37. Bunyan, *Grace Abounding*, 14.
38. Bunyan, *Grace Abounding*, 14–15.

continual meditating on them, and on all other good things which at any time I heard or read of.[39]

Thus began a five-year battle for assurance that saw Bunyan fighting against fear, unbelief, and temptations to blaspheme, as well as the gnawing dread—at times a debilitating persuasion—that he had sinned against the Holy Spirit, that he had "sold Christ," and like Esau, that he faced certain damnation for his unpardonable apostasy. It was a war waged on the battlefield of Scripture, as legal threats and gospel promises engaged in mortal combat for the fate of Bunyan's soul.[40] In the end, however, the promises won out. In a delightful section near the end of the account of his conversion travail, Bunyan recounted how he faced down the passages of Scripture that tormented him most:

> I durst venture to come nigh unto those most fearful and terrible Scriptures, with which all this while I had been so greatly affrighted, and on which indeed before I durst scarce cast mine eye, (yea, had much ado an hundred times to forbear wishing

---

39. Bunyan, *Grace Abounding*, 15.

40. Greaves examines the role of psychosis in Bunyan's prolonged spiritual struggle, concluding, "The evidence strongly suggests that Bunyan suffered from recurrent, chronic dysthymia on which a major depressive episode was imposed about late 1653 or early 1654. The onset of the illness would have occurred about early 1651 and terminated, by Bunyan's reckoning, in approximately late 1657 or early 1658. There would be at least one further apparent recurrence, triggered by anxiety about late 1663 or 1664 during his imprisonment. During his illness in the 1650s, he suffered from pronounced dysphoria, marked feelings of worthlessness and excessive guilt, periodic fatigue, physical restlessness, feelings of hopelessness, impaired rational ability at times, apparent insomnia, and diminished pleasure in normal activities" (Greaves, *Glimpses of Glory*, 57). For Greaves's discussion of Bunyan's alleged mental illness, see *Glimpses of Glory*, 31–61. It is possible that mental illness exacerbated Bunyan's spiritual struggle; however, three cautions are in order. First, it is highly speculative to attribute mental illness to historical figures, as Greaves himself admits: "Although the use of psychology to study people who have long been deceased is fraught with difficulty, it is a valuable, almost indispensable tool for biographers, and I have therefore cautiously used it in this work" (vii). Second, one must not allow speculation of mental illness to obscure the causes to which Bunyan himself attributed his struggle, namely, troubling texts of Scripture and the temptations of Satan. And third, mental illness cannot account for the fact that Bunyan's despair was rooted in the fear of eternal damnation, and that, having achieved a settled measure of assurance by 1657/8, this fear does not seem to have recurred, with the sole exception of a brief season early in Bunyan's imprisonment when he was "in a very sad and low condition for many weeks," during which time he faced the very real possibility of martyrdom (Bunyan, *Grace Abounding*, 91). But this isolated and comparatively brief episode represents an anomaly during the last thirty years of Bunyan's life, and was quickly resolved by the "key . . . called Promise." See Bunyan, *Pilgrim's Progress*, 1:114.

of them out of the Bible, for I thought they would destroy me) but now, I say, I began to take some measure of incouragement, to come close to them, to read them, and consider them, and to weigh their scope and tendence.

The which when I began to do, I found their visage changed; for they looked not so grimly on me as before I thought they did.[41]

One by one, the giants fell: Hebrews 6, Hebrews 10, and finally, Hebrews 12, with its terrifying warning about the hopeless state of Esau, who sold his birthright for a single meal and was beyond repentance. The promises of the gospel conquered the threats of judgment, the tension of the texts was resolved, and Bunyan saw that he had not rejected Christ, but rather was accepted of God, despite the weakness of his faith, and that because of Christ's imputed righteousness.

But one day, as I was passing in the field, and that too with some dashes on my Conscience, fearing lest yet all was not right, suddenly this sentence fell upon my Soul, *Thy righteousness is in heaven*; and methought withal, I saw, with the eyes of my Soul Jesus Christ at Gods right hand, there, I say, as my Righteousness; so that wherever I was, or whatever I was a doing, God could not say of me, *He wants my righteousness*, for that was just before him. I also saw moreover, that it was not my good frame of Heart that made my Righteousness better, nor yet my bad frame that made my Righteousness worse: for my Righteousness was Jesus Christ himself, *the same yesterday, and to day, and for ever*, Heb. 13. 8.

Now did my chains fall off my Legs indeed, I was loosed from my afflictions and irons, and my temptations also fled away: so that from that time those dreadful Scriptures of God left off to trouble me; now went I also home rejoicing, for the grace and love of God.[42]

Reading through the account of Bunyan's spiritual travail, one could get the impression that it was a battle Bunyan fought alone, in the dark recesses of his own mind. This was not the case. After recounting his spiritual awakening that sunny day in 1650 as he listened to the Bedford women speak about their evangelical faith and experience, Bunyan wrote that he was irresistibly drawn into the fellowship of the Bedford saints. "Therefore I should often make it my business to be going again and again

---

41. Bunyan, *Grace Abounding*, 63.
42. Bunyan, *Grace Abounding*, 65–66.

into the company of these poor people; for I could not stay away."[43] They even invaded his dreams.

> About this time, the state and happiness of these poor people at *Bedford* was thus in a Dream or Vision represented to me: I saw as if they were set on the Sunny side of some high Mountain, there refreshing themselves with the pleasant beams of the Sun, while I was shivering and shrinking in the cold, afflicted with frost, snow, and dark clouds; methought also betwixt me and them I saw a wall that did compass about this Mountain; now thorow this wall, my Soul did greatly desire to pass, concluding that if I could, I would goe even into the very midst of them, and there also comfort myself with the heat of their Sun.[44]

Initially, Bunyan's interactions with the church occurred outside of their corporate worship gatherings, for it was sometime later that Bunyan was introduced to their pastor, John Gifford, who invited Bunyan to his house where he presided over spiritual conversation and offered spiritual counsel.[45] The church nurtured Bunyan during his prolonged struggle, though Bunyan confessed that in his state it was to little avail. "Sometimes I would tell my condition to the people of God; which when they heard, they would pity me, and would tell me of the Promises; but they had as good have told me that I must reach the Sun with my finger, as have bidden me receive or relie upon the Promise."[46] In time, Bunyan found himself in regular attendance at the church's worship.

> At this time also I sat under the Ministry of holy Mr. *Gifford*, whose Doctrine, by Gods grace, was much for my stability. This man made it much his business to deliver the People of God from all those false and unsound rests that by Nature we are prone to take and make to our Souls; he pressed us to take special heed, that we took not up any truth upon trust, as from this or that or another man or men, but to cry mightily to God, that he would

---

43. Bunyan, *Grace Abounding*, 15.
44. Bunyan, *Grace Abounding*, 18–19.
45. "About this time I began to break my mind to those poor people in *Bedford*, and to tell them my condition: which, when they had heard, they told *Mr. Gifford* of me, who himself also took occasion to talke with me, and was willing to be well perswaded of me, though I think but from little grounds; but he invited me to his house, where I should hear him confer with others about the dealings of God with the Soul" (Bunyan, *Grace Abounding*, 24).
46. Bunyan, *Grace Abounding*, 25.

convince us of the reality thereof, and set us down therein by his own Spirit in the holy Word.[47]

During the narration of his conversion, Bunyan mentioned three other potential influences. Two were negative. Soon after his 1650 awakening, Bunyan "met with some *Ranters* books, that were put forth by some of our Country men; which Books were also highly in esteem by several old Professors."[48] Feeling inadequate to judge the truth of them, Bunyan prayed for wisdom and discernment. Encountering his former friend who had first introduced him to the Scriptures, but had now "turned a most devilish *Ranter*, and gave himself up to all manner of filthiness," Bunyan was convinced of their error. "Wherefore abominating those cursed principles, I left his company forth with, and became to him as great a stranger as I had been before a familiar."[49]

Bunyan also encountered the Quakers, whose influence again was negative, for "the *Quakers* did oppose his Truth, as God did the more confirm me in it, by leading me into the Scriptures that did wonderfully maintain it."[50] Both the Ranters and the Quakers espoused extremely low-church ecclesiologies that had little in common with the Nonconformist ecclesiology which Bunyan would soon adopt.

A third, and far more positive, influence upon Bunyan came in the form of a book. Bunyan wrote that during his struggle,

> the God in whose hands are all our days, did cast into my hand (one day) a book of *Martin Luther*; his Comment on the *Galathians*, so old that it was ready to fall piece from piece, if I did but turn it over. Now I was pleased much that such an old Book had fallen

---

47. Bunyan, *Grace Abounding*, 34.

48. Bunyan, *Grace Abounding*, 16. On the Ranters, see Hill, *Tinker and a Poor Man*, 75–84; Greaves, *Glimpses of Glory*, 69–74.

49. Bunyan, *Grace Abounding*, 16. Nor was this Bunyan's only interaction with Ranters. "Neither was this man onely a temptation to me, but my calling lying in the countrey, I happened to light into several peoples company; who though strict in Religion formerly, yet was also swept away by these Ranters. These would also talk with me of their ways, and condemn me as legal and dark, pretending that they onely had attained to perfection that could do what they would and not sin." Bunyan confessed to being tempted by such a doctrine, but God "kept me in the fear of his name, and did not suffer me to accept of such cursed principles" (Bunyan, *Grace Abounding*, 16).

50. Bunyan, *Grace Abounding*, 36. Bunyan proceeded to enumerate eight errors of the Quakers. In 1656, he published two treatises against them, *Some Gospel-Truths Opened* and *A Vindication of . . . Some Gospel-Truths Opened*, which was a response to Edward Burrough's *The True Faith of the Gospel of Peace*.

into my hand; the which, when I had but a little way perused, I found my condition in his experience, so largely and profoundly handled, as if his Book had been written out of my heart; . . . I do prefer this Book of Mr. *Luther* upon the *Galathians*, (excepting the Holy Bible) before all the Books that ever I have seen, as most fit for a wounded Conscience.[51]

It has become axiomatic in Bunyan scholarship that Luther exercised a dominant influence upon Bunyan's theology, particularly Luther's theology of law, grace, and justification.[52] Such claims are overstated; Luther's influence upon Bunyan was more experiential and pastoral than theological.[53] What influence Luther did exercise upon Bunyan did not extend to Bunyan's ecclesiology; on this all scholars agree.

The dominant influence upon Bunyan's theology and ecclesiology came from John Gifford and the Bedford Church. It was through the

---

51. Bunyan, *Grace Abounding*, 38.

52. For instance, Richard Greaves argues that Luther "cast an indelible imprint upon [Bunyan's] concept of Christianity," and that Bunyan "built an essentially Calvinist superstructure" upon a "Lutheran foundation" (Greaves, *John Bunyan*, 18, 156). Greaves bemoans the "fallacious tendency of most of Bunyan's critics and historians to speak of him simply as a Calvinist" (153). He asserts that "Luther exercised appreciable influence on Bunyan in the closely related areas of the nature of God, the basic concept of salvation *per se*, the necessity of justification *sola gratia* and *sola fide*, and the unalterable opposition of the law and grace" (156). Yet Greaves also affirms, "No single theological label without careful qualification will fit Bunyan. . . . His foundation principles were basically Lutheran, but most of his theology was in full accord with the orthodox Calvinism of his period" (159). See also Greaves, *Glimpses of Glory*, 108–9, written forty years later, for similar sentiments. Samuel Coleridge wrote in his marginalia, "Bunyan may have been one [i.e., a Calvinist]; but I have met with nothing in his writings (except his anti-paedobaptism, to which too he lays no saving importance) that is not much more characteristically Lutheran" (Coleridge, *Literary Remains*, 3:398, quoted in Talon, *John Bunyan*, 272n4). Jonathon Shears quotes the same passage, stating, "Coleridge had previously produced fifteen marginalia on Luther's *Colloquia Mensalia*, and everywhere in Bunyan he saw the thought of Luther" (Shears, "Bunyan and the Romantics," 569).

53. "However, to describe Bunyan as Lutheran in his theology is an exaggeration: Luther inspired him and abetted his escape from legalism, but, immersed as he was in the theology of the Bedford meeting and of his Puritan and Dissenting heritage, Bunyan read Luther in a Calvinist context and put the inspiration he received from him at the service of a high Calvinist double-covenant theology" (Wallace, "Bunyan's Theology and Religious Context," 84). Gordon Wakefield writes, "Bunyan was not concerned with Luther's sacramental or political theology, both of which the majority of English divines deplored. He may not have been aware of them. But Luther's experience was similar to that of Bunyan in his psychological traumas and his struggles for assurance which no external aids could bring" (Wakefield, *Bunyan the Christian*, 24).

testimony and conversation of the "three or four poor women sitting at a door in the Sun" that Bunyan was awakened to evangelical doctrine and his need of evangelical experience.[54] It was through his continual interactions with and irresistible attraction to "these poor people" of Bedford that Bunyan was made to "fall under the conviction of what by Scripture they asserted."[55] It was his dream of "these poor people at *Bedford*" that produced in him a great longing to enter into their blessed fellowship through that "wonderful narrow" gap in the wall that he might be "comforted with the light and heat of their Sun."[56] When Bunyan confided in them about his despairing condition, it was "those poor people in *Bedford*" who brought him to John Gifford, who discoursed with Bunyan on evangelical doctrines and offered evangelical counsel.[57] It was under Gifford's ministry in the Bedford Church that Bunyan found some measure of "stability," as Gifford impressed upon his hearers evangelical doctrine and exhorted them to "cry mightily to God, that he would convince us of the reality thereof, and set us down therein by his own Spirit in the holy Word."[58] It may well have been from Gifford's own library that the tattered copy of Luther's *Commentary on Galatians* fell into Bunyan's hand. And it was into the fellowship of the Bedford Church that Bunyan was formally received as a member in 1655: "After I had propounded to the Church, that my desire was to walk in the Order and Ordinances of Christ with them, and was also admitted by them."[59] Though Bunyan never wrote about his baptism, it may be assumed that he was baptized at this time, given his stated convictions about the validity (though not the necessity) of credobaptism.[60]

54. Bunyan, *Grace Abounding*, 14.
55. Bunyan, *Grace Abounding*, 15.
56. Bunyan, *Grace Abounding*, 18–19.
57. Bunyan, *Grace Abounding*, 24.
58. Bunyan, *Grace Abounding*, 34.

59. Bunyan, *Grace Abounding*, 72. Brown dated Bunyan's membership to 1653 (Brown, *John Bunyan*, 92). Charles Doe, writing in 1692, asserted that Bunyan professed faith and was baptized sometime between 1651 and 1653 (Doe, *Struggler*, 3:765). Brown may have based his date upon Doe's account. However, Greaves dates Bunyan's membership to 1655 (Greaves, *Glimpses of Glory*, 54). Nearly all scholars opt for the later date. The *Minutes* of the Bedford Church do not begin until 1656, so the dates must be surmised from the internal evidence in *Grace Abounding*.

60. The anonymous author of *A Continuation of Mr. Bunyan's Life* (1692) stated that Bunyan was baptized at the time he joined the Bedford Church (Anonymous, *Continuation of Mr. Bunyan's Life*, 1:64). For Bunyan's convictions regarding credobaptism, see Bunyan, *Holy Life*, 9:259; *Confession of My Faith*, 4:164; *Differences in Judgment*, 4:214, 226. Bunyan's baptismal theology is addressed in the following chapters.

The Origin and Founding Principles of the Bedford Church

As the Bedford Church exercised the dominant, formative influence upon Bunyan's theology, and particularly his ecclesiology, it is prudent to inquire as to the origin and convictions of this Nonconformist congregation. In "A Brief Account of the 1st Gathering of the Church of Christ at Bedford," found at the beginning of the *Minutes*, an anonymous author recorded the Semi-Separatist origins of the Bedford Church:

> In this towne of Bedford, and the places adjacent, there hath of a long time bene persons godly, who in former times, (even while they remained without all forme and order as to visible church communion according to the Testament of Christ) were very zealous according to their light, not onely to edify themselves, but also to propogate the Gospell, and help it forward, both by purse and presence, keeping always a door open and a table furnished and free, for all such ministers, and Christians, who shewed their zeal for, and love to, the Gospell of Christ. Among these that reverend man Mr. John Grew was chief, also Mr. John Eston, senior, and brother Anthony Harrington, with others: men that in those times were enabled of God to adventure farre in shewing their detestation of the bishops and their superstitions. But as the saide these persons, with many more, neither were, not yet desired to be, imbodied into fellowship according to the order of the Gospel, onely they had in some measure separated themselves from the prelaticall superstition, and had agreed to search after non-conforming men, such as in those days did beare the name of Puritanes.[61]

The mention of "prelaticall superstition" locates the origins of this Semi-Separatist gathering in the time of the Laudian reforms, which abruptly ended with Laud's impeachment in late 1641.[62] Thus, it is reasonable to conclude that this group began meeting by the late 1630s.[63] And though they met for mutual edification, for evangelism, and to show hospitality to traveling evangelicals ("non-conforming men, such as in those days did beare the name of Puritanes"), they had no intention as yet of forming a Separatist church.

61. *Minutes*, 15.

62. For Laud's ascendency, reforms, and demise, see Watts, *Dissenters*, 62–77; Kishlansky, *Monarchy Transformed*, 128–37, 143; Hall, *Puritans*, 206–60.

63. Greaves states, "The congregation Bunyan joined had roots extending almost certainly to the 1630s" (Greaves, *Glimpses of Glory*, 61).

The Palace Beautiful

Nevertheless, a strong Nonconformist sentiment emerged in Bedfordshire during the revolutionary years.[64] They were as unimpressed by Westminster Presbyterianism as they had been by Laudian Episcopalianism.[65] For instance, William Dell, rector of Yelden and Fellow of Emmanuel College, Cambridge, "strenuously resisted the establishment of any national form of religion. He held strong views on the spirituality of the Church of Christ, and was averse to all stereotyped uniformity in its organization and worship."[66] John Brown wrote that Dell's opinions "greatly influenced the course of Free Church life in the neighbouring town of Bedford."[67] Additionally, the Particular Baptist Benjamin Coxe founded a short-lived congregation in Bedford in 1643, but his strict communion views were not shared by the Bedford saints.[68]

Sometime in 1648/1649, John Gifford arrived in Bedford. Gifford's story is included in the prefatory account attached to the *Minutes*. Gifford, a native of Kent, was a "great royalist, and an officer (*viz.* a major) in the King's army."[69] He was arrested in the June 1648 uprising in Maidstone, and was sentenced to death with eleven other prisoners.[70] But on the eve of his execution, he made a daring escape with the help of his sister, and because the guards were "heavy through drinke" and "a deep sleep from the Lord [was] upon them."[71] After three days of hiding in a ditch, Gifford made his way first to London, and then to Bedfordshire, where he was hidden

---

64. For an account of the ecclesiastical history of Bedford during the years 1640–1650, see Brown, *John Bunyan*, 69–95.

65. "Many were beginning to think that the Presbyterianism of that time was not as wide and tolerant as it might be, and that there was little use in merely exchanging one form of yoke for another. These opinions found strong support in Bedfordshire at a very early stage in the national conflict" (Brown, *John Bunyan*, 78).

66. Brown, *John Bunyan*, 78–79.

67. Brown, *John Bunyan*, 80.

68. Brown, *John Bunyan*, 80. Coxe was jailed later in 1643 in Coventry after a debate with Richard Baxter over baptism. Brown wrote that Coxe "appears not to have returned to Bedford, for three years later we find him in prison in London, for distributing to the members of Parliament a Confession of Faith held by himself and his brethren on the questions of the time" (80). Greaves adds, "Cox[e] was seemingly again active at Bedford in 1648, but his insistence on believer's baptism as a condition of church membership did not strike a responsive chord with the semi-separatists" (Greaves, *Glimpses of Glory*, 63).

69. *Minutes*, 15.

70. Greaves identifies the unnamed "rising" as the uprising of Maidstone, Kent in June 1648 (Greaves, *Glimpses of Glory*, 63, citing Everitt, *Community of Kent*, 261–63).

71. *Minutes*, 15–16.

by royalist sympathizers. Eventually, Gifford came to Bedford where "he professed and practiced physicke," and lived a "very vile and debauched" lifestyle, "being a great drinker, gamester, swearer etc."[72] One night, having accrued a fifteen-pound gambling debt, Gifford flew into a rage and "he thought many desperate thoughtes against God."[73] But picking up a book by the Puritan Robert Bolton, he was awakened, and within a month was fully converted. He presented himself to the Semi-Separatists of Bedford, who at first did not believe his testimony of conversion. They can hardly be blamed for their incredulity, for not long before, Gifford had "bene a very vile man" with "a very rude manner," who "often had thoughts to kill brother Harrington, meerly from the great antipathy that was in his heart against the people of God and the holyness of the Gospell."[74] Eventually, however, Gifford won over the small fellowship of saints.

It was not long before Gifford sensed a call to preach, doing so first in private before the saints, and then in public. His preaching was immediately attended with evangelical fruit: "whose word God so blessed that even at the first he was made through grace a father to some through the Gospell."[75] Gifford also sought to gather the Semi-Separatist fellowship into a constituted church, but met with some resistance: "Now having continued preaching a while, and receiving some light into the Congregationall way, after some acquaintance also with other ministers, he attempted to gather into Gospell fellowship the saintes and brethren in and about this towne, but the more antient professors, being used to live as some other good men of these times, without regard to such separate and close communion, were not at first so ready to fall into that godly order."[76] Nevertheless, after much prayer and counsel, they "determined to walke together in the fellowship of the Gospell, and so to build an house for the name of our God, who were most expedient to begin to be laide in this building as foundation stones."[77]

---

72. *Minutes*, 16.

73. *Minutes*, 16.

74. *Minutes*, 16.

75. "For instance sister Cooper, a woman whose memory is yet precious among us, was converted by the first sermon he preached in publicke" (*Minutes*, 16).

76. *Minutes*, 17.

77. *Minutes*, 17. Greaves mistakenly interprets this last phrase as a reference to a physical building, stating that they resolved to "construct a building in which to worship" (Greaves, *Glimpses of Glory*, 63). The reference, rather, is to the mystical temple of Ephesians (Eph 2:19–22). The "foundation stones" are identified as "twelve of the holy brethren and sisters" who "began this holy worke: *viz.* Mr. John Grew and his wife, Mr.

They unanimously selected Gifford to be their pastor, who agreed to "walke with them, watch over them, and dispense the misteryes of the Gospell among them."[78] *The Minutes of . . . Bunyan Meeting* are explicit concerning the manner of their constituting as a church: "The manner of their putting themselves into the state of the Church of Christ was:—after much prayer and waiting upon God and consulting one with another, by the Word, they, upon the day appointed for this solemne worke, being met, after prayer and seeking God as before, with one consent they joyntly first gave themselves to the Lord, and one to another by the will of God."[79] The authority to constitute as a church did not come from any external ecclesiastical or governmental body, but directly from Scripture itself ("by the Word"). And the basis of their thus constituting was a mutual covenant (they "gave themselves to the Lord, and one to another"). This two-dimensional covenant, having both vertical and horizontal dimensions, has deep roots in the covenant ecclesiology of early English Separatists.[80]

The following paragraph, included in this prefatory history of the Bedford Church, is of the utmost significance to this monograph:

> Now the principle upon which they thus entered into fellowship one with another and upon which they did afterwards receive those that were added to their body and fellowship was faith in Christ and holines of life, without respect to this or that circumstance or opinion in outward and circumstantiall things. By which meanes grace and faith was incouraged: love and amity maintained: disputings and occasion to janglings and unprofitable questions avoided, and many that were weake in faith confirmed in the blessings of eternall life.[81]

John Eston the elder, Anthony Harrington and his wife, Mr. John Gifford, sister Coventon, sister Bosworth, sister Munnes, sister Fenne and sister Norton and sister Spencer, all antient and grave Christians well knowne one to another" (*Minutes*, 17).

78. *Minutes*, 17.

79. *Minutes*, 17.

80. Paul Fiddes explores this two-dimensional covenant ecclesiology in Fiddes, "Covenant and the Inheritance of Separatism," 63–91. Fiddes makes the intriguing suggestion that, "During the course of the seventeenth century it seems that the actual act of covenant-making dropped out of practice in some Baptist congregations, both General and Particular, since receiving baptism as a believer was deemed sufficient for church membership" (79). As the Bedford Church did not require baptism for membership, the explicit covenant remained a necessity.

81. *Minutes*, 17.

Thus, open communion was a foundational principle of the Bedford Church, deemed essential ("by which meanes") to the faith of the saints and the unity of the church. "This principle was maintained in the Church to her mutual comfort and edification, even till the death of brother Gifford, who also of his care to the congregation while he was fetching his last breath, wrote an epistle to the congregation, to perswade them to continue in the faithfull maintaining of the abovenamed principle among them."[82]

This parting epistle from John Gifford, just prior to his death in September 1655, is likewise included in the preface to the *Minutes*.[83] After briefly exhorting the church to keep "the mystery of the faith in a pure conscience," Gifford proceeded to write concerning "your Church affairs, which I feare have bene little considered by most of you; which things, if not minded aright and submitted unto according to the will of God, will by degrees bring you under divisions, distractions, and at last to confusion of that Gospell order and fellowship which now through grace you enjoy."[84] First, Gifford reminded them of their covenant with Christ and with one another. Because of this binding covenant, "neither have any of you liberty to joyne

---

82. *Minutes*, 17–18. An interesting wrinkle in this story is that in the summer of 1653, the Bedford Common Council named John Gifford rector of St. John's parish church in Bedford, as well as master of its hospital. John Brown relates the story of how this historical anomaly ("This could not, of course, have happened at any other time than between the years 1653 and 1660") came about (Brown, *John Bunyan*, 87–92). See also Greaves, *Glimpses of Glory*, 65. Brown does not address whether the small congregation of saints was incorporated into the parish church, or whether it remained separate whilst Gifford ministered to both. Greaves raises the question, but is uncertain as to the answer. However, Gifford's statement in his parting epistle that, "If the members at such a time will go to a publick ministry, it must first be approved of by the Church," assuming that "publick ministry" refers to a parish church (as Greaves contends in *Glimpses of Glory*, 66), insinuates that the two congregations remained strictly separate, as does Gifford's exhortation that the church wait a year or two before electing its next pastor (as the rector of the parish church was appointed by the Council). See *Minutes*, 21. Following Gifford's death, after the Council's appointment of William Hayes was appealed by the town, Oliver Cromwell appointed John Burton rector of St. John's and master of its hospital in January 1656 (Greaves, *Glimpses of Glory*, 66). By the time the *Minutes* begin in May 1656, Burton was already a member and apparently functioning as the church's pastor.

83. On Gifford's death, see Brown, *John Bunyan*, 92–93. Brown eulogized Gifford, the Evangelist to Bunyan's Pilgrim: "After signing this letter in the presence of two of the brethren, Gifford went home to be with God. No stone marks the spot where he was buried in the churchyard of St. John's, but there his dust lies—mingling with that of the long line of masters and rectors, of bedesman and brethren, stretching through more than six hundred years, and of whom he was one" (95).

84. *Minutes*, 18.

your selves to any other society, because your pastor is removed from you, for you were not joyned to the ministery, but to Christ and the Church."[85] Next, he urged them to be faithful to the assemblies and ministries of the Church. Third, Gifford addressed the admission of members:

> After you are satisfyed in the worke of grace in the party you are to joyne with, the saide party do solemnly declare (before some of the Church at least), that union with Christ is the foundation of the saintes' communion, and not any ordinances of Christ, or any judgement or opinion about externalls. And the saide party ought to declare, whether a brother or sister, that through grace they will walke in love with the Church, though there should happen any difference about other things.[86]

Admission into the membership of the Bedford Church thus required three fundamentals: (1) a satisfactory testimony of evangelical experience (presumably validated by some new measure of "holines of life"); (2) an affirmation that union with Christ is the only foundation of church membership along with the corresponding denial that disagreement over "externalls" (in the next paragraph Gifford listed "baptisme, laying on of hands, anoynting with oyle, psalmes, or any other externalls") is a bar to such communion; and (3) a commitment to walk in love and not to divide over such matters, which Gifford called a "great evill" that "some have committed and that through a zeale for God, yet not according to knowledge," and thus "have erred from the lawe of the love of Christ, and have made a rent from the true Church which is but one."[87] Following these three exhortations are various instructions regarding corporate worship, church discipline, prayer, the election of pastors, and more.[88] It is evident from this pastoral letter that the Bedford Church practiced congregational polity, for the admission of members, the discipline of members, and the election of officers required church consent.[89] There is also evident concern for the regulative principle

---

85. *Minutes*, 18.
86. *Minutes*, 19.
87. *Minutes*, 19.
88. *Minutes*, 19–21.

89. The covenanting member had to "solemnly declare" his submission to the doctrine and principles of the Church "before some of the Church at least" (*Minutes*, 19). No brother who walked "disorderly" could be "shut out from any ordinance before Church censure" (20). And Gifford hoped that the church would wait a year or two "before election" of their next pastor (21).

of worship, however liberally that may have been applied.[90] Bunyan would come to champion each of these distinctives.

The Continuing Principles of the Bedford Church

That these founding principles (the necessity of evangelical faith and holiness, a mutual covenant as the form of the church, congregational polity, the regulative principle of worship, and especially, open communion) were in place in 1655 when Bunyan became a member of the Bedford Church is evident from Gifford's letter. That they remained the principles of the Bedford Church throughout Bunyan's membership and under his leadership is evident from the continuing witness of the *Minutes*, which is replete with the records of congregational action, examinations of the testimonies and lives of prospective members, and acts of discipline upon those who walked in a disorderly manner.[91] But there are three lines of evidence in the history of the Bedford Church before, during, and soon after Bunyan's ministry that are particularly relevant to the thesis of this monograph, as they demonstrate the church's ongoing commitment to open communion, and their corresponding rejection of seventeenth-century Baptist identity.

First, the Bedford Church repeatedly refused to recommend or transfer members to strict-communion Baptist churches, recommending them instead to paedobaptist Congregationalist churches. The first such instance occurred in July 1671. Sister Tilney had moved to London, and desired a transfer of membership to the church of her son-in-law, Mr. Blakely. However, the church (and Bunyan's is the first signature appended to the letter) took its responsibility very seriously, fearing that a mistake in such a matter would imperil her immortal soul. "Wherefore we may not, neither dare, give our consent that you feed and fold with such whose principles and practices, in matters of faith and worshippe, we as yet are strangers to, and have not received commendations concerning, either from workes of theires or epistles from others. . . . Wherefore we beseech you, that for the love of our Lord Jesus Christ, you give us leave

---

90. "I exhort you brethren, in your comings together, let all things be done decently and in order according to the Scriptures" (*Minutes*, 19).

91. As the minutes of the Bedford Church from the first entry in May 1656 intersect with Bunyan's own ecclesiology, these congregational actions are considered in detail in the following chapter.

to informe our selves yet better, before we grant your request."[92] Instead, the church encouraged her to attend the churches of "brother Cockin, brother Griffith, brother Palmer, or other who of long continuance in the city have shewed forth their faith, their worship, and good conversation by the word."[93] Or, if this was displeasing to Sister Tilney, she could procure "a commendatory epistle from brother Owen, brother Cocking, brother Palmer or brother Griffith, concerning the faith and principles of the person and people whom you mention."[94] George Cokayne, George Griffith, Anthony Palmer, and John Owen, all Congregationalists, were the only London ministers deemed trustworthy for a Bedford saint. This letter evidently did not find favor with Sister Tilney, for a second letter was required from the church attributing her stubbornness to temptation, praying for her forgiveness from the Lord, and again insisting that she attend the churches of the "brethren there mentioned [in the first letter], being men of such worth and reverence among all the Churches of Christ in this land, as we know not of any the like."[95] On the other hand, the church was happy to transfer Sister Martha Grew to Anthony Palmer's London congregation.[96] At a June 1674 meeting, it was decided that "a letter be sent to that church of whom brother Jesse once was pastor, to know whether it be their church principle still to hold communion with saints as saint[s] though differing in judgment about watter baptizm, that we may the better know what to doe as to our sister Martha Cumberland as to her joyning with them or not."[97] Jessey's former church responded, but failed to report their convictions regarding baptism and communion. Therefore, at a December 1676 meeting, the Bedford Church wrote again:

> We receaved your letter and by it a signification of your readiness to receave our sister Martha Cumberland, but before we can with such fredome as we desire, deliver hir up to you, we must take leave to propound to you, and to desire your faithfull answer therto, to witt whether that good old principle once professed by you in the time of our honored brother Jese, that communion, church

---

92. *Minutes*, 66.
93. *Minutes*, 66.
94. *Minutes*, 66.
95. *Minutes*, 69.
96. *Minutes*, 71.
97. *Minutes*, 77.

communion of saints, not withstanding difference in judgment about water baptisme, be yet a church principle with you.[98]

The Church then reported that they had unsuccessfully attempted to persuade Sister Cumberland to attend the churches of "our honored brother Coken, brother Palmer or brother Owen, but non of these congregations would content hir, the which we have taken very ill, especially since those of our members which are in London are receaved by and hold communion with them, they being also of that Christian principle afore mentioned, to hold communion with saints as saints."[99] Before and during Bunyan's pastorate, the Bedford Church refused to associate with Baptist churches, only permitting their members to transfer to Congregationalist churches or open-communion Independent churches like themselves.[100]

The second evidence of the Bedford Church's ongoing commitment to open communion and their corresponding rejection of Baptist identity is the May 1672 application for licenses under the Declaration of Indulgence that Bunyan filed on behalf of himself and twenty-five other preachers, the result of a plan hatched while in the Bedford jail to establish a network of churches throughout Bedfordshire and surrounding counties.[101] According to John Brown, the application is in Bunyan's own handwriting.[102] Every one of these licenses was filed as "Congregationall." Bunyan could have

---

98. *Minutes*, 79.

99. *Minutes*, 79–80. The letter proceeds to explain that they have reason to believe open communion was no longer a principle of the church, for a "brother Forly" had dissuaded a certain Christian sister from joining the Bedford Church because of their open-communion convictions (80).

100. For transfers of membership, see *Minutes*, 30 (Sister Fryer to John Simpson's London church), 34 (Katharine Hustwhat to Simpson's London church), 37 (Sister Foxe to Simpson's London church), 70–71 (Martha Grew to Palmer's London church), 82 (Samuel Hensman to the Braintree open-communion church), 87 (William Breeden to Cokayne's London church), 92 (Samuel Hocrafft to Matthew Mead's London church).

101. Brown, *John Bunyan*, 232–33; Greaves, *Glimpses of Glory*, 286–89; "Organizational Response of Nonconformity," 1–13; Nuttall, "Church Life in Bunyan's Bedfordshire," 305–13. Greaves writes, "In addition to Bunyan, the key figures in this scheme appear to have been [John] Donne, [Nehemiah] Coxe, the Fennes [John and Samuel], [John] Wright, and Thomas Cooper" (Greaves, *Glimpses of Glory*, 287). For the 1672 Declaration of Indulgence, see Watts, *Dissenters*, 257–60; Kishlansky, *Monarchy Transformed*, 246–48. A copy of the Declaration of Indulgence is provided in Offor, *Works of John Bunyan*, 3:21–22.

102. A transcription of the application is found in Brown, *John Bunyan*, 232–33.

applied for a license as a Baptist. Many did; Bunyan did not.[103] Furthermore, when in 1674 one of the men for whom Bunyan applied for a license, Nehemiah Coxe, the son of the Particular Baptist Benjamin Coxe, began creating divisions within the church, he was censured. His confession, presented in writing to the church, may imply that his sin was advocating for believer's baptism or strict communion:

> Whereas several words and practises have bin uttered and performed by me that might justly be construed to have a tendencie to make rents and devisions in the congregation, I doe declare my self unfeignedly repentant and sorry for the same.—Nehemiah Coxe[104]

Within two years, Coxe moved to London, where he was ordained at the Petty France Particular Baptist Church.[105] Coxe's censure, along with the aforementioned evidence of the Bedford Church's ecclesiastical affiliations in London, indicates that Bunyan intended all of these churches within the network of which Bedford was the hub and Bunyan the "bishop" to be open-communion Independent (not Baptist) churches.[106]

A third evidence of the Bedford Church's ongoing commitment to its founding principle of open-communion is its decision after Bunyan's death to call Ebenezer Chandler, a paedobaptist, as its next pastor. Chandler came to Bedford from Richard Taylor's London Church in 1691.[107] His appointment caused some consternation with a sister church at Gamlingay that was troubled not only about the institution of "publick singing" at Bedford, but also about the installation of a paedobaptist pastor. Evidently, the Gamlingay church was open to communion with paedobaptists, but not to the practice of paedobaptism within the network. In response, Chandler sent the church a letter that was transcribed into the *Minutes*.

---

103. Paul Fiddes writes that under the 1672 Declaration of Indulgence "many Baptists registered their meeting houses, and among 1,434 Nonconformist pastors who applied for preaching licenses, 202 declared themselves to be Baptists" (Fiddes, "Baptists and 1662," 183–204).

104. *Minutes*, 77. For Bunyan and the Bedford Church, no issue was more prone to make "rents and devisions in the congregation" than strict communion. James Renihan likewise suggests that Coxe's censure may have been "related to the issue of open or closed membership, so hotly debated at the time" (J. Renihan, *Edification and Beauty*, 23–24).

105. Greaves, "Organizational Response," 478.

106. "[Bunyan] quickly became the organizing bishop of the whole district" (Brown, *John Bunyan*, 232).

107. The letter of dismissal from Taylor's church is found in the *Minutes*, 93.

> Our brethren have determined that those that are perswaded in there consciences that publick singing is an ordinance of God, shall practice it on the Lord's Day in our meeting in Bedford. Those that are of differing judgment have there liberty whether they will sing, ye or noe, or whether they will be presant whilst we sing, so that they do not turn there backs on other parts of God's worship. Nether is it at all designed to be imposed or proposed to any other meeting of the Church. Againe, with respect to baptisme, I have liberty to baptise infants without making it my business to promote it amonst others, and every member to have his liberty in beleivers' baptisme, onely to forbare discourse and debates on it that may have a tendency to break the peace of the Church. When thought expedient the Church doth designe to choose an administrator of believers' baptisme, we doe not designe to make baptisme, whether of belivers' or infants, any bar to communion.[108]

The Gamlingay Church responded cordially, and agreed to extend to one another liberty to preach and to practice according to conscience.[109] Clearly, the election of a paedobaptist pastor is not a move towards Baptist identity, but away from it.

The Decisive Influence of the Bedford Church

The foregoing account has demonstrated that none of Bunyan's early religious encounters exercised decisive influence upon his ecclesiology. The Ranters and Quakers Bunyan rejected out of hand. The Church of England functioned only as a negative influence, convincing Bunyan of the vapidity of its liturgy and the carnality of its clergy. The Westminster Presbyterianism he encountered at Newport Pagnell seems to have had little impact upon his young soul. The Puritan divines he read early in his marriage piqued his spiritual interest, but did not prove decisive in his theological or ecclesiological development. The Calvinistic Puritan theological framework which Bunyan would eventually adopt was mediated to him through

---

108. *Minutes*, 93–94.

109. "We, the brethren of this Church in and about Gamlingay, doe heartily and cordeally aquiesce in this letter, only desire to have liberty to spake or preach belivers' baptisme if the Lord shall sett it upon our hearts, yet with that tenderness as being far from any such designe as to tend at least to the breaking the peace of the Church, and do heartily grant our brother Chandler the same liberty to speak of or preach infant baptisme, provided with the same tendernesse" (*Minutes*, 94).

Nonconformity. Even Luther's influence was more experiential than theological, more evangelical than ecclesiological. The law-free gospel Bunyan found in Luther's *Commentary on Galatians* helped Bunyan make sense of his experience and overcome his doubts, but did not prove decisive in his theological development nor contribute to his ecclesiological convictions. Next to the Scriptures themselves, there is only one source that proved decisive in Bunyan's theological and ecclesiological development.[110] Bunyan is the product of the teaching ministry of John Gifford and the fellowship of saints in the Bedford Church.

Bunyan adopted the founding principles of the Bedford Church as his own. The necessity of evangelical faith and holiness, a mutual covenant as the form of a visible church, congregational polity, the regulative principle of worship liberally applied, and especially, open communion, became the core of his own doctrine of the church. From the time of his membership in 1655 until his death on August 31, 1688, he never deviated from those principles first established by John Gifford and the founding members of the Bedford Church. On the contrary, he defended them vigorously and propagated them far and wide, as Bunyan became the voice and leader of a small movement of open-communion Independent churches in Bedfordshire and beyond. The following chapter will examine Bunyan's ministry amongst these churches and the content of his ecclesiology.

---

110. Bunyan frequently asserted that the Scriptures were his only teacher. In the same work in which he praised Luther's *Commentary on Galatians*, he later wrote, "I never endeavoured to, nor durst make use of other men's lines, Rom 15:18. (though I condemn not all that do) for I verily thought, and found by experience, that what was taught me by the Word and Spirit of Christ, could be spoken, maintained and stood to, by the soundest and best established Conscience" (Bunyan, *Grace Abounding*, 80). Bunyan wrote in *Solomon's Temple Spiritualiz'd*, "I have not for these things fished in other mens *Waters*, my Bible and Concordance are my only Library in my writings" (Bunyan, *Solomon's Temple Spiritualiz'd*, 7:9). Bunyan is employing hyperbole; his writings contain numerous references to other works. See Greaves, *Glimpses of Glory*, 603–6. Nevertheless, if he may be forgiven the exaggeration, his point remains. He wrote in his preface to *Light for Them That Sit in Darkness*, "I have not writ at venture, nor borrowed my Doctrine from Libraries. I depend upon the sayings of no man: I found it in the Scriptures of Truth, among the true sayings of God" (Bunyan, *Light for Them*, 8:51). Though Alison Searle calls such claims "somewhat tendentious," and Roger Pooley thinks them "a polemical point more than a true confession," yet the truth of such statements is borne out in his doctrinal works, which bear the marks of original thought (whether for good or for ill) and are almost exclusively exegetical. Similarly, his allegorical works contain biblical quotations or allusions on nearly every page. See Searle, "Bunyan and the Word," 90; Pooley, "Bunyan's Reading," 101.

Chapter 3

The Palace Beautiful: Bunyan's Evangelical Independent Ecclesiology

The *Builder's* God, *Materials* his Elect;
His *Son's* the *Rock,* on which it is Erect;
The *Scripture* is his Rule, Plummet or Line,
Which gives proportion to this *House divine*;
His *Working-Tools* his Ordinances are,
By them he doth his *Stones* and *Timber* square,
Affections *knit* in *Love*, the *Couplings* are;
Good Doctrine like to *Morter* doth cement
The whole together, *Schisme* to prevent:
His *Compass*, his *Decree*; his *Hand's* the *Spirit*
By which he *Frames* (what he means to inherit)
A *Holy Temple*, which shall far excell
That very place, where now the Angels dwell.[1]

---

1. Bunyan, *Discourse of the Building*, 6:274.

The Palace Beautiful

Bunyan's Membership and Ministry in the Bedford Church

JOHN BUNYAN WAS ADMITTED into the membership of the Bedford Church in 1655. Because the records of *The Minutes of . . . Bunyan Meeting* do not begin until May 1656, there is no entry for either his admission or his baptism.[2] His name appears twenty-sixth on the list of members at the front of the *Minutes*.[3] Almost immediately, Bunyan sensed a call to preach, for by the October 1657 church meeting, he was so preoccupied with preaching that the congregation determined it would be unwise to appoint him to serve as a deacon even though he had been nominated.[4] Bunyan located his call to preach around 1656, and described it in *Grace Abounding*:

> For after I had been about five or six years awakened, and helped to see both the want and worth of Jesus Christ our Lord, and inabled to venture my Soul upon him: some of the most able among the Saints with us, I say the most able for Judgement, and holiness of Life, as they conceived, did perceive that God

---

2. No record of Bunyan's baptism exists, other than his paedobaptism on November 30, 1628 in the Elstow parish church. See the facsimile of the baptismal registry entry in Brown, *John Bunyan*, 32. But given Bunyan's personal conviction regarding credobaptism, it may be assumed that he received baptism at or near the time of his admission to the church. The Bedford Church did not record baptisms in its church book, a further indication of the church's *laissez-faire* attitude toward the ordinance.

3. Intriguingly, Bunyan's unnamed first wife is not included in the list of members of the Bedford Church, nor does she appear anywhere in the *Minutes* (assuming she would have been entered under her married name of Bunyan). She died in 1658, leaving Bunyan with four children: his blind daughter Mary (b. 1650), Elizabeth (b. 1654), John (b. 1655), and Thomas (b. 1656). Bunyan then married a young woman named Elizabeth in 1659, who bore him a daughter, Sarah (b. 1666), and one son, Joseph (b. 1672). See Brown, *John Bunyan*, 238–39, 401–10; Greaves, *Glimpses of Glory*, 30, 34, 142, 211, 546–48. Neither does Bunyan's second wife, Elizabeth, appear in the records of the church book as Elizabeth Bunyan. Prior to their 1659 marriage, five women named Elizabeth were received into membership: Elizabeth Munnes, Elizabeth Yorke, a first Elizabeth Cooper, Elizabeth Rush, and a second Elizabeth Cooper. It is possible one of these women became Elizabeth Bunyan (*Minutes*, 214).

4. "Whereas there hath heretofore bene time spent in seeking God to direct us in the choyce of officers necessary for the congregation, according to the order of the Gospell, and whereas heretofore there were nominated and appointed for tryall, our brother Spensely, brother Bunyan, brother Coventon and brother Robert Wallis, to exercise the office of deacons, and brother Bunyan being taken off by the preaching of the Gospel, we are agreed that, our brother Bunyan being otherwise imployed, our three brethren beforenamed be continued" (*Minutes*, 28). John Fenne was appointed to take Bunyan's place in the diaconate.

had counted me worthy to understand something of his Will in his holy and blessed Word, and had given me utterance in some measure to express, what I saw, to others for edification; they desired me, and that with much earnestness, that I would be willing at sometime to take in hand in one of the Meetings to speak a work of Exhortation unto them.[5]

Bunyan consented to their entreaty, "though at the first it did much dash and abash my spirit."[6] His gift was immediately affirmed by the congregation: "At which they not onely seemed to be, but did solemnly protest as in the sight of the great God, they were both affected and comforted, and gave thanks to the Father of Mercies for the grace bestowed upon me."[7] The next step was to publicly and formally set Bunyan apart for the ministry of the gospel:

> Wherefore, to be brief, at last, being still desired by the Church, after some solemn prayer to the Lord, with fasting, I was more particularly called forth, and appointed to a more ordinary and publick preaching of the Word, not onely to and amongst them that believed, but also to offer the Gospel to those who had not yet received the faith thereof: about which time I did evidently find in my mind a secret pricking forward thereto: (tho I bless God not for desire of vain-glory, for at that time I was most sorely afflicted with the firy darts of the devil, concerning my eternal state).[8]

This public appointment to the gospel ministry must have transpired before May 1656, for there is no record of it in the *Minutes*.

Bunyan's ministry was attended with immediate fruit: "For I had not preached long, before some began to be touched by the Word, and to be greatly afflicted in their minds at the apprehension of the greatness of their sin, and of their need of Jesus Christ. . . . At this therefore I rejoyced; yea, the tears of those whom God did awaken by my preaching, would be both solace and encouragement to me."[9] Bunyan needed solace and

---

5. Bunyan, *Grace Abounding*, 75.
6. Bunyan, *Grace Abounding*, 75.
7. Bunyan, *Grace Abounding*, 76.
8. Bunyan, *Grace Abounding*, 76. Bunyan continued, "But yet [I] could not be content unless I was found in the exercise of my Gift" (76).
9. Bunyan, *Grace Abounding*, 77. Bunyan later wrote that he seemed most gifted and fervent in "awakening and converting-Work" (81).

encouragement, for at first he preached through continued turmoil over the state of his own soul.

> Indeed I have been as one sent to them from the dead; I went my self in chains to preach to them in chains, and carried that fire in my own conscience that I perswaded them to beware of. I can truly say, and that without dissembling, that when I have been to preach, I have gone full of guilt and terrour even to the Pulpit-Door, and there it hath been taken off, and I have been at liberty in my mind until I have done my work, and then immediately, even before I could get down the Pulpit-Stairs, have been as bad as I was before. Yet God carried me on, but surely with a strong hand: for neither guilt nor hell could take me off my Work.[10]

Bunyan added, "Thus I went for the space of two years, crying out against mens sins, and their fearful state because of them. After which, the Lord came in upon my own Soul with some staid peace and comfort thorow Christ; for he did give me many sweet discoveries of his blessed Grace thorow him."[11] With this new sense of confidence came a new focus of his preaching. Before, Bunyan's preaching centered upon the curse of the law (an "awakening word"); now, he preached on "Jesus Christ in all his Offices, Relations, and Benefits unto the World, and did strive also to discover, to condemn and remove those false supports and props on which the World doth both lean, and by them fall and perish."[12] To these two points of emphasis, Bunyan added a third.

> After this, God led me into something of the mystery of union with Christ: wherefore that I discovered and shewed to them also. And when I had travelled thorow these three chief points of the Word of God, about the space of five years or more; I was caught

---

10. Bunyan, *Grace Abounding*, 78. Bunyan's anxieties over his eternal state would continue for some years after his call to preach. He considered such doubts and anxieties his "thorn in the flesh (2 Cor 12:8, 9) the very mercy of God to me" that prevented his being overtaken by pride (83).

11. Bunyan, *Grace Abounding*, 78.

12. Bunyan, *Grace Abounding*, 78. Of his earlier preaching of sin and the curse of the law, Bunyan wrote, "Now this part of my work I fulfilled with great sence; for the terrours of the Law, and guilt for my transgressions, lay heavy on my Conscience. I preached what I felt, what I smartingly did feel, even that under which my poor Soul did groan and tremble to astonishment." Of his preaching after receiving some measure of confidence, he wrote, "wherefore now I altered in my preaching (for still I preached what I saw & felt); now therefore I did much labour to hold forth Jesus Christ in all his Offices, Relations, and Benefits unto the world" (78).

in my present practice, and cast into Prison, where I have lain as long, to confirm the Truth by way of Suffering, as I was before in testifying of it according to the Scriptures, in a way of Preaching.[13]

On May 8, 1660, Parliament proclaimed Charles II King of England.[14] Despite the promises of tolerance made in the Declaration of Breda, the suppression of religious radicals began almost immediately in London and soon spread to the outlying counties. The Bedford Church felt the mounting pressure. They lost access to St. John's Parish Church, where they had gathered for worship since 1653, and were forced to meet in private homes.[15] On November 12, 1660, Bunyan fell prey to the royalist purge. He had been invited to preach in the small Bedfordshire hamlet of Samsell. But the local justice, Francis Wingate, hearing of it issued an arrest warrant. Bunyan was alerted to the danger prior to the gathering, but was determined to continue. When urged to depart and evade arrest, Bunyan replied, "By no means, I will not stir, neither will I have the meeting dismissed for this. Come, be of good chear, let us not be daunted, our cause is good, we need not be ashamed of it, to preach Gods word, it is so good a work, that we shall be well rewarded, if we suffer for that."[16] And suffer he did, spending the next twelve years imprisoned in the Bedford gaol, located in cramped quarters on the bridge over the river Ouse.[17]

Bunyan's twelve-year imprisonment hindered but did not halt his evangelical ministry. The prison years proved fruitful for writing. Bunyan

13. Bunyan, *Grace Abounding*, 78–79.

14. Greaves, *Glimpses of Glory*, 128. See also Watts, *Dissenters*, 215–16; Kishlansky, *Monarchy Transformed*, 213–39.

15. Greaves, *Glimpses of Glory*, 130–31.

16. Bunyan, *Relation of the Imprisonment*, 98. *A Relation of the Imprisonment of Mr. John Bunyan* "is a document—made up of five reports or letters from the imprisoned Bunyan to the church—about his arrest, prosecution, and imprisonment; unpublishable in the time when it was written. The manuscript of *A Relation of the Imprisonment* was in the hands of Bunyan's descendants until 1765, when it was first published" (Stachniewski and Pacheco, *Grace Abounding*, xxvii). For the historical context of Bunyan's arrest and trials, see Greaves, *Glimpses of Glory*, 127–45.

17. John Brown, *John Bunyan*, 160. Bunyan would endure another imprisonment in 1676-1677. He was excommunicated by the Church of England in April 1675 and was required to appear before the archdeacon within forty days. When he did not show, he was arrested on a writ *de excommunicato capiendo* by the sheriff of Bedfordshire, and confined in the Bedford gaol for six months, from December 1676 to June 1677. He obtained his release on June 21, 1677, with the help of John Owen (Greaves, *Glimpses of Glory*, 342–45). Information on Bunyan's release from prison comes from John Asty's memoir of John Owen (Asty, "Memoirs" [1721], xxx).

published at least twelve original works during his imprisonment, and authored at least three more, including *The Pilgrim's Progress, Part One*.[18] Furthermore, the severity of his incarceration fluctuated, affording him periods of relative freedom, such that he remained an active member of the Bedford Church, even taking on an increasingly prominent leadership role as the end of his imprisonment drew near.[19] By the time he emerged from prison in May 1672, Bunyan was an elder in the Bedford Church, was a leading voice within Nonconformity, and was engaged in a controversy with the Baptists that would prove his most influential ecclesiological contribution.[20]

Bunyan's Evangelical Independent Ecclesiology

This chapter provides a systematic overview of Bunyan's ecclesiology. Its analysis takes into account every extant work of Bunyan's corpus, a corpus that exceeds sixty published works.[21] A further valuable source for

---

18. Bunyan's works published during his imprisonment are *Profitable Meditations* (1661), *I Will Pray with the Spirit and with the Understanding Also* (1662), *Prison Meditations* (1663), *Christian Behaviour* (1663), *A Mapp Shewing the Order and Causes of Salvation and Damnation* (1663/1664), *The Holy City* (1665), *One Thing Is Needful* (1665), *The Resurrection of the Dead* (1665), *Ebal and Gerizim* (1665), *Grace Abounding to the Chief of Sinners* (1666), *A Confession of My Faith, and a Reason of My Practice* (1672), and *A Defence of the Doctrine of Justification by Faith in Jesus Christ* (1672). In addition, Bunyan authored *A Relation of the Imprisonment of Mr. John Bunyan* (w. 1660–1662; p. 1765), *The Heavenly Foot-Man* (w. 1667/1668; p. 1698), and *The Pilgrim's Progress, Part One* (w. 1668–1671; p. 1678). Bunyan also oversaw subsequent editions of several works during his imprisonment. See Greaves, *Glimpses of Glory*, 637–38.

19. For Bunyan's involvement in church activities during his imprisonment, see *Minutes*, 37 [1661], 39–73 [1668–1672]. The *Minutes* contain no records from March 1664 to October 1668.

20. Bunyan's call to the pastorate of Bedford Church in January 1672 is discussed in the introduction to the following chapter on the communion controversy.

21. Two works once attributed to Bunyan are of questionable provenance: *Reprobation Asserted* and *An Exhortation to Peace and Unity*. The former work is likely authentic, yet has little relevance to the study of Bunyan's ecclesiology. *Reprobation Asserted* aligns with Bunyan's other works in content, style, and tone, and is included in Charles Doe's 1692 catalogue of Bunyan's works. See Doe, *Struggler*, 3:763. See also Greaves's arguments against its authenticity in Greaves, "John Bunyan and the Authorship of Reprobation Asserted," 126–31, and Paul Helm's response in Helm, "John Bunyan and 'Reprobation Asserted,'" 87–93. The latter work, *An Exhortation to Peace and Unity*, first published in 1688 after Bunyan's death, advocates strict communion, a position antithetical to the one argued by Bunyan during the communion controversy of the 1670s and maintained until his death. The treatise also advocates the laying on of hands,

Bunyan's ecclesiology is *The Minutes of . . . Bunyan Meeting*, which relate the church's activities before, during, and after Bunyan's pastorate. The following overview analyzes Bunyan's ecclesiology under nine heads: the nature, unity, membership, purpose, polity, officers, worship, ordinances, and discipline of the church. This analysis demonstrates that the driving concern of Bunyan's ecclesiology is the promotion of evangelical faith and holiness. Justification by faith in the imputed righteousness of Christ and Spirit-wrought obedience to the "moral law gospelized" is the thread that ties Bunyan's doctrine of the church together.

The Nature of the Church

Bunyan conceived of the church almost exclusively in two senses. On the one hand, the church is universal and invisible, consisting of every saint, in every age, in every place, who possesses evangelical faith and holiness and is included in the covenant of grace by God's sovereign election.[22] On the other hand, the church is particular and visible, consisting of all those saints who profess evangelical faith and holiness, and are in covenant with one another to walk together according to *"the laws and government of Christ in his Church."*[23] In "A Brief Account of the 1st Gathering of the Church of Christ at Bedford" at the front of the *Minutes*, the anonymous

---

a practice Bunyan nowhere else mentions. *An Exhortation to Peace and Unity* differs significantly from Bunyan's other works in content, style, and tone, and will not be considered in this analysis. See Bunyan [apocryphal], *Exhortation to Peace and Unity*, 2:744–45. George Offor listed eight reasons Bunyan is not the author of *An Exhortation to Peace and Unity*, and instead suggested Henry Danvers may have been the author (Offor, "Advertisement by the Editor," in *Works of John Bunyan*, 2:763). *An Exhortation to Peace and Unity* did not appear in Charles Doe's 1692 catalogue of Bunyan's works (Doe, *Struggler*, 3:763). Neither work is included in the Oxford critical edition of Bunyan's works, but may be found in Bunyan, *Reprobation Asserted*, 2:335–58; *An Exhortation to Peace and Unity*, 2:742–54.

22. Expounding upon John 6:37 and the phrase, "All that the Father giveth me shall come to me," and relating it to the body of Christ spoken of in Eph 4:13 ("till we all come in the unity of the faith"), Bunyan wrote, "Mark, as in the Text, so here he speaketh of *All*; *Untill we* All *come. We* All! All who? Doubtless, *All* that the Father giveth to *Christ*. This is further insinuated, because he calleth *this* All, The *Body* of Christ, the Measure of the Stature of the Fulness of *Christ*: By which he means the Universal Number given, to wit, The true Elect Church" (Bunyan, *Come & Welcome*, 8:293).

23. Bunyan, *Confession of My Faith*, 4:162. "I tell you again, That a discovery of the Faith and Holiness, and a Declaration of the willingness of a Person to subject himself to the Laws and the Government of Christ in his Church, is a ground sufficient to receive such a Member" (Bunyan, *Differences in Judgment*, 4:199–200).

author related the gathering and constitution of the Bedford Church: "The manner of their putting themselves into the state of a Church of Christ was: after much prayer and waiting upon God and consulting one with another, by the Word, they, upon the day appointed for this solemne worke, being met, after prayer and seeking God as before, with one consent joyntly first gave themselves to the Lord, and one to another by the will of God."[24] To use the terminology of the day, the matter of a particular/visible church is a saint professing evangelical faith made visible and credible by evangelical holiness, and the form of a particular/visible church is its mutual covenant.[25] Bunyan and the Bedford Church possessed what Paul Fiddes refers to as a "covenant ecclesiology," in which the church is gathered by means of a two-dimensional covenant—i.e., vertical and horizontal (they "with one consent joyntly first gave themselves to the Lord, and one to another by the will of God").[26] Beyond the initial covenant language cited

---

24. *Minutes*, 17.

25. Commenting on the debates over baptism and communion that embroiled the JLJ Church and its offshoots in the early 1640s, Matthew Ward writes, "Church leaders defined the church by two parameters: matter and form. The 'matter' of a church was someone 'professing faith in the righteousness of Jesus Christ'; the 'form' of a church was 'that by which these are united and knit together in one fellowship.' Everyone agreed on those definitions in general but interpreted them in different ways. For example, the form of a church could refer to any number of things. Was a church united by its profession of faith? Its baptism? Its covenant? Many of the leaders we now call 'Baptist' concluded believer's baptism by immersion to be the form of a church" (Ward, "Baptism as Worship," 20). The definitions employed by Ward come from Spilsbury, *Treatise* [1643], 41. Ward also cites Henry Jessey, who wrote, "Where is *matter* and *forme*, there is a true Church; the *Matter* of a true Church, to be Saints visibly; the *Forme*, a gathering of these out from the world and *joyning of them together* to worship the Lord in truth" (Jessey, *Storehouse of Provision* [1650], 102).

26. Paul Fiddes writes about the "covenant ecclesiology" of English Separatism: "In my own essay, I trace two 'tensions' of oversight or authority within the covenant theology of the English Separatists—between members of a congregation and their officers, and between the local congregation and a fellowship or association of congregations. These, I suggest, arise from the priority given within covenant to the rule of Christ, and I propose that the tensions remain characteristic of a covenantal ecclesiology in the successors to Separatism, including the Baptists. . . . My argument is that the two tensions and the two dimensions are endemic to a church established by covenant, and wherever they appear we may recognize a covenant ecclesiology *regardless of whether a covenant document is used to gather the church*. A characteristic linguistic sign of the tensions, with or without the term 'covenant,' is the language of 'walking together' and 'watching over one another'" (Fiddes, "Introduction," 6, italics added). See Fiddes's essay on the covenant ecclesiology of English Separatism in Fiddes, "Covenant and the Inheritance of Separatism," 63–91. See also Lee, "Baptism and Covenant," 119–36.

above from the account of its constitution, the *Minutes* contain numerous examples of the Bedford Church's covenant ecclesiology.[27] Bunyan's writings are likewise permeated with the notion of Christians "walking together" in covenant with the Lord and with one another.[28]

A saint is baptized by the Spirit into the invisible church (1 Cor 12:13).[29] However, the parallel does not hold: a saint is not baptized into a visible church by water baptism, for baptism is not the form of a particular/visible church. "I told you also, That Baptism makes thee no Member of the Church, neither doth it make thee a visible Saint; *It giveth thee, therefore, neither right to, nor being of Membership at all.*"[30] There are a few instances in which Bunyan seemed to entertain a *tertium quid*: a non-particular/visible expression of the universal church. For instance, Bunyan could refer to the universal/invisible church as the church mystical, and to particular/visible churches collectively as the church politic. "As Christ then, has a

---

27. See *Minutes*, 27 (new members were admitted after "resolving in the strength of Christ to walk with the Church"), 41 (the church disciplined brother Coventon for refusing to "maintaine his communion with the Church, contrary to solemn covenant"), 73 (the church commissions the "elders and gifted brethren" to draw up a confession of faith, "that after the Churche's approbation thereof it may be propounded to all that shall hereafter give up themselves to the Lord and us by the will of God, and their unfeigned consent thereto required"), 85 ("the Church did sollemnely give themselves up to the Lord and to one another, and did promise in the strength of Crist to walke more in love one with another, and to perform the dutyes of ther relation more carfully then formerlie they had done"), 94 (sister Honour and sister Julian Browne are admonished to "maintayne there communion and fellowship with the Church according to there inishall covenant and Christian duty").

28. For example, the mutual covenant is depicted in *The Pilgrim's Progress* when, after Faithful's martyrdom in Vanity Fair, Hopeful joins Christian on his pilgrimage: "Now I saw in my Dream, that *Christian* went not forth alone, for there was one whose name was *Hopeful*, (being made so by the beholding of *Christian* and *Faithful* in their words and behaviour, in their sufferings at the *fair*) who joyned himself unto him, and, entring into a brotherly covenant, told him that he would be his Companion" (Bunyan, *Pilgrim's Progress*, 1:95, 97).

29. "Sir [i.e., Thomas Paul], you mistake me, I treat not here of our being baptized with the Spirit, with respect to its coming from Heaven into us; but of that act of the Spirit, when come, *which baptizeth us into a Body, or Church*: It is one thing to be baptized *with* the Spirit in the first sense; and another to be baptized *by* it in the sense I treat of: for the Spirit to come down upon me, is one thing; and for that when come, to implant, imbody, or baptize me into the body of Christ, is another" (Bunyan, *Differences in Judgment*, 4:210).

30. Bunyan, *Differences in Judgment*, 4:200. It is the mutual covenant, not baptism, that binds the saints together, uniting them into a church. "Affections *knit* in *Love*, the Couplings are" (Bunyan, *Discourse of the Building*, 6:274).

Body *Mystical*, which is called his *Members*, his *Flesh*, and his *Bones*, *Ephes.* 5. 30. So he has a Body *Politick*, Congregations modelled by the skill that his Ministers have in his Word, for the bearing up of his Name, and the preserving of his Glory in the World against *Antichrist*."[31] Employing a different metaphor, Bunyan also divided the church into the church triumphant in heaven, and the church militant upon the earth.[32]

But in his controversy with the Baptists, Bunyan presented the church in strictly binary terms: the church is either universal/invisible or particular/visible. Thomas Paul posited that baptism was the initiating ordinance into the "*universal, orderly, Church-visible*," a position evidently held by Henry Danvers as well.[33] Bunyan found this absurd.

> *Answ. Universal*, that is, the *whole* Church; This word now comprehendeth all the parts of it, even from *Adam* to the very world's end, whether in Heaven or Earth, &c. Now that Baptism makes a man a member of this Church, I do not yet believe, nor can you shew me why I should.
>
> 2. The *Universal, Orderly Church*: What Church this should be (if by orderly, you mean Harmony or Agreement in the outward parts of Worship) I do not understand neither.
>
> And yet thus you should mean, because you add the word *VISIBLE* to all at the last; *The Universal, Orderly, Visible Church*. Now I would yet learn of this Brother where this church is; for if it be *Visible*, he can *tell* and also *shew* it. But to be short, there is no such Church: The universal Church cannot be visible; a great part of that vast Body being already in Heaven, and a great part as yet (perhaps) unborn.
>
> But if he should mean by *Universal*, the whole of that part of this Church that is on Earth, then neither is it *Visible* nor *Orderly*.

---

31. Bunyan, *Case of Conscience Resolved*, 4:322–23.

32. In *Solomon's Temple Spiritualiz'd*, Bunyan related the holy place to the church militant, and the most holy place to the church triumphant. "That commonly called the Temple of God at *Jerusalem*, considered as standing of two parts, was called the *outward*, and *inward* Temple, or, the *holy*, and *most* holy place. They were builded upon *one*, and the *same* foundation, neither could one go into the Holiest, but as thorow the holy place. . . . The *first* house, namely, that which we have been speaking of, was a type of the Church-*militant*, and the place *most holy* a type of the Church-*triumphant*, as it is now. So then, The house standing of these two parts, was a shadow of the Church both in *Heaven* and *Earth*. And for that they are joyned together by *one* and the *same* foundation, it was to shew, that *they above*, and *we below*, are yet *one* and the *self-same* house of God" (Bunyan, *Solomon's Temple Spiritualiz'd*, 7:85).

33. Bunyan, *Peaceable Principles and True*, 4:273.

> 1. Not *Visible*; for the greatest part remains alwayes to the best mans eye utterly invisible.
>
> 2. This Church is not *Orderly*; that is, hath not Harmony in its outward and visible parts of worship; some parts opposing and contradicting the other most *severely*. . . .
>
> So then by *Universal, Orderly, Visible Church*, this Brother must mean those of the Saints only, that have been, or are baptized as we; this is clear, because Baptism (saith he) maketh a Believer a member of *this Church*; his meaning then is, that there is an *Universal, Orderly, Visible Church*, and they *alone* are the *Baptists*; and that every one that is baptized, is by that made a member of the *Universal, Orderly, Visible Church of Baptists*, and that the whole number of the rest of Saints are utterly excluded.
>
> But now if other men should do as this man, how many Universal Churches should we have? An *Universal, Orderly, Visible Church of Independents*; an *Universal, Orderly, Visible Church of Presbyterians*, and the like.[34]

Bunyan recognized that his Baptist opponents had carved out a third category of the church. It was universal in the sense that it was not confined to a particular congregation. And it was visible in that it was militant and earthly; it did not comprehend the church triumphant in heaven. This church was spread over the whole earth, or at least over a particular region.[35] Throughout the baptism debate, Bunyan rejected this *tertium quid*, though his references in later writings to the "Body *Politick*" and the "Church-*militant*" bear some resemblance to the Baptist conception in that they refer to a non-particular/visible expression of the universal church.[36] However, even though Bunyan later allowed for a non-particular/visible expression of the universal church, he strenuously denied that baptism was the initiating ordinance into such a "Body *Politick*" or "Church-*militant*," for the true visible churches that make up this body practice opposing forms of baptism. Thus, throughout the baptism debate, Bunyan refused to consider the church in anything other than binary categories. The church is either universal/invisible or particular/visible, and baptism cannot be the initiating ordinance into either one.

---

34. Bunyan, *Peaceable Principles and True*, 4:273–74.

35. Matthew Ward writes, "Kiffin's vision clearly meant one great Baptist church in each city" (Ward, "Baptism as Worship," 30). Ward notes that Hanserd Knollys held a similar position, and cites Knollys, *World That Now Is*, 8, 44, 45.

36. Bunyan, *Case of Conscience Resolved*, 4:322–23 ("Body *Politick*"); *Solomon's Temple Spiritualiz'd*, 7:85 ("Church-*militant*").

Bunyan found numerous types of the church throughout the Old Testament.[37] In his *Exposition of the First Ten Chapters of Genesis*, Bunyan saw in Adam and Eve a type of Christ and the Church. "All the glory of this World, had not *Adam* had a Wife, could not have compleated this Man's blessedness; he would yet have been wanting: so all the Glory of Heaven, consider Christ as Mediator, could not, without his Church, have made him up compleate."[38] Later in the same work he wrote, "When *Adam* was created, the Lord created two in one: So when Christ, the Head of the Church, was chosen, the Church was also chosen in him. *And blessed them*. With the Blessing of *Generation:* A Type of the Blessing of *Regeneration* that was to be by Christ in the Church."[39] Indeed, all Christian marriages are a type of the relationship between Christ and the church. "This is one of God's chief ends in instituting Marriage, that Christ and his Church, under a figure, might be wherever there is a Couple that believe through Grace."[40] Noah's ark is likewise a type of the church: "I told you before, That the Ark was a Type of Christ, and also of the Works of the Faith of the Godly. And now he seems to bring in more, and to make it a Type of the Church of Christ; as indeed the Prophet also does, when he calls the Church, *One afflicted, and tossed with tempests*; and compareth her Troublers to the *Waters of Noah*, saying, *This is as the Waters of Noah*."[41] Bunyan teased out this metaphor by noting that the ark had: (1) light ("the *Word* and the *Spirit* of God"); (2) a door ("a Type of Christ"); (3) stories of lower and higher rank ("1. *Apostles*: 2. *Evangelists*: 3. *Pastors* and *Teachers*").[42] And just like the visible church, so the ark had both clean and unclean beasts within it, a type of regenerate and unregenerate persons.[43] In *Solomon's Temple Spiritualiz'd*, Bunyan viewed Solomon's temple as a type of the church, and derived from its design, construction, furniture, vessels, and worship abundant ecclesiological instruction.[44] Likewise, in *A*

---

37. Though Bunyan viewed the universal church as comprised of all the elect of every age, and could even speak of the congregation of Israel as the "church" of the Jews (Bunyan, *Saints Privilege and Profit*, 13:188, 195), yet when it came to Old Testament typology, by "church" Bunyan meant the church of the new covenant.

38. Bunyan, *Exposition of the First Ten Chapters*, 12:125.

39. Bunyan, *Exposition of the First Ten Chapters*, 12:182.

40. Bunyan, *Christian Behaviour*, 3:27.

41. Bunyan, *Exposition of the First Ten Chapters*, 12:202.

42. Bunyan, *Exposition of the First Ten Chapters*, 12:202–3.

43. Bunyan, *Exposition of the First Ten Chapters*, 12:211.

44. "But I have, in the ensuing Discourse, confined my self to the *Temple*, that

Discourse of the House of the Forest of Lebanon, Bunyan viewed the house of the forest of Lebanon as a type of the persecuted church.

> I will therefore take it for granted, That the House of the Forest of *Lebanon* is a significative thing, yea, a Figure of the Church, as the Temple at *Jerusalem* was, though not under the same consideration. The Temple was a Figure of the Church under the Gospel, *as She relateth to Worship*; but the House of the Forest of *Lebanon* was a Figure of that Church, as she is assaulted for her worship, as she is persecuted for the same. Or take it more expresly thus: *I take this House of the Forest of* Lebanon *to be a Type of the Church in the Wilderness*, or as she is in her *sack-cloth* state.[45]

Besides these biblical images, Bunyan also described the church under a number of allegorical depictions in *The Pilgrim's Progress*. The Palace Beautiful is the most recognizable portrait of a particular/visible church, but it is not the only ecclesiological image in Bunyan's allegory.[46] The "stately Palace," the fifth emblem shown to Christian in the House of Interpreter into which the "man of a very stout countenance" enters amidst much persecution, is a picture of a Nonconformist church.[47] The House of Interpreter, which on Christian's journey functions primarily as an image of the Bible illuminated by the Spirit, functions as a church during Christiana's pilgrimage.[48] Likewise, Gaius's house, at which the pilgrims lodge

---

immediate place of God's Worship; of whose Utensils in particular, as I have said, I have spoken, (though to each with what brevity I could) For that none of them are without a Spiritual, and so a Profitable Signification to us. And here we may behold much of the Richness of the Wisdom and Grace of God; namely, That he, even in the very place of Worship of old, should ordain Visible Forms, and Representations, for the Worshippers to learn to Worship him by. Yea, the Temple it self was, as to this, to them a good Instruction" (Bunyan, *Solomon's Temple Spiritualiz'd*, 7:6).

45. Bunyan, *Discourse of the House*, 7:122 (see also 7:169).

46. For the Palace Beautiful, see Bunyan, *Pilgrim's Progress*, 1:45–55; 2:207–21. The various aspects of the church found within the Palace Beautiful are discussed in the following sections.

47. Bunyan, *Pilgrim's Progress*, 1:33. This identification was suggested by Joseph Ivimey. See Offor's notes in Offor, *Works of John Bunyan*, 3:100.

48. For instance, in *The Pilgrim's Progress, Part Two*, Bunyan stated that this "House [of Interpreter] was built for the relief of Pilgrims," language identical to the way the Porter describes the Palace Beautiful in *The Pilgrim's Progress, Part One*: "The *Porter* answered, This House was built by the Lord of the Hill: and he built it for the relief and security of Pilgrims" (Bunyan, *Pilgrim's Progress*, 2:186; cf. 1:47). Furthermore, Christiana, Mercy, and the children enjoy fellowship with the inhabitants of the House of Interpreter, whom Bunyan noted in the margin are "Old Saints" (2:188). The pilgrims partake of a supper

between the Valley of the Shadow of Death and Vanity Fair, and Mnason's house, where they stay while in Vanity Fair, both function as allegories of the church.[49] A convincing argument can be made for understanding Christiana and her ever-expanding company of pilgrims, under the steady leadership of Great-heart, as an allegory of the church.

Finally, Bunyan wrote concerning the history and perpetuity of the church. The church came into being with Adam. "*Universal*, that is, the *whole* Church; This word now comprehendeth all the parts of it, even from *Adam* to the very world's end, whether in Heaven or Earth, *&c.*"[50] The church continued from Adam to Abraham, as is evident throughout Bunyan's *An Exposition of the First Ten Chapters of Genesis*, in which Bunyan pitted the faithful offspring of Seth against the wicked descendents of Cain, the seed of the woman against the seed of the serpent. Despite this opposition, the church must survive. "For let the Number and Wickedness of Men be never so great in the World, there must be also a Church, by whose Actions the Ways of the Wicked must be condemned."[51] From its inception, the church has always existed in both its invisible and visible forms. But in Abraham's physical seed the visible church began to take institutional shape. The invisible church is henceforth equated with the spiritual offspring of Abraham, the children of promise, the children of faith; while the visible church is the physical seed of Abraham, the children of the flesh, first the congregation of the patriarchs, followed by the congregation of Israel.[52] Bunyan saw far more continuity than discontinuity

---

during which they share their testimonies (as Christian also did at the Palace Beautiful), and they receive what many have interpreted as baptism (the "Bath of Sanctification") and the Lord's Supper ("the contents and sum of the Passover which the Children of *Israel* did eat when they came out from the Land of *Egypt*") (2:192–96). For a discussion of this potential allusion to the ordinances, see the introduction to chapter 5.

49. For Gaius's house, see Bunyan, *Pilgrim's Progress*, 2:241–53, 257; for Mnason's house, see Bunyan, *Pilgrim's Progress*, 2:254–59.

50. Bunyan, *Peaceable Principles and True*, 4:273.

51. Bunyan, *Exposition of the First Ten Chapters*, 12:272–73. See also Bunyan, *Discourse of the Building*, 6:277–78; *Discourse of the House*, 7:166.

52. In *Israel's Hope Encouraged*, Bunyan's exposition of Psalm 130:7, Bunyan distinguished between "*Israel* [as it] is to be taken for those that are such after the flesh; that is, for those that sprang from the loins of *Jacob*, and are called, ISRAEL, after the Flesh, the Children of the Flesh," and "*Israel* . . . [as it] is Israel after God or the Spirit; hence they are called the *Israel* of God, because they are made so of him, not by Generation, nor by Fancy, but by Divine Power" (Bunyan, *Israel's Hope Encouraged*, 13:25–26). Note Bunyan's use of "church" for the visible congregation of Israel in the following text: "First then, the Mercy-seat was for the Church, not for the World; for a Gentile could not go

between the old covenant church and the new covenant church; the two were different historical administrations of the one covenant of grace.[53] However, Bunyan did distinguish the two, speaking of "both the Churches, that is, both of the Jewish and Gentile Church of God," which is a reference to the (mostly Jewish) church under the old covenant and the (mostly Gentile) church under the new covenant.[54] Bunyan conceived of the New Testament church as existing in three historical states, analogous to the three historical states of Old Testament Jerusalem.

> But again, as [the new] *Jerusalem* is thus generally to be understood, so also she is to be considered more particularly: 1. Either as she relates to her first and purest state; or, 2, As she relates to her declined and captivated state; or, 3. With reference to her being recovered again from her apostatized and captivated condition: Thus it was with *Jerusalem* in the Letter; which threefold state of this City shall be most exactly answered by our *Gospel-Jerusalem*, by our New-Testament-Church. Her first state was in the days of Christ and his Apostles, and answered to *Jerusalem* in the days of *Solomon*; her second state is in the days of Antichrist, and answereth to the carrying away of the Jews from their City into *Babylon*; and her third state is this in the Text [i.e., Rev 21], and answereth to their return from Captivity, and rebuilding their City and Walls again: All which will be fully manifest in this Discourse following.[55]

---

immediately from his natural state to the Mercy-seat, by the High-priest, but must first, orderly joyn himself, or be joyned to the Church, which then consisted of the body of the *Jews*. The stranger then must first be circumcised, and consequently profess Faith in the *Messias* to come, which was signified by his going from his Circumcision directly to the Passover, and SO orderly to other privileges, specially to this of the Mercy-seat, which the High-priest was to go but once a year into" (Bunyan, *Saints Privilege and Profit*, 13:195).

53. Bunyan's conception of the covenant of grace is beyond the scope of this monograph, but his covenant theology is expounded at length in *The Doctrine of the Law and Grace Unfolded*, and remained his theological framework throughout his life, permeating all of his writings. See Bunyan, *Doctrine of the Law*, 2:1–226; Greaves, *John Bunyan*, 97–121; Wallace, "Bunyan's Theology and Religious Context," 69–85 (esp. 84), where Wallace concludes that Bunyan was "immersed . . . in the theology of the Bedford meeting and of his Puritan and Dissenting heritage," and that his foundational theological grid was that of "a high Calvinist double-covenant theology."

54. Bunyan, *Saints Privilege and Profit*, 13:188.

55. Bunyan, *Holy City*, 3:78–79 (see also Bunyan's discussion of these three states on 134–36).

The third state is the church in the millennium, symbolized by the New Jerusalem of Revelation 21.[56]

In summary, Bunyan viewed the church in two senses. The universal/invisible church comprehends all the elect who are included in the covenant of grace, all who possess or will possess evangelical faith and holiness. The particular/visible church comprehends those visible saints professing evangelical faith and holiness (the matter) and joined together by mutual covenant (the form). Bunyan found numerous types of the church throughout the pages of the Old Testament, and often portrayed the church in his allegorical writings. Bunyan saw continuity in the distinction between the Israel of God (Abraham's spiritual seed) and the congregation of Israel (Abraham's physical seed) in the Old Testament, and the universal/invisible church (all the elect) and the particular/visible church (all covenanted members) in the New Testament. He interpreted the history of the church through a postmillennial hermeneutic that saw the New Testament church recapitulating the history of Old Testament Jerusalem.

The Unity of the Church

Bunyan's convictions regarding the unity of the visible church (or better, the unity of visible *churches*) must be understood within two different spheres. On the one hand, Bunyan was a Separatist. He refused to sacrifice doctrinal fidelity upon the altar of ecclesiastical unity. His controlling principle of evangelical faith and holiness drove him to dissent from a church that propagated false doctrine and impure worship, and that communicated with unbelieving and unholy people. He wrote in *A Confession of My Faith*, "*Indeed my principles are such, as lead me to a denial to communicate in the things of the Kingdom of Christ, with the ungodly and open prophane; neither can I in, or by the superstitious inventions of this world, consent that my Soul should be governed, in any of my approaches to God,*

---

56. *The Holy City* (1665) is the first and longest exposition of Bunyan's postmillennial eschatology (see esp. Bunyan, *Holy City*, 3:82, 128, 156, 158, 174, 177). Bunyan's postmillennialism may also be discerned in: Bunyan, *Holy War* [*passim*; postmillennialism is the allegory's redemptive-historical framework]; *Of Antichrist*, 12:434–35, 488; *Christ a Compleat Savior*, 13:329; *Solomon's Temple Spiritualiz'd*, 7:19; *Discourse of the House*, 7:172–73. See also the discussion of Bunyan's eschatology in Ross, "Paradise Regained," 73–90; Owens, "John Bunyan and English Millenarianism," 91–92; Greaves, *Glimpses of Glory*, 180–88 [on postmillennialism in *Holy City*], 426–28 [on postmillennialism in *Holy War*].

*because commanded to the contrary, and commended for so refusing.*⁵⁷ Yet he was sensitive to charges of schism and sedition:

> Wherefore excepting this one thing, for which I ought not to be rebuked; I shall, I trust in despite of slander and falsehood, discover my self at all times a peaceable, and an obedient Subject. But if nothing will do, unless I make of my conscience a continual butchery, and slaughter-shop, unless putting out my own eyes I commit me to the blind to lead me, (as I doubt is desired by some) I have determined the Almighty God being my help, and shield, yet to suffer, if frail life might continue so long, even till the moss shall grow on mine eye-browes rather then thus to violate my faith and principles.⁵⁸

In response to Edward Fowler, the Latitudinarian minister at Northill in Bedfordshire and later bishop of Gloucester, who had suggested that the "scandalous lives" of some of the clergy was the main cause of Dissent, Bunyan wrote, "I will grant it, if you respect these poor carnal People, who yet have been shamed from your Assemblies, by such Vicious Persons you mention; But the truly Godly, and Spiritually Judicious have left you from other Arguments."⁵⁹ The true cause of Dissent was that the Church of England preached a different gospel and taught a different holiness. Bunyan's response to Fowler, *A Defence of the Doctrine of Justification by Faith in Jesus Christ* is a vehement denial of justification by the inherent righteousness of man and a vigorous defense of justification by the imputed righteousness of

---

57. Bunyan, *Confession of My Faith*, 4:136.

58. Bunyan, *Confession of My Faith*, 4:136. For Bunyan's profession of loyalty during his trial before the magistrate, see Bunyan, *Relation of the Imprisonment*, 115: "We had much other discourse which I cannot well remember, about the laws of the nation, submission to governments; to which I did tell him, that I did look upon myself as bound in conscience to walk according to all righteous laws, and that whether there was a King or no; and if I did any thing that was contrary, I did hold it my duty to bear patiently the penalty of the law, that was provided for such offenders; with many more words to that effect." See also Bunyan, *Confession of My Faith*, 4:153: "Many are the mercyes we receive, by a well qualified Magistrate, and if any shall at any time be otherwise inclined, *let us shew our christianity in a patient suffering for well doing, what it shall please God to inflict by them.*" Patient suffering under persecution for conscientious dissent is the entire subject of Bunyan, *Seasonable Counsel*, 10:5–104.

59. Bunyan, *Defence of the Doctrine of Justification*, 4:103. Fowler had written, "And I am very certain from my own observation, that no one thing hath so conduced to the prejudice of our Church of *England*, and done the separating parties so much service, as the scandalous lives of some that exercise the ministerial function in her" (Fowler, *Design of Christianity*, 258).

Christ. In Bunyan's opinion, Fowler had grossly overestimated the ability of natural man to produce a righteousness acceptable to God.

> But I say, these principles thus stated by you, being the principles, and the goodness of this World, and such as have not faith, but the law, not the holy Ghost, but humane nature in them; they cannot be those which you affirm, was or is the design, the great, the only, and ultimate design of Christ, or his Gospel to promote, and propagate in the World; neither with respect to our justification before God from the curse; neither with respect to the workings of his Spirit, and the faith of Jesus in our hearts, the true Gospel or evangelical Holiness.[60]

The only righteousness that justifies is Christ's righteousness; the only righteousness that sanctifies is that which is produced by the Spirit through faith.[61] Bunyan's commitment to evangelical faith and holiness was the cause of his separatism.

On the other hand, Bunyan's commitment to evangelical faith and holiness also drove him to a passionate advocacy for evangelical unity. Bunyan could not conceive of nor tolerate separation from those who possessed evangelical faith and manifested evangelical holiness. He spoke derisively of those who segregated along the lines of such external and secondary matters as church governance or baptism.

> Here's a *Presbyter*, heres an *Independent*, an *Anabaptist*, so joyned each man to his own opinion, that they cannot have that communion one with another, as by the testament of the Lord Jesus, they are commanded and injoyned. What is the cause? Is the Truth? No? God is the author of no confusion in the Church of God. It is then because every man makes too much of his own opinion, abounds too much in his own sence, and takes not care to separate his opinion from the iniquity that cleaveth thereto. . . .

---

60. Bunyan, *Defence of the Doctrine of Justification*, 4:22.

61. Bunyan understood the justifying righteousness of Christ as comprehending both his active and passive obedience: his answering "the Demands of the Law, in Thought, Word, and Deed, without the least Commixture of the least Sinful thought, in the whole Course of his Life," and his giving by his death, "even by the Death that hath the Curse of God in it, a compleat satisfaction to the Law for the breach thereof. Now this could none but Christ accomplish; none else having Power to do it" (Bunyan, *Defence of the Doctrine of Justification*, 4:55). Likewise, Bunyan understood evangelical holiness as comprised of three essential components: "There are three things which are essential to the inward gospel holiness . . . 1. *The holy Ghost*. 2. *Faith in Christ*. 3. *A new Heart, and a new Spirit*" (4:27–31). Both themes permeate the treatise.

> I have often said in my heart, what is the reason that some of the brethren should be so shy of holding communion, with those every whit as good, if not better, than themselves? Is it because they think themselves unworthy of their holy fellowship? No, verily: it is because they exalt themselves, they are leavened with some iniquity that hath mixed it self with some good opinions that they hold, and therefore it is that they say to others, *stand by thy self, come not near me, for I am holier than thou*.[62]

Bunyan found the effects of division among evangelical churches devastating. In *A Confession of My Faith*, Bunyan listed eighteen negative consequences of such division, the last of which is that it brought God's judgment down upon the nonconforming churches in the form of persecution, a charge that incensed his Baptist opponents during the communion controversy.[63] Bunyan heeded John Gifford's charge to the Bedford Church not to divide over external matters:

> Concerning separation from the Church about baptisme, laying on of hands, anoynting with oyle, psalmes, or any externalls, I charge every one of you respectively, as you will account for it to our Lord Jesus Christ, who shall judge both quick and dead at his coming, that none of you be found guilty of this great evil, which while some have committed and that through a zeale for God, yet not according to knowledge, they have erred from the lawe of the love of Christ, and have made a rent from the true Church which is but one.[64]

---

62. Bunyan, *Holy Life*, 9:327–28. Along the same lines are his words in *Peaceable Principles and True*: "And since you would know by what Name I would be distinguished from others; I tell you, I would be, and hope I am *a Christian*; and chuse, if God should count me worthy, *to be called a Christian, a Believer* or other such Name which is approved by the Holy Ghost. And as for those Factious Titles of *Anabaptists, Independents, Presbyterians*, or the like, I conclude, that they came neither from *Jerusalem*, nor *Antioch*, but rather from *Hell* and *Babylon*; for they naturally tend to divisions, *you may know them by their Fruits*" (Bunyan, *Peaceable Principles and True*, 4:270). See also Bunyan, *Heavenly Foot-Man*, 5:152.

63. "Shall I add, Is it not that which greatly prevailed to bring down these judgments, which at present we feel and groan under; I will dare to say, it was the cause thereof" (Bunyan, *Confession of My Faith*, 4:183). See also Bunyan, *Vindication*, 1:126: "Another reason why so many are carried away with delusions, is, those differences that are among the Children of God about smaller matters. . . . I say it makes them to say within themselves, and one to another; There are so many sects and judgments in the World, that we cannot tell which way to take."

64. John Gifford's death-bed letter in *Minutes*, 19.

This explains why Bunyan was so appalled at the Baptists' willingness to divide evangelical churches over credobaptism. Like Gifford, he thought it a "great evil" that rendered one liable to the severe judgment of Christ. Evangelical faith and holiness were the marks of a true visible church, and must be the only standard of fellowship and communion, both amongst believers and amongst churches.

> For those that have *private* opinions too
> We must *make* room, or shall the Church undo;
> Provided they be *such* as don't impair
> Faith, Holiness, nor with good Conscience jar;
> Provided also *those that hold them shall*
> Such Faith hold to themselves, and not let fall
> Their fruitless Notions in their Brothers way,
> Do thus, and Faith and Love will not decay.[65]

Evangelical unity promotes evangelical faith and holiness; evangelical disunity hinders the same.

Nevertheless, Bunyan was confident that the unity of the visible church (the church militant) would one day be attained. In Bunyan's postmillennial vision of the New Jerusalem, Bunyan opined,

> That at the day of New *Jerusalem*, there shall be no Doctrine accepted, nor no Preachers regarded, but the Doctrine, and the Preachers of the Doctrine of the Twelve: for in that he saith, That *in them are found the Names of the twelve Apostles of the Lamb*, he doth implicitly exclude all other, of whatever Tribe they pretend themselves: It shall not be then as now, a Popish Doctrine, a Quakers Doctrine, a Prelatical Doctrine, and the Presbyter, Independent, and Anabaptist, thus distinguished, and thus confounding and destroying: but the Doctrine shall be one, and that one the Doctrine where you finde the Names of the twelve Apostles of the Lamb.[66]

When Antichrist is defeated, the visible church will truly be one.

Bunyan wrote in his preface to *A Confession of My Faith*, "*Faith and Holiness, are my professed principles, with an endeavour, so far as in me*

---

65. Bunyan, *Discourse of the Building*, 6:311.

66. Bunyan, *Holy City*, 3:115 (see also 3:184; cf. *Solomon's Temple Spirituliz'd*, 7:85, in which Bunyan asserted a unity between the church triumphant and the true [evangelical] church militant).

lyeth, to be at peace with all men."⁶⁷ Those principles led him to separate from those who preached an unholy gospel and led unholy lives, but it also led him to chastise those who separated from evangelical brethren for any reason, especially baptism.⁶⁸

The Membership of the Church

Bunyan's overarching concern for the promotion of evangelical faith and holiness also determined his views on membership in a particular/visible church. Bunyan was a vigorous advocate of regenerate church membership. Evangelical faith and holiness are the indispensable requirements for membership in a particular/visible congregation. As demonstrated above, this was one of the reasons for Bunyan's dissent from the Church of England (the other being false doctrine). "*I dare not have communion with them that profess not faith and holiness*; or that are not visible Saints by calling.... Now he that is visibly or openly prophane, cannot be then a visible Saint, for he that is a visible Saint must profess faith, and repentance, and consequently holyness of life: And with none else dare I communicate.*"⁶⁹ In *A Confession of My Faith*, Bunyan provided seven reasons he insisted upon regenerate church membership:

1. From the beginning God has separated the unfaithful from the faithful, as evidenced by his separation of Cain from Seth, and the wicked world from Noah.

2. Separation from the ungodly is commanded in the Scriptures (e.g., Lev 11:44).

3. The New Testament churches provide the pattern for a community of visible saints.

4. The nature of the church is such that it is impossible it should have "true and spiritual communion" with unbelievers.

---

67. Bunyan, *Confession of My Faith*, 4:135–36.

68. It is somewhat ironic that Bunyan separated from the Baptists because they separated over baptism. Either Bunyan was unaware of the irony and this is an inconsistent point of his practice, or he did not regard those who did so as truly evangelical. The following chapter demonstrates that either conclusion is possible.

69. Bunyan, *Confession of My Faith*, 4:154. See also Bunyan, *Strait Gate*, 5:77: "In at the gate *of the Church*, none may enter *now*, that are open profane and scandalous to religion; no, though they pleade they are beloved of God."

5. Communion of the godly and the ungodly is unnatural and forced, like "plowing with an Ox, and an Ass together" (Deut 22:10).

6. Communion with the openly profane is "most pernicious and destructive," as evidenced by Israel's corruption by her pagan neighbors. It "polluteth the ordinances of God," "*violateth the law*," "profaneth the holyness of God," and "defileth the truly Gracious."

7. Communion with the ungodly provokes God to severe judgments. Bunyan was adamant that "it is all one with the Church to Communicate with the prophane; and to sacrifice, and offer their gifts to the Divel."[70]

These seven arguments reflect the standard Nonconformist defense of the principle of separation.

Bunyan echoed these sentiments throughout his written corpus. In his exposition of Genesis 6, he wrote:

> The first great quarrel therefore that God had with his Church, it was for their holding unwarrantable Communion with others. The Church should always *dwell alone*, and not be *reckoned among the Nations*. The Church is *a chosen Generation, a royal Priesthood, an holy Nation, a peculiar People*: Therefore the work of the Church of God, is not to fall in with any sinful Fellowship, or receive into their Communion the ungodly World, but to *shew forth the praises and vertues of him who hath called them* out from among such Communicants into *his marvellous Light*.[71]

The danger of mixed communion is great. "They that profess the name of Christ, or that name it religiously, should to their utmost depart from iniquity, *because of the Church of Christ which is holy*.... One black sheep is quickly espied among five hundred white ones, and one mangie one will soon infect many. One also among the Saints, that is not clean, is a blemish to the rest, and, as *Solomon* says, *one sinner destroyeth much*

---

70. These seven reasons are found in Bunyan, *Confession of My Faith*, 4:154–60. Bunyan later made another plea for separation from the ungodly (4:185–86). See also Bunyan, *Differences in Judgment*, 4:199: "You ought to receive no man, but upon a comfortable satisfaction to the Church, that you are now receiving a Believer."

71. Bunyan, *Exposition of the First Ten Chapters*, 12:192. Bunyan pressed home the same point in regard to the Tower of Babel: "Hence Note, That the First and Primitive Churches were safe and secure, so long as they kept intire by themselves; but when once they admitted of a mixture, a Great *Babel*, as a Judgment of God, was admitted to come into their mind" (12:276).

good."⁷² When Faithful's incisive questioning of Talkative angers the latter and drives him away, Christian affirms Faithful's conduct:

> You did well to talk so plainly to him as you did; there is but little of this faithful dealing with men now a days, and that makes Religion to stink so in the nostrils of many, as it doth: for they are these *Talkative* Fools, whose Religion is only in word, and are debauched and vain in their Conversation, that (being so much admitted into the Fellowship of the Godly) do stumble the World, blemish Christianity, and grieve the Sincere. I wish that all Men would deal with such, as you have done, then should they either be made more conformable to Religion, or the company of Saints would be too hot for them.⁷³

Likewise, Wiseman tells Attentive that "those that are guilty of wronging, corrupting or defrauding of any, should not be admitted to the fellowship of the Saints, no nor into the common catalogue of Brethren with them."⁷⁴ Failing to maintain a regenerate church membership hinders the promotion of faith and holiness among the saints and in the world, and exposes the church to the judgment of God.

But neither faith nor holiness can be observed in their essence. How, then, is a church to determine who is regenerate? Bunyan faced this question head-on. "*I dare not have communion with them that profess not faith and holiness*; or that are not visible Saints by calling: but note that by this assertion, I meddle not with the elect; but as he is a visible Saint by calling; neither do I exclude the secret Hypocrite, *if he be hid from me by visible Saint ship.*"⁷⁵ Bunyan meddled not with that which is invisible: election, regeneration, and faith. Rather, a visible church is concerned only with visible sainthood. Faith is made visible by a profession of faith, a profession requiring both doctrinal and experiential content, and by a life of holiness.

---

72. Bunyan, *Holy Life*, 9:300.

73. Bunyan, *Pilgrim's Progress*, 1:83. When asked whether the pilgrims might lodge in his house, Gaius replies, "Yes Gentlemen, if you be true Men, for my House is for none but Pilgrims" (Bunyan, *Pilgrim's Progress*, 2:242).

74. Bunyan, *Life and Death of Mr. Badman*, 98.

75. Bunyan, *Confession of My Faith*, 4:154. "Now visible Church-Communion doth not absolutely call for onely invisible Saints, neither can it: for if the Church were to joyn with none but those whom they knew to be the very Elect of God (as all invisible Saints are) then she must joyn with none at all; for it is not possible that any Church should be so infallible to judge in that manner of the Elect, as to discern them always, and altogether from the non-Elect, which cannot be an invisible Saint" (Bunyan, *Holy City*, 3:175; see the entire discussion on 3:173–78).

> *Quest.* But by what rule, then would you gather persons into Church-communion?
>
> *Answ. Even by that rule, by which they are discovered to the Church to be visible Saints; and willing to be gathered into their body and fellowship. By that word of God therefore, by which their Faith, experience and conversation (being examined) is found Good; by that the Church should receive them into fellowship with them.*[76]

In dialogue with Talkative, Faithful discusses how to discern a "work of grace in the soul." Doctrinal content is essential, but not sufficient. Doctrine must be joined to experience.

> Indeed to know, is a thing that pleaseth Talkers and Boasters; but to do, is that which pleaseth God. Not that the heart can be good without knowledge; for without that the heart is naught: There is therefore knowledge, and knowledge. Knowledge that resteth in the bare speculation of things, and knowledge that is accompanied with the grace of faith and love, which puts a man upon doing even the will of God from the heart: the first of these will serve the Talker; but without the other the true Christian is not content.[77]

Thus, according to Faithful, a work of grace is discovered by two essential components:

> 1. By an experimental confession of his faith in Christ. 2. By a life answerable to that confession, to wit, a life of holiness; heart-holiness, family-holiness (if he hath a Family) and by Conversation-holiness in the world: which in the general teacheth him, inwardly to abhor his sin, and himself for that, in secret, to suppress it in his Family, and to promote holiness in the World; not by talk only, as a Hypocrite or Talkative person may do: but by a practical Subjection in Faith, and Love, to the power of the word.[78]

Evangelical faith (comprised of both evangelical doctrine and experience) and evangelical holiness (obedience to the moral law, by the Spirit, through faith, from a new heart) are the *sine qua non* of church membership.[79]

---

76. Bunyan, *Confession of My Faith*, 4:165. For a poetic description of the requirements for church communion, see Bunyan, *Discourse of the Building*, 6:279–81.

77. Bunyan, *Pilgrim's Progress*, 1:80.

78. Bunyan, *Pilgrim's Progress*, 1:81.

79. In the same year that Bunyan wrote *A Confession of My Faith* (1672), he also wrote *A Defence of the Doctrine of Justification*, in which he provided the following definition of evangelical holiness: "There are three things which are essential to the inward

"Therefore I say, the rule by which we receive Church-members; it is the word of the Faith of Christ, and of the moral precept Evangelized."[80] Nevertheless, though the matter of a church is a visible saint whose profession of faith is rendered observable and credible by a life of holiness, the form of a church is its mutual covenant. Therefore, in addition to evangelical faith and holiness, Bunyan added a third membership requirement.

> Quest. *But by what rule would you receive them into fellowship with your selves?*
>
> Answ. Even by a discovery of their faith and holyness; *and their declaration of willingness to subject themselves to the laws and government of Christ in his Church.*[81]

Examples abound in the *Minutes* of new members received by profession of faith, the evidence of a holy life, and a commitment to "walk with the Church" in mutual covenant, a covenant to which they were held accountable through discipline.[82]

To the congregation belongs the responsibility, under the watchful eye of its elders, to examine the professions of faith of candidates for membership.

> Now in order to the discovery of this faith and holiness, and so to fellowship in Church communion: I hold it requisite that a faithful relation be made thereof by the party thus to be received; yea, if need be by witnesses also, *for the satisfaction of the church, that she may receive in faith and judgment,* such as best shall suit her holy profession.... For no man may intrude himself upon,

---

Gospel holiness ... 1. The holy Ghost. 2. Faith in Christ. 3. A new Heart, and a new Spirit" (Bunyan, *Defence of the Doctrine of Justification*, 4:27). On the distinction between legal and evangelical holiness, see Bunyan, *Few Sighs from Hell*, 1:381: "Then if the law thou readest of, tell thee in thy conscience, thou must do this and the other good work of the Law, if ever thou wilt be saved. Then answer plainly, that for thy part thou art resolved now not to work for life, but to believe in the vertue of that blood shed upon the Crosse upon Mount *Calvary*, for the remission of sins: and yet, because Christ hath justified thee freely by his Grace, thou wilt serve him in Holinesse and Righteousnesse all the dayes of thy life, yet not in a legall Spirit, or in a covenant of Works, but mine obedience (say thou) I will endeavour to have it free, and chearful, out of love to my Lord Jesus."

80. Bunyan, *Confession of My Faith*, 4:166. Earlier, Bunyan stated that the righteousness required is obedience "to the royal Law, the perfect Law which is the moral precept Evangelized or delivered to us by the hand of Christ" (4:166).

81. Bunyan, *Confession of My Faith*, 4:162. For a nearly identical statement, see Bunyan, *Differences in Judgment*, 4:199–200.

82. See the explicit covenant language in *Minutes*, 27, 41, 73, 85, 94.

or thrust himself upon, or thrust himself into a Church of Christ: without the Church have first the knowledge, and liking of the person to be received.[83]

Bunyan illustrated such examinations for membership at a number of points in *The Pilgrim's Progress*. For instance, Christian must give testimony of his faith and experience to Discretion, one of the "Virgins of this place," before he is allowed entrance into the Palace Beautiful.

> The *Porter* answered, This man is in a Journey from the City of *Destruction* to Mount *Zion*, but being weary, and benighted, he asked me if he might lodge here to night; so I told him I would call for thee, who after discourse had with him, mayest do as seemeth thee good, even according to the Law of the House.
>
> Then she asked him whence he was, and whither he was going, and he told her. She asked him also, how he got into the way and he told her; Then she asked him, What he had seen, and met with in the way, and he told her; and last, she asked his name, so he said, It is *Christian*; and I have so much the more a desire to lodge here to night, because, by what I perceive, this place was built by the Lord of the Hill, for the relief and security of Pilgrims. So she smiled, but the water stood in her eyes: And after a little pause, she said, I will call forth two or three more of the Family. So she ran to the door, and called out *Prudence*, *Piety* and *Charity*, who after a little more discourse with him, had him in to the Family; and many of them meeting him at the threshold of the house, said, Come in thou blessed of the Lord; this house was built by the Lord of the Hill, on purpose to entertain such Pilgrims in. Then he bowed his head, and followed them into the House.[84]

The shepherds of the Delectable Mountains similarly examine Christian and Hopeful before welcoming them into their care.[85] On the other hand, By-Ends is refused fellowship with Christian and Hopeful because he would not "*own Religion in his Rags, as well as when in his Silver Slippers, and stand by him too, when bound in Irons, as well as when he walketh the*

---

83. Bunyan, *Confession of My Faith*, 4:160–61. Similarly, "By that word of God therefore, by which their Faith, experience, and conversation (being examined) is found Good; by that the Church should receive them into fellowship with them" (4:165).

84. Bunyan, *Pilgrim's Progress*, 1:47–48. Christiana and her company have much easier access to the Palace Beautiful, perhaps due to Great-heart's testimony that vouched for the sincerity of their faith (Bunyan, *Pilgrim's Progress*, 2:207–9).

85. Bunyan, *Pilgrim's Progress*, 1:117.

Streets with applause."[86] When By-ends protests, "You must not impose, nor Lord it over my Faith; leave me to my liberty, and let me go with you," Christian responds, *"Not a step further, unless you will do in what I propound, as we."*[87] Examples of congregational examination of prospective members are found throughout the *Minutes*.[88] It was not uncommon for petitions for membership to be postponed until there was "farther satisfaction" of evangelical faith and holiness. For instance, on May 24, 1656, "Mrs Waller's desire was also considered, but the church not being satisfied in her, did appoint brother Harrington to go to her and to deale closely with her about the worke of grace in her soule." The next month, on June 28, "Mrs Waller was according to her appointment spoken with, and advised yet to [waite]."[89] At the meeting on January 25, 1657, the congregation determined to codify the membership process:

> We do also agree that such persons as desire to joyne in fellowship, if upon the conference of our friends with them, who shall be sent for that purpose, our saide friends be satisfied of the truth of the worke of grace in their heartes, then they shall desire them to come to the next church-meeting, and so waite neare the place assigned for that meeting, that they may be called in. And if, notwithstanding that first satisfaction, it be afterwards thought fitt, that any person so appearing, be yet delayed, that then some of the brethren go forth, and have conference with them, and labour in the wisedome, and spirit of the Gospell, to incourage them to farther waiting, and indeavour the prevention of any temptation, that by the denyall of admittance they may be exposed to. But if the brethren sent forth be not satisfied in the worke of grace in the persons they are sent to, then they shall not desire their coming to the church meeting.[90]

It was not sufficient that one member be satisfied with the candidate's profession of faith and holiness; unless the whole congregation was satisfied with the work of grace in his heart, his membership was delayed. The congregation was aware, however, of the potential for discouragement at

---

86. Bunyan, *Pilgrim's Progress*, 1:98.

87. Bunyan, *Pilgrim's Progress*, 1:99.

88. For example, the examinations of Sister Cooper, Humphrey Merrill and his wife, Roger Crompe, Sister Witt, and Sister Hodell (*Minutes*, 21–22).

89. *Minutes*, 22 (see also 24 [Friend Harper], 28 [Sister Wells], 29 [Brother Skelton and Sister Chamberlaine]).

90. *Minutes*, 24.

such a denial, and took special care to encourage and exhort the delayed prospect. Nevertheless, despite the abundance of caution exercised in congregational examination, there are still tares sown among the wheat. Sometimes the church discerns wrongly, and false converts are received into church communion.

> The discerning of the heart, and the infallible proof of the truth of saving-grace, is reserved to the Judgment of Jesus Christ at his coming; the Church and best of saints, sometimes hit, and sometimes miss in their judgments about this matter; and the cause of our missing in our judgment is; 1. partly because we cannot infallibly, at all times, distinguish grace that saveth, from that which doth but appear to do so. 2. partly also because some men have the art to give right names to wrong things. 3. and partly because we, being commanded to receive *him that is weak*, are afraid to exclude the least Christian.[91]

Bunyan's concern for the promotion of evangelical faith and holiness drove him to his conviction regarding regenerate church membership. The membership of a visible church must be restricted to visible saints—those who profess an evangelical and experiential faith, whose lives manifest evangelical holiness, and who enter into a mutual covenant to promote and preserve the same. The membership of a particular/visible church is managed by the congregation, which bears the responsibility to examine candidates to see whether they meet these qualifications. Yet Bunyan's concern for evangelical faith and holiness worked in both directions. While membership in a visible church must be restricted to visible saints, it must at the same time be open to all visible saints. Not only are faith and holiness the indispensable terms of membership in a visible church, they are the *only* terms of membership.[92] The membership requirements of a particular/visible church must mirror the membership requirements of the universal/invisible church. As Bunyan would argue throughout the communion

---

91. Bunyan, *Strait Gate*, 5:118–19. For similar statements, see Bunyan, *Holy City*, 3:173–78; *Barren Fig-Tree*, 5:15–17.

92. Bunyan and the Bedford Church also required an affirmation of open communion. No one could join the Bedford Church who did not profess this principle, and the Bedford Church would not transfer members to those churches that denied it. However, it can be argued that Bunyan viewed strict communion as a denial of evangelical faith and holiness, such that an affirmation of open communion was simply regarded as a profession of the gospel, and its denial a repudiation of the gospel. Likewise, Bunyan understood the mutual covenant as merely the corporate expression of evangelical faith and holiness.

controversy, the church must receive all whom God receives, on the same basis upon which God receives them—namely, on the basis of evangelical faith made visible and credible by evangelical holiness.

The Purpose of the Church

The church exists for the purpose of promoting evangelical faith and holiness. It accomplishes this purpose in two ways: through the evangelization of sinners and the edification of saints. While Bunyan did not write explicitly upon the topic of evangelism, this does not signal a lack of concern for the conversion of souls. There is hardly a work in his written corpus that does not contain fervent warnings to the unconverted, and passionate calls to repentance and faith in Christ.[93] In fact, it could be argued that Bunyan viewed himself more as an evangelist than a pastor. But even as an evangelist, he always viewed himself as sent forth from the Bedford Church, "appointed to a more ordinary and publick preaching of the Word, not onely to and amongst them that believed, but also to offer the Gospel to those who had not yet received the faith thereof."[94] The evangelistic efforts of the Bedford Church were instrumental in Bunyan's own conversion. It was through the evangelical conversation of the "three or four poor women sitting at a door in the Sun, and talking about the things of God" that Bunyan was awakened to his need of regeneration and justifying righteousness.[95] These saints brought Bunyan to their pastor, John Gifford, who continued to evangelize the young tinker: "he invited me to his house, where I should hear him confer with others about the dealings of God with the Soul."[96] This concept of congregational evangelism is portrayed at numerous places throughout *The Pilgrim's Progress*, not only in the character of Evangelist, who points Christian to the Wicket Gate and later rescues him from legalism at Mount Sinai, but also in the evangelical conversations that take place along the way between the pilgrims and other travelers.[97] The church's

---

93. More than a few works are dedicated to the evangelism of the unconverted. See Bunyan, *Few Sighs from Hell*, 1:231–382; *Barren Fig-Tree*, 5:9–64; *Light for Them*, 8:50–160; *Come & Welcome*, 8:239–392; *Life and Death of Mr. Badman*; *Greatness of the Soul*, 9:137–245; *Discourse upon the Pharisee*, 10:111–235; *Jerusalem Sinner Saved*, 11:7–92. Many other works include addresses and appeals to the unconverted.

94. Bunyan, *Grace Abounding*, 76.

95. Bunyan, *Grace Abounding*, 14.

96. Bunyan, *Grace Abounding*, 24.

97. Bunyan, *Pilgrim's Progress*, 1:11–13, 20–25. For examples of evangelistic

The Palace Beautiful

evangelistic mission will continue until Antichrist is defeated and eternity dawns. "For while the day of time doth last, even the World it self hath need of the shining of the Church."[98] Nevertheless, the primary responsibility for evangelism lies with gospel ministers. While the church is represented by the moon in Bunyan's exposition of Revelation 21:23, reflecting the light of the gospel upon a sin-darkened world, the sun is "the good and pure Word of the Gospel of Christ, unfolded, opened, and explained by the Servants of Christ; . . . The Ministers of the Gospel are of use so long as there is either Elect to be converted, or any converted soul to be perfected by that measure of Perfection that God hath appointed on this side of Glory; but when this Work is done, their Ministry ceaseth."[99]

Bunyan did, however, write explicitly upon the role of the church in the edification of the saints. The church exists to encourage and exhort one another to evangelical faith and holiness. In a particularly poignant passage, Bunyan pictures the church as a garden. "Christians are like the several flowers in a Garden, that have upon each of them the Dew of Heaven, which being shaken with the wind, they let fall their Dew at each others roots, whereby they are joyntly nourished, and become nourishers of one another."[100] Such mutual edification is repeatedly portrayed in the frequent discourses among fellow pilgrims, and its necessity depicted in the way Hopeful prevents Christian from committing suicide in Doubting Castle by reminding him of his perseverance through past dangers:

> My Brother, said he, rememberest thou not how valiant thou hast been heretofore; Apollyon could not crush thee, nor could all that thou didst hear, or see, or feel, in the Valley of the shadow of Death; what hardship, terror, and amazement hast thou already gone through, and art thou now nothing but fear? Thou seest that I am in the Dungeon with thee, a far weaker man by nature than

---

conversations, see the interactions with Simple, Sloth, and Presumption (1:39); with Formalist and Hypocrisy (1:39–41); with Mistrust and Timorous (1:42–44); with Talkative (1:74–82); with Ignorance (1:120–21, 137–41); and with Mercy (2:175–77).

98. Bunyan, *Holy City*, 3:161. This comes from Bunyan's exposition of Rev 21:23, where Bunyan identified the sun as the light of the gospel, and the moon as the church which reflects that gospel light into the dark night of the world (3:158–61). For the church's mission against Antichrist, see Bunyan, *Discourse of the House*, 7:167: "Wherefore, since the Church is set for defence of Religion, and to be as a battery to beat down Antichrist, 'tis requisite, that she should be made up of Pillars of strong and stanch Materials."

99. Bunyan, *Holy City*, 3:159–60.

100. Bunyan, *Christian Behaviour*, 3:54.

The Palace Beautiful

> thou art: Also, this Giant has wounded me as well as thee; and hath also cut off the Bread and Water from my mouth; and with thee I mourn without the light: but let's exercise a little more patience. Remember how thou playedst the man at Vanity-Fair, and wast neither afraid of the Chain nor Cage; nor yet of bloody Death: wherefore let us (at least to avoid the shame, that becomes not a Christian to be found in) bear up with patience as well as we can.[101]

Similarly, Christian keeps Hopeful from falling asleep on the Enchanted Ground:

> CHR. *Do you not remember, that one of the Shepherds bid us beware of the Inchanted ground? He meant by that, that we should beware of sleeping; wherefore let us not sleep as do others, but let us watch and be sober.*
>
> HOPE. *I acknowledge my self in a fault, and had I been here alone, I had by sleeping run the danger of death. I see it is true that the wise man saith,* Two are better than one. *Hitherto hath thy Company been my mercy; and thou shalt have a good reward for thy labour.*[102]

Again, Hopeful helps Christian to die in faith when Christian fears that the waves of death might drown him:

> *Hopeful* therefore here had much adoe to keep his Brothers head above water, yea sometimes he would be quite gone down, and then ere a while he would rise up again half dead. *Hopeful* also would endeavour to comfort him, saying, Brother, I see the Gate, and men standing by to receive us. But *Christian* would answer, 'Tis you, 'tis you they wait for, you have been *Hopeful* ever since I knew you: and so have you, said he to *Christian*. Ah Brother, said he, surely if I was right, he would now arise to help me; but for my sins he hath brought me into the snare, and hath left me. Then said *Hopeful*, My Brother, you have quite forgot the Text, where its said of the wicked, *There is no band in their death, but their strength is firm, they are not troubled as other men, neither are they plagued like other men.* These troubles and distresses that you go through in these Waters, are no sign that God hath forsaken you, but are sent to try you, whether you will call to mind that which heretofore you have received of his goodness, and live upon him in your distresses.[103]

---

101. Bunyan, *Pilgrim's Progress*, 1:113.

102. Bunyan, *Pilgrim's Progress*, 1:130–31.

103. Bunyan, *Pilgrim's Progress*, 1:148–49. Note also the way the company of pilgrims in the second part help one another to die in faith (2:282–90).

The Palace Beautiful

Bunyan appears to have intentionally structured the narrative in such a way as to drive home the point that neither Christian nor Hopeful would have arrived at the Celestial City without the encouragement and edification provided by the other.

The necessity of congregational edification shines through in Bunyan's lesser-known works as well. In reference to Esther's preparation in the house of the women in order to appear before the king, Bunyan wrote, "God also hath appointed, that those that come into his Royal presence, should first go to the House of the Women, the Church, and there receive of the Eunuchs things for purification, things to *make us meet to be partakers of the inheritance of the Saints in light*."[104] Bunyan considered the ministry of the church to be essential preparation for eschatological salvation. "Wherefore, they are deceived that think to go into the *holiest*, which is Heaven, when they dye; who yet abandon, and hate the *holy place*, while they live. Nay, Sirs, The way into the *holiest*, is thorow the *holy place*; the way into Heaven, is thorow the Church on Earth; for that Christ is there by his Word to be received by faith, before he can by us in Person be received in the *beatical* vision."[105] Bunyan viewed the church as "an Hospital of sick, wounded, and afflicted People."[106] The church's commission to help the sick and weak in faith is vividly depicted in Great-heart's invitation to Feeble-mind, whom he had rescued from the Giant Slay-good, to join their pilgrim company.

> But Brother, said Mr. *Great-heart*. I have it in Commission, to comfort the *feeble minded*, and to support the weak. You must needs go along with us; we will wait for you, we will lend you our help, we will deny our selves of some things, both *Opinionative* and *Practical*, for your sake; we will not enter into doubtful Disputations before you, we will be made all things to you, rather than you shall be left behind.[107]

The church's responsibility to encourage their afflicted brethren is beautifully demonstrated in four letters sent from the Bedford congregation in February 1671 to members who for various reasons, including persecution,

---

104. Bunyan, *Greatness of the Soul*, 9:233.
105. Bunyan, *Solomon's Temple Spiritualiz'd*, 7:86.
106. Bunyan, *Of Justification*, 12:336.
107. Bunyan, *Pilgrim's Progress*, 2:252. This conversation is immediately followed by the appearance of Mr. Ready-to-halt, who walks on crutches, yet is gladly welcomed into the pilgrim company (2:252–53). Similarly, see the pilgrims' treatment of Mr. Despondency and Mrs. Much-afraid (2:264–66, 276, 285, 287).

were geographically separated from the church.[108] The letters are filled with exhortations to bear up under suffering, to receive tribulation as from the hand of a sovereign God, and to persevere in faith and holiness.

The church's ministry of edification extends to all ages. The church promotes evangelical faith and holiness by catechizing its children, as is portrayed by Prudence's catechizing of Christiana's four sons at the Palace Beautiful.[109] The edification of the church even extends to soliciting congregational wisdom regarding marriage. Speaking of Mr. Badman's godly wife and her ill-fated marriage, Wiseman says, "And besides I verily think (since in the multitude of Counsellors there is safety) that if she had acquainted the Congregation with it, and desired them to spend some time in prayer to God about it, and if she must have had him, to have received him as to his godliness, upon the Judgment of others, rather than her own."[110]

The church is able to edify the saints because of the river of the water of life that flows through it. "All the warmth that we have in our Communion, it is the warmth of the Spirit. When a company of Saints are gathered together in the Name of Christ, to perform any spiritual Exercise, and their Souls be edified, warmed and made glad therein, it is because this Water, this River of Water of Life, has in some of the Streams thereof, ran into that assembly."[111]

According to Bunyan, the church exists for the promotion of evangelical faith and holiness. The church promotes faith and holiness in the world through the evangelization of sinners, primarily by gospel ministers whom the church commissions and sends out, but also through congregational involvement as they present the gospel in word and deed. But Bunyan's primary focus was upon the church as the garden of the Lord, the place where members promote faith and holiness in one another through mutual encouragement and exhortation. The church is the necessary place of preparation for eschatological salvation. *The Pilgrim's Progress* is not an account of the solitary Christian's journey to heaven. No one makes it to the Celestial City alone. "This House," says the Porter to

---

108. *Minutes*, 56–58 (to brother Harrington), 58–59 (to sister Foxe), 59–61 (to Katharine Hustwhat), 61–62 (to John Wilson). Bunyan signed his name to all but the second of these letters.

109. Bunyan, *Pilgrim's Progress*, 2:211–18. See also Bunyan's own catechism, *Instruction for the Ignorant*, 8:7–44, which is addressed "To the Church of Christ in and about Bedford" for their "*Edification and Consolation*" (8:7).

110. Bunyan, *Life and Death of Mr. Badman*, 73.

111. Bunyan, *Water of Life*, 7:205.

Christian, "was built by the Lord of the Hill: and he built it for the relief and security of Pilgrims."[112]

The Polity of the Church

Bunyan's views on church polity were likewise informed by his concern for the promotion of evangelical faith and holiness. While Bunyan never wrote explicitly on the merits of congregationalism relative to a presbyterian or episcopalian form of government, the Bedford Church was clearly congregational in its polity. It was constituted by mutual covenant, rather than by ecclesiastical authority.[113] Its officers were elected by a vote of the congregation, and removed by the same.[114] Members were received by authority of the congregation, and dismissed by the same.[115] All the privileges of the church were available to all members, and none could be barred from the

---

112. Bunyan, *Pilgrim's Progress*, 1:47.

113. "The manner of their putting themselves into the state of a Church of Christ was: after much prayer and waiting upon God and consulting one with another, by the Word, they, upon the day appointed for this solemne worke, being met, after prayer and seeking God as before, with one consent joyntly first gave themselves to the Lord, and one to another by the will of God" (*Minutes*, 17).

114. At the November 1658 meeting, the *Minutes* read, "Debate also being farther had this day about the choyce of elders, it was agreed that two should be chosen, and our brethren and sisters were required to consider what persons the Lord shall direct them to in the society that they shall judge fit to choose, and that they give in their names in writing at the next monthly meeting" (*Minutes*, 31). Three months later it was reported, "By the brethren now assembled, and by the papers containing the votes of those absent, our brother Grew and our brother Whiteman were chosen elders" (32). For other instances of the election of elders, see *Minutes*, 21, 34, 36–37, 38–39, 68, 71–72, 90, 91, 93–94. For the election of deacons, see *Minutes*, 28, 41, 71–72, 87. In September 1669, "The Church also having taken notice of the utter neglect of brother Coventon and brother Wallis in the executing of the office of deacon, whereunto they had formerly bene appointed, did judge them unworthy of that honourable imployment and divest[ed] them of all authority and trust of that nature committed to them formerly" (40).

115. "The congregation being satisfied concerning brother Merrill and his wife [received] them into fellowship. Our sister Cooper was likewise received into comm[union]" (*Minutes*, 22). "It was agreed that sister Creake of Wotton be admitted a member of this congregation" (23). Such language pervades the *Minutes*. For examples of congregational approval of transfer of membership, see *Minutes*, 30, 34, 37, 65–69 [request denied], 70–71, 77–80 [request denied], 82, 87, 92.

ordinances apart from church censure.[116] The church is the final authority, yet is itself under the authority of Christ by his Word.[117]

> *The Temple was higher than the Pillars*, and so is the Church than her Officers; I say, consider them singly as Officers (though inferiour as to gifts and office) for as I said before of Ministers in general, so now I say the same of the Apostles, though as to office they were the highest, yet the *Temple* is above them. . . . 'Tis the Church as such, that is the *Lady*, a *Queen*, the *Bride*, the Lamb's *Wife*; and Prophets, Apostles, and Ministers &c. are but *Servants, Stewards, Labourers* for her good. . . . As therefore the *Lady* is above the *Servant*, the *Queen* above the *Steward*, or the *Wife* above all her Husband's *Officers*, so is the Church, *as such*, above these Officers.[118]

One reason Bunyan insisted upon congregational authority is because he saw a direct link between ecclesiastical hierarchy and the corruption of evangelical faith and holiness. Bunyan was ever wary of Antichrist, and he believed that Antichrist took the form of a counterfeit church wielding hierarchical ecclesiastical authority allied with coercive state power.[119]

> For we find that the King of *Babylon*, who was a Type of our Antichrist, when he came up against *Jerusalem*, the Type of our Primitive Church, he brake down their City, destroyed their Walls,

---

116. "If any brother should walke disorderly, he cannot be shut out from any ordinance before Church censure" (*Minutes*, 20). "*Come, Sir, said good* Gaius [to Feeblemind], *be of good Chear, you are welcome to me, and to my House; and what thou hast a mind to, call for freely; and what thou would'st have my Servants do for thee, they will do it with a ready Mind*" (Bunyan, *Pilgrim's Progress*, 2:250).

117. On Christ as the head of the church, see Bunyan, *Discourse of the Building*, 6:282–85.

118. Bunyan, *Solomon's Temple Spiritualiz'd*, 7:31–32.

119. For Bunyan's definition of Antichrist, see Bunyan, *Of Antichrist*, 13:432: "*Antichrist therefore is a mystical Man, so made, or begotten of the Devil, and sent into the World, himself being the chief and highest of him. Three things therefore go to the making up of Antichrist; the Head, Body*, and *Soul. The Devil, he* is the Head; the *Synagogue of Satan, that* is the Body; that wicked Spirit of Iniquity, *that* is the Soul of Antichrist. Christ then is the Head of his Church; the Devil is the Head of Antichrist; the Elect are the Body of Christ; the reprobate Professors are the Body of Antichrist; the Holy Ghost is the Spirit of Life that acteth Christ's Body; that wicked Spirit of Iniquity, is that which acteth the Body of Antichrist." A few pages later he wrote, "Now, by *Ordinances of Antichrist*, I do not intend things that *only* respect Matters of Worship in *Antichrist's* Kingdom, but those Civil Laws that impose and enforce *them* also; yea, that inforce THAT Worship with Pains and Penalties" (13:439).

The Palace Beautiful

rifled their Houses, and killed their Children; whose steps, I say, our Antichrist follows to a hair, in treading down the Primitive Church, corrupting her Doctrines (which are her Safeguard and Wall) also robbing and spoiling the Houses of God, and killing his Children with a thousand Calamities; turning all that heavenly Frame and Order of Church-government into an heap of Rubbish, and a confused Dunghil.[120]

Faith and holiness flourish where the church is free from coercive authority.

Let us therefore state the matter right; No man needs be afraid to let Jesus Christ be chief in the world, he envies no body, he designs the hurt of none: His Kingdom is not of this world, nor doth he covet temporal matters; Let but his wife his Church alone, to enjoy her purchased privileges, and all shall be well. Which privileges of hers, since they are soul-concerns, make no infringement upon any mans Liberties: let but Faith and Holiness walk the Streets without controule, and you may be as happy as the world can make you.[121]

Bunyan was adamant that the church should not bear the sword; neither should the state wield the sword on behalf of the church.[122] Rather, Bunyan pleaded with the magistrate to act toward the church as did Artaxerxes act toward the Jews. From the letter of Artaxerxes of Persia recorded in Ezra 7 Bunyan drew the following three conclusions:

1. That this King imposed no Law, no Priest, no People upon these Jews; but left them wholly to their own Law, their own Ministers, and their own People: All which were the Laws of God, the Priests of God, the People of God, as to their Building of their Temple, and the Worship of their God.

2. He forced not *THIS* People, no, not to their Land, their Temple, nor their Worship, by his or their Law; but left them free to their own mind, to do thereabout as they would.

---

120. Bunyan, *Holy City*, 3:132.

121. Bunyan, *Discourse of the House*, 7:153.

122. Speaking of Cain's murder of Abel, Bunyan wrote, "It is therefore hence to be observed, That it is a Sign of an Evil way, be it covered with the Name of the Worship of God, when it cannot stand without the shedding of Innocent Blood" (Bunyan, *Exposition of the First Ten Chapters*, 12:164). The weapons wielded by the church are spiritual: "Here is therefore no mans *person* in danger by *this* war [between the Church and Antichrist]. And I say again, so far as any mans person is in danger, *it is by wrong managing of this war*" (Bunyan, *Discourse of the House*, 7:153). The church is not interested in earthly kingdoms (cf. Bunyan, *Discourse of the House*, 7:128; *Holy City*, 3:96).

3. He added not any Law therefore of his own, either to prescribe Worship, or to enforce it upon the Jews.[123]

If the magistrate will leave the conscience free, and let the church alone to worship as the Scripture directs, he will find Christians his most loyal subjects.[124] Nevertheless, if the church should suffer under an unjust magistrate, it must do so with faith and patience. "Many are the mercyes we receive, by a well qualified Magistrate, and if any shall at any time be otherwise inclined, *let us shew our christianity in a patient suffering for well doing, what it shall please God to inflict by them.*[125] Bunyan steadfastly opposed the violent overthrow of persecutors.[126]

Furthermore, congregationalism is the polity most conducive to the promotion of faith and holiness because the gifts of the Spirit are given to the congregation of the saints for the edification of the saints. No other system of governance fosters such mutual edification. Once again, Bunyan's imagery of the church as a garden is instructive: "Christians are like the several flowers in a Garden, that have upon each of them the Dew of Heaven, which being shaken with the wind, they let fall their Dew at each other's roots, whereby they are joyntly nourished, and become nourishers of one

---

123. Bunyan, *Of Antichrist*, 13:424–25.

124. "Indeed my principles are such, as lead me to a denial to communicate in the things of the Kingdom of Christ, with ungodly and openly prophane; neither can I in, or by the superstitious inventions of this world, consent that my Soul should be governed, in any of my approaches to God, because commanded to the contrary, and commended for so refusing. Wherefore excepting this one thing, for which I ought not to be rebuked; I shall I trust in despite of slander and falsehood, discover my self at all times a peaceable, and an obedient Subject" (Bunyan, *Confession of My Faith*, 4:136).

125. Bunyan, *Confession of My Faith*, 4:153. See also Bunyan's seven exhortations to the suffering church in Bunyan, *Seasonable Counsel*, 10:100–104.

126. Speaking of the threat of seven-fold vengeance upon those who kill Cain in revenge for Abel's murder, Bunyan wrote, "It would not be hard to shew how little they have prevailed, who have taken upon them to take Vengeance for the Blood of Saints, on them that have been the Spillers of it. But my business here is brevity, therefore I shall not launch into that deep, only shall say to such as shall attempt it hereafter, *Put up thy Sword into his place; for they that take the Sword shall perish with the sword!* and here is the Patience and Faith of the Saint. Let *Cain* and God alone, and do you mind Faith and Patience; suffer with *Abel*, until your Righteous Blood be spilt: Even the Work of Persecutors, is, for the present, Punishment enough; the Fruits thereof being the provoking of God to Jealousie, a denying of them the knowledge of the Way of Life, and a binding of them over to the Pains and Punishment of Hell" (Bunyan, *Exposition of the First Ten Chapters*, 12:173).

another."[127] Bunyan adopted Gifford's view of congregational gifts and their purpose: "Let the gifts of the Church be exercised according to order. Let no gift be concealed which is for edification: yet let those gifts be chiefly exercised which are most for the perfecting of the saints. Let your discourses be to build up one another in your most holy faith and to provoke one another to love and good works."[128] In *The Pilgrim's Progress*, the Reliever tells Christiana, "*To go back again, you need not. For in all places where you shall come, you will find no want at all, for in every of my Lord's Lodgings, which he has prepared for the reception of his Pilgrims, there is sufficient to furnish them against all attempts whatsoever.*"[129]

One final note in Bunyan's ecclesiastical polity demands attention. The Bedford Church maintained with neighboring churches in Bedfordshire and its surrounding counties an association so close that it approached a modern multi-site church governance. The first mention of such an association was in July 1656: "Some brethren at Woollaston desiring to joyne in fellowship with us it was agreed that before the next meeting a day should be set apart to seek the Lord concerning it."[130] This appears to be a request from the congregation of Dissenters at Wollaston to either associate or merge with the Bedford Church, as Wollaston was fifteen miles from Bedford, too distant to be merely a request for membership. In June 1657, the church set apart time "to seeke God for direction in discoursing with any of our dissenting friends."[131] In October 1658 it was recorded: "And as for the continuing of unity and preventing of differences among the congregations walking with Mr. Donne Mr. Wheeler and Mr. Gibbs, and ourselves it was agreed that brother Burton, brother Grew, brother Harrington, brother Whiteman and brother Bunyan, should within [a] few days meet together to consider of some things that may conduce to love and unity amongst us

---

127. Bunyan, *Christian Behaviour*, 3:54.

128. *Minutes*, 19. Bunyan was aware that his gifts were for the good of the church, and that the remembrance of this was the antidote to pride: "He hath also cause to walk humbly with God, and be little in his own eyes, and to remember with all, that his Gifts are not his own, but the Churches; and that by them he is made a servant to the Church; and he must give at last an account of his Stewardship unto the Lord Jesus; and to give a good account, will be a blessed thing!" (Bunyan, *Grace Abounding*, 84).

129. Bunyan, *Pilgrim's Progress*, 2:185.

130. *Minutes*, 23.

131. *Minutes*, 26.

all."[132] The meeting was successful, for an association of congregations was formalized in May 1659.

> Whereas at the last Church meeting it was agreed (according to the 8th proposall of our agreement with other congregations adjacent *viz.* that in matters of difficulty we should advise with each other) that the advise of the other congregations should be had about John Childe's business; it was now farther ordered that letters should be sent unto them, to desire the pastors of each congregation, and some other deputed members, to come to Bedford the 16th of the next moneth, to consult together what is to be done in this case. It is also agreed that brother Burton, brother Grew, brother Whiteman, brother Whitebread, brother Harrington and brother John Fenne be deputed of the Church to meet with them.[133]

At the October 1659 meeting, more proposals from messengers of neighboring churches regarding associational unity were read, approved, and entered into the *Minutes*.[134] After the death of John Burton in 1660, in accordance with their associational agreement, the Bedford Church solicited the advice of associated churches regarding the future choice of a pastor.[135] In January 1670, "The congregation also having taken into consideration the desire of the Gamlingay friends to joyne with us, did agree that next meeting they should come over, and give in their experience."[136] The Bedford Church's connection with the Gamlingay congregation appears to be more than the association of two autonomous churches. For from that time on, church meetings began to be held periodically at Gamlingay, as

---

132. *Minutes*, 31. Five months later, in March 1659, it was recorded: "There having bene some meetings of the friends of the several adjacent congregations to conferre of some things for the furthering of unity and love amongst us, and another meeting being appointed for the finishing of some conclusions to that end, we do agree that our brother Bunyan, brother Grew, brother Harrington do meet with the brethren of the other churches about this matter" (32).

133. *Minutes*, 33.

134. *Minutes*, 34.

135. *Minutes*, 36. The church desired that Mr. Wheeler (Tibbutt writes in the notes that this was probably William Wheeler of Cranfield in Bedfordshire) should be their next pastor. But Wheeler was a member of Mr. Gibbs's church, which was reluctant to give him up, and Wheeler himself was reluctant to accept. Thus, "the Church here afterwards thought it not convenient to presse it, least it might indeed prove a disadvantage to their brethren aforesaide." Instead, Samuel Fenne and John Whiteman were appointed as elders, "to minister the word and ordinances of Jesus Christ to them" (36–37, 38–39, 207n18).

136. *Minutes*, 42.

well as at Haynes, Kemptson, Edworth, Cotton End, Maulden, and Limercy.[137] Such meetings were not specific to these neighboring congregations, but dealt with Bedford Church matters as well. For instance, it was at a "generall assembly of the Church at Hanes" in November 1671 that, "The Church was also minded to seeke God about the choyce of brother Bunyan to the office of an elder, that their way in that respect may be cleared up to them."[138] Bunyan was then appointed as an elder two months later at a "full assembly of the Church at Bedford the 21th of the 10th moneth."[139] In February 1672, "It was also agreed upon that the 16th of this instant should be set apart for seeking God by prayer with fasting, for our children and carnall relations, and for the tempted and afflicted and for the Lord's blessing upon the ministery: and that this be in each part of the congregation, viz. as well at Hanes and Gamlinghay as here."[140] When, after Bunyan's death, the Bedford Church called Ebenezer Chandler as their next pastor, the brethren at Gamlingay were disturbed over Chandler's paedobaptist convictions and the new practice of psalm-singing, Chandler wrote a letter to the Gamlingay congregation. The language of the letter further suggests a kind of multi-site polity.

> Our brethren have determined that those that are perswaded in their consciences that publick singing is an ordinance of God, shall practice it on the Lord's Day in our meeting in Bedford. Those that are of differing judgments have there liberty whether they will sing, ye or noe, or whether they will be presant whilst we sing, so that they do not turn there backs on other parts of God's worship. *Nether is it at all designed to be imposed or proposed to any other meeting of the Church.* Againe, with respect to baptisme, I have my liberty to baptise infants without making it my business to promote it amonst others, and every member to have his liberty in believers' baptisme, onely to forbare discourse and debates on it that may have a tendency to break the peace of the Church.

---

137. For church meetings at Gamlingay during Bunyan's lifetime, see *Minutes*, 44, 48, 65, 67, 68, 73, 75, 76, 77, 78, 80, 81, 83, 84, 87, 88, 89; for meetings at Haynes, see *Minutes*, 39, 41, 44, 48, 51, 52, 68, 70, 73, 78, 81; for meetings at Kempston, see *Minutes*, 73; for meetings at Edworth, see *Minutes*, 76; for meetings at Cotton End, see *Minutes*, 76, 81, 83, 84, 85, 88; for meetings at Maulden, see *Minutes*, 82; for meetings at Limercy, see *Minutes*, 84.

138. *Minutes*, 70.

139. *Minutes*, 71.

140. *Minutes*, 72. Note carefully the wording "in each part of the congregation [singular]," which evidently included the gatherings at Haynes, Gamlingay, and Bedford.

> When thought expedient the Church doth designe to choose an administrator of believers' baptisme, we doe not designe to make baptisme, whether of belivers' or infants, any bar to communion, only the Church hath promised that none shall hear after to my greeffe or truble or dissatisfaction be admitted.[141]

The response from Gamlingay employed the same language, speaking of the singular "Church" in reference to multiple congregations.

> We, the brethren of this Church in and about Gamlingay, doe heartily and cordeally aquiesse in this letter, only desire to have liberty to spake or preach belivers' baptisme if the Lord shall sett it upon our hearts, yet with that tenderness as being far from any such designe as to tend at least the breaking of the peace of the Church, and do heartily grant our brother Chandler the same liberty to speak of or preach infant baptisme, provided with the same tendernesse.[142]

From the preceding evidence, it is apparent that the Bedford congregation and at least eight other nearby congregations were closely associated.[143] Initially, these associations maintained the autonomy of the local congregations. Each congregation had its own ministers, and though counsel was sought in the calling of a new pastor and in other matters of difficulty (e.g., John Child's apostasy), the language does not suggest that such counsel was binding. This began to change, however, first with the congregation at Haynes in 1664, and especially with the congregation at Gamlingay in 1670. The association grew tighter, and the boundaries of local church autonomy were blurred. Church meetings were held at each of these locations, and decisions were made that affected parties known to be in the Bedford congregation (e.g., the consideration of Bunyan as elder). Sometimes the words "generall assembly" or "full assembly" are used for these church meetings, indicating the involvement of multiple congregations.[144] The associated congregations were informed of excommunications, and were expected to

---

141. *Minutes*, 93–94, italics added.

142. *Minutes*, 94.

143. The number is likely much higher, as Bunyan applied for "Congregationall" licenses for himself and twenty-five others (including Wollaston, Haynes, Gamlingay, Kemptson, and Maulden) in May 1672. A transcription of the application is found in Brown, *John Bunyan*, 232–33.

144. See, for instance, "a generall assembly of the Church at Hanes" in November 1671 (*Minutes*, 70), and, "a full assembly of the Church at Bedford" in January 1672 (71). Both assemblies dealt with the appointment of Bunyan as elder of the Bedford Church.

uphold these decisions.[145] Bunyan applied for "Congregationall" preaching licenses for twenty-five local congregations besides the Bedford Church.[146] Finally, both Chandler and the brethren at Gamlingay used the language of one church with multiple congregations ("Nether is it at all designed to be imposed or proposed to any other meeting of the Church"). Whether Bunyan thought of the association as a single church with multiple congregations is doubtful, given his aversion to the concept of a non-particular/visible church. The blurring of autonomous lines was likely due to external circumstances rather than ecclesiological convictions.[147] But it does speak to the question of Bunyan's Baptist identity, for all of these churches were open-communion, licensed as "Congregationall," and it may be surmised that, like the Bedford Church, they refused association with strict-communion Baptists. It is better to classify this association of churches, though small in number, as something other than seventeenth-century Baptists.

The Officers of the Church

While the responsibility for the promotion of evangelical faith and holiness rests with the whole congregation, Bunyan recognized that those primarily engaged in this task will be the officers of the church. While the apostolic church had five offices, only two offices continue to the present day, the "extraordinary" offices of apostle, prophet, and evangelist having ceased once the foundation of the church was complete.[148] The other two offices are elder/

---

145. See the announcements of the excommunications of Humphrey Merrill and Robert Nelson (*Minutes*, 45, 64–65).

146. Brown, *John Bunyan*, 232–33.

147. Greaves understands the relationship between churches to be that of "principal churches" and their "satellite meetings." In an essay examining the 1672 license application under the Declaration of Indulgence, Greaves writes, "The 1672 application lists twenty-seven men in twenty-six towns and villages in six counties. These numbers reflect five principal churches: Bedford, Stevington, Keysoe, Newport Pagnell, and Cranfield. Bedford sought approval for teachers for no less than twelve of its satellite meetings: Blunham, Goldington, Oakley, Kempston, Cardington, Stagsden, Haynes, Maulden, Edworth, Gamlingay, Toft, and Ashwell" (Greaves, "Organizational Response," 482). Later, Greaves writes, "The basis for this organizational concept likely lies in the earlier use of visitors to reach church members in the scattered communities" (483). If true, this reflects a form of multi-site ecclesiology.

148. "Timothy, unto whom this Epistle was writ, was an *Evangelist*, that is, inferior to Apostles and extraordinary Prophets, and above ordinary Pastors and Teachers. And he with the rest of those under his circumstances was to go with the Apostles hither, and thither, to be disposed of by them as they saw need for the further edification of those

The Palace Beautiful

pastor and deacon. To these may be added a third category, that of "gospel minister," that is not quite an office, yet still an ordained role.

Bunyan had much to say about the call, character, and charge of a pastor/elder.[149] A man is called and appointed to the office of elder by a particular/visible congregation that recognizes his gifts and godliness. Ultimately, though, the calling and authority comes from God. "The Ministers of the Gospel have each of them all that authority that belongs to their calling and office, and need not to stay for power from Men to put the Laws of Christ in his Church into due and full Execution."[150] A minister of the gospel needs no episcopal ordination or license from the state, least of all an education from Oxford or Cambridge.[151] All he needs

---

who by the Apostolical Ministry were converted to the Faith: And hence it is, that *Titus* was left at *Creet*, and that this *Timothy* was left at *Ephesus*" (Bunyan, *Holy Life*, 9:261). "Besides *Timothy* and *Titus* being extraordinary officers, stood as members and officers in every Church where they were received. Likewise *Barnabas*, and *Saul*, *Judas* and *Silas*, abode as members and officers where they were sent" (Bunyan, *Confession of My Faith*, 4:161). "The Apostles were sent *immediately*, their Call was *extraordinary*, their *Office* was *Universal*; they had *alike* power in all Churches, and Doctrine was infallible" (Bunyan, *Solomon's Temple Spiritualiz'd*, 7:27). See also Bunyan, *Holy City*, 3:109–15.

149. Bunyan viewed "pastor" and "elder" as the same office. He made no distinction between lay elders and vocational elders, nor between teaching elders and ruling elders. In May 1670, the Bedford Church rebuked William Whitebread for withdrawing from communion because of his dissatisfaction with lay preaching. Whitebread wanted an "able pastor," to which the church responded, "We know not what you meane by an able pastor. We have such as we hope the Holy Ghost hath made overseers and guides among us, to feed us in the word and doctrine, to whom that title of pastor belongeth, as well as of bishops and ministers. But if you suppose that to the terme pastor there is intailed authority superior to those that office-wise do as before, we are ignorant of any such office" (*Minutes*, 50; see also 45). In *A Discourse of the Building, Nature, Excellency, and Government of the House of God*, Bunyan appeared to draw a distinction between teaching and ruling elders, the latter being responsible for ensuring the holy conversation of the church ("Here are of Rulers, yet another sort, / Such as direct our *manners* to comport"), but this is best understood as a functional rather than an ontological distinction (Bunyan, *Discourse of the Building*, 6:285–90).

150. Bunyan, *Paul's Departure and Crown*, 12:358.

151. For Bunyan's 1659 controversy with the Cambridge don Thomas Smith over Bunyan's right to preach without ordination or education, see Greaves, *Glimpses of Glory*, 121–24. Henry Denne defended Bunyan's right to preach in the preface to H. Denne, *The Quaker No Papist*. See Bunyan, *Few Sighs from Hell*, 1:306. See also John Gibbs's prefatory epistle affixed to the beginning of Bunyan, *Few Sighs from Hell*, 1:242–43. John Burton claimed that Bunyan "is not chosen out of an earthly, but out of the heavenly University, the Church of Christ, which Church, as furnished with the spirit, gifts, and graces of Christ, was in the beginning, and still is, and will be to the end of the world, that out of which the word of the Lord, and so all true gospel Ministers must proceed, whether

is a call from God and an appointment by his church.[152] This also implies that no minister has authority outside of the church that ordained him. Ordination is rooted in the particular/visible church.

Bunyan spoke of the elder's charge by way of explicit instruction and allegorical example. A pastor/elder is to preach the gospel and teach the Word.

> Call them your *Cooks*, they're skill'd in dressing Food,
> To nourish Weak, and Strong, and cleanse the *Blood*:
> They've *Milk* for *Babes*, strong *Meat* for *Men* of Age;
> Food fit for who are *Simple*, who are *Sage*.[153]

Evangelist is a portrait of a pastor, pointing sinners to the Wicket Gate and the King's Highway beyond, turning them from the futile attempt to remove the burden of guilt through works of the law rather than through faith in the cross of Christ, and preparing the saints to suffer persecution in Vanity Fair.[154] The first emblem shown to Christian in the House of Interpreter, the painting of the "very grave Person," is a portrait of a pastor. Interpreter states,

> The Man whose Picture this is, is one of a thousand, he can beget Children, Travel in birth with Children, and Nurse them himself when they are born. And whereas thou seest him with his eyes lift up to Heaven, the best of Books in his hand, the Law of Truth writ on his Lips: it is to shew thee, that his work is to know, and unfold dark things to sinners; even as also thou seest him stand as if he Pleaded with Men: And whereas thou seest the World as cast behind him, and that a Crown hangs over his head; that is, to shew thee, that slighting and despising the things that are present, for

---

learned or unlearned, as to humane learning.... *He hath, through grace, taken these three heavenly degrees, to wit, union with Christ, the anointing of the spirit, and experience of the temptations of Satan, which doe more fit a man for that weighty work of preaching the Gospell, then all University Learning and degrees that can be had*" (John Burton's prefatory epistle in Bunyan, *Some Gospel-Truths Opened*, 1:11).

152. For the account of Bunyan's call to gospel ministry, see Bunyan, *Grace Abounding*, 75. For the congregational calling of elders in the Bedford Church, see *Minutes*, 21, 32, 38–39, 71–72, 90–91, 93.

153. Bunyan, *Discourse of the Building*, 6:286–87.

154. Bunyan, *Pilgrim's Progress*, 1:11–13, 20–25, 83–85.

The Palace Beautiful

the love that he hath to his Masters service, he is sure in the world that comes next to have Glory for his Reward.[155]

When Gifford was elected pastor of the Bedford Church, he "accepted of the charge, and gave himself up to the Lord, and to his people, to walke with them, watch over them, and dispense the misteryes of the Gospell among them."[156] Christian and Hopeful sang of the Shepherds of the Delectable Mountains:

> *Thus by the* Shepherds, *Secrets are reveal'd,*
>
> *Which from all other men are kept conceal'd:*
>
> *Come to the* Shepherds *then, if you would see*
>
> *Things deep, things hid, and that mysterious be.*[157]

Each of these examples, "unfold[ing] dark things to sinners," "dispens[ing] the misteryes of the Gospell," and coming to the shepherds for "*things deep, things hid, and that mysterious be,*" are allusions to the preaching and teaching ministry of elders.

An elder is responsible for watching over the souls of those entrusted to his charge, defending them from dangers, and guiding them to their eternal home. The preeminent portrait of this pastoral function is the character of Great-heart, who is assigned by Interpreter (a figure of the Holy Spirit) to provide safe conduct for Christiana and her ever-growing band of pilgrims. Without a conductor, pilgrims are exposed to all manner of dangers; but safety is found in the care of a capable guide.[158] Great-heart leads the pilgrims from the House of Interpreter to the Palace Beautiful, teaching them Christology as they go.[159] When they arrive at the Palace, Great-heart slays

---

155. Bunyan, *Pilgrim's Progress*, 1:29–30.

156. *Minutes*, 17.

157. Bunyan, *Pilgrim's Progress*, 1:119.

158. Christiana and Mercy learn this lesson the hard way when they are assaulted by "two very *ill-favoured ones*" immediately upon leaving the King's palace at the Wicket Gate, and are rescued just in time by Reliever (Bunyan, *Pilgrim's Progress*, 2:183–85). Great-heart twice expounds upon his pastoral calling. He tells the Giant Maul, "I am a Servant of the God of Heaven, my business is to perswade sinners to Repentance, I am commanded to do my endeavour to turn Men, Women, and Children, from darkness to light, and from the power of Satan to God" (2:229). When Great-heart relates his prior journey with Mr. Fearing, Honest asks, "Then you knew him to be a troublesom one?" To which Great-heart replies, "*I did so, but I could very well bear it: for Men of my Calling are often times intrusted with the Conduct of such as he was*" (2:233).

159. Bunyan, *Pilgrim's Progress*, 2:197–200.

The Palace Beautiful

the Giant Grim, the persecutor who would keep pilgrims out of the Nonconformist church.[160] He then leads them safely past the lions and introduces them to the Porter. He vouches for the pilgrims' sincerity (they face far less examination than does Christian, who had no conductor), and they enter the Palace, while Great-heart returns to the House of Interpreter.[161] When the time comes for the pilgrims to depart the Palace, they send to Interpreter and ask that Great-heart might be sent to guide them the rest of the way to the Celestial City.[162] Interpreter willingly assents, and Great-heart leads them safely, slaying giants all along the way.[163] It is no coincidence that their journey is considerably easier than was Christian's before them.[164] Such is the benefit of a capable and courageous pastor.[165]

An elder is charged with guarding the door of the church, and maintaining a regenerate church membership. While the ultimate responsibility lies with the church, the elders oversee the membership process. The character of the Porter, who guards the gate of the Palace Beautiful, is an illustration of this pastoral function.[166] Bunyan explicitly referred to pastors as porters of the church. "And hence it is that the true Ministers in their right administration, are called *Porters*; because as Porters stand at the Gate, and there open to, or shut upon those that make an attempt to enter in; so the Ministers of Christ, by the Doctrine of the Twelve, do both open

---

160. Bunyan, *Pilgrim's Progress*, 2:206–7.
161. Bunyan, *Pilgrim's Progress*, 2:207–8.
162. Bunyan, *Pilgrim's Progress*, 2:218–20.

163. Great-heart possesses a "Map of all ways leading to, or from the Celestial City," and is careful to consult the map and keep to the way. Bunyan explained in the margin that the map is "God's Book" (Bunyan, *Pilgrim's Progress*, 2:277).

164. Great-heart tells Christiana while they are walking through the Valley of the Shadow of Death, "You cannot imagine how many are killed here about, and yet men are so foolishly venturous, as to set out lightly on Pilgrimage, and to come without a *Guide*. Poor *Christian*, it was a wonder that he here escaped. but he was beloved of his God" (Bunyan, *Pilgrim's Progress*, 2:228).

165. One may also view Valiant-for-truth as a pastoral apprentice, for he is placed by Great-heart as the rear guard of the pilgrim company and is assigned the care of Mr. Despondency. See Bunyan, *Pilgrim's Progress*, 2:276. Later, he is assigned the care of Christiana's sons and their families (2:284). At Christiana's death, both Great-heart and Valiant-for-truth "played upon the well tuned Cymbal and Harp for Joy. So all returned to their respective Places," a probable reference to funeral sermons (2:285).

166. Bunyan, *Pilgrim's Progress*, 1:45–47; 2:207–8, 220–21.

to, and shut the Gates against the Persons that will be attempting to enter in at the Gates of this City [the New Jerusalem]."[167]

Pastors have charge over the ordinances and worship of the church. Elders are watchmen. "*Watchman, Watchman*, see to thy Duty, look well to the manner of Worship that is to be performed according to thy commission."[168] One of the reasons Bunyan opposed women's prayer meetings (against William Kiffin, who had written in their favor), was that elders were not present to ensure that worship was conducted in a proper manner. "Yea more, why are the Elders of the Churches called Watchmen, Overseers, Guides, Teachers, Rulers, and the like? If this kind of Worship may be performed, without their Conduct and Government?"[169]

As to their character, elders are to be men of godliness and grace. While pilgrims need a conductor, and sheep need shepherds, the church should take great care what kind of shepherd they follow.

> Is it so? is the Soul such an excellent thing, and is the Loss thereof so unspeakably great? then, *This should teach people to be very careful to whom they commit the teaching and guidance of their souls.* . . .
>
> Yet this I will say unto thee, take heed of that Shepherd that *careth not for his own Soul*; that walketh in wayes, and doth such things as have a direct tendency *to damn his own Soul*; I say, take heed of such an one, come not near him, let him have nothing to do with thy Soul, for if he be not faithful to *that* which is his own Soul, be sure he will not be faithful to that which is another mans. He that feeds his own Soul with *ashes*, will scarce feed thine with the *bread of life*.[170]

---

167. Bunyan, *Holy City*, 3:105. Similarly, Bunyan, *Solomon's Temple Spiritualiz'd*, 7:42: "The opening of the Gates did also belong to the Porters, to shew that the power of the Keys, to wit, of opening and shutting, of letting in and keeping out of the Church, doth ministerially belong to these Watchmen." Earlier, Bunyan wrote, "I told you the Porters were types of our Gospel-Ministers" (7:41).

168. Bunyan, *Case of Conscience Resolved*, 4:309.

169. Bunyan, *Case of Conscience Resolved*, 4:308. "But I say, if they *must* do as Mr. K[iffin] says they are *in duty bound*, to witt, meet by themselves apart from their Men, and as so met, perform this most solemn Worship to God: How shall the Elders and Overseers, the Watchmen, Rulers, and Guides in Worship, perform their Duty to God, and to the Church of God, in this, since from this kind of Worship they are quite excluded, and utterly shut out of Dores" (4:309). See also Bunyan, *Solomon's Temple Spiritualiz'd*, 7:41–42.

170. Bunyan, *Greatness of the Soul*, 9:227–28.

Elders ought to be examples to the church of love, charity, and good works.[171] Ministers must be free from covetousness. Though Bunyan was not averse to elders receiving wages, he detested hireling ministers.[172] In short, "A Pastour must himself be exemplary in Faith and Holiness."[173] This means that along with great godliness must be great grace. "And Lord, I am willing to be made a Preacher my self, for that I have been a horrible Sinner; wherefore, if thou shalt forgive my great Transgressions, I shall be a fit man to tell of thy wondrous Grace to others."[174] An elder must be a man of evangelical faith and experience.

Bunyan had much less to say about the office of deacon. In September 1657, he was nominated by the congregation, along with three other men, and "appointed for tryall . . . to exercise the office of deacons," but withdrew with the consent of the congregation because he was "otherwise imployed," presumably in the preaching of the gospel.[175] Like the elders, the deacon's call comes from the local congregation.[176] Their character must be of the same exemplary quality as the elders.[177] The main charge entrusted to deacons is the care of the poor.

---

171. "And let Ministers do this: they are now Pillars of the Churches, and they stand before the Porch of the House, let them also shew their *Lilie-work* to the House, that the Church may learn of them to be without carefulness, as to worldly things, and also to be rich in love, and charity towards the brethren" (Bunyan, *Solomon's Temple Spiritualiz'd*, 7:36).

172. On pastoral wages, see Bunyan, *Pilgrim's Progress*, 2:220–21 [Christiana's gift to the Porter of a "Gold Angel"]; *Holy War*, 38 [the Captains of Shaddai's army "lived upon the Kings cost in all the way they went"]; *Minutes*, 21 ["Muzzle not the mouth of the oxe that treads out the corn to you. Search the Scriptures. Let some of them be read to you about this thing"]. On hireling preachers, see Bunyan, *Vindication*, 1:205; *Few Sighs from Hell*, 1:314: "How many souls hath *Bonner* [Edmund Bonner, Bishop of London during the Marian persecutions] to answer for think you? and several filthy blind Priests? How many souls have they been the means of destroying by their ignorance, and corrupt doctrine? preaching that that was no better for their souls, than Rats-bane to the body, for filthy lucres sake."

173. Bunyan, *Christian Behaviour*, 3:23. In this passage, Bunyan affirmed and applied the qualifications of overseers stated in 1 Tim 3:1–7.

174. Bunyan, *Jerusalem Sinner Saved*, 11:33. In this text, Bunyan expounded upon Psalm 51.

175. *Minutes*, 28.

176. *Minutes*, 28, 40, 41, 71–72, 87.

177. Bunyan, *Christian Behaviour*, 3:22–23.

> Another sort of Officers we have,
>
> *Deacons* we call them, 'cause their work's to save
>
> And distribute those Crumbs of Charity
>
> Unto the Poor, for their Subsistency,
>
> That contributed is for their relief,
>
> Which of their bus'ness is indeed the chief.[178]

Gifford exhorted the congregation, "Let your deacons have a constant stock by them to supply the necessities of those who are in want."[179] When John Fenne was appointed as a deacon, the *Minutes* record, "The same time also, the congregation having had long experience of the faithfulnes of brother John Fenne in the care of the poor, did after the same manner solemnly choose him to the honourable office of a deacon, and committed their poor and purse to him, and he accepted thereof and gave up himself to the Lord and to them in that service."[180] This was designed to take the burden of caring for the poor off of the elders, who had other responsibilities to fulfill. "For a Pastour to be exercising the office of a Deacon instead of the office of a Pastour, it is misplacing of works."[181]

Bunyan also recognized a third category, one that is not strictly an office of the church but is nevertheless an ordained role, that of "gospel minister." Bunyan recounted in *Grace Abounding*:

> For after I had been about five or six years awakened [ca. 1656], and helped to see both the want and worth of Jesus Christ our Lord, and inabled to venture my Soul upon him: some of the most able among the Saints with us, I say the most able for Judgement, and holiness of Life, as they conceived, did perceive that God had counted me worthy to understand something of his Will in his holy and blessed Word, and had given me utterance in some measure to express, what I saw, to others for their edification; therefore they desired me, and that with much earnestness, that I would be willing at sometime to take in hand in one of the Meetings to speak a word of Exhortation unto them.[182]

---

178. Bunyan, *Discourse of the Building*, 6:290.
179. *Minutes*, 20.
180. *Minutes*, 71–72.
181. Bunyan, *Christian Behaviour*, 3:19.
182. Bunyan, *Grace Abounding*, 75.

The Palace Beautiful

Evidently, the Bedford Church conducted an itinerant preaching ministry, and Bunyan soon joined them in this task.

> After this, sometimes when some of them did go into the Countrey to teach, they would also that I should go with them; where, though as yet I did not, nor durst not make use of my Gift in an open way, yet more privately still, as I came amongst the good People in those places, I did sometimes speak a word of Admonition unto them also; the which they, as the other, receiving with rejoicing at the mercy of God to me-ward, professing their Souls were edified thereby.[183]

Eventually, the church ordained Bunyan to the gospel ministry: "Wherefore, to be brief, at last, being still desired by the Church, after some solemn prayer to the Lord, with fasting, I was more particularly called forth, and appointed to a more ordinary and publick preaching the Word, not onely to and amongst them that believed, but also to offer the Gospel to those that had not yet received the faith thereof."[184] Bunyan regarded himself as duly appointed to preach the gospel by the authority of the Bedford congregation. The implication is that it is the particular/visible church that is commissioned to preach the gospel, it is the particular/visible church that bears the responsibility to send forth gospel preachers, and to preach without such a commission from a particular/visible church is to preach without legitimate authority.[185] Yet Bunyan held no office in the church until 1672, when he was appointed an elder.[186] While "gospel minister" should not be regarded as a separate office of the church, it was an ordained role similar to the itinerant ministers that proliferated during the Evangelical Awakening, yet with the distinction of being commissioned by and accountable to a particular/visible church.

Bunyan held the offices of the church in high esteem, particularly the pastoral office. Being under the care of capable and courageous elders was essential to a successful pilgrimage. Therefore, Bunyan exhorted the church: "The Conclusion is, Then let the Churches love their Pastors, hear their Pastors, be ruled by their Pastors, and suffer themselves to be

---

183. Bunyan, *Grace Abounding*, 76.

184. Bunyan, *Grace Abounding*, 76.

185. See above on Bunyan's controversy with Thomas Smith over his authority to preach without episcopal ordination or ecclesiastical education, but solely upon the authority of ordination by the Bedford congregation.

186. *Minutes*, 71–72.

watched over, and to be exhorted, counselled, and if need be, reproved, and rebuked by their Pastors. And let the Ministers not sleep, but be watchful, and look to the Ordinances, to the Souls of the saints, and the Gates of the Churches. Watchman, Watchman, watch."[187]

The Worship of the Church

The worship of the church is the primary means of promoting evangelical faith and holiness in the saints. "Gospel-Worship" is the place where "the Saints in the times of the New Testament, both meet and edifie each other; and also meet their God, and are blessed and refreshed by him."[188] Attendance upon the means of grace is essential to the health and welfare of the soul. "*Praying, Hearing, Reading; for what are these things Ordained, but that we might by the godly use of them, attain to more of the knowledge of God, and be strengthened by his Grace to serve him better according to his moral Law? Baptism, Fellowship, and the Lords Supper, are Ordained for these ends also.*"[189] But the means of grace must be used for their appointed ends of increasing evangelical faith and holiness. "*For all these things we should use to Support our Faith, to mortifie the Flesh, and strengthen us to walk in newness of Life by the rule of the moral Law.*"[190] The means of grace must be attended with fear and reverence. "There flows from *this* Fear of God, great reverence of his Majesty, in and under the use and enjoyment of God's holy Ordinances. His Ordinances are his Courts, and Palaces, his Walks and Places where he giveth his presence to those that wait upon him in them, in the fear of his name."[191] Not only must the means of grace be used in godly fear, they must be used in faith. "First then, that man that doth take up any of the ordinances of God, namely, as prayer, baptisme, breaking of bread, reading, hearing, alms-deeds, or the like; I say, he that doth practice any of these or such like, supposing thereby to procure the

---

187. Bunyan, *Solomon's Temple Spiritualiz'd*, 7:42.

188. Bunyan, *Holy City*, 3:156.

189. Bunyan, *Holy Life*, 9:254.

190. Bunyan, *Holy Life*, 9:254. "Only here will thy wisdom be manifested, to wit, that thou grow in grace, and that thou use lawfully and diligently the means to do it" (Bunyan, *Greatness of the Soul*, 9:238). Those come rightly who "come to God by Christ for a blessing upon that means of grace which God has afforded for the succour of the soul, and the building of it up in the faith; knowing that as the means, so a blessing upon it, is from God" (Bunyan, *Christ a Compleat Saviour*, 13:305).

191. Bunyan, *Treatise on the Fear of God*, 9:65 (see also 9:13). Note Bunyan's comments on impropriety during sermons. See Bunyan, *Life and Death of Mr. Badman*, 41.

love of Christ to his own soul; he doth do what he doth from a Legal, and not from an Evangelical, or Gospel Spirit."[192] To neglect the means of grace is to call into question the sincerity of one's faith. "Not that faith and hope are deficient, if they be right, but they are both of them counterfeit when not attended with a reverent use of all the means: upon the reverent use of which the soul is put, by this grace of fear."[193]

Besides baptism and the Lord's Supper, which are examined in the next section, Bunyan affirmed two primary means of grace: preaching and prayer. Bunyan wrote surprisingly little on the act of preaching. Nevertheless, many of his published works have the appearance of expanded sermons and from them one may readily discern his hermeneutical and homiletical method.[194] Furthermore, the emphasis placed upon the responsibility of elders to preach and teach the Word, noted above, testifies to the centrality of preaching in Bunyan's conception of the church's worship.

Bunyan did write a considerable amount on prayer. This was the subject of one of his earliest publications, *I Will Pray with the Spirit*, written from prison in 1662. In this work, Bunyan provided the following definition of prayer: "Prayer is a sincere, sensible, affectionate pouring out of the heart or soul to God through Christ, in the strength and assistance of the holy Spirit, for such things as God hath promised, or, according to the Word, for the good of the Church, with submission, in Faith, to the Will of God."[195] For Bunyan, this meant that true prayer must be extemporaneous. Bunyan loathed the Book of Common Prayer. In his trial before Judge Keeling, Keeling argued that "we might pray with the spirit, and with the understanding, and with the Common Prayer-book also." Bunyan replied that "those prayers in the Common Prayerbook, was such as was made by other men, and not by the motions of the Holy Ghost, within our Hearts; and as I said the Apostle saith, he will pray with the spirit and with the understanding; not with the spirit and the Common Prayerbook."[196] The apostle Paul, or any other apostle, could have written a prayer book if they had wanted the church to pray by rote.[197]

---

192. Bunyan, *Doctrine of the Law*, 2:72.

193. Bunyan, *Treatise on the Fear of God*, 9:73–74.

194. For example, Bunyan, *Saved by Grace*, 8:165–228; *Come & Welcome*, 8:239–392; *Jerusalem Sinner Saved*, 11:7–92.

195. Bunyan, *I Will Pray with the Spirit*, 2:235.

196. Bunyan, *Relation of the Imprisonment*, 106.

197. "Surely there is no man but will confess, that *Paul* and his Companions were as

To employ written prayers is a violation of Romans 8:26–27 and a denial of the Spirit's ministry of intercession; to pray as one ought is to pray by the Spirit's help, which cannot be done when repeating written prayers.[198] Bunyan went so far as to state that written prayers are expressly forbidden by God, an abomination in his sight:

> There is none can take away the same [i.e., ignorance], nor give you spiritual understanding. The *Common-Prayer-Book* will not do it, neither can any man expect that it should be instrumental that way, it being none of God's Ordinances; but a thing since the Scriptures were written, patched together, one piece at one time, and another at another; a meer humane invention and institution, which God is so far from owning of, that he expressly forbids it, with any other such like, and that by manyfold sayings in his most holy and blessed Word. . . . For right prayer, must as well in the outward part of it, in the outward expression, as in the inward intention, come from what the soul doth apprehend in the Light of the Spirit; otherwise it is condemned as vain and an abomination (*Mark 7.*); because the heart and tongue do not go along joyntly in the same, *Prov.* 21. 9. *Isa.* 29. 13. neither indeed can they, unless the Spirit help our infirmities.[199]

Bunyan detested vain repetition. This included repetition of the Lord's Prayer, which he did not think was intended to be repeated verbatim.[200] An awakened man has no need of written prayers, for "he hath his understanding well exercised; to discern between good and evil, and in it placed a sence, either of the misery of man, or the mercy of God; that soul hath no need of the Writings of other men, to teach him by Forms of Prayer."[201] Therefore, those Anglican bishops sin grievously who require the Book of Common Prayer and forbid extemporaneous prayers by the Spirit. "Did God send his holy Spirit into the hearts of his People to that end that you should taunt at it? is this to serve God? And doth this demonstrate

---

able to have done any work for God, as any *Pope* or proud *Prelate* in the Church of *Rome*, and could as well have made a *Common-Prayer Book*, as those who at first composed this; as being not a whit behind them, either in grace or gifts" (Bunyan, *I Will Pray with the Spirit*, 2:247).

198. Bunyan, *I Will Pray with the Spirit*, 2:248–49.
199. Bunyan, *I Will Pray with the Spirit*, 2:249–50.
200. Bunyan noted, "We do not find that the Apostles did ever observe it as such, neither did they admonish others so to do" (Bunyan, *I Will Pray with the Spirit*, 2:270).
201. Bunyan, *I Will Pray with the Spirit*, 2:264.

the Reformation of your Church? Nay, is it not the mark of implacable Reprobates? O fearful! can you not be content to be damned for your sins against the Law, but you must sin against the Holy Ghost?"[202] Bunyan also warned against the opposite danger, that of extemporaneous prayers that are devoid of the Spirit, and simply a show of one's supposed piety and an imitation of another's style.

> I have often observed, that that which is natural, and so comely in one, looks odiously when imitated by another: I speak as to *Gestures* and *Actions* in Preaching and Prayer. Many, I doubt not, but will imitate the Publicane, and that both in the *prayer* and *gestures* of the Publicane, whose persons and actions will yet stink full foully in the nostrils of him that is holy and just, and that searcheth the Heart and the Rains.[203]

True prayer must flow from an evangelical heart, and be offered in an evangelical spirit.[204] For Bunyan, corporate prayer is not only worship, it is teaching. "As teaching by Prayer in Assemblies, is thus set on foot; so every one also that shall in such Meetings be the mouth of the whole, to God, Ministereth, SO, Doctrine to that Assembly, as well as presenteth petitions to God."[205] And as corporate prayer is teaching, it is a ministry reserved for men.[206]

---

202. Bunyan, *I Will Pray with the Spirit*, 2:282. "As this is the doom of those who do openly blaspheme the holy Ghost, in a way of disdain and reproach to its office and service: So also it is sad for you, who resist this Spirit of Prayer, by a Form of man's inventing" (2:283). Bunyan proceeded to rail against the entire Anglican liturgy.

203. Bunyan, *Discourse upon the Pharisee*, 10:223–24 (see also 10:129). Likewise, Bunyan warned against the use of "high, flaunting, swelling words of vanity"; true prayer consists of "humble Hearts, and sensible words" (10:234).

204. The prayers of the unconverted are sin, as without the Spirit "men are senceless, so hypocritical, cold, and unseemly in their prayers; and so, they with their prayers, are both rendred abominable to God" (Bunyan, *I Will Pray with the Spirit*, 2:250). Therefore, only those who know themselves to be disciples should pray (2:271).

205. Bunyan, *Case of Conscience Resolved*, 4:305–6.

206. "Because *This kind of Worship, when done in and by a Company, is MINISTERIAL to that Company, as well as petitionary to God. That is, they that as the mouth in Assemblies Pray to God, teach that Assembly, as well as beg mercies of him. And I finde not that Women may Assemble to do thus*" (Bunyan, *Case of Conscience Resolved*, 4:304). According to John Gifford, corporate prayer is not only restricted to men, but to those men who are gifted to do so: "God hath not gifted, I judge, every brother to be a mouth to the Church. Let such as have most of the demonstration of the Spirit, and of power, shut up all your comings together, that ye may go away with your heartes comforted, and quickened" (*Minutes*, 20). Gifford also thought that the congregation

A hotly-contested element of worship in the seventeenth century was psalm-singing. Psalm-singing was discussed in the Bedford Church for the first time in 1674. The issue was still not settled in 1690: "About the 5 of October 1690 it was apoynted that noatice be giveing for a generall Church meeting to be heild at Bedford on the 20 day of this instant, to seek unto God and debate about the singing of Psalms in publick on the Lord's Day."[207] When that day came, "it was debated and agreed that publick singing of Psalms be practised by the Church, with a cuashion that non others peforme it but such as can singe with grace in there hearts according to the command of Christ."[208] Like prayer, acceptable singing in the sight of God requires evangelical faith. Although Bunyan did not offer an explicit statement of his position, there is evidence that he was in favor of the practice. In *A Treatise on the Fear of God*, he mentioned the singing of Psalm 128 and included Sternhold and Hopkins's 1635 edition of the psalm.[209] He spoke of the saints singing songs of praise in *Israel's Hope Encouraged*.[210] His words in *Solomon's Temple Spiritualiz'd* seem conclusive:

> But we are confined to the Songs of the Temple, a more distinct type of ours in the Church under the Gospel. . . .
> These Singers of old were to sing their Songs *over the burnt-offering*, which were types of the Sacrificed Body of Christ, a *Memorial* of which Offering we have at the Lord's Table, the Consummation of which, *Christ and his Disciples celebrated with a Hymn. Matt. 26. 30.*

---

should stand to pray: "I beseech you forbeare sitting in prayer, except parties be any way disabled. Tis not a posture that suites with the majesty of such an ordinance. Would you serve your prince so?" (20).

207. *Minutes*, 91–92.

208. *Minutes*, 92. The decision was not unanimous, however, for Ebenezer Chandler wrote a few months later, "Our brethren have determined that those that are perswaded in their consciences that publick singing is an ordinance of God, shall practice it on the Lord's Day in our meeting in Bedford. Those that are of differing judgments have there liberty whether they will sing, ye or noe, or whether they will be presant whilst we sing, so that they do not turn there backs on other parts of God's worship. Nether is it at all designed to be imposed or proposed to any other meeting of the Church" (93).

209. Bunyan, *Treatise on the Fear of God*, 9:88–89. See Offor's note in Offor, *Works of John Bunyan*, 1:473.

210. "This also should teach the Saints when they Sing or Praise the Lord, they should not sing of Mercy only, but of Mercy and Judgment too" (Bunyan, *Israel's Hope Encouraged*, 13:83).

And as of old they were the Church that did sing in the Temple, according to Institution, to God; So also they are by God's appointment to be sung in the Church in the New.[211]

Two final components of Bunyan's doctrine of worship require examination. First, Bunyan was committed to the regulative principle of worship, at least in theory. Bunyan affirmed that, "God's command must be the Rule whereby we order all our Actions, especially when we pretend to Worship that is divine and religious."[212] Likewise, "I therefore take little notice of what a man saith, though he flourisheth his matter with many brave words, if he bring not with him, *Thus saith the Lord*. For that, and that onely, ought to be my ground of Faith as to how my God would be worshipped by me."[213] Likewise, "The more outward and External Part, as well as that more Internal Worship to be performed to God, should be grounded upon Apostolical Doctrine and Appointments."[214] The glory that attends the church's worship depends upon the purity of its worship. "For that Glory doth attend the Church upon the account of her Purity of Worship, of Temple-Worship, and doth either abide on her, or withdraw it self, according to her exact observing the Rule, or declining from it."[215]

However, Bunyan was not always consistent in his application of the regulative principle. In his writings during the communion controversy (1672–1674), Bunyan repeatedly urged the regulative principle in support of his open-communion position. The Baptists had neither "*Precept, President nor Example in all the Scripture for our excluding our holy Brethren that differ in this point from us; therefore we ought not dare to do it*, but contrariwise to receive them; because God hath given us sufficient proof

---

211. Bunyan, *Solomon's Temple Spiritualiz'd*, 7:83–84. Mercy exclaims at the Palace Beautiful, "Wonderful! Musick in the House, Musick in the Heart, and Musick also in Heaven, for joy that we are here" (Bunyan, *Pilgrim's Progress*, 2:209). See also Bunyan, *Holy War*, 115–16.

212. Bunyan, *Exposition of the First Ten Chapters*, 12:202.

213. Bunyan, *Questions*, 4:341. Also, "Take heed of letting the name, or good shew of a thing, begett in thy Heart a Religious reverence of that thing; but look to the Word for thy bottom, for it is the Word that Authorizeth, what ever may be done with Warrant in Worship, to God; without the Word, things are of human invention, of what Splendor or Beauty soever they may appear to be" (Bunyan, *Case of Conscience Resolved*, 4:321–22).

214. Bunyan, *Solomon's Temple Spiritualiz'd*, 7:20. For similar plain statements of Bunyan's commitment to the regulative principle, see Bunyan, *Solomon's Temple Spiritualiz'd*, 7:8, 27; *Seasonable Counsel*, 10:28, 47–48; *Relation of the Imprisonment*, 108. Gifford exhorted the Bedford Church in a similar fashion (*Minutes*, 19–20).

215. Bunyan, *Holy City*, 3:161.

that himself hath received them, whose example in this case he hath commanded us to follow."[216] The Baptists pointed to the precept, precedent, and example of Scripture for the baptizing of converts as justification for their exclusion of the unbaptized from church communion. Bunyan disagreed. "That Water-baptism hath formerly gone first [i.e., before church communion] is granted: But that it ought of necessity so to do, I never saw proof."[217] The New Testament precept, precedent, and example of credobaptism prior to church communion was insufficient to justify the exclusion of the unbaptized. Yet a decade later, in *Questions about the Nature and Perpetuity of the Seventh-Day-Sabbath* (1685), Bunyan argued for the Christian Sabbath in precisely the same manner as the Baptists had argued for strict communion.

> Now why should the Holy Ghost thus precisely speak of their assembling together upon the *first day*, if not to conform us in this, that the Lord had chosen *that* day for the *new* Sabbath of his Church? Surely the Apostles knew what they did in their meeting together upon that day; yea, and the Lord Jesus also; for that he used SO to visit them when SO assembled, made his *practice a Law unto them*: For Practice is enough for us New Testament Saints, specially when the Lord Jesus himself is in the head of that practice, and that after he rose from the dead.[218]

The New Testament lacks any explicit command to the church to assemble on the first day of the week, nor does it contain any explicit teaching regarding the establishment of that day as the Christian Sabbath. Yet in this case, the practice of the apostolic church was sufficient to ground the rule. The meaning and application of the regulative principle in regard to baptism was a major source of contention in the communion controversy with the Baptists, and is discussed in the following chapter.

The final issue related to Bunyan's doctrine of worship was his conviction that the first day of the week, the Lord's Day, has replaced the seventh day as the Sabbath. Bunyan wrote an entire treatise on the subject in response to Seventh-Day Baptists who contended that because the seventh-day Sabbath was instituted before the fall of man, it was part of the

---

216. Bunyan, *Peaceable Principles and True*, 4:270 (see also 4:276). See also Bunyan, *Confession of My Faith*, 4:172–74; *Differences in Judgment*, 4:216–19.

217. Bunyan, *Confession of My Faith*, 4:169 (see also 4:162). See Bunyan, *Differences in Judgment*, 4:263; *Peaceable Principles and True*, 4:269–70.

218. Bunyan, *Questions*, 4:364.

moral law that transcended the various covenant dispensations; hence, its inclusion in the Ten Commandments.[219] Bunyan argued that the Sabbath Day is no part of natural or moral law, but rather an ordinance imposed by God upon Israel at Mt. Sinai. While it is part of natural or moral law to set aside time for worship, what time that must be is not natural or moral and must be dictated by revelation.[220] No such revelation was given from Adam to Moses, nor were any punished for its violation during that time.[221] Even after the Sabbath law was given, it was not incumbent upon the Gentiles, but upon Israel alone.[222] Furthermore, the ministration of the Sabbath was, like the rest of the old covenant law, a shadow and type of the new covenant antitype. The old covenant ministration has given way to the new covenant ministration, established by Jesus Christ, the Lord of the Sabbath.[223] Finally, the Lord of the Sabbath has established, by precept and precedent, that the instituted day of worship under the new covenant is the first day of the week.

> This then is the Conclusion, that *TIME* to worship God in is required by the Law of Nature; but that the Law of Nature doth, as such, fix it on the *Seventh day* from the Creation of the World, that I utterly deny, by what I have said already, and have yet to say on that behalf: Yea, I hope to make it manifest, as I have, that *this* Seventh day is removed; that God, by the ministration of the Spirit, has changed the time to another day, to wit, *The first day of the week.* Therefore we conclude the time is fixed for the worship of the New Testament-Christians, or Churches of the Gentiles, unto *that* day.[224]

Bunyan argued this last point from seven texts that imply this point, followed by five texts "that are more express."[225] Corporate worship is com-

---

219. "Historians have found no evidence of seventh-day sabbatarians in Bedfordshire, although some were in counties Bunyan visited, including Suffolk, Essex, and Berkshire. More likely, he came into personal contact with sabbatarians in London, where three Seventh-day Baptist congregations were in existence at this time" (Greaves, *Glimpses of Glory*, 519). Greaves provides helpful background to Bunyan's treatise (519–25).

220. Bunyan, *Questions*, 4:337–40.

221. Bunyan, *Questions*, 4:340–45.

222. Bunyan, *Questions*, 4:345–48.

223. Bunyan, *Questions*, 4:348–56.

224. Bunyan, *Questions*, 4:358.

225. Bunyan, *Questions*, 4:358–74. The five "explicit" texts [(1) Luke 24/John 20; (2) John 20:20; (3) Acts 2:1–4; (4) Acts 20:7; (5) 1 Cor 16:1–2] still fall short of precept, resting upon precedent alone.

manded on the Christian Sabbath, because the worship on that day "has a divine stamp upon it."[226] The day sanctifies the worship: "And I believe, that things done on the Lords day, are better done, than on other days of the week, in his Worship."[227] It is the day on which the heavenly manna is given.[228] For Bunyan, worship on the Lord's Day is vital to evangelical faith and holiness. Furthermore, the Lord's Day reveals faith and holiness, or the lack thereof. Wiseman informs Attentive:

> Yes doubtless; and a man shall shew his Heart and his Life what they are, more by one Lords-day, than by all the days of the week besides: And the reason is, because on the Lords-day there is a special restraint laid upon men as to Thoughts and Life, more than upon other days of the week besides. Also, men are enjoyned on that day to a stricter performance of holy Duties, and restraint of worldly business, than upon other days they are; wherefore, if their hearts incline not naturally to good, now they will shew it, now they will appear what they are. The Lords Day is a kind of an Emblem of the heavenly Sabbath above, and it makes manifest how the heart stands to the perpetuity of Holiness, more than to be found in a transient Duty, does.[229]

God "*hath put sanctity and holiness upon it* [i.e., the Lord's Day]."[230] This is why the corporate means of grace (preaching, prayer, psalm-singing), when received according to God's rule, on God's day, are the church's primary means of promoting evangelical faith and holiness.

The Ordinances of the Church

Bunyan viewed baptism and the Lord's Supper as means of grace, special vehicles through which the saints are built up in evangelical faith and holiness.

> Do you think that *Love-letters* are not *desired* between Lovers? Why these, God's Ordinances, they are His *Love-letters*, and *Love-tokens* too: no marvel then if the righteous do SO desire them. . . .

---

226. Bunyan, *Questions*, 4:382.

227. Bunyan, *Questions*, 4:371.

228. "The *Lords day*, as was said, is to the Christians the principal Manna-day" (Bunyan, *Questions*, 4:385).

229. Bunyan, *Life and Death of Mr. Badman*, 25.

230. Bunyan, *Life and Death of Mr. Badman*, 24.

> FOR this cause therefore are the Ordinances of God so much desired by the Righteous. In them they meet with God; and by them they are builded, and nourished up to Eternal life....
>
> He made himself known to them in breaking of Bread: Who would not then, that loves to know him, be present at such an Ordinance?
>
> Oft times the Holy Ghost, in the comfortable influence of it, has accompanied the Baptized in the very act of Administring it.[231]

The ordinances are "servants ... and our mystical Ministers, to teach and instruct us, in the most weighty matters of the Kingdom of God: I therefore here declare my reverent esteem of them."[232]

Nevertheless, their importance must not be overstated. They are "Shadowish Sacraments" and "outward circumstances."[233] They have no inherent value or efficacy in themselves apart from God's appointment.[234] They must not be made "Co-Saviours, Co-Advocates" with Jesus Christ.[235] They cannot justify in the sight of God. In an interesting passage in *The Doctrine of the Law and Grace Unfolded*, Bunyan seemed to have his eye upon the Baptists:

> But (say you) our practices in the worship of God shall testifie for us, that we are not under the Law; for we have by Gods goodness attained to as exact a way of walking in the ordinances of God, and as near the examples of the Apostles, as ever any Churches since the primitive times, as we judge.

231. Bunyan, *Desire of the Righteous Granted*, 13:129–30. See also Bunyan, *Holy Life*, 9:254; *Holy City*, 3:150. "I believe that Christ hath ordained but two [ordinances] in his Church, viz., Water baptism and the Supper of the Lord: both which are of excellent use to the Church, in this world; they being to us representations of the death and resurrection of Christ; and are as, God shall make them, helps to our faith therein" (Bunyan, *Confession of My Faith*, 4:160). "Baptism and the Lord's-Supper both, were made for us, not we for them; wherefore both were made for our Edification, but no one for our destruction" (Bunyan, *Differences in Judgment*, 4:223; similarly, Bunyan, *Book for Boys and Girls*, 6:212–13).

232. Bunyan, *Confession of My Faith*, 4:160.

233. Bunyan, *Exposition of the First Ten Chapters*, 12:153 ("Shadowish Sacraments"); *Confession of My Faith*, 4:172 ("outward circumstance") (see also 4:180).

234. Bunyan, *Paul's Departure and Crown*, 12:376.

235. "For if Christ be my *Righteousness*, and not Water; if Christ be my *Advocate*, and not Water; if there be that good and blessedness in Christ, that is not in Water; then is Jesus Christ better than Water; and also in these to be eternally divided from Water; unless we will make them Co-Saviours, Co-Advocates, and such as are equally good, and profitable to men" (Bunyan, *Differences in Judgment*, 4:215).

> *Answ.* What then? do you think that the walking in the order of the Churches of old, as to matter of outward worship, is sufficient to clear you of your sins at the judgement day?[236]

And when used in the wrong spirit, as though they were meritorious works of the law and not signs and seals of the righteousness that is by faith, they are positively deadly. "And again though they be in themselves Gospel ordinances, as baptisme, breaking of bread, hearing, praying, meditating, or the like: yet I say if they be not done in a right spirit, they are thereby used as a hand by the devil, to pull thee under the Covenant of Works; as in former times he used circumcision, which was no part of the Covenant of Works, the ten Commands, but a seal of the righteousness of Faith."[237]

As Bunyan's doctrine of baptism is discussed in detail in the following chapter, a few brief points will suffice here. Bunyan was a credobaptist, yet he denied that baptism was the initiating ordinance into the church, whether the universal/invisible church or the particular/visible church. "The person then that is baptized stands by that, a member of no Church at all, neither of the visible, nor yet of the invisible. A visible Saint he is, but not made so by Baptism; for he must be a visible Saint before, else he ought not to be baptized."[238] In fact, Bunyan denied that baptism was a church ordinance at all; that is, baptism is not an element of the church's worship as a church. "For albeit that Baptism be given by Christ our Lord to the Church, yet not for them to worship Him by as a Church."[239] "That Water-baptism giveth neither being, nor well-being to a Church, neither is any part of that Instituted Worship of God, that the Church, as such, should be found in the Practice of."[240] It is strictly for the benefit of the individual, for personal edification, and not to be used as an evidence of grace; for the act of baptism cannot demonstrate the sincerity of one's faith

---

236. Bunyan, *Doctrine of the Law*, 2:71. Nor is baptism regenerative (2:150).

237. Bunyan, *Doctrine of the Law*, 2:181.

238. Bunyan, *Confession of My Faith*, 4:164. Bunyan did not make many such explicit statements regarding the proper subjects and mode of baptism, but for inferential references to credobaptism, see Bunyan, *Confession of My Faith*, 4:172; *Holy Life*, 9:258–59; *Differences in Judgment*, 4:215, 225–26, 246; *Desire of the Righteous Granted*, 13:130; *Come & Welcome*, 8:294 (against paedobaptism). On baptism not being the initiating ordinance, see Bunyan, *Confession of My Faith*, 4:162; *Differences in Judgment*, 4:198, 222–23, 240.

239. Bunyan, *Differences in Judgment*, 4:200. For similar statements on baptism not being a church ordinance, see Bunyan, *Differences in Judgment*, 4:208, 222, 223, 240.

240. Bunyan, *Differences in Judgment*, 4:221.

and holiness.²⁴¹ In fact, baptism should be temporarily set aside if it causes church division.²⁴² In terms of positive baptismal theology, baptism is a profession of one's death to the world and resurrection in Christ, as well as a symbol of one's regeneration.²⁴³ Finally, any Christian can baptize. "No man baptizeth by virtue of his Office in the Church; no man is baptized by virtue of his Membership there."²⁴⁴

While baptism is no part of the church's worship, the Lord's Supper is. "There is more to be said in that case [the Lord's Supper] than the other [baptism]: for that is a part of that Worship which Christ hath Instituted for his Church, to be Conversant in as a Church; presenting them as such, with their Communion with their Head, and with one another as Members of him."²⁴⁵

> Breaking of Bread, not Baptism, being a Church-Ordinance, and *that* such also, as must be *often* reiterated; yea, it being an Ordinance SO full of blessedness, as lively to present Union and Communion with Christ to all the Members that worthily eat thereof; I say, The Lord's-Supper being *such*, that while the Members sit at that feast, they *shew* to each other the Death and Blood of the Lord; as they ought to do, *till he comes*, . . . the Church, as a Church, is much more concerned in THAT, than in *Water-Baptism*, both as to her Faith, and *Comfort*; both as to her Union, and *Communion*.²⁴⁶

The Lord's Supper can be an intensely spiritual experience. In *Grace Abounding*, Bunyan recounted his first Lord's Supper as a member of the Bedford Church:

---

241. On baptism's value for personal edification, see Bunyan, *Confession of My Faith*, 4:164, 172; *Differences in Judgment*, 4:200, 222. On baptism as an insufficient testimony to one's faith and holiness, see Bunyan, *Confession of My Faith*, 4:168–69, 172; *Differences in Judgment*, 4:200, 216, 241, 245.

242. "Again; if Water-baptism, as the circumstances with which the Churches were pestered of old, trouble their peace, wound the consciences of the Godly; dismember and break their fellowships, it is although an ordinance for the present to be shunned; for the edification of the Church as I shall shew anon, is to be preferred before it" (Bunyan, *Confession of My Faith*, 4:171). See also Bunyan, *Differences in Judgment*, 4:224.

243. Bunyan, *Confession of My Faith*, 4:172; *Exposition of the First Ten Chapters*, 12:237; *Of Justification*, 12:292 [baptism the "Symbol of Regeneration"].

244. Bunyan, *Differences in Judgment*, 4:203.

245. Bunyan, *Differences in Judgment*, 4:202 (for similar statements, see 4:203, 223).

246. Bunyan, *Differences in Judgment*, 4:245.

> After I had propounded to the Church, that my desire was to walk in the Order and Ordinances of Christ with them, and was also admitted by them; while I thought of that blessed Ordinance of Christ, which was his last Supper with his Disciples before his death, that Scripture, *Do this in remembrance of me*, Luk. 22. 19. was made a very precious word unto me; for by it the Lord did come down upon my conscience with the discovery of his death for my sins, and as I then felt, did as if he plunged me in the vertue of the same.[247]

At all times, the Supper must be approached with repentance and remembrance.[248] Although Bunyan never explicitly took a position on the presence of Christ in the Supper, there is at least one passage that suggests that he believed Christ to be spiritually present. "His Ordinances are his Courts, and Palaces, his Walks and Places where he giveth his presence to those that wait upon him in them, in the fear of his name."[249]

Bunyan practiced a form of closed communion, in that one must be a member of the church by covenant in order to be admitted to the Lord's Table.[250] But as baptism is not a prerequisite to church membership, neither is it requisite to the Lord's Supper. Bunyan rejected the parallel between Passover and the Lord's Supper, just as he rejected the parallel between circumcision and baptism. The antitype of the circumcision of the flesh is the circumcision of the heart; the antitype of the Passover is the body and blood of Christ.[251] Therefore, any argument for excluding the unbaptized

---

247. Bunyan, *Grace Abounding*, 72.

248. "It would be well also, if these Instruments were at all times laid upon *our* Tables, for our more humbling for our sins in every thing we do, especially upon the *Lord's* Table, when we come to eat and drink before him. I am sure the Lord Jesus doth more than intimate, that he expects that we should do so, where he saith, When ye eat that Bread, and drink that Cup, *Do this in remembrance of me*. In remembrance that I died for your sins, and consequently, that they were the meritorious cause of the shedding of my blood" (Bunyan, *Solomon's Temple Spiritualiz'd*, 7:61).

249. Bunyan, *Treatise on the Fear of God*, 9:65 (see also 9:14: "Besides, this glorious Majesty is himself present to behold his Worshippers in their worshiping him").

250. In January 1670, the *Minutes* record, "It was agreed also that brother Bunyan and brother Man should reason with Mr. Sewster about his desire of breaking bread with this congregation, without sitting downe as a member with us" (*Minutes*, 42). In May 1662, the church "enquired of the pastors in London, whether the pastor of one congregation do administer the ordinance of the Supper to another congregation, and on what Scripture grounds they do it or refuse" (38).

251. For baptism not being the antitype of circumcision, see Bunyan, *Confession of My Faith*, 4:162–63; *Peaceable Principles and True*, 4:276. For the Lord's Supper not

from the Lord's Supper based upon the exclusion of the uncircumcised from the Passover is invalid. There are several potential allusions to the Lord's Supper in Bunyan's allegories, but they yield little information as to his theology of the ordinance beyond potential inferences.[252]

The ordinances of the church are to be received with an evangelical faith and are given for the increase of such faith and its fruit of holiness. Furthermore, as is demonstrated in the following chapter, it was Bunyan's commitment to evangelical faith and holiness that determined his position on the relationship between the ordinances.

The Discipline of the Church

Finally, the faith and holiness of the church is guarded by the discipline of the church. While Bunyan wrote relatively little on the topic of church discipline, there are a handful of passages that establish the authority of the church to admonish and, if necessary, excommunicate its members. In *Solomon's Temple Spirituliz'd*, Bunyan outlined the relationship between the judgment of the church and the judgment of God:

> But what are we to understand in Gospel-days, by going out of the house of the Lord, for, or by sin?
>
> *I answer*, If it be done *voluntarily*, then sin leads you out, if it be done by the *holy compulsion* of the Church, then 'tis done by the Judicial Judgment of God; That is, they are cut off, and cast out from thence, as a Just reward for their transgressions. . . .
>
> Well, but whether do they go, that are thus gone out of the Temple or Church of God?
>
> *I answer*, not to the *Dunghil* with *Athaliah*, nor to the *Pesthouse* with *Uzziah, but to the Devil,* that is the first step, and *so to Hell*, without repentance. But if their sin be not unpardonable, they may by repentance be recovered, and in mercy tread these Courts again.[253]

---

being the antitype of the Passover, see Bunyan, *Differences in Judgment about Water Baptism*, 4:224.

252. See Bunyan, *Pilgrim's Progress*, 1:48 (examination and discipleship should precede one's admittance to the Lord's Supper), 52 (the Lord's Supper should be accompanied by instruction about Christ and his saving work); 2:195–96 (the Lord's Supper is a "*Seal*" that "greatly added to their Beauty, for it was an Ornament to their Faces. It also added to their gravity, and made their Countenances more like them of Angels"); *Holy War*, 115–16 (the Lord's Supper should be accompanied by music and preaching), 148 (the Lord's Supper should be observed weekly).

253. Bunyan, *Solomon's Temple Spirituliz'd*, 7:82.

In *The Barren Fig-Tree*, Bunyan wrote, "God doth sometimes cut down the *barren Fig-tree* by the Church, by the Churches due execution of the Laws and Censures, which Christ for that purpose hath left with his Church."[254] Church discipline is essential, not only for the purity of the church, but for the sanctification of its individual members.

> As it is said, *This mischief to prevent,*
> Let all men watch, yea, and be diligent
> Observers of its motions, and then flie,
> *This is the way to live and not to die.*
> He that would never fall, must never slip,
> Who would obey the Call, must fear the Whip.
> God would also that *every stander by,*
> That in the Grass doth see the *Adder lie,*
> Should cry as he did, *Death is in the Pot,*
> That many by its Poyson, perish not.[255]

The Minutes of . . . Bunyan Meeting tell the story of a congregation that took seriously its authority and responsibility to discipline its members. The church followed a three-step process of discipline. First, the sinning brother was admonished by members of the congregation commissioned for the task. Next, if the sinning brother did not respond, he was "withdrawn from," meaning communion was withheld until the church was satisfied with his repentance. This second step could last months, even years. The church, while quick to admonish, was remarkably patient and cautious in taking the third and final step of excommunicating the unrepentant. A case in point is the account of Richard Deane. In November 1668, Samuel Fenne and John Croker were sent to admonish Deane, and "rebuke him for his withdrawing from the assemblyes of the saints, and to inquire into the truth of those scandalous reports that we heare concerning him."[256] In September 1669, Deane was ordered to appear before

---

254. Bunyan, *Barren Fig-Tree*, 5:36. "If they be such as eat out the bowels of a Church, so soon as they are detected, he must either be kept out, while out, or cast out, if in: For it must be the prudence of every community, to preserve its own unity and peace and truth: The which the Churches of Christ may do" (Bunyan, *Confession of My Faith*, 4:184; see also 4:159).

255. Bunyan, *Discourse of the Building*, 6:307. See the extended poetic treatment of church discipline in Bunyan, *Discourse of the Building*, 6:304–13.

256. *Minutes*, 39.

the church, "to give an account of [his] carriages towards God and his Church."²⁵⁷ Deane did not respond well.

> At their first speaking with Richard Deane, he seemed forward and willing to come, till his former offences were laide before him, and he certifyed that the Church did looke for good evidence of his repentance for them, and then he brake out into high language, but they told him that would not satisfy the Church neither; their desire was to see him brought to repentance, and then he seemed againe to be yielding, and promised conditionally to be there, but came not. These things considered, the Church thought it good to send brother Bunyan and brother John Whiteman once more to admonish them.²⁵⁸

Two months later, "Richard Deane did acknowledge himself not sensible as yet but desired the prayers and patience of the Church." So Bunyan and Whiteman were again dispatched to admonish him.²⁵⁹ In May 1670, John Fenne reported that he and Bunyan had attempted to speak again with Deane, "but (he continually indeavouring to avoide their delivering their message by keeping out of the way) they could by no meanes accomplish it, whereupon the Church did agree shortly to proceed farther with him."²⁶⁰ The following month, the church sent two more men to Deane, "to admonish and advertise him of their intentions speedily to deale with him according to Christ's testament, unles his unfeigned repentance prevent it."²⁶¹ Finally, in April 1671, Deane was "cut off from, and cast out of this congregation."²⁶² The charges against him were as follows:

> 1. A wicked withdrawing from the Church, and the worship of God in the Church, contrary to solemne covenant.
>
> 2. A loose and ungodly life, accompanied with defrauding in his calling, selling to severall persons deceivable goods, to the great dishonour of God, and scandall of our profession.
>
> 3. For speaking contemptuously against the Church, pretending he had something to lay to their charge, yet, contrary to *Matthew*

---

257. *Minutes*, 40.
258. *Minutes*, 41.
259. *Minutes*, 42.
260. *Minutes*, 51.
261. *Minutes*, 52.
262. *Minutes*, 63.

18 withdrew without declaring to the Church beforehand his dissatisfaction, neither could he be brought to give any account thereof since.

4. That he went without the consent or knowledge of the Church, in the Churche's name, particularly naming John Bunyan and Samuel Fenne, to some good people in St. Neots, requesting their benevolence for the supply of his family.[263]

From 1656–1688, the Bedford Church placed over twenty-five individuals under discipline, excommunicating five.[264] The most frequent offense that occasioned the church's censure was absenteeism. But other offenses included sheep-stealing, "evill carriages," joining another congregation without permission, disorder, conformity to the Church of England, "scandalous reports," "railing and other wicked practices," indebtedness, immodesty, disobedience to parents, causing division, immorality, gossip, child abuse, wife-beating, "unseemly language," and slander.[265] In one instance, the Bedford Church refused to uphold a Cambridge church's excommunication of Brother Waite, demonstrating that the congregation operated autonomously, reserving the right to judge matters of discipline for themselves.[266]

The goal of church discipline is always the promotion of faith and holiness. The member who walks in sin must be cut off from the church, like dead branches from the vine, that the rest of the branches might bear much fruit. But discipline is also designed to promote faith and holiness in the life of the erring brother, that he might be restored to the fellowship of the saints.

---

263. *Minutes*, 63.

264. These figures are based upon the incomplete records found in the *Minutes*; actual figures are likely to be higher.

265. *Minutes*, 25–37 (Oliver Dicks—sheep stealing), 25–27, 30–31 (Martha Radwell—"evill carriages"), 31–34 (John Childe—joining another congregation without permission), 37–64 (Robert Nelson—disorder, absenteeism), 40–45 (Humphrey Merrill—conformity to the Church of England), 40–42, 68 (Brother Coventon—absenteeism), 39–64 (Richard Deane—absenteeism, scandalous reports) 39–40, 44 (Sister Warner—absenteeism, scandalous reports), 43–70 (William Whitbread—absenteeism), 76 (Sister Witt—"railling and other wicked practices," indebtedness), 76–77 (Elizabeth Bisbie—immodesty), 76 (Elizabeth Maxey—disobedience to parents), 76–77 (Nehemiah Coxe—causing division), 80 (Sister Cooper—attending Anglican services), 83 (Edward Dent—financial neglect; indebtedness), 84 (Mary Fosket—gossip), 84 (John Stanton—child abuse, wife-beating), 85 (Sister Hauthorn—"unseemly language"), 85–90 (John Wildeman—slander).

266. *Minutes*, 48–49, 52–53, 54–56, 68.

If he *falls not*, but in the second charge,
Spread not his wickedness abroad at large.
But, if thou think his *sorrow to be sound*,
Forgive his sin, *and hide it under ground.*
 If he shall stand the *first* and *second* shot?
If he before the *Church*, repenteth not?
Deal with him *as the matter shall require*,
Let not the House for him be set on fire.
If after *all*, he shall *repent and turn*
To God, and you, *you must not let him burn*
For ever under sense of sin and shame,
You must his sin forgive in Christ his name.[267]

Bunyan: The Lonely Pilgrim?

The eminent Baptist scholar B. R. White claimed that while Bunyan's "membership of the congregation of Independents at Bedford and their influence upon him played an important part" in Bunyan's own spiritual pilgrimage as detailed in *Grace Abounding to the Chief of Sinners*, yet "Christian, Bunyan's pilgrim, was essentially a lonely figure. Admittedly he had counsellors such as Evangelist and the Interpreter and, importantly, friends on the way such as Faithful and Hopeful, but the sense of the surrounding presence of a church fellowship was almost completely absent."[268] White contended that this "strange disjunction between Bunyan's own experience and that of his pilgrim ... illustrates the deep cleft between the two cardinal aspects of both Calvinism itself and Puritan theology more generally, for they were both deeply concerned with the theology of individual faith and salvation and also with the nature and constitution of the visible church."[269] Bunyan was indeed deeply concerned with both "the theology of individual faith and salvation" and "the nature and constitution of the visible church," but he did not view these issues as separated by a "deep cleft." In fact, they were very much in harmony. Bunyan's Christian is only "essentially a lonely

---

267. Bunyan, *Discourse of the Building*, 6:307–8. The "second charge" refers to the second admonishment (Matt 18:16).

268. White, "Fellowship of Believers," 1.

269. White, "Fellowship of Believers," 2.

figure" if one views the Palace Beautiful as the only image of the church to be found in *The Pilgrim's Progress*, but this is far from the case. Christian was not alone on his pilgrimage. He was helped along by pastoral figures and Christian friends, many of whom represent real people found within the congregation of the Bedford Church.[270]

For Bunyan, the church was essential to individual faith and salvation. Pilgrims do not make it to the Celestial City without the means of grace supplied through the ministry of a particular/visible church. Everything in Bunyan's doctrine of the church was informed by the fundamental aim of aiding individual faith and salvation by promoting evangelical faith and holiness. The particular/visible church is the assembly of all those professing faith and holiness, covenanted together to promote the same. The reason for Bunyan's separation from the Church of England was its inability to promote faith and holiness, yet the unity of all true believers compelled Bunyan to hold communion with all who possessed evangelical faith and holiness, regardless of differences of opinion on "circumstantial matters" like baptism. The membership of a particular/visible church must be confined only to the regenerate, else faith and holiness suffer. To the particular/visible church is granted the responsibility of promoting faith and holiness in the lives of sinners through evangelization, and in the lives of saints through edification. The reason Bunyan insisted upon congregational polity is because ecclesiastical hierarchy hinders the promotion of faith and holiness. Furthermore, the gifts of the Spirit are given to the congregation for the edification (increase of faith and holiness) of the saints. The officers of the church lead the congregation in promoting faith and holiness by teaching, watching, guiding, guarding, and caring for the saints. The means of promoting faith and holiness are found in the worship and ordinances of the church, in preaching and prayer, in baptism and the Lord's Supper. Finally, the faith and holiness of the church is guarded through the careful exercise of congregational discipline.

---

270. White acknowledges, "Partly, no doubt, the idea of a personal pilgrimage made the possibility of a community in pilgrimage difficult to handle," but then claims that "the strange disjunction between Bunyan's own experience and that of his pilgrim has a more fundamental explanation [i.e., the 'deep cleft' noted above]" (White, "Fellowship of Believers," 2). This critique of White's portrait of "the lonely pilgrim" is first suggested in Archer, "Like Flowers in the Garden," 280–93, esp. 287–88, 292. Archer writes, "Bunyan the Christian was ever Bunyan the Churchman. In his earlier preaching ministry Bunyan did not set out solely to win converts but to make disciples who would find their place in the local church" (280).

The promotion of evangelical faith and holiness was the controlling principle in Bunyan's ecclesiology. And in the 1670s, it brought him into irreconcilable conflict with the Baptists, whose own controlling principle of ecclesiological purity led them to a different conclusion regarding the relationship between baptism and church communion.

Chapter 4

Bunyan vs. the Baptists: The Communion Controversy

Baptism makes thee no member of the Church, neither particular nor universall: neither doth it make thee a visible Saint: It therefore gives thee neither right to, nor being of membership at all.[1]

The Origin of the Controversy

ON NOVEMBER 24, 1671, the Bedford Church considered the question of whether to appoint John Bunyan to the office of elder.[2] By this time, Bunyan had distinguished himself as a popular preacher, a prolific writer, and a powerful voice for persecuted Nonconformists in post-Restoration England. Though officially imprisoned from the time of his arrest on November 12, 1660, Bunyan enjoyed sporadic periods of relative freedom during his nearly twelve-year incarceration, as indicated by his appearance in the *Minutes* in the years 1661 and 1668–1672.[3] Bunyan was already performing pastoral functions within the church at the time of his appointment,

---

1. Bunyan, *Confession of My Faith*, 4:164.

2. "The Church was also minded to seeke God about the choyce of brother Bunyan to the office of an elder, that their way in that respect might be cleared up to them" (*Minutes*, 70).

3. For Bunyan's account of his arrest and trials, see Bunyan, *Relation of the Imprisonment*, 98–122. For Bunyan's involvement in church activities during his imprisonment, see *Minutes*, 37 [1661], 39–73 [1668–1672].

including writing letters on behalf of the congregation and admonishing wayward members.[4] It was therefore natural, especially given the liberties he enjoyed toward the end of his imprisonment, that the congregation should appoint him as an elder, which they did on January 21, 1672, two months before the Declaration of Indulgence and at least four months before Bunyan's release.[5]

It was his concern for the safety and welfare of the flock over which he would soon be appointed an elder that provoked Bunyan in late 1671 to launch the first salvo in his controversy with the Baptists: *A Confession of My Faith, and a Reason of My Practice*.[6] Bunyan wrote in his 1673 follow-up, *Differences in Judgment about Water-Baptism, No Bar to Communion*:

---

4. For Bunyan's authorship of the congregational letters found in the *Minutes*, see Davies, "Spirit in the Letters," 331.

5. "After much seeking God by prayer, and sober conference formerly had, the congregation did at this meeting with joynt consent (signifyed by solemne lifting up their hands) call forth and appoint our brother John Bunyan to the pastorall office or eldership. And he accepting therof gave up himself to serve Christ and his church in that charge, received of the elders the right hand of fellowship" (*Minutes*, 71). There is a difference of opinion regarding the dates inscribed in the minutes. H. G. Tibbutt's transcription of the *Minutes* explains, "In common with early records of other Nonconformist and Quaker causes there are in the earlier minutes in this volume references to 'First Month,' 'Second Month,' etc. In this context, 'First Month' is 'April,' the second is 'May' and the last, or 'Twelfth month' is 'March.' For this dating see the entry of 26 February 1674 with its description of the '11 month called February'" (*Minutes*, 7). John Brown's biography agrees with this schema, placing Bunyan's appointment as elder of the Bedford Church on January 21, 1672 (Brown, *John Bunyan*, 228). Greaves, however, dates the event to December 21, 1671. The same discrepancy of one month occurs elsewhere in Greaves's work, for instance when he dates Bunyan's reception of Edward Fowler's *The Design of Christianity*, which Bunyan said occurred on "the 13th of this 11th month," as January 13, 1672 rather than February 13, 1672 (Greaves, *Glimpses of Glory*, 271, 287–88). This monograph will follow the dating schema presented by Tibbutt, in which the "first month" of the church year corresponds to April of the calendar year.

6. Greaves dates the composition of *A Confession of My Faith* to October–December 1671, published in early 1672 (Greaves, *Glimpses of Glory*, 638). This date is based upon two lines of internal evidence. First, *A Confession of My Faith* must have preceded Bunyan's *A Defence of the Doctrine of Justification*, his response to Edward Fowler's *The Design of Christianity*, because *A Confession of My Faith* is among Bunyan's works listed in an appendix to *A Defence of the Doctrine of Justification*. In *A Defence of the Doctrine of Justification*, Bunyan stated that he obtained Fowler's work on "the 13*th* of this 11*th* Month [February 13, 1672]," and completed it "*From Prison, the* 27. *of the* 12 *Month.* 1671 [March 27th, 1672]" (Bunyan, *Defence of the Doctrine of Justification*, 4:10, 11). Second, Bunyan concluded his dedicatory epistle in *A Confession of My Faith*, "Thine in Bonds for the Gospel" (Bunyan, *Confession of My Faith*, 4:136). Bunyan likely obtained his release from prison in May 1672, and thus, *A Confession of My Faith* must have been composed prior to that date. See Greaves, *Glimpses of Glory*, 287–88.

> Be intreated to believe me, I had not set Pen to Paper about this Controversie, had we been let alone at quiet in our Christian Communion. But being assaulted for more than sixteen years; wherein the Brethren of the Baptized-way (as they had their opportunity) have sought to break us in pieces, meerly because we are not in their way all baptized first: I could not, I durst not, forbear to do a little, if it might be, to settle the Brethren, and to arm them against the attempts, which also of late they begin to revive upon us.[7]

A few pages later, Bunyan again stated:

> And even *now*, before I go any further, I will give you a touch of the Reason of my publishing that part thereof you so hotly oppose.
>
> It was because of those continual Assaults that the rigid Brethren of your way, made, not only upon this Congregation, to rend it; but also upon many others about us: if peradventure they might break us in pieces, and draw from us Disciples after them.
>
> Assaults (I say) upon this Congregation by times, for no less than these sixteen or eighteen years....
>
> Now, Sir, to settle the Brethren (the Brethren of our Community) and to prevent such disorders among others, was the cause of my publishing my Papers.[8]

Bunyan's reference to "these sixteen or eighteen years" coincides with two events noted in the minutes of the meeting of the Bedford Church on June 28, 1656: "Our brother Cromp desires to stay still upon the account of baptisme.... Our sister Linford having upon the account of baptisme, (as she pretended) withdrawn from the congregation, was required to be at this meeting to render a reason for her so doing, but being come, shee refused so to doe her self alone, unles shee had her husband and another with her."[9] The reference to Brother Cromp desiring to "stay still upon the account of baptisme" likely means that he decided he would not make an issue of baptism, which would have been a clear violation of the founding principles of the Bedford Church. Sister Linford was not willing to "stay still," and likely withdrew from the congregation because of its open-communion stance, perhaps the result of Baptist influence. That the question

---

7. Bunyan, *Differences in Judgment*, 4:193.

8. Bunyan, *Differences in Judgment*, 4:196–97 (see also 4:248; *Peaceable Principles and True*, 4:271). Evidently, the proselytizing efforts of the Baptists had not been in vain. "Neither did they altogether fail of their purpose, for some they did rent and dismember from us; but none but those, of whom they begin to be ashamed" (Bunyan, *Differences in Judgment*, 4:197).

9. *Minutes*, 22.

of baptism occupied the attention of the Bedford Church throughout this period is evident from the 1655 letter written by the dying John Gifford in which he implored the church to maintain its open-communion position, an unnecessary plea if Gifford did not sense their convictions were under attack.[10] Nor were these 1656 references isolated events, for Bunyan referred to "continual assaults" made by the Baptists, not only upon the Bedford Church, but upon the network of open-communion churches in and around Bedfordshire, a network Bunyan was eager to expand with the twenty-five "Congregationall" licenses for which he applied on behalf of his like-minded brethren in May 1672.[11] The time had come to state and defend his open-communion principles in print, thus igniting a controversy that helped to define the boundaries of seventeenth-century Baptist ecclesiology.

The Works of the Controversy

This chapter will analyze the seven extant works that emerged out of the communion controversy, and then synthesize seven essential points at which Bunyan deviated from the ecclesiology of his Baptist opponents. This analysis will reveal that the difference between Bunyan and the Baptists on the relationship of baptism to church communion was neither superficial nor a matter of semantics, but symptomatic of a deep ecclesiological divide. Differing conceptions of the nature, worship, and composition of the visible church drove each side to their respective positions. But beneath all such considerations lay fundamentally different views on the purpose of the visible church. Is the church's fundamental aim the display of evangelical unity, or of ecclesiological purity? Their respective answers to this question revealed the unbridgeable chasm between Bunyan and the Baptists.

A Confession of My Faith, and a Reason of My Practice

To whom this first published foray in the communion controversy was addressed remains a mystery. The dedicatory epistle opens simply with "Sir."[12] The epistle is a brief but vigorous defense of Bunyan's dissent from the established Church. Bunyan wrote,

---

10. *Minutes*, 19.

11. A transcription of the application is found in Brown, *John Bunyan*, 232–33.

12. Bunyan, *Confession of My Faith*, 4:135.

> Indeed my principles are such, as lead me to a denial to communicate in the things of the Kingdom of Christ, with ungodly and openly prophane; neither can I in, or by the superstitious inventions of this world, consent that my Soul should be governed, in any of my approaches to God, because commanded to the contrary, and commended for so refusing. Wherefore excepting this one thing, for which I ought not to be rebuked; I shall I trust in despite of slander and falsehood, discover myself at all times a peaceable, and an obedient Subject. But if nothing will do, unless I make of my conscience a continual butchery, and slaughter-shop, unless putting out my own eyes I commit me to the blind to lead me, (as I doubt is desired by some) I have determined, the Almighty God being my help, and shield, yet to suffer, if frail life might continue so long, even till the moss shall grow on mine eye-browes rather then thus to violate my faith and principles.[13]

Such statements are unnecessary if addressed to a fellow Nonconformist. No Baptist needed to be convinced of the principle of religious liberty or regenerate church membership. No Baptist would encourage Bunyan to conform to the established Church in order to secure his freedom.[14] Nevertheless, well over half the treatise is a defense of open communion, which could only be relevant to a Baptist. Add to this the evidence cited above of Bunyan's statements in *Differences in Judgment about Water-Baptism* about his purpose in writing, and it appears that either the treatise is addressed to a Baptist who assumed that Bunyan's lengthy imprisonment was due to some gross doctrinal heterodoxy, or else the "Sir" is a rhetorical device and not an actual recipient.[15] In either case, Bunyan's Baptist

---

13. Bunyan, *Confession of My Faith*, 4:136.

14. "I Marvail not that both your self, and others do think my long Imprisonment strange (or rather strangely of me for the sake of that) for verily I should also have done it my self, had not the Holy Ghost long since forbidden me" (Bunyan, *Confession of My Faith*, 4:135).

15. Greaves writes that Bunyan's epistle, written "to an unidentified man who had questioned his lengthy imprisonment, suggests an external target, at least in part. This hypothesis is strengthened by the fact that the book's main thrust is a defense of those nonconformists who refused to make water-baptism a condition of church membership and communion" (Greaves, *Glimpses of Glory*, 271–72). Brown, on the other hand, suggested that the intended audience was those who had the power to set him free: "It was written in the early part of 1672, at the end of his imprisonment, and its main purpose was to vindicate his teaching, and, if possible, to secure his liberty" (Brown, *John Bunyan*, 239).

opponents assumed it was addressed to them, and it provoked a decade of furious controversy.

The first portion of the treatise is an orthodox, if somewhat idiosyncratic, confession of the Protestant faith.[16] It contains nine articles on theology/Christology, justification, election, calling, faith, repentance, love, the Scriptures, and the magistracy.[17] There is nothing in its pages that a Particular Baptist would find objectionable.[18] Indeed, there is nothing to which an Anglican subscribing to the Thirty-Nine Articles should have objected, save perhaps the final line with its call to conscientious dissent: "Many are the mercyes we receive, by a well qualified Magistrate, and if any shall at any time be otherwise inclined, *let us shew our christianity in a patient suffering for well doing, what it shall please God to inflict by them.*"[19] Conspicuously missing from Bunyan's *Confession* is an article on the church.

Bunyan's ecclesiological concerns are addressed in the second portion of the treatise, which is divided into two sections: "*With whom I dare not hold communion,*" and "*With whom I dare.*"[20] In the first section, Bunyan defended the Nonconformist principle of separation. "Now, Then, I

---

16. It is intriguing to note that a quarter-century after the publication of the Westminster Standards, Bunyan did not model his *Confession* upon the Westminster Confession, as did the Congregationalists in the Savoy Declaration (1658) and the Baptists in the Second London Baptist Confession (1677/1689). Bunyan was undoubtedly familiar with the Westminster Confession; therefore, this is likely another example of Bunyan's fierce assertion of doctrinal independence. "True, I have not for these things fished in other mens *Waters*, my Bible and Concordance are my only Library in my writings" (Bunyan, *Solomon's Temple Spiritualiz'd*, 7:9).

17. Only one edition of *A Confession of My Faith* was published during Bunyan's lifetime, and only two copies are extant. Intriguingly, the article on the magistracy does not occur in one of the two original copies. T. L. Underwood suggests that "some changes were apparently made during production, for the copy at Union Theological Seminary in New York City contains a paragraph which is not in the Manchester Central Library copy" (Underwood, *Miscellaneous Works of John Bunyan*, 4:133). See also Greaves, *Glimpses of Glory*, 273n26.

18. However, as noted below, the General Baptist John Denne found the pervasive Calvinism of Bunyan's *Confession* abhorrent.

19. Bunyan, *Confession of My Faith*, 4:153.

20. Bunyan, *Confession of My Faith*, 4:154. Bunyan defined what he meant by "communion": "Only, first, Note, that by the word Communion, I mean fellowship *in the things of the Kingdom of Christ*, or that which is commonly called Church communion, the Communication of Saints" (4:154). For Bunyan, as well as the other participants in this debate, "communion" referred to admission to both membership and the Lord's Supper. In the seventeenth century, the terms of membership and communion were one and the same.

dare not have communion with them that profess not faith and holiness; or that are not visible Saints by calling. . . . Now he that is visibly or openly prophane, cannot then be a visible Saint, for he that is a visible Saint must profess faith, and repentance, and consequently holyness of life: And with none else dare I communicate."[21] Faith and holiness are the marks of a visible saint; thus, a profession of faith made visible and credible by a life of holiness were Bunyan's terms of communion. Bunyan defended this principle with seven arguments that represent the standard Nonconformist defense of separation.[22]

The second section ignited the firestorm as Bunyan loaded his cannon with arguments in favor of open communion and blasted them in the direction of the Baptists. Bunyan's thesis was that not only are faith and holiness essential terms of communion, they are the *only* terms of communion. "*Baptism makes thee no member of the Church, neither particular nor universall: neither doth it make thee a visible Saint: It therefore gives thee neither right to, nor being of membership at all.*"[23] Baptism is not the initiating ordinance into the church; rather, a church should examine candidates for membership by their profession of faith, their experience of conversion, and their godly conversation conforming to the Ten Commandments, the "moral duties gospelized," the "moral precept evangelized."[24]

> Now that which by Christ is made the door of entrance into the Church, by that we may doubtless enter; and seeing Baptism is not that ordinance, we ought not to seek to enter thereby, but may with good conscience enter without it.

21. Bunyan, *Confession of My Faith*, 4:154. Bunyan added, "But note that by this assertion, I meddle not with the elect; but as he is a visible Saint by calling; neither do I exclude the secret Hypocrite, *if he be hid from me by visible Saint ship*" (4:154). Bunyan refused to pry into the hidden decree of God's election, or the invisible nature of saving faith. When it comes to communion, the visible church is concerned only with visible sainthood.

22. These seven arguments are stated in chapter 3 of this monograph under the discussion of regenerate church membership (the unity of the church).

23. Bunyan, *Confession of My Faith*, 4:164.

24. "And if Churches after the confession of faith, made more use of the ten commandments, to judge of the fitness of persons by; they might not exceed by this seeming strictness christian tenderness towards them, they receive to communion. I will say therefore, that by the word of faith and of good works, moral duties Gospelized; we ought to judge of the fitness of members by, by which we ought also to receive them into fellowship. . . . Therefore I say, the rule by which we receive Church-members; it is the word of the Faith of Christ, and of the moral precept Evangelized" (Bunyan, *Confession of My Faith*, 4:165–66).

Quest. But by what rule, then would you gather persons into Church-communion?

Answ. Even by that rule, by which they are discovered to the Church to be visible Saints; and willing to be gathered into their body and fellowship. By that word of God therefore, by which their Faith, experience, and conversation (being examined) is found Good; by that the Church should receive them into fellowship with them.[25]

Anyone can be baptized; holiness, on the other hand, cannot easily be counterfeited. "And when men have juggled what they can, and made never such a prattle about religion; yet if their greatest excellency, as to the visibility of their Saintship, lyeth in an outward conformity, to an outward circumstance in religion; their profession is not worth two mites."[26] Furthermore, the New Testament lacks an explicit precept making baptism the initiating ordinance into the New Testament church, nor does the New Testament comprehend the situation in Bunyan's day in which there was so much "darkness" surrounding the ordinance. And as none ought to be baptized apart from "light," it is therefore wrong to deny membership to those still in the dark regarding this "shaddowish, or figurative" ordinance.[27]

Bunyan supported this thesis with ten arguments:

1. The true visible saint possesses the righteousness of God through faith in Christ, whether or not he is baptized.[28]

2. The true visible saint has been baptized by the Spirit, whether or not he has been baptized in water, and this is a sufficient basis for church unity. Bunyan based this argument upon his reading of Ephesians 4:4–6, regarding the baptism there spoken of as the baptism of the Spirit rather than baptism in water.[29]

---

25. Bunyan, *Confession of My Faith*, 4:164–65.

26. Bunyan, *Confession of My Faith*, 4:168–69.

27. "But they could not render a bigger reason than this. *I have no light therein*: which is the cause at this day that many a faithful man denyeth to take up the ordinance of Baptism, But I say what ever the hindrance was, it mattereth not; our brethren have a manifest one, an invincible one, one that all the men on earth nor Angels in heaven can remove: *For it is God that createth light*; and for them to do it without light would but prove them unfaithfull to themselves, and make them sinners against God; *For whatsoever is not of Faith is sin*" (Bunyan, *Confession of My Faith*, 4:170). For baptism as a "shaddowish, or figurative" ordinance, see Bunyan, *Confession of My Faith*, 4:160.

28. Bunyan, *Confession of My Faith*, 4:171.

29. Bunyan, *Confession of My Faith*, 4:171.

3. The true visible saint has the "doctrine of baptisms" (i.e., the substance which baptism signifies), whether or not he is baptized.[30]

4. God has communion with the true visible saint, regardless of baptism. The church dares not reject one whom God has accepted. "*God hath received him, Christ hath received him*, therefore do you receive him."[31]

5. Failure to be baptized "doth not unchristian us." Bunyan practically dared his opponents to question the sincerity and faith of the martyrs who populated the pages of his beloved *Acts and Monuments*: "This must needs be granted, not onely from what was said before; but for that thousands of thousands that could not consent thereto, as we, have more gloriously, then we are like to do, acquitted themselves and their Christianity before men, and are now with the innumerable company of Angels, and with spirits of just men made perfect."[32]

6. The "edification of Souls in the Faith and holyness of the Gospell," is of greater importance than "an agreement in outward things," such as baptism. Those who disagreed, Bunyan accused of a lack of charity: "But to contest with gracious men, men that walk with God; to shut such out of the Churches; because they will not sin against their Souls, rendereth thee uncharitable."[33]

7. Love is of greater importance than baptism. "*Love is also more discovered when it receiveth for the sake of Christ, and grace; then when it*

---

30. "For here you must note, I distinguish between the doctrin and practise of Water-baptism; The Doctrin being that which by the outward sign is presented to us, or which by the outward circumstance of the act is preached to the believer: *viz. The death of Christ; My death with Christ; also his resurrection from the Dead, and mine with him to newness of life.* This is the doctrin which Baptism preacheth, or that which by the outward action is signifyed to the believing receiver. Now, I say, he that believeth in Jesus Christ; that [hath] richer and better than that, *viz.* is dead to sin, and that lives to God by him, he hath the heart, power, and doctrine of Baptism: all then that he wanteth, is but the sign, the shadow, the outward circumstance thereof" (Bunyan, *Confession of My Faith*, 4:172).

31. Bunyan, *Confession of My Faith*, 4:173. "I am bold to hold communion with visible Saints as afore [described]; because God hath communion with them; whose example in the case, we are streightly commanded to follow" (4:172).

32. Bunyan, *Confession of My Faith*, 4:174. Foxe's *Acts and Monuments* was one of the few books Bunyan possessed in prison. He quoted from or alluded to it at least fourteen times in his writings. On Bunyan's love for and use of Foxe's *Acts and Monuments*, see Pooley, "Bunyan's Reading," 114–16.

33. Bunyan, *Confession of My Faith*, 4:175–76.

refuseth for want of Water.... It is Love, not Baptism that discovereth us to the world to be Christs Disciples."[34]

8. The apostle Paul rebuked the church at Corinth for dividing over baptism, calling them "*carnal, and the actors herein babyish Christians.*"[35]

9. To deny true visible saints the privileges of church communion is to deprive the children of God of their birthright.[36]

10. To deny church communion to a visible saint is to heap the greatest contempt upon him. Bunyan accused his opponents of hypocrisy for being willing to "pray and Preach with these, and hold them Christians, Saints, and Godly," and yet "not count them meet for other Gospel priviledges."[37]

Bunyan closed his treatise with a brief exhortation to separate from the openly profane, but to unite with the visible saint: "I return now to those that are visible Saints by Calling, that stand at a distance one from another, upon the accounts before specifyed: Brethren: Close; Close; Be one as the Father and Christ is one."[38]

---

34. Bunyan, *Confession of My Faith*, 4:177–78. Bunyan continued, "It is Love that is the undoubted character of our interest in, and sonship with God: I mean when we Love as Saints, and desire communion with others, because they have fellowship with God the Father, and his Son Jesus Christ" (4:178).

35. Bunyan, *Confession of My Faith*, 4:179. "Ah Brethren! Carnall Christians with outward circumstances, will if they be let alone, make sad work in the Churches of Christ, against spiritual growth of the same" (4:180).

36. Bunyan, *Confession of My Faith*, 4:182–83. It is under this heading that Bunyan wrote, "Shall I add, Is it not that which greatly prevailed to bring down these judgments, which at present we feel and groan under; I will dare to say, it was *the* cause thereof" (italics added). However, Bunyan explained elsewhere that this was a typographical error: "*A*, was in my Copy, instead whereof the Printer put in *the*; for this, although I speak only the truth, I will not beg of you belief; besides, the Bookseller desired me, because of the Printers haste, to leave the last sheet to be over-looked by him, which was the cause it was not among the Errata's" (Bunyan, *Differences in Judgment*, 4:233). This line, erroneously printed though it was, incensed Bunyan's Baptist opponents. Thomas Paul called it "one of the most Prodigiousest Sentence that ever I heard pass from the Mouth, or fall under the Pen, of the worst of Truths Enemies" (Paul, *Some Serious Reflections*, 3). Paul later added, "Sir, who made you so privy to the secrets of Gods Judgements, that you must assign this alone, as the cause of (not some but) all the Judgements that have befallen us?" (43).

37. Bunyan, *Confession of My Faith*, 4:183.

38. Bunyan, *Confession of My Faith*, 4:186.

Bunyan vs. the Baptists

Some Serious Reflections on that Part of Mr. Bunion's Confession of Faith

Bunyan's *A Confession of My Faith* provoked an immediate and incendiary response from the London Baptist Thomas Paul. A Particular Baptist and likely member of William Kiffin's Devonshire Square congregation, Paul published *Some Serious Reflections on that Part of Mr. Bunion's Confession of Faith* early in 1673, to which Kiffin contributed a preface.[39] In his preface, Kiffin charged Bunyan with theological novelty, stating that Bunyan had argued for "A Doctrine not known or practiced in the first Gospel Churches, or by any others of what perswasion ever, that have professed Christian Faith, since that time to this very age."[40] Furthermore, he accused Bunyan of logical inconsistency:

> If this Argument be good (as I believe it is) that causeth him to forsake the practice of Baptizing Children; why should it not be as good at least to him in the case in hand? but to cause in him the same belief, that none ought to be admitted to the Lords Supper, but such as are Baptized with Water, seeing there cannot be shown any Precept [text illegible] or Example in the Scriptures that any Unbaptized-person was ever admitted to the Lords Supper.[41]

Finally, Kiffin expressed his "Honour and Reverence" to those "many faithful Christians that differ from us, who notwithstanding value this Ordinance of Christ, only mistake the subject, and are far from placing Religion only in this or any other institution of Christ; but finding the Scriptures shew no other Rule in the Order of instituted Worship, then upon believing, to be first Baptized, then added to the Church, we dare not be wise above what is Written."[42]

---

39. Thomas Paul published a second reply to Bunyan's *Differences in Judgment about Water-Baptism* in late 1673 or early 1674 that is no longer extant. Paul's affiliation with Kiffin's Devonshire Square Particular Baptist Church is based upon two lines of circumstantial evidence: first, that Kiffin wrote a preface to *Some Serious Reflections* suggests such an affiliation; second, Paul was not a signatory of either the 1644 or 1689 London Baptist Confessions, suggesting that he was not a pastor of a Baptist church in either of those years. Greaves agrees that Paul was "probably a member of Kiffin's church" (Greaves, *Glimpses of Glory*, 291).

40. Kiffin, "Epistle to the Reader," in Paul, *Some Serious Reflections*, A3.

41. Kiffin, "Epistle to the Reader," in Paul, *Some Serious Reflections*, A3–A4.

42. Kiffin, "Epistle to the Reader," in Paul, *Some Serious Reflections*, A5.

The controversy may have died with Bunyan's *Confession* and Paul's response had Paul not adopted an insulting and elitist tone to which Bunyan took offense.[43] Yet despite his inflammatory rhetoric, Paul provided the most substantive critique of Bunyan's views in the entire controversy. Paul started by setting the record straight as to what the Baptists actually believe: "Your great noise about an Initiating Ordinance, wherein you spend time enough, I shall take no notice of, I know none that assert it to be the Inlet into perticular Churches, though it prepares them for Reception: It's consent ON all hands, and nothing else, that makes them Members of this or that perticular Church, and not Faith and Baptism."[44] Paul then adduced some of the strongest arguments in the Baptist arsenal. Bunyan had posed the question, by what rule should persons be received into church fellowship? And he had answered, "Even by a discovery of their faith and holiness; *and their declaration of willingness to subject themselves to the laws and government of Christ in his Church.*"[45] Paul pounced, exposing one of the weaknesses in Bunyan's position: "And pray you tell me, is obeying Baptism, no part of a Christians Holiness? is Baptism none of the Laws of Christ, the Law-giver? must this, with others have no place of discovery? but must it altogether be shut out from being a witness to the truth of Faith?"[46] Another strong argument was Paul's rebuttal of Bunyan's assertion that a person ought not receive baptism without "light," that it is God that gives light, and therefore that an unbaptized believer ought to be received into church communion: "Is it a Persons light, that gives being to a Precept? is it not his sin, though he want light? . . . Suppose

43. Paul opened his work by stating, "Should all of your rank, take occasion to tell the World what they do, and do not believe or practice, it might give them more imployment then they can or need to attend: I should little have troubled my self, to take notice of the rest of your offers, in your Confession, had you not under the head before expressed, shewed your self so bold to assert that which is unproved; neither should I have medled with the controversie at all, had I found any, of parts, that would divert themselves from more weighty occasions, to take notice of you" (Paul, *Some Serious Reflections*, 1–2). Bunyan responded, "In that you closely disdain my Person, because of my *low* descent among men, stigmatizing me for a Person of THAT Rank, that *need* not to be heeded, or attended unto. . . . What need you, before you have shewed one syllable of a reasonable Argument in opposition to what I Assert, thus trample my Person, my Gifts, and Grace (have I any) so disdainfully under your feet? What kind of a YOU am I? And why is MY Rank so mean, that the *most* gracious and godly among you, may not duly and soberly consider of what I have said?" (Bunyan, *Differences in Judgment*, 4:195–96).

44. Paul, *Some Serious Reflections*, 3–4.

45. Bunyan, *Confession of My Faith*, 4:162.

46. Paul, *Some Serious Reflections*, 5–6.

men plead want of light in other Commands, must they be excused?"[47] A third strong argument in Paul's introduction regarded Bunyan's assertion that the New Testament contains no precept declaring that baptism must precede church communion. Bunyan had written, "That Water-baptism hath formerly gone first is granted: But that it ought of necessity so to do, I never saw proof."[48] Paul responded, "But sir, pray you tell us, in your next, whether any of those you mean, were Unbaptized beleivers, that were concerned in those Epistles: forasmuch as you confess, in those times Baptism followed immediately upon Conversion: if they were not Unbaptized Believers, it is without our question."[49] In other words, the New Testament does not contain an explicit precept requiring baptism in order to church communion, because no such a precept was necessary, for all to whom the letters were written were already baptized.

Paul then responded point-for-point to Bunyan's ten arguments for open communion.

1. Paul did not address the main point of Bunyan's first argument.[50] Rather, he took Bunyan to task for insinuating that baptism could ever be a pest or plague to the people of God, and therefore ought to be shunned. "Is this the best Title you can give to one of Christs Commands? did God ever send an Ordinance, as a Pest and Plague to his People? are not all the Ordinances of the Gospel Blessings?"[51]

2. The baptism referenced in Ephesians 4:5 is not the baptism of the Spirit but water baptism, for the apostle had already mentioned the

---

47. Paul, *Some Serious Reflections*, 7.
48. Bunyan, *Confession of My Faith*, 4:169.
49. Paul, *Some Serious Reflections*, 9–10.
50. Bunyan took notice of this fact: "And now *Reader*, although this Author hath thus objected against *some* passages in this my first Argument for Communion with Persons unbaptized; yet the *body* of my Argument he misseth, and passeth over, as a thing not worth the Answering; whether because he forgot, or because he was conscious to himself, that he knew not what to do therewith, I will not now determine" (Bunyan, *Differences in Judgment*, 4:206–7).
51. Paul, *Some Serious Reflections*, 10–11. Paul was referring to Bunyan's statement: "Again; if Water-baptism, as the circumstances with which the Churches were pestered of old, trouble their peace, wound the consciences of the Godly; dismember and break their fellowships, it is although an ordinance for the present to be prudently shunned" (Bunyan, *Confession of My Faith*, 4:171).

Spirit as one of the church's foundations for unity in v. 4, and to mention the Spirit again would be redundant.[52]

3. The doctrine of baptism cannot be separated from the practice of baptism. This severing of the sign from the thing signified was not permissible in the typological worship of the Old Testament, and neither is it permissible in the New Testament antitype. Furthermore, the true doctrine of baptism is the command of Christ to be baptized in his name.[53] "Who taught you to devide between Christ and his Precepts?"[54]

4. Romans 14–15 was written to those already baptized and in church communion, and therefore does not apply to the matter at hand. The issues at stake in that passage relate to matters of indifference in Old Testament law, not to a New Testament ordinance such as baptism. Furthermore, God receives sinners on the basis of faith, but churches must receive them on the basis of fruit, namely, obedience to Christ's ordinances.[55]

5. To Bunyan's claim that failure in baptism "doth not unchristian" a man, Paul retorted,

---

52. "If *Paul* intended Spirit Baptism, in this place, as the last thing he urgeth upon them, for Union: what doth he mean by Spirit and Faith, which are urged before by him, as Arguments?" (Paul, *Some Serious Reflections*, 14).

53. "This is one of the strangest Paradoxes that I have lightly observed; is it enough to hold practical Doctrines, to know them so as to hold them, and yet not do them?" (Paul, *Some Serious Reflections*, 15). Paul also took issue with Bunyan referring to baptism as an "outward circumstance": "From whom have you Authority to nick-name any of Christ's precepts? is this according to the form of sound words? will you be wise above what is written, and call Commands Circumstances, only meer shews? do you pretend your self a Minister of the Gospel, and dare you thus disparage Gospel truths by such low Titles, to discharge men of their obedience to them? Verily Sir, what ever you think of your self, I am confident Christ will not take this well at your hands" (18).

54. Paul, *Some Serious Reflections*, 19.

55. Paul, *Some Serious Reflections*, 20–22. Also under this section, Paul took the opportunity to register his complaint regarding Bunyan's depiction of the Baptists as "vain" men ("Is this the best Title you have for them?") who imagine that by the "straightness of thine Order in outward and bodily Conformity to outward & shadowish Circumstances" ("I never knew straightness in Order to be a crime, but rather a praise") to have peace with God ("But you say our peace is not maintained hereby, but by the Blood of the Cross: I know our peace is made for us by the Blood of Christ's Cross, but is not our peace maintained and kept alive in the way of obedience?") (22–23).

Who saith it doth? Persons ought to be Christians before they are Baptized; and once a Christian, and always a Christian: but in pursuit of this Argument you are pleased to rank Water-Baptism with eating, or not eating, that if a man do it, he is not the better, or neglect it, he is not the worse.

Verily Sir, if Gospel-Precepts must be ranked with Old Testament Ceremonies that are abrogated by the death of Christ, I know not upon what account you practice instituted Worship now, unless upon the same account as *Paul* practiced Circumcision upon *Timothy*, or shaving on others, not as a Command from God, but as a prudential consideration as to others, which is below that confession, or profession, that hitherto you have made about Baptism.[56]

6. To Bunyan's assertion that edification is superior to baptism, Paul asked, What could be more edifying than to obey Christ's ordinances?[57]

7. To Bunyan's claim that love is greater than baptism, Paul queried, What could be more loving than to aid a brother in his obedience to Christ by refusing to countenance his neglect of baptism?[58]

8. The divisions mentioned in the Corinthian letter did not pertain to exclusions from the church, but to divisions within the church. Baptism was not the cause of division (for all in the church were baptized); false apostles were the cause of division. Furthermore, the apostle cannot be said to have belittled the importance of baptism when he said he could not remember who he had baptized, or that the Lord had not

---

56. Paul, *Some Serious Reflections*, 25.

57. "But you say Edification is greater than consenting to Water-Baptism: To which I answer, I had thought that a Preaching and opening Baptism, might have been reckoned as a part of our Edification" (Paul, *Some Serious Reflections*, 27). "Why may you not as well say that Edification is greater then breaking Bread? then any part of Church rule, or Government? and so at once shut out all instituted Worship?" (25). "Is not the least of truths worth contending for?" (27–28).

58. "But must our love to these, indulge them in any act of disobedience? cannot we love their Persons, Parts, Graces, but we must love their Sins, and disorders? I take it to be the highest act of friendship to be faithful to these professors, and to tell them they want this one thing in Gospel order, which ought not to be left undone; and I doubt your favour towards them, in descrying before them one of Christs Commands, as a Circumstance, meer shew, that that may, or may not be done; for which we are neither better nor worse (in your sence) making it no more than eating, or not eating, as men are perswaded: Is this your faithfulness to your friends, that you pretend so much love to? I doubt when it comes to be weighed in God's Balance, it will be found no less than Flattery, for which you will be reproved" (Paul, *Some Serious Reflections*, 30–31).

The Palace Beautiful

sent him to baptize but to preach. Could Bunyan remember everyone he had baptized? Does the apostle's emphasis upon his preaching ministry by necessity denigrate the importance of baptism?[59]

9. To deny church communion to the unbaptized is not to deprive them of their birthright, but rather to "keep them from a disorderly practice of Gospel Ordinances: we offer them their priviledge in the way of Gospel order, as all the Scripture Saints received their Priviledges."[60]

10. The world has no authority to judge the church's rule and order; therefore, Bunyan's tenth argument—that such division causes the world to hold the church in contempt—was irrelevant.[61]

Paul followed these ten rebuttals with fourteen arguments in favor of strict communion:

1. The Great Commission, from which every minister derives his authority, clearly establishes the Gospel order: "Ministers are, first to Disciple, and then Baptize them, so made Disciples; and afterward to teach them to observe all that Christ has commanded, as to other Ordinances of Worship."[62]

2. Under the old covenant, God was severe in his punishment of those who disobeyed his prescribed order of worship. Should the new covenant church, which has the substance rather than the shadow, expect any less?[63]

3. The first gospel ministers, who drank from the fountainhead of Christ's own mouth and therefore understood best what Christ meant

---

59. Paul, *Some Serious Reflections*, 32–40.

60. Paul, *Some Serious Reflections*, 40. Under this heading, Paul also responded to the eighteen effects of strict communion which Bunyan charged to the Baptists' account: "I durst commit this cause to the worst of our Enemies, and doubt not they themselves being Judges, would clear us in the things laid to our charge; that none but your self could ever find an innocent truth, big with so many monstrous obsurdities, as you do. You have carried like one of *Machevel's* Schollers, to purpose, *Throw dirt enough, and some of it will be sure to stick*" (42).

61. "I grant, the World are in some cases Judges of our conversation; and it becomes us to carry it well in those things, wherein they are capable to be Judges: but I deny, that the World are proper Judges of the grounds of our Profession, or Communion, as to Church-fellowship" (Paul, *Some Serious Reflections*, 45).

62. Paul, *Some Serious Reflections*, 47.

63. Paul, *Some Serious Reflections*, 47–48.

in his Great Commission, did not circumvent the prescribed order, as discovered by the Acts of the Apostles.[64]

4. No "Scripture Saints" ever entered into church communion before baptism.[65]

5. If Christ was manifested as sent by God by his baptism, why should not his saints be manifested as his disciples in the same manner?[66]

6. According to Hebrews 6:1–2, baptism is among the foundations of the church, "the A B C of a Christian, and the beginnings of Christianity," and therefore ought to be placed at the beginning of the Christian life and church communion.[67]

7. The apostle Paul recognized the Galatians as the sons of God by faith by means of their baptism (Gal 3:26–27).[68]

8. Baptism is a putting on of Christ (Gal 3:27). It is the Christian's "Livery," that which makes a saint visible.[69]

9. The church at Thessalonica was commended for following the pattern set by the churches of Judea (1 Thess 2:14), which churches added only baptized believers to their communion.[70]

10. The apostle Paul's arguments from baptism found in his letters to the churches of Corinth, Galatia, Colossae, and Rome, as well as those in Peter's first epistle, are senseless if the members thereof were not baptized.[71]

11. If the unbaptized may be admitted to the church on the basis of a lack of light, then why not those who have neglected other gospel ordinances? "So then, as the Consequence of this Principle, Churches may be made up of visible Sinners, instead of visible Saints."[72]

---

64. Paul, *Some Serious Reflections*, 48–49.
65. Paul, *Some Serious Reflections*, 49.
66. Paul, *Some Serious Reflections*, 50.
67. Paul, *Some Serious Reflections*, 50.
68. Paul, *Some Serious Reflections*, 51.
69. Paul, *Some Serious Reflections*, 51–52.
70. Paul, *Some Serious Reflections*, 52–53.
71. Paul, *Some Serious Reflections*, 53–54.
72. Paul, *Some Serious Reflections*, 54.

12. Baptism is not so vague as men make it out to be. "Hath not mans wisdom interposed, to darken this part of Gods Counsel, by which professors seem willingly led, though against so many plain commands and examples, written as with a Sun beam, that he that runs may read?"[73]

13. If obedience is the evidence of faith, "why must Baptism be shut out, as if it were not part of Gospel obedience?"[74]

14. To deny the necessity of Christian baptism is to place it beneath the dignity of John's baptism. For those who received John's baptism are said to have received his doctrine, and those who rejected his baptism are said to have rejected his doctrine.[75]

These arguments represent the standard seventeenth-century Baptist defense of strict communion. Many of Paul's arguments had been made by Baptists before and would appear again in the years (and centuries) to come.[76]

Paul concluded his treatise with seven queries to Bunyan in which he accused Bunyan of pride, incivility, divisiveness, a love of conflict, and theological novelty: "Do you delight to have your hand against every man?"[77]

---

73. Paul, *Some Serious Reflections*, 55.

74. Paul, *Some Serious Reflections*, 56.

75. Paul, *Some Serious Reflections*, 56–57.

76. Two notable examples of Baptist defenses of strict communion preceding Paul's *Some Serious Reflections* are Allen, *Some Baptismal Abuses Briefly Discovered* (1654), and Lambe, *Truth Prevailing Against the Fiercest Opposition* (1654), both of which were responses to John Goodwin's *Water-Dipping No Firm Footing for Church Communion* (1653). These treatises, as well as other seventeenth-century defenses of strict communion, are examined in the following chapter.

77. Paul, *Some Serious Reflections*, 61. Regarding pride: "Ask your heart whether popularity, and applause of variety of professors, be not in the bottom of what you have said" (58). Regarding incivility, Paul accused Bunyan of refusing to speak with the London Baptists face-to-face, though he had opportunity to do so, instead attacking them in print. "Doth your carriage answer the Law of Love, or Civility, when the Brethren used means to send to you for a conference, and their Letter was received by you, that you should go out again from the City, after knowledge of their desires, and not vouchsafe a meeting with them, when the Glory of God, and the vindication of so many Churches, is concerned?" (59). Paul further complained of the Bedford Church's refusal to communicate with the London Baptist churches, though the Baptists were willing to communicate with Bedford: "Is this your way of retaliation? or are you afraid lest the truth should in this matter invade your Quarters?" (60). Regarding theological novelty, Paul asked Bunyan to consider "Whether your Principle & Practice is not equally against others, as

Bunyan vs. the Baptists

Differences in Judgment about Water-Baptism, No Bar to Communion

Shortly after the appearance of Thomas Paul's *Some Serious Reflections*, Bunyan issued a blistering response. *Differences in Judgment about Water-Baptism, No Bar to Communion* was not a new statement of Bunyan's position, but rather a point-for-point defense of his original ten arguments set forth in *A Confession of My Faith* against Paul's rebuttals, as well as responses to Paul's fourteen arguments in favor of strict communion. It is clear from the introduction that Bunyan was offended by Paul's elitist tone. "Need I reade you a Lecture? *Hath not God chosen the foolish, the weak, the base, yea and even things that are not, to bring to nought things that are?* Why then do you despise my *rank*, my *state*, and *quality* in the World."[78] Bunyan also felt Paul had questioned his motives, impugned his character, and misrepresented his views. Bunyan's tone was unapologetic and defiant.[79]

In the opening section of the treatise, Bunyan turned to the question of whether baptism is the initiating ordinance into the church. In *A Confession of My Faith*, Bunyan claimed this was the Baptist position; in *Some Serious Reflections*, Paul denied this to be the case. Bunyan thus accused Paul of being either ignorant of or insincere about the Baptist view:

> How ignorant you are of such as hold it the initiating Ordinance I know not: nor how long you have been of that perswasion I know not. This I know, that men of your own Party, as serious, godly, and it may be, more learned than your self, have within less than this twelve-month urged it. Mr. D. in my hearing, did from *Rom.* 6. 1,

well as us? *viz.* Episcopal, Presbyterian, and Independent, who are all of our side for our practice (though they differ with us about the subject of Baptism)" (61).

78. Bunyan, *Differences in Judgment*, 4:196.

79. "That I deny the Ordinance of Baptism, or that I have placed one piece of an Argument against it, (though they feign it) is quite without colour of truth. All I say is, That the Church of Christ hath not Warrant to keep out of their Communion the Christian that is discovered to be a visible Saint by the Word, the Christian that walketh according to his Light with God" (Bunyan, *Differences in Judgment*, 4:193). Bunyan also accused Paul of falling "*far short* of a candid Replication" of his views (4:195) and later repeated the accusation (4:229). To Paul's contention that Bunyan had published his confession out of a desire for fame, Bunyan responded, "If you, and the Brethren of your way, did think it convenient to shew to the World what you held; if perhaps by that means you might escape the Prison [a reference to the 1644 London Baptist Confession]: why might not I, after above 11 years indurance there, give the World a view of my Faith and Practice; if peradventure, wrong Thoughts, and false Judgments of me, might by that means be abated, and removed" (4:196).

2. in the Meeting in *Lothbury* affirm it: also my much esteemed Mr. D. A. did twice in a Conference with me Assert it.

But whatever you say, whether for, or against, 'tis no matter; for while you deny it be the entering Ordinance, you account it the Wall, Bar, Bolt, and Door; even that which must separate between the righteous and the righteous.[80]

In denying that Baptists believe baptism to be the initiating ordinance, Paul had overstated his case, claiming it was "consent ON all hands, and nothing else, that makes them Members of this or that perticular Church, and not Faith and Baptism."[81] Bunyan pounced. "What? Consent and nothing else? But why do YOU throw out FAITH?"[82] It is doubtful this was Paul's intention, but his language was incautious and provided Bunyan the opportunity to pummel the straw man and claim the doctrinal high ground. "The Church hath no such Liberty to receive men without respect to Faith; yea Faith and Holiness, must be the Essentials, or Basis, upon, and for the sake of which you receive them: Holiness (I say) yet not such as is circumstantial, but that which is such in the very heart of it."[83] Paul asked, "Is Baptism none of the Laws of Christ, the Law-giver? must this, with others have no place of discovery? but must it altogether be shut out from being a witness to the truth of Faith?"[84] Bunyan responded that although baptism is an ordinance of the church, it was not given to the church for the purpose of discovering faith and holiness. "I find not (as I told you in my first) that Baptism is a sign to any, but the Person that is baptized. The Church hath her satisfaction of the Person, from better proof."[85] That better proof is the "*Moral Duties*

---

80. Bunyan, *Differences in Judgment*, 4:198. "Mr. D." is likely Daniel Dyke, copastor of William Kiffin's Devonshire Square Church, and Mr. D. A. is likely Henry Danvers (or D'Anvers) (Greaves, *Glimpses of Glory*, 296). T. L. Underwood suggests that "Mr. D" was John Denne (Underwood, *Miscellaneous Works of John Bunyan*, 4:400).

81. Paul, *Some Serious Reflections*, 4.

82. Bunyan, *Differences in Judgment*, 4:199.

83. Bunyan, *Differences in Judgment*, 4:199. Bunyan knew he was taking advantage of Paul's incautious words, for he added, "Pray you in your next therefore word it better" (4:199). A few paragraphs later, Bunyan added a third condition to church membership: "I tell you again, That a discovery of the Faith and Holiness, and a Declaration of the willingness of a Person to subject himself to the Laws and the Government of Christ in his Church, is a ground sufficient to receive such a Member" (4:199–200).

84. Paul, *Some Serious Reflections*, 5–6.

85. Bunyan, *Differences in Judgment*, 4:200. "[Baptism] is none of those Laws, neither any part of them, that the Church, as a Church, should shew her Obedience by. For albeit that Baptism be given by Christ our Lord to the Church, yet not for them to worship him

Gospelized ... whereby we ought to judge of the fitness of Members."[86] Does not this make the Christian more beholden to Moses than to Christ, as Paul claimed? No, said Bunyan, for "the Faith of Christ, with the Ten Commandments, are as much now Gospel-Commands as Baptism," and furthermore, evangelical holiness does more to discover true faith than does baptism.[87] The other major issue of contention from Bunyan's introduction in *A Confession of My Faith* was his claim that a man ought not be baptized apart from "light." Bunyan dug in his heels, attempting to impale Paul upon the horns of a dilemma between the command to be baptized and the principle that "whatever is not of faith is sin" (Rom 14:23):

> But I will suppose a case; There is a man wants Light in Baptism, yet by his Neighbour is pressed to it: he saith he seeth it not to be his Duty; the other saith, he sins if he doth it not: Now seeing *whatsoever is not of Faith, is Sin*; what should this man do? If you say, Let him use the means: I say so too. But what, if when he hath used it, he still continueth dark about it; what will you advise him now? If you bid him wait, do you not encourage him to live in sin, as much as I do? Nay, and seeing you will not let him for want of Light in that, obey God in other his Institutions, what is it, but to say, Seeing you live for want of Light in the neglect of Baptism, we will make you, while you continue so, live (though quite against your Light) in the breach of all the rest.[88]

Having defended his introduction, Bunyan turned next to the defense of his ten arguments.

1. A point of contention under Bunyan's first argument was his claim that the New Testament epistles, most notably 1 Corinthians, James,

---

by as a Church.... Again, That submitting to Water-Baptism, is a sign or note, that was ever required by any of the Primitive Churches, of him that would hold Fellowship with them; or that it infuseth such Grace and Holiness into those that submit thereto, as to capacitate them for such a Priviledge; or that they did acknowledge it a sign thereof, I find not in all the Bible" (4:200).

86. Bunyan, *Differences in Judgment*, 4:200.

87. Bunyan, *Differences in Judgment*, 4:201. "The Church then must first look to Faith, then to good Living according to the Ten Commandments; after that she must respect those Appointments of our Lord Jesus, that respects her outward order and discipline, and then she walks as becomes her, sinning if she neglecteth either; sinning if she overvalueth either" (4:201). Bunyan stated in *A Confession of My Faith*, "A visible Saint he is, but not made so by Baptism; for he must be a visible Saint before, else he ought not to be baptized" (Bunyan, *Confession of My Faith*, 4:164).

88. Bunyan, *Differences in Judgment*, 4:203–4.

1–2 Peter, and 1 John, were not written to particular churches, but to all the saints. This was to refute a foundational point in the Baptist position, namely, that the epistles were written to churches of baptized believers, and therefore the absence of an explicit precept establishing baptism as a prerequisite for church communion could not be used in support of open communion.[89] Not only did Bunyan argue again his position with greater force, but with an impressive bit of rhetorical sleight of hand, he accused the Baptists of wresting the Scriptures away from all paedobaptists, as though the New Testament Epistles were written only to Baptist churches.[90] Bunyan likewise reasserted his position that if baptism becomes a cause of division or affliction in the church, it should be temporarily suspended.[91]

2. Bunyan provided an expanded exposition of Ephesians 4:4–6, and gave two reasons why the "one baptism" refers to the baptism of the Spirit and not to baptism in water. First, "Water-Baptism hath nothing to do in a Church, as a Church, nor is any part of our Worship when we come there; how then can the Peace and Unity of the Church depend upon Water-Baptism?"[92] Second, "That other Text [1 Cor 12:13], that treateth of our being *baptized into a body*, saith expressly it is done by the Spirit."[93]

[89] "Some indeed do object that what the Apostles wrote, they wrote to gathered Churches, and so to such as were baptized. And therefore the arguments that are in the Epistles about things circumstantial, respect not the case in hand" (Bunyan, *Confession of My Faith*, 4:171).

[90] "But I would ask these men, *If the word of God came out from them? or if it came to them only?* Or, whether Christ hath not given his *whole* Word to every one that believeth, whether they be baptized, or in, or out of Church Fellowship. . . . Would to God they had learnt more modesty, than thus to take from all others, and appropriate to themselves, and that for the sake of their observing a Circumstance in Religion, *so high*, and glorious a Privilege" (Bunyan, *Differences in Judgment*, 4:204–5).

[91] "I said not that God did send it for any such end at all [i.e., 'a Pest and Plague' upon the church]; God's Ordinances are none of this, in themselves: nor if used as, and for the end for which God sent them" (Bunyan, *Differences in Judgment*, 4:206).

[92] Bunyan, *Differences in Judgment*, 4:208. Bunyan continued, "Besides, he saith expressly, It is the *Unity of the Spirit*, (not Water), that is here intended" (4:209).

[93] Bunyan, *Differences in Judgment*, 4:209. Bunyan accused Paul of inconsistency on this point: "But behold, while here you would have this to be Baptism with Water, how you contradict and condemn your own Notion: You say Water-baptism is not the *entering* Ordinance; yet the Baptism here is such as baptizeth us *into* a Body: Wherefore before you say next time that this in *1 Cor* 12. 16. [1 Cor 12:13] is meant of Water-baptism; affirm, that Water-baptism is the *initiating* or *entering* Ordinance, that your Opinion and Doctrine may hang better together" (4:210–11).

3. Paul claimed not to know what Bunyan meant by the "doctrine of baptism." Therefore, Bunyan provided some instruction: "Your ignorance of the Truth makes it not an Error: But I pray you, what is the *Doctrine of Baptism*, if not that which Baptism teacheth, even that which is signified thereby?"[94] Paul and the rest of the Baptists were unwilling to sever the sign from the thing signified, the physical act of baptism from the spiritual truth it symbolized. Bunyan traced their stance to its logical conclusion: "But what? Because they are not baptized; have they not Jesus Christ?"[95] Paul castigated Bunyan for calling baptism a "circumstance" and an "outward shew." Bunyan replied, "Deep reproof! But why did you not shew me my evil in thus calling it, when opposed to the Substance, and the thing signified? Is it the Substance, *is it the thing signified*? And why may I not give it the Name of *a Shew*; when you call it a symbole, and compare it to a Gentleman's Livery?"[96] The doctrine of baptism is that which baptism signifies, not the command and practice thereof; and one may have the former by faith without having the latter by water.[97]

4. Paul made two rebuttals to Bunyan's argument from Romans 14–15: first, that the epistle to the Romans was written to a baptized congregation, and therefore did not respect church communion; second, that the matter in hand pertained to issues of Jewish law, not to a command of Christ. Bunyan responded to the first rebuttal, but not the second. Rather, he focused upon the dictum that the church must receive all whom God receives (Rom 15:7), on the same basis upon which God receives them, that is, through faith in his Son. "*You must have Communion with visible Saints, because God hath Communion with them, whose Example in the Case we are strictly Commanded to follow.*"[98]

---

94. Bunyan, *Differences in Judgment*, 4:212.

95. Bunyan, *Differences in Judgment*, 4:213.

96. Bunyan, *Differences in Judgment*, 4:215.

97. "And take notice, I do not plead for a *despising* of Baptism, but a bearing with our Brother, that *cannot* do it for *want* of Light. The *best* of Baptism he hath, *viz.* the signification thereof; he wanteth only the outward *shew*, which if he *had*, would *not* prove him a truly *visible* Saint; it would not tell *me* he had the Grace of God in *his* heart; it is no Characteristical note to another of *my* Sonship with God" (Bunyan, *Differences in Judgment*, 4:216).

98. Bunyan, *Differences in Judgment*, 4:218.

5. Paul denied that the neglect of baptism could "unchristian" a man. However, he claimed that by his insistence that baptism was a matter of "light," Bunyan had relegated baptism to the same position as an Old Testament ordinance. Bunyan refused to back down. "What was said of Eating, or the contrary, may *as to this* be said of Water-baptism; Neither if I be baptized, am I the better? neither if I be not, am I the worse? not the better before God, not the worse before Men; still meaning as *Paul*, Provided I walk according to my Light with God; otherwise 'tis false."[99]

6. Paul claimed that baptism was essential to edification: "Edification as to Church-Fellowship, being a building up, doth suppose the being of a Church, before they can be thus Edified or built up: But pray you, shew us a Church without Baptism, approved of by the New Testament, and then edifie them as much as you can."[100] Bunyan again took Paul's words to their logical conclusion.

> See here the spirit of these Men, who for want of Water-Baptism, have at once un-Churched all *such* Congregations of God in the World; but against this I have, and do urge, That Water-baptism giveth neither being, nor well-being to a Church, neither is any part of that Instituted Worship of God, that the Church, as such, should be found in the Practice of. Therefore her Edification as a Church may, yea and ought to be attained unto without it.[101]

7. Paul asserted that love would not indulge a man in his disobedience, but rather exhort him to obedience to Christ. Bunyan did not agree. "That Love is more discovered when we receive for the sake of Christ, than when we refuse his Children for want of Water."[102] Once again, Bunyan argued that baptism is a matter of light. "But what acts of disobedience do we indulge them in? *In the Sin of Infant-baptism.*

---

99. Bunyan, *Differences in Judgment*, 4:220.

100. Paul, *Some Serious Reflections*, 26. Bunyan quoted Paul accurately, but stopped after "but pray you shew us a Church without baptism," leaving off "approved of by the New Testament" (Bunyan, *Differences in Judgment*, 4:221). Whether Paul intended to "unchurch" all paedobaptist churches is doubtful, but is a fair conclusion from his words.

101. Bunyan, *Differences in Judgment*, 4:221. Bunyan continued to press his point: "But, Sir, Are none but those of your way the publick Christians? Or, ought none but them that are baptized to have the publick means of Grace? . . . And, are there no publick Christians, or publick Christian-Meetings, but them of your way? I did not think that all but Baptists, should only abide in holes" (4:222).

102. Bunyan, *Differences in Judgment*, 4:225.

Answ. We indulge them not; but being Commanded to bear with the Infirmities of each other, suffer it; it being indeed in our eyes such; but in theirs they say a duty, till God shall otherwise perswade them."[103] Bunyan simply could not comprehend the Baptist position. "Strange! Take two Christians equal in all Points but this; nay, let one go beyond the other in Grace and Goodness, as far as a Man is beyond a Babe, yet Water shall turn the Scale, shall open the Door of Communion to the less; and command the other to stand back."[104]

8. For his eighth argument, Bunyan simply restated his major points: the church at Corinth was charged with carnality and immaturity for dividing over weightier matters than baptism, the abuse of baptism was a part of the problem at Corinth, and the apostle Paul did not make a major issue out of baptism. *"But if Baptism had been the initiating-Ordinance, (and I now add) Essential to Church-Communion; then no doubt he had made more Conscience of it, than thus lightly to pass it by."*[105]

9. Paul denied that restricting communion to baptized believers was to deprive them of their birthright, but rather to offer them their privileges according to Christ's rule and order. Bunyan once again demanded chapter and verse for such a restriction. "Where have you one word of God, that forbiddeth a person, so qualified, as is signified in mine Argument, the best Communion of Saints for want of Water? There is not a syllable for this in all the Book of God."[106] The exemplary pattern of the primitive church is not sufficient; Bunyan demanded explicit precept. Bunyan also refused to apologize for the eighteen charges he laid upon the Baptists for their uncharitable position. "But, I say, where is the Proposition offensive? Is it not a wicked thing to make *bars* to Communion, where *God* hath made *none*? Is it not a wickedness, to make that a Wall of Division betwixt us, which

---

103. Bunyan, *Differences in Judgment*, 4:226.

104. Bunyan, *Differences in Judgment*, 4:228.

105. Bunyan, *Differences in Judgment*, 4:230. Under this heading, Bunyan again denied that he denigrated baptism. "I have no Argument against its place, worth, or continuance, although thus you seek to scandalize me. But this kind of sincerity of yours, will never make me one of your Disciples. Have not I told you even in this Argument, That I speak not as I do, to perswade men or teach men to break the least of God's Commandments; but that my Brethren of the Baptized-way may not hold too much THEREUPON, may not make it an Essential of the Gospel, nor yet of the Communion of Saints" (4:229).

106. Bunyan, *Differences in Judgment*, 4:231.

God never commanded to be so. If it be not, justifie your practice; if it be, take shame."[107]

10. Bunyan added little to his tenth argument, but repeated it emphatically. To refuse communion amounts to preemptive excommunication. "And now I add, Is not this to deliver them to the Devil, 1 *Cor.* 5. or to put them to shame before all that see your acts?"[108]

In the third section of his treatise, Bunyan responded to Paul's fourteen arguments for strict communion.

1. The Great Commission does not explicitly forbid teaching before baptism.[109]

2. The Old Testament examples to which Paul pointed all regard the violation of explicit prohibitions in the law. The New Testament lacks such an explicit prohibition against receiving unbaptized believers into church communion.[110]

3. Apostolic practice does not amount to an explicit precept.[111]

4. Early church precedent does not amount to an explicit precept.[112]

5. Christ was not manifest as being sent of God through baptism, for He was recognized as the Messiah by John the Baptist before He was baptized. Furthermore, Scripture never refers to baptism as the "fruit of faith," or the "first step of gospel-obedience," as Paul claimed.[113]

6. Baptism is no part of the church's foundation, for the church has one foundation, which is Jesus Christ himself.[114]

---

107. Bunyan, *Differences in Judgment*, 4:233.

108. Bunyan, *Differences in Judgment*, 4:234. The phrase "preemptive excommunication" comes from John Piper, who argues the same in his case for open communion; (Piper, "Response to Grudem").

109. "That the Ministers are to Disciple and Baptize, is granted. But that they are prohibited (by the Commission; *Matt* 28) to Teach the Disciples other parts of Gospel-Worship, that have not Light in Baptism, remains for you to prove" (Bunyan, *Differences in Judgment*, 4:235).

110. Bunyan, *Differences in Judgment*, 4:236–37.

111. Bunyan, *Differences in Judgment*, 4:237–38.

112. Bunyan, *Differences in Judgment*, 4:238.

113. Bunyan, *Differences in Judgment*, 4:238–39.

114. Bunyan, *Differences in Judgment*, 4:239–40. Paul was referring to Heb 6:1–2. Bunyan, however, asserted that the "Baptisms are not here mentioned, with respect to the Act in Water, but of the Doctrine, that is, the signification thereof. *The Doctrine of*

7. The apostle Paul does not say that the Galatians were known to him by baptism, but that they were known to themselves thereby. Only God and the individual being baptized can know if the baptism was an act of faith, or a work of the flesh.[115]

8. Thomas Paul used Gal 3:27 to assert that those who have not been baptized have not put on Christ. Baptism is the livery of the church, that which makes the Christian visible. Bunyan was appalled: "Now that none have put on Christ in *Paul's* sense; yea, in a saving, in the best sense; but them that have, as you would have them, gone into Water, will be hard for you to prove, yea, is ungodly for you to assert."[116] Because only God and the individual being baptized can know if baptism was an act of faith, baptism in water cannot be that which makes the Christian visible. Love, not baptism, is the livery of the church, the distinguishing mark of the Christian.[117]

9. The Thessalonian church was indeed commended for following the example of the Judean church. But that the Judean church refused communion to unbaptized believers remains to be proven.[118]

10. That the apostle Paul grounded his argument for the resurrection and his exhortation to holiness in baptism is no proof that he excluded unbaptized believers from church communion.[119]

11. Thomas Paul worried that allowing an unbaptized person into the church would lead to the neglect of other gospel ordinances, or the admittance of visible sinners instead of visible saints. Bunyan responded that baptism is not a church ordinance, essential to a church's constitution, and therefore is not to be put in the same category as

---

Baptisms" (4:240). Bunyan's sixth response is a specious argument, for Paul was speaking of baptism as a part of the foundation of church order, and would not have denied that Christ was the church's one foundation.

115. "[Paul] puts them upon concluding themselves the Sons of God, if they were baptized into the Lord Jesus, which could not (ordinarily) be known but unto themselves alone; because, being thus baptized, respecteth a Special Act of Faith, which onely God, and him that hath, and acteth it, can be privy to. It is one thing for him that administreth, to Baptize in the Name of Jesus, and another thing for him that is the Subject, by that to be baptized INTO Jesus Christ" (Bunyan, *Differences in Judgment*, 4:241).

116. Bunyan, *Differences in Judgment*, 4:241.

117. Bunyan, *Differences in Judgment*, 4:241–42.

118. Bunyan, *Differences in Judgment*, 4:242–43.

119. Bunyan, *Differences in Judgment*, 4:243.

preaching, prayer, or the Lord's Supper. A church without preaching is no church; a church without baptism may be a church still. Furthermore, Bunyan was not pleading for the admittance of all unbaptized persons, but only those whose lives testify to their faith.[120]

12. "*Why should Professors have more Light in breaking of Bread, than Baptism?*" asked Paul. "Must God be called to an account by you, why he giveth more Light about the Supper, than Baptism?" replied Bunyan.[121] Furthermore, the Lord's Supper, being often reiterated and an ordinance in which the whole church participates, is by its nature of greater clarity than baptism.[122]

13. Paul asked why baptism is no part of that obedience by which true faith is discovered? "This is but round, round, the same thing over and over: That my obedience to Water, is *not* a discovery of my faith to others, is evident, from the body of the Bible, we find nothing that affirms it. And I will now add, That if a man cannot shew himself a Christian without Water-baptism, *He shall never shew either Saint, or Sinner, that he is a Christian by it.*"[123]

14. To Paul's assertion that those who rejected John's baptism were reckoned God's enemies, Bunyan replied that John's baptism "did not demonstrate by that SINGLE act, the receiving of the whole Doctrine of God as you suggest." Rather, "Yea, it is evident, that a man may be desirous of Water that man may be baptized, and neither own the Doctrine of Repentance, nor know on whom he should believe."[124]

---

120. "There are some of the Ordinances that, be they neglected, the being of a Church, as to her visible Gospel-Constitution, is taken quite away; but Baptism is none of them, it being no Church-Ordinance as such, nor any part of Faith, nor of that Holiness of heart, or life, that sheweth me to the Church to be a visible Saint. The Saint is a Saint before, and may walk with God, and be faithful with the Saints, and to his own Light also, though he never be baptized. Therefore to plead for his admission, makes no way at all for the admission of the open prophane" (Bunyan, *Differences in Judgment*, 4:244).

121. Bunyan, *Differences in Judgment*, 4:244.

122. Bunyan, *Differences in Judgment*, 4:244–45.

123. Bunyan, *Differences in Judgment*, 4:245.

124. Bunyan, *Differences in Judgment*, 4:246–47. Bunyan pointed to the Pharisees in Matt 3:7 and the Ephesian disciples in Acts 19:2–4 as examples. "That our denomination of Believers, and our receiving the Doctrine of the Lord Jesus, is not to be reckoned from our Baptism, is evident; Because according to our Notion of it, they only that have before received the Doctrine of the Gospel, and so shew it us by their Confession of Faith, they only ought to be baptized" (4:246).

Bunyan vs. the Baptists

Bunyan's responses to Paul's seven concluding questions added heat to the debate, but contributed little light. Where Paul accused him of pride, incivility, divisiveness, and a love of conflict, Bunyan reminded Paul that it was the Baptists who sought to "rend . . . in pieces" the Bedford Church through their "provocation of sixteen years long." It was the Baptists who had the true "Spirit of Diotrephes" as they cast dirt on unbaptized saints. It was the Baptists who were truly those who disrupt the "Union, Concord, and Communion" of the saints.[125] Paul claimed Anglicans, Presbyterians, and Independents were in agreement with the Baptists in requiring baptism before church communion. In response, Bunyan pointed out that it was he, and not the Baptists, who would welcome such into church communion.[126]

To *Differences in Judgment about Water-Baptism*, Bunyan appended a brief essay by Henry Jessey. "*I have also here presented thee with the Opinion of Mr.* Henry Jesse, *in the Case, which providentially I met with, as I was coming to* London *to put my Papers to the Press, and that it was his Judgment is Asserted to me, known many years since to some of the Baptists, to whom it was sent, but never yet Answered; and will be yet Attested if need shall require.*"[127]

Jessey managed to maintain an open-communion church in London until his death in 1663 and published his views in *A Storehouse of Provision* (1650).[128] When this essay was written, or how Bunyan obtained a copy of

---

125. Bunyan, *Differences in Judgment*, 4:247–50.

126. "I own Water-baptism to be God's Ordinance, but I make no Idol of it. Where you call now the *Episcopal* to side with you, and also the *Presbyterian*, &c. you will not find them easily perswaded to conclude with you against me. They are against your manner of Dipping, as well as the Subject of Water-baptism; neither do you, for all you flatter them, agree together in all but the Subject. Do you allow their Sprinkling? Do you allow their signing with the Cross? Why then have you so stoutly, an hundred times over, condemned these things as Antichristian. I am not against every man, though by your abusive language you would set every one against me, but am for Union, Concord, and Communion with Saints, as Saints, and for that cause I wrote my Book" (Bunyan, *Differences in Judgment*, 4:250).

127. Bunyan, *Differences in Judgment*, 4:193.

128. Jessey, *Storehouse of Provision*, 93–122, 174–203. Though this work was published over twenty years prior to the beginning of the communion controversy, it did not factor into the debate. While Jessey probably influenced Bunyan's open-communion views via the Bedford Church's connection with Jessey's church in London (see Greaves, *Glimpses of Glory*, 273–74), no author in the controversy referenced Jessey's arguments. After Jessey's death, the "JLJ Church" shifted to a strict communion position (see *Minutes*, 77, 79–80).

it, remains a mystery.[129] The essay is an application of Romans 14–15 to the question of baptism and church communion. Contrary to what the Baptists contended, Jessey argued that these chapters of Romans concern gospel institutions, and not just Jewish ordinances, and that they concern receiving into church communion, and not just into mutual affection within the already-baptized congregation.[130] Jessey then raised and answered nine objections to this interpretation, some more convincing than others. Jessey made many of the same arguments as Bunyan (e.g., the Baptists lack an explicit prohibition against receiving unbaptized saints; apostolic practice and early church precedent are not sufficient to overturn the explicit precept of Romans 15:7 to receive those whom God has received; the baptisms of 1 Cor 12:13 and Eph 4:5 refer to the baptism of the Spirit; baptism does not form the visible body of a particular church; etc.). Nevertheless, Jessey did add three novel arguments to Bunyan's case for open communion.

1. When it comes to the gospel, there are no real matters of indifference. Adhering to the statutes of Old Testament law regarding meats and days amounted to a devaluing of the death of Christ, by which such ordinances had been abolished. The question is not whether baptism is a matter of indifference or the neglect thereof a sin, but whether the Lord receives those with an imperfect faith and obedience.[131]

2. Jessey argued that if the rule to receive all whom God receives (Rom 15:7) were true in the apostolic age, when the church "had infallible helps to expound Truths unto them, much more now, the Church hath been so long in the Wilderness and in Captivity, and not that

---

129. Greaves suggests that "Bunyan, in London to deliver the manuscript to the printer John Wilkins, obtained a copy of Jessey's 5,000-word statement defending open-communion, open-membership principles. Jessey had died in 1663, but Bunyan may have acquired his statement from their mutual friend, the bookseller Francis Smith" (Greaves, *Glimpses of Glory*, 297).

130. Jessey, "Appendix," in Bunyan, *Differences in Judgment*, 4:252–53. Like Bunyan, Jessey regarded Paul's epistle to the Romans as written "Not only to the Church there, but unto all that were beloved of God, and called to be Saints in all Ages" (4:253).

131. Jessey, "Appendix," in Bunyan, *Differences in Judgment*, 4:255–56. "For if it were but in things wherein they had not sinned, it were no great matter for the Lord to receive, and it would have been as good an Argument or Motive to the Church, to say things were indifferent as to say the *Lord had received them*. Whereas the Text is to set out the Riches of Grace to the Vessels of Mercy, as *Rom*. 9. 15. That as at first he did freely chuse and accept them; so when they fail and miscarry in many things, yea about his Worship also, although he be most injured thereby, yet he is first in passing it by, and perswading others to do the like" (4:255–56).

his People should be *driven away in the dark day*, though they are sick and weak."[132] The primitive church simply was not confronted with the issue that confronts churches today, that is, what to do with paedobaptist believers.

3. Bunyan argued that paedobaptist churches were true churches, and paedobaptist Christians were true Christians; but he yet regarded them as "unbaptized." Jessey suggested that paedobaptists ought to be regarded as truly, though imperfectly, baptized, and therefore received into communion, "especially in *such as own it for an Ordinance, though in some things miss it, and do yet shew their love unto it, and unto the Lord, and unto his Law therein, that they could be willing to die for it rather than to deny it; and to be baptized in their blood.*"[133]

Truth Outweighing Error

The year 1673 saw another response to Bunyan's *A Confession of My Faith*, this time from the Huntingdonshire and Cambridgeshire General Baptist John Denne.[134] Denne was perhaps known to Bunyan, as it was his father, Henry Denne, who had defended Bunyan in his 1659 controversy with the Cambridge don Thomas Smith over Bunyan's right to preach without ordination.[135] Denne's tone is even more incendiary than Thomas Paul's; he called Bunyan a minister of Satan, a false prophet, a wolf in sheep's clothing, an "Anti-Baptist" who endeavored to "vilify" and "explode" the

---

132. Jessey, "Appendix," in Bunyan, *Differences in Judgment*, 4:260.

133. Jessey, "Appendix," in Bunyan, *Differences in Judgment*, 4:261. William Kiffin, on the other hand, could not comprehend a credobaptist affirming that paedobaptism is a true, if imperfect, form of baptism: "Now our Dissenting Brethren with whom we have to do, look upon this way [paedobaptism] to be absolutely invalid, and so no Baptism (else they would not be Baptized themselves) and consequently esteem all such as Unbaptized" (Kiffin, *Sober Discourse*, 9).

134. Bunyan's *Differences in Judgment about Water-Baptism* was published prior to Denne's *Truth Outweighing Error*, but Denne evidently had not yet seen Bunyan's second work. Thus, Denne's response was to Bunyan's *A Confession of My Faith*, and Bunyan does not respond to Denne until his 1674 *Peaceable Principles and True*. For this reason, this monograph places *Truth Outweighing Error* after *Differences in Judgment* in its analysis (Greaves, *Glimpses of Glory*, 294).

135. For an account of the controversy, see Greaves, *Glimpses of Glory*, 121–24. Henry Denne's defense of Bunyan's right to preach is found in the preface to H. Denne, *Quaker No Papist*.

holy ordinance of baptism.[136] On the other hand, Denne styled himself as Phineas, who vindicated the truth and defended the glory of God by slaying the sinning Israelite (Num 25).[137]

The first half of Denne's treatise was a response to the articles of Bunyan's *A Confession of My Faith* that Denne found troubling, including Bunyan's emphasis upon redemption by the "personal acts of Christ" rather than the sufferings of Christ, Bunyan's incautious language concerning the union of Christ's two natures at the cross that Denne rather uncharitably took for a form of patripassianism, and especially, Bunyan's doctrines of election and effectual calling, which the General Baptist found particularly abhorrent.[138]

The second half of Denne's treatise addressed Bunyan's defense of open communion. Denne attacked Bunyan at many of the same points as Thomas Paul. Bunyan said that people ought to be received into communion by the discovery of faith and holiness. Denne replied, "*Is not Faith discovered by Works?* Jam. 2.17. And by what works, if not obedience to Christ's Ordinances, to holy Ordinances, to enjoyned duties, I know not, surely what, if not this, discovers Faith?"[139] Bunyan admitted that in the apostolic church, baptism preceded church communion. Denne asked, "Is not the Primitive pattern, their general Practice, a sufficient testimony? Doth not the word of Scripture enjoyn us to follow that Example?"[140] Bunyan claimed that in the early church, none were excluded from church membership over neglect of baptism, and that baptism does not make one a member of the church, whether universal or particular. Denne responded,

> First, how can *J. Bunyan* expect any instance to be given of the debarring of any unbaptized Person, when that (by his own Confession, . . .) in the Primitive times they were (generally even all Disciples) baptized upon Conversion? And if so, much less can it be expected to find any threatened to be cut off from the Church, because not first baptized, there not being in those days such an Heretick hatch'd as would so explode Baptism.[141]

---

136. J. Denne, *Truth Outweighing Error*, A2–A4, 9–10, 50. Denne's treatise abounds with such invectives.

137. J. Denne, *Truth Outweighing Error*, A3.

138. J. Denne, *Truth Outweighing Error*, 12–16 (redemption by the sufferings of Christ), 16–20 (patripassianism), 20–41 (election and effectual calling).

139. J. Denne, *Truth Outweighing Error*, 44.

140. J. Denne, *Truth Outweighing Error*, 47.

141. J. Denne, *Truth Outweighing Error*, 49.

Non-subjection to baptism indeed debars men from church communion, for it is a "walking disorderly, not according to the Traditions received from the Apostles," "a sin against God, a rejecting of the Counsel of God against our selves," a departure from the example of the primitive church, and a violation of the express command of Christ in the Great Commission.[142] Bunyan claimed that baptism requires light, that God gives light, and that whoever wants light ought not be required to be baptized. Denne replied,

> The question is not, who have Light therein, but who ought to have Light therein? . . . He hath often cryed out against others for saying, *The Light within is the Rule for Christians to walk by*; but now he himself confidently affirms it, yea, in opposition to positive Commands, and express Prohibitions, making it the great reason for and against a Practice. . . . But let me ask *J. Bunyan*, Whether Light makes a thing to be a Duty or no Duty? Is God's Law subservient to our Light?[143]

These arguments and more appeared in Paul's *Some Serious Reflections*, as well as other Baptist contributions to the communion controversy.

Denne did, however, marshal a number of novel arguments that were not found in Paul's work. For instance, Denne insisted, contrary to Paul, that baptism is indeed an initiating ordinance into the visible church. "For that which ought to be administered upon Conversion, before Church-membership, is an initiating Ordinance."[144] Bunyan claimed that the rule by which faith and holiness is discovered is by "the moral precept evangelized." This is impractical and dangerous, claimed Denne. It is impractical, because baptism ought to be administered upon conversion, but new converts have no good works whereby to commend them.[145] It is dangerous, because obedience to the moral law can be counterfeited by the

---

142. J. Denne, *Truth Outweighing Error*, 55, 56, 57–58.

143. J. Denne, *Truth Outweighing Error*, 73, 78–79. Denne was referencing Bunyan's controversies with Edward Burrough and the Quakers during the latter half of the 1650s. See Bunyan, *Some Gospel-Truths Opened*, 1:5–115; *Vindication*, 1:121–220.

144. J. Denne, *Truth Outweighing Error*, 51.

145. "Wherein let me ask *J. Bunyan*, or any rational Christian, how this is possible in divers cases: as First, upon Conversion, when men are presently (upon the Preaching of the Word) turned from darkness to light, and so are received as Church-members, as soon as they are Converted, who before were Fornicators, Murtherers, Thieves, and what not, 1 *Cor*. 6. 11, but upon their Conversion are received as Church-members even the same day, *Acts* 2. 41. What experience can there be of their Conversion who were Adulterers the day before?" (J. Denne, *Truth Outweighing Error*, 61).

natural man, as Scripture so often warns.[146] Furthermore, why did Bunyan exalt the moral law, even the moral law "evangelized" (a phrase Denne rejected—"for, where do you read in Scripture of the Law Evangelized? Surely the contrary is found") above the rule of Christ?[147]

Having interacted with Bunyan's primary thesis, Denne then responded to each of Bunyan's ten arguments (which reminded Denne of "the Red Dragon with his ten horns").[148] These responses echoed those of Paul, with five exceptions:

- To Bunyan's second argument that the "one baptism" of Ephesians 4:5 is the baptism of the Spirit and not baptism in water, Denne argued that this baptism could not be the baptism of the Spirit because "the baptism of the Spirit was not general, and so could not be intended by one Baptism."[149]

- Bunyan's third argument, that one may have the doctrine of baptism apart from the practice, Denne said he readily affirmed.[150] But Denne and Bunyan were using the "doctrine of baptism" in different senses. For Bunyan, the "doctrine of baptism" meant the reality which baptism signifies: "*viz. The death of Christ; My death with Christ; also his resurrection from the Dead, and mine with him to newness of life.*"[151] But for Denne, the "doctrine of baptism" meant the command to credobaptism.[152] Therefore, according to Denne, one may have the doctrine

---

146. J. Denne, *Truth Outweighing Error*, 61–62.

147. J. Denne, *Truth Outweighing Error*, 65. At this point, Denne disputed Bunyan's understanding of the place of the moral law in the new covenant. Bunyan's covenant theology saw much continuity between the old and new covenants within the one covenant of grace; Denne saw little continuity, and therefore had little place for the Ten Commandments in the life of the church. The debate centered upon the meaning of "the perfect law of liberty" (Jas 1:25) and the "royal law" (Jas 2:8) (J. Denne, *Truth Outweighing Error*, 65–72).

148. J. Denne, *Truth Outweighing Error*, 80.

149. J. Denne, *Truth Outweighing Error*, 86. This is not the standard Baptist reply that the "baptism" in Eph 4:5 could not be Spirit baptism because the "one Spirit" was already mentioned in Eph 4:4.

150. "We readily allow that, and oftentimes find that many have the Doctrine (although not without light) without the Practice" (J. Denne, *Truth Outweighing Error*, 87).

151. Bunyan, *Confession of My Faith*, 4:172.

152. "He may well say, *Bold*, for he hath no Scripture-warrant for it, and it is a great boldness to adventure in Church-Communion beyond what is written, yea, contrary to what is written; for our Saviour saith, *Luk.* 12. 49. *He that knew his lord's will* (that had the Doctrine of a Duty) *and prepared not himself* (to Practise) *neither did according to his will, shall be beaten with many stripes*" (J. Denne, *Truth Outweighing Error*, 87).

of baptism apart from its practice; that is, one may understand the command to be baptized as a disciple and yet disobey that command. But such a one is hardly fit for church communion.

- To Bunyan's fourth argument from Romans 14–15, Denne echoed Paul's responses, adding only that Bunyan's assertion that the church must receive those whom God receives was false, for God may receive whom He will, yet the church is required to walk according to his rule.[153]

- Of Bunyan's fifth argument, that failure in baptism does not "unchristian" a man, Denne was not convinced. "I say, this Reason which is grounded upon a false Position: for although Baptism doth not make a Christian, yet the want of it may mar a Christian, and the neglect thereof unchristian men."[154]

- To Bunyan's ninth argument, that to refuse church communion to an unbaptized yet visible saint is to deprive him of his birthright, Denne replied, "Can a man (considering what hath been said) be a visible Saint that denyeth Christ's Holy Ordinances? Can we be assured that a man hath Communion with God, who rejects his Counsel?"[155] For Denne, an "unbaptized Christian" amounted to a contradiction in terms.

A Treatise of Baptism

Within months of the 1673 publication of *Differences in Judgment about Water-Baptism*, the London General Baptist Henry Danvers responded to Bunyan in a postscript to his *A Treatise of Baptism*.[156] *A Treatise of Baptism* is a lengthy historical-theological defense of credobaptism. Danvers did not intend a substantive reply to Bunyan, rather "leaving his manifold *Absurdities*, Contradictions, unbrotherly Tauntings and Reflections,

---

153. J. Denne, *Truth Outweighing Error*, 90–91, 96.

154. J. Denne, *Truth Outweighing Error*, 97–98.

155. J. Denne, *Truth Outweighing Error*, 122. Denne proceeded to ask, "Can they truly desire Communion, that refuse to obey Baptism when required?" (122).

156. Danvers, *Treatise of Baptism*. There is some confusion over whether Danvers was a General or Particular Baptist. Sometimes, Richard Greaves refers to Danvers as a General Baptist (Greaves, "Henry Danvers [2008]"; *Saints and Rebels*, 157–78). Other times, Greaves calls Danvers a Particular Baptist (Greaves, "Henry Danvers [1982]," 210–11; *Glimpses of Glory*, 146). Because his associations were predominantly with General Baptists, this monograph regards Danvers as such.

Contemptions, traducing the wisdome of Christ, and his holy Appointments, to be called to account by that hand, that hath so well begun to reckon with him [i.e., Thomas Paul]."[157] Rather, Danvers contented himself to respond to six "Fundamental Mistakes" in Bunyan's *Differences in Judgment about Water-Baptism*.

1. Bunyan asserted his position without "*footing* nor *Foundation* in the Word of God, and for which neither *Precept* nor *Example* is produced to warrant it."[158]

2. Open communion not only contradicts Christ's command given in the Great Commission, but also the constant practice of the early church in obedience to the Great Commission. The reason of the order set forth in the Great Commission is plain: "Because [baptism] was the *Listing, Espousing, Covenanting, Ingrafting, Implanting* Ordinance."[159]

3. Ignorance does not absolve anyone of sin. Bunyan's position "not only justifies the *neglect* of the *true*, but the Exercise of *false* Worship."[160]

4. Bunyan elevated the Ten Commandments above the ordinance of Christ, "as though it were possible to be guilty of *false Worship* and *Idolatry* [i.e., paedobaptism], and not violate the *first* and *second* Commandment."[161]

5. Bunyan asserted that not all in the churches to which the New Testament epistles were written were baptized, which is manifestly false.[162]

6. Baptism is a church ordinance, the "*entrance* and *door* into the Visible Church."[163] Under this heading, Danvers offered an analogy:

> For by that publick *Declaration* of consent is the *Marriage* and solemn *Contract* made betwixt Christ and the Believer

---

157. Danvers, *Treatise of Baptism* postscript [p.s.] 41. The postscript begins on page 41 of an appendix to *A Treatise of Baptism* entitled, "The History of Christianity Amongst the Ancient Britains and Waldenses."

158. Danvers, *Treatise of Baptism* p.s. 42.

159. Danvers, *Treatise of Baptism* p.s. 44. Danvers repeated the standard Baptist reply that Bunyan's position was historically novel: "[Strict communion] hath obtained an *universal Consent* by most that have owned the Christian Religion, and in any Form professed the same, whether *Papists, Protestants, Independents, Baptists*" (p.s. 45).

160. Danvers, *Treatise of Baptism* p.s. 48.

161. Danvers, *Treatise of Baptism* p.s. 49.

162. Danvers, *Treatise of Baptism* p.s. 49–51.

163. Danvers, *Treatise of Baptism* p.s. 52.

in Baptisme, as before at large. And if it be *preposterous* and *wicked* for a Man and a Woman to cohabit together, and to enjoy the Privileges of a *Marriage-State*, without the passing of that publick *Solemnity*, so it is no less *disorderly* upon a *Spiritual* account, for any to claim the Priviledges of a Church, or be admitted to the same till the passing of this *Solemnity* by them.[164]

Peaceable Principles and True

Bunyan's third and final contribution to the communion controversy was his 1674 *Peaceable Principles and True*, a response to Paul's second reply (no longer extant) and Danvers's *A Treatise of Baptism*.[165] Bunyan refused to respond to Denne's *Truth Outweighing Error*, although he counted Denne's arguments superior to those of either Paul or Danvers. This was evidently because of Denne's scurrilous reputation:

For Mr. *Den*, if either of the three [Kiffin, Paul, and Danvers] will make his Arguments their own, *they may see what their Servant can do*: but I shall not bestow Paper and Ink upon *Him*, nor yet upon Mr. *Lamb*; the one already, *having given his profession the lye*, and for the other perhaps they that know his Life, will see little of Conscience in the whole of his Religion, and conclude him not worth the taking notice of.[166]

Peaceable Principles and True did little to advance the argument for open communion, but was a forceful restatement of Bunyan's position

---

164. Danvers, *Treatise of Baptism* p.s. 52–53.

165. "Apparently no copy of Paul's work, not even the title, has survived, though its theses can be reconstructed from those points Bunyan refuted in *Peaceable Principles and True* (1674)" (Greaves, *Glimpses of Glory*, 297).

166. Bunyan, *Peaceable Principles and True*, 4:288. Bunyan earlier stated concerning Denne, "But considering him, and comparing his Notions with his Conversation, I count it will be better for him to be better in Morals, before he be worthy of an Answer" (4:285). Greaves writes with regard to Denne's immorality, "Unfortunately, the church book of Denne's congregation at Caxton and Fenstanton for this period, which might have cast light on his reputed offenses, has not survived. Sometime before 1672 Denne moved to St. Ives, Huntingdonshire, where he was licensed to preach the same year. Margaret Spufford suggests that 'some disaster' struck the Caxton part of the congregation in this period, for the church had no members there by 1676. This crisis may have involved the immoral conduct of Denne to which Bunyan alludes" (Greaves, *Glimpses of Glory*, 300; cf. Spufford, *Contrasting Communities*, 291–92). Danvers referenced Thomas Lambe's *Truth Prevailing Against the Fiercest Opposition* in his *A Treatise of Baptism* (Danvers, *Treatise of Baptism* p.s. 53).

and defense of Bunyan's character. Though Bunyan was tempted merely to quote Romans 14–15 and be done with it, he instead attempted an answer to Paul's argument, "because, perhaps, should I thus conclude, some might make *an ill use* of my brevity; I shall therefore briefly step after you, and examine your *short Reply*; at least, where shew of Argument is."[167]

The first five pages of Paul's second work were evidently an attack on Bunyan's character ("to prove me either *proud* or a *liar*").[168] Paul then questioned Bunyan's Baptist *bona fides* ("How long 'tis since I was a Baptist? . . . 'Tis an ill Bird that bewrays his own Nest"), to which Bunyan famously responded,

> I must tell you (avoiding your *slovenly* Language) I know none to whom that Title is so proper as *to the Disciples of* John. And since you would know by what Name I would be distinguished from others; I tell you, I would be, and hope I am, *a Christian*; and chuse, if God shall count me worthy, *to be called a Christian, a Believer* or other such Name which is approved by the Holy Ghost. And for those Factious Titles of *Anabaptists, Independents, Presbyterians*, or the like, I conclude, that they came neither from *Jerusalem*, nor *Antioch*, but rather from *Hell* and *Babylon*; for they naturally tend to divisions, *you may know them by their Fruits*.[169]

Paul also asserted his good relations with other London Nonconformists of differing opinions, to which Bunyan replied that his relations could not be that good if he refused *"to admit them* to their Father's Table."[170]

The following section of Bunyan's treatise contains some interesting comments that provide color and context to the communion controversy. Evidently, Bunyan asked John Owen to write a prefatory epistle to *Differences in Judgment about Water-Baptism*, and Owen agreed. But several Baptists persuaded Owen to desist from doing so.[171] Paul wrote that "some

---

167. Bunyan, *Peaceable Principles and True*, 4:270. Bunyan wrote, *"That there being no Precept, President nor Example in all the Scripture for our excluding our holy Brethren that differ in this point from us; therefore we ought not dare to do it,* but contrariwise to receive them; because God hath given us sufficient proof that himself hath received them, whose example in this case he hath commanded us to follow, *Rom* 14:15. This might serve for an Answer to your Reply" (4:270).

168. Bunyan, *Peaceable Principles and True*, 4:270.

169. Bunyan, *Peaceable Principles and True*, 4:270.

170. Bunyan, *Peaceable Principles and True*, 4:271.

171. "And perhaps, 'twas more for the Glory of God that Truth should go naked into the world, then as seconded by so mighty an Armour-bearer as he" (Bunyan, *Peaceable Principles and True*, 4:272).

of the sober Independents" had not approved of *Differences in Judgment.* "What then?" Bunyan replied. "If I should also say, as I can without lying, *that several of the Baptists have wished yours burnt before it had come to light*; is your Book ever the worse for that?"[172] Such comments indicate that the Nonconformist community in London was quite agitated over this controversy between the London Baptists and the Bedford tinker. Furthermore, if Bunyan is to be believed, not all Baptists were happy with Paul's representation of the Baptist position.

In a key passage, Bunyan pressed Paul on his assertion, made in *Some Serious Reflections*, that baptism is not an initiating ordinance. Bunyan called him out on this point in *Differences in Judgment*, and Paul backtracked a bit on his claim, saying that while baptism was not an initiating ordinance into a particular church, it was an initiating ordinance into the "*universal, orderly, Church-visible.*" Danvers evidently agreed.[173] Bunyan was astounded by this statement. How could baptism be the initiating ordinance into the universal church, when those from Adam to Christ knew nothing of baptism? How could the universal church be orderly—that is, in "Harmony or Agreement in the outward parts of Worship"—when the outward forms of worship had substantively changed throughout the church's various dispensations, and even today there are differences of opinion on baptism, the Lord's Supper, and other matters of worship?[174] And whoever heard of the universal church being visible? "Now I would yet learn of this Brother where this church is; for if it be *Visible*, he can *tell* and also *shew* it. But to be short, there is no such Church: The universal Church cannot be visible; a great part of that vast Body being already in Heaven, and a great part as yet (perhaps) unborn."[175] Bunyan traced this claim to its logical conclusion: if only Baptists are baptized, and baptism is the initiating ordinance into the "*universal, orderly, Church-visible*," then this church must be a Baptist church comprised of Baptists alone.[176] Furthermore, Bunyan once

---

172. Bunyan, *Peaceable Principles and True*, 4:272.

173. "You seem to retract your denial of Baptism to be the initiating Ordinance. And indeed Mr. *Danvers* told me, that you must retract that Opinion, and that he had or would speak to you to do it . . . But it seems though you do not now own it to be the inlet into a particular Church; yet (as you tell us in *p.* 14 of your last) *you never denied that Baptism doth not make a Believer a member of the universal, orderly, Church-visible.* And in this Mr. *Danvers* and you agree" (Bunyan, *Peaceable Principles and True*, 4:273).

174. Bunyan, *Peaceable Principles and True*, 4:273.

175. Bunyan, *Peaceable Principles and True*, 4:273.

176. "So then by *Universal, Orderly, Visible Church*, this Brother must mean those

again reminded the Baptists that by their own admission, one must be a visible saint prior to baptism, else he ought not be baptized. Clearly, then, it is not baptism that makes a saint visible.[177]

Bunyan again asserted his right to demand a precept for excluding the unbaptized, and defended at length his use of Israel's setting aside of circumcision during its forty years in the wilderness to justify the claim that baptism may be set aside for a season if circumstances warrant it. As the church is still in the wilderness, having not yet fully returned from its exile in Babylon, it is not wise to demand baptism of every visible saint that differs in opinion on the ordinance.[178] Bunyan charged Paul with failing to address his argument about the command to love being greater than the command to baptize, and restated the seventeen absurdities that follow from dividing over baptism.[179]

Next, Bunyan responded to Paul's vindication of his fourteen arguments that he advanced in *Some Serious Reflections*, again pressing the point that when asked for a precept or precedent, all Paul offered was presumption. Evidently, Paul claimed that he had humbly submitted his arguments "*to others much above me.*"[180] To which Bunyan replied that Paul obviously had not submitted them to the Independents or Presbyterians of London, for they would not have affirmed him in his views.[181] It is easy to receive affirmation if you seek it only from those already in agreement.

---

of the Saints only, that have been, or are baptized as we; this is clear, because Baptism (saith he) maketh a Believer a member of *this Church*; his meaning then is, that there is an *Universal, Orderly, Visible Church*, and they *alone* are the *Baptists*; and that every one that is baptized, is by that made a member of the *Universal, Orderly, Visible Church of Baptists*, and that the whole number of the rest of the Saints are utterly excluded. But now if other men should do as this man, how many Universal Churches should we have? An *Universal, Orderly, Visible Church of Independents*; an *Universal, Orderly, Visible Church of Presbyterians*, and the like" (Bunyan, *Peaceable Principles and True*, 4:274).

177. "His visibility is already; he is already a Visible Member of the Body of Christ, and after that baptized. His Baptism then neither makes him a Member, nor Visible Member, of the Body of Jesus Christ" (Bunyan, *Peaceable Principles and True*, 4:274).

178. Bunyan, *Peaceable Principles and True*, 4:275–79.

179. Bunyan, *Peaceable Principles and True*, 4:279–82. In *A Confession of My Faith*, Bunyan listed eighteen such "absurdities," but in *Peaceable Principles and True* he switched the order of the eighth and ninth and left out the fifteenth ("It giveth Occasion to many to turn aside to most dangerous heresies") (Bunyan, *Confession of My Faith*, 4:182–83).

180. Bunyan, *Peaceable Principles and True*, 4:283.

181. Bunyan, *Peaceable Principles and True*, 4:283–84.

Bunyan then turned his attention to Danvers's analogy between baptism and the solemnization of marriage. If allowing the unbaptized into church communion is akin to allowing a man and woman to enjoy the conjugal benefits of marriage without the covenant of marriage, as Danvers claimed, then this is to charge Jesus with fornication, for He has communion with the unbaptized who are yet visible saints. Bunyan was appalled by the analogy. "Brother, God give him Repentance. I wot that through ignorance, and a preposterous Zeal he said it: unsay it again with tears, and by a publick renunciation of so wicked and horrible words."[182]

In the conclusion, Bunyan brought all his polemical firepower to bear upon the debate, accusing the Baptists of mischief in sowing discord and attempting to steal away members from other dissenting churches, accusing Paul of confusing slanders with arguments, and asserting that Paul and Danvers would have been better off making Denne's arguments their own.[183] In the end, Bunyan claimed victory: "In the mean-while, I affirm, that Baptism with Water, *is neither a Bar nor Bolt to Communion of Saints, nor a Door nor Inlet to Communion of Saints.* The same which is the Argument of my Books; and as some of the moderate among themselves have affirmed, that neither Mr. *K.* Mr. *P.* nor Mr. *D'anvers*, have made invalid, though sufficiently they have made their assault."[184]

A Sober Discourse of Right to Church Communion

Peaceable Principles and True provoked two responses. The first appeared the same year, John Denne's *Hypocrisies Detected, or Peaceable and True Principles* (1674), but no copy is extant.[185] William Kiffin offered the final word in the debate with his 1681 *A Sober Discourse of Right to Church Communion*, a treatise written with all the skill and diplomacy of an elder statesman.[186] While Paul's *Some Serious Reflections* is the most substantive

---

182. Bunyan, *Peaceable Principles and True*, 4:285.
183. Bunyan, *Peaceable Principles and True*, 4:285–89.
184. Bunyan, *Peaceable Principles and True*, 4:287–88.
185. Greaves, *Glimpses of Glory*, 301.
186. Though Kiffin never mentioned Bunyan by name, it is clear that he was Kiffin's primary sparring partner. Bunyan evidently violated polite conventions by not only naming Kiffin specifically, but writing his name at length. "You blame me for writing his Name at length; but I know he is not ashamed of his Name" (Bunyan, *Peaceable Principles and True*, 4:271). Kiffin did not commit the same *faux pas*.

critique of open communion to emerge from the controversy, Kiffin offered the debate's most substantive defense of strict communion.

Kiffin began with an epistle to the Christian reader, in which he asserted that open communion was a dangerous and novel invention, "A Notion, *not only* Contrary *to the* Primitive *Pattern, but the* Constant *Practice of all that ever professed the Christian Religion, or that own the Scriptures to be the Rule of Faith and Practise.*"[187] Kiffin was careful neither to overstate nor underemphasize the importance of baptism: "*Knowledge of the Truth, and Obedience to it in outward performances, will as little save a mans soul as the Covenant of Works. Yet every man that hath an interest in Christ, is bound by the Word of God to be obedient to all his Commands.*"[188] Obedience to the Word of God and worship according to his rule were the driving concerns of Kiffin's work: "*I have no other design, but the preserving the Ordinances of Christ, in their purity and Order as they are left unto us in the holy* Scriptures *of Truth; and to warn the Churches* To keep close to the Rule, *least they being found not to Worship the Lord according to His prescrib'd Order he make a* Breach *amongst them.*"[189]

In a brief preface, Kiffin expounded upon the importance of worship according to the rule of Christ. "It is a superlative and desperate piece of audacity for men to presume to mend anything in the Worship of God; for it supposes the All-wise Law giver capable of error, and the attempter wiser than his Maker."[190] Peace and unity are no excuse for disobedience.

> When that question shall be askt, *Who hath required this at your hands?* I doubt it will be no sufficient plea to say, That if we have erred in any Punctilio's of Divine Truth, it was for Peace and Unions sake, &c. For, *No motions of peace are to be made or received with the loss of Truth*: Nor may the Laws, Orders, and Prescriptions of Christ be altered, or varyed, in any tittle, upon any pretense whatsoever, God having never given any such Prerogative to mankind, as to be Arbitrators how he may be best and most decently Worshiped.[191]

Kiffin then professed his love for those who disagree, a love that is best expressed by endeavoring to inform them of their error, "in a meek and

---

187. Kiffin, *Sober Discourse*, A3.
188. Kiffin, *Sober Discourse*, A4.
189. Kiffin, *Sober Discourse*, A6.
190. Kiffin, *Sober Discourse*, B4.
191. Kiffin, *Sober Discourse*, B6–B7.

sober way; and if we fail of success, then to leave them to the Lord, who in his own due Season will uncloud those Sacred Mysteries, which yet are hidden to a great many."[192]

In the first chapter, Kiffin addressed himself to the question, quoting from Bunyan without naming him: "We shall therefore direct this Discourse to our Dissenting Brethren, of the Baptized way only, who reason thus, *That there being no Precept, President nor Example in all the Scripture, for our excluding our Holy Brethren that differ in this Point from us, therefore we ought not to dare to do it.*"[193] Kiffin responded first by pointing out the danger of such a rule. There are no explicit precepts forbidding a number of practices, including "Popish Purgatory, and Monkery and ten thousand other things."[194] The question is not whether there is explicit precept, but whether the truth is established by necessary inference. "If it be meant what may be inferred *by direct and plain consequence* in the true *Logical* Notion of it, without Sophistry or Quibble, I am satisfied we can produce *Precept, President,* and *Example*, that it is our Duty to withdraw from disorderly Walkers."[195] Kiffin then stated five convictions upon which strict communion is founded:

1. All believers ought to be baptized.
2. Only believers ought to be baptized.
3. All other practices deviate from the Scriptural rule.
4. All such deviations are dangerous and disorderly.
5. Baptists are not guilty of schism for holding to the truth.[196]

---

192. Kiffin, *Sober Discourse*, b8. Kiffin later wrote that Baptists "exclude such as disorderly practice the Ordinance of Baptism, from our immediate Communion at the Lords Table, though not from our Love and Affection, for we hope they walk according to their Light, and the Error being not so fundamental as to endanger their Eternal state, we esteem them Christian Brethren and Saints, for whose further illumination we dayly put up our Prayers" (6). This was a striking departure from Denne's stance.

193. Kiffin, *Sober Discourse*, 3. The quote is from Bunyan, *Peaceable Principles and True*, 4:270. Though Kiffin referred to Bunyan (anonymously) as "of the Baptized way," this should not be admitted as evidence that Kiffin regarded Bunyan as a Baptist, at least not in the way that Kiffin regarded himself as a Baptist; Kiffin is merely affirming Bunyan's personal commitment to credobaptism.

194. Kiffin, *Sober Discourse*, 4.

195. Kiffin, *Sober Discourse*, 4.

196. Kiffin, *Sober Discourse*, 6–8.

In chapter 2, Kiffin provided three reasons to reject open communion. First, Kiffin exposed the dangerous consequences of such a practice. Open communion "tends to destroy the Nature, Ends and Uses of these Gospel Ordinances."[197] It leads inexorably to the laying aside of baptism altogether, for it fails to provide a compelling reason to be baptized.[198] It will cause Baptists to be reviled and persecuted, for it paints Baptist separation as "frivolous, our Separation Schismatical, and our Suffering the Penalties of Humane Laws, foolish."[199] Second, Kiffin argued from the relationship of baptism to the Lord's Supper. Those advocating open communion are inconsistent in welcoming those who neglect baptism, but not those who neglect the Lord's Supper. Does not Scripture place baptism on equal standing with the Lord's Supper? Does not Scripture give baptism "precedency in *order of time*, as being the Sacrament of the Spiritual *Birth*, and the other of Spiritual *Nourishment* and *Growth*?"[200] "As the *Supper* is a Spiritual participation of the *Body* and *Blood* of Christ by Faith, and so (not meerly by the work done) is a means of Salvation; so *Baptism Signs* and *Seals* our Salvation to us, which lies in *Justification* and discharge of sin, *&c.*"[201] Finally, Kiffin argued that the pattern for baptism is plainly established by both positive command and prescriptive example of the primitive church. This was perhaps Kiffin's most significant contribution to the communion controversy. Bunyan repeatedly demanded "precept or precedent" for excluding the unbaptized from church communion. Kiffin responded that the positive precept and precedent necessarily imply the negative prohibition.

> All Sound and Orthodox Writers with one mind agree (and meer Reason teaches it) that where a *Rule* and *express Law* is prescribed to men, that very *Prescription*, is an express prohibition of the contrary: Here we have the Order of the Gospel Administration,

---

197. Kiffin, *Sober Discourse*, 10. These ends and uses Kiffin identified as: (1) "To represent to the Eye and Understanding by a visible sign or figure what hath been Preacht to the Ear and Heart"; (2) "To witness Repentance"; (3) "To evidence Regeneration"; (4) to be "a Symbol of our dying unto sin, and living again to Christian newness of life" (Kiffin, *Sober Discourse*, 31–32).

198. "For if Unbaptized Persons may be admitted to all Church Priviledges, does not such a practice plainly suppose that it is unnecessary?" (Kiffin, *Sober Discourse*, 13).

199. Kiffin, *Sober Discourse*, 16.

200. Kiffin, *Sober Discourse*, 23 (see also 115).

201. Kiffin, *Sober Discourse*, 25–26. "And if the advantage inclines to either of them, it is evident that the New Testament more frequently mentions the Command and Practice of Baptism than of the Supper" (26).

not only Commanded, but Practiced. First they Preached; and such as were Converted, were Baptized; such as were Baptized, walkt in Church-Fellowship, *&c*. Breaking of Bread and Prayers; which being so express, what necessity is there to be wise above what is written, and to clamor for *Precept* or *Example*, to prove that Baptism is a bar to Communion, since we read every where (where Gospel order is set down) that all such as were received, were first Baptized; and not one instance in the whole Bible, that any were received without it.[202]

In his third chapter, Kiffin made four theological arguments in favor of strict communion. First, because Christ has ordered his church and its ordinances, observing those ordinances according to his rule exalts his wisdom. On the contrary, when we alter his ordinances "we cast a blemish upon the Wisdom of Christ, as if we were wiser to order things than he."[203] Second, the ordinances belong to Christ and are given to the church in trust, and must therefore be observed by the church in exact accordance with the rules given.[204] Third, observing the ordinances according to the rule of Christ preserves the beauty of the church, "For whatsoever is prescribed by the Lord Jesus, with respect to his Worship, is full of Beauty, Harmony, and Order, every thing answering its respective end, and what is signified thereby."[205] Under this heading, Kiffin also argued from the significance of baptism. If regeneration is the first grace received and the doorway into all other gospel graces, and if baptism is the sign of regeneration, then baptism must be the first ordinance received, the initiation into all other gospel ordinances.[206] Not only does the precedence of regeneration to participation in the new covenant blessings demonstrate the precedence of baptism to the Lord's Supper, but so does its non-repeatability. "As Baptism is not to be Repeated, because it is the Sacrament of Regeneration, Initiation, and Incorporation, which are not capable of Reiteration,

---

202. Kiffin, *Sober Discourse*, 28–29.

203. Kiffin, *Sober Discourse*, 36.

204. "For as in Humane Affairs, the exact conscientious and upright management of a Trust, is a certain note of the Integrity and Honesty of the Trustee, so the violation of it is a high breach and violation of Sincerity and Faithfulness" (Kiffin, *Sober Discourse*, 37).

205. Kiffin, *Sober Discourse*, 38.

206. "Also, how *Baptism* being the first Ordinance to be Administered, answers to the first Grace Received; From whence it appeareth, That as the Grace of Regeneration gives a Right to the Enjoyment of Gospel Institutions; so *Baptism*, with respect to Priority and Order, is the first Institution, without which, none may regularly partake of other Church-Ordinances" (Kiffin, *Sober Discourse*, 47).

so neither can the Seal and Sign thereof; so whatsoever makes for the not Repeating it in the ordinary use of it, makes also for this as fully or more, that it should be the first."[207] Fourth, observing the ordinances according to the rule of Christ "prevents the creeping in of the Inventions of Men in the Worship of God."[208] Anything less than exact obedience in this first gospel institution is a step toward Antichrist, "which is indeed no wonder, for if a Church swerves from the Rule in one thing, a Foundation is thereby laid of doing so in many things."[209]

In the fourth chapter, Kiffin presented an historical survey from the time of the apostles to his own day in order to demonstrate that open communion is an historical novelty, while strict communion has been the continuous practice of the church throughout the ages. This historical survey asserts that in the third century the error of paedobaptism crept into the church under the pretense of love (lest infants die in a state of damnation), and on its heels followed all manner of heresy. But even in the midst of this error, paedobaptists still held the ordinance of baptism in high esteem, requiring it for admission to full communion in the church. "*Pado-Baptism* is but a perverting or an abuse of the Ordinance of Baptism, but this Opinion [i.e., open communion] quite abolishes it, which is the necessary effect and Consequence of their declaring it to be needless in order to admission into a Church, *&c.*"[210]

In the final chapter, Kiffin responded to eleven objections to strict communion.

1. To the objection that there is "*no Rule, or express Warrant*" for excluding saints from church communion, Kiffin responded that this turns the regulative principle on its head, for it supposes "that whatsoever is not forbidden in Scripture, is Lawful."[211] This, said Kiffin, "is a Perni-

---

207. Kiffin, *Sober Discourse*, 59.
208. Kiffin, *Sober Discourse*, 48.
209. Kiffin, *Sober Discourse*, 54.

210. Kiffin, *Sober Discourse*, 79. In Kiffin's fourth chapter, he cited numerous contemporary authors in support of strict communion, most if not all of whom were paedobaptists, to prove that strict communion had the universal approbation of Protestants (81–117). Intriguingly, given the ambiguity of the 1677 London Baptist Confession on this issue of strict communion, Kiffin quoted from the 1646 London Baptist Confession to prove that strict communion was the Baptist position (109–10).

211. Kiffin, *Sober Discourse*, 120.

cious way of Argument . . . tending to bring all Humane Inventions into Gods Worship."[212]

2. To the objection that paedobaptists think themselves baptized, Kiffin responded that the ordinances are not ruled by man's opinion, but by God's word.[213]

3. To the objection that Rom 14:1 says to receive those who are weak in faith, Kiffin replied: first, that Paul is speaking to matters of conscience, and baptism is a matter of command; and second, that Paul is speaking to a baptized congregation about mutual fellowship, not church communion.[214]

4. To the objection that 1 Cor 12:13 refers to the baptism of the Spirit, Kiffin replied that the apostle Paul is speaking of water baptism, for in the same verse he refers to drinking of one Spirit, which is a reference to the Lord's Supper.[215]

5. To the objection that Rom 6:3 and Gal 3:27 imply that not all in Rome or Galatia were baptized, Kiffin demonstrated that these verses actually imply the opposite.[216]

6. To the objection that nobody inquired into Paul's baptism when he arrived in Jerusalem after his conversion (Acts 9:26–27), Kiffin argued that the Scripture does not record everything said and done. "For how should they know him to be a Disciple of Christ and so meet for Communion with them, but by knowing that he had at least done the first things of a Disciple . . . ?"[217]

---

212. Kiffin, *Sober Discourse*, 120.

213. Kiffin, *Sober Discourse*, 125–29.

214. Kiffin, *Sober Discourse*, 129–32.

215. "The Apostle shews the Communion which Believers have with the Holy Spirit in the Two Ordinances, *Baptism* and the *Lords Supper*. For what else can be intended by Drinking into one Spirit, but the Saints Communion in the Spirit, in, and by the Supper [*Drinking*] by a *Synecdoche* being put both for Eating and Drinking; And if so, why must we not as well understand the First Ordinance in its proper Sense for Water Baptism in the former part, as the Later Ordinance, the Supper in the first part of the Text" (Kiffin, *Sober Discourse*, 133–34).

216. Kiffin, *Sober Discourse*, 139–46.

217. Kiffin, *Sober Discourse*, 147.

7. To the objection that this rule only applied in the infancy of the church, but is not binding any longer, Kiffin asked, "If that be no Rule to us, let it be shown where there is another Rule?"[218]

8. To the objection that union with Christ alone gives a right to all his ordinances, Kiffin responded that this union is signified through baptism. If union with Christ apart from baptism sufficed, then why the command to be baptized?[219]

9. To the objection that excluding the unbaptized saint is divisive and uncharitable, Kiffin retorted that those obedient to the truth are not the cause of division, but rather those who are disobedient to the rule of Christ. Nevertheless, Kiffin denied that strict Baptist communion serves to "Unchristian or Unchurch" paedobaptists.[220]

10. To the objection that those who have the other six foundations of unity mentioned in Eph 4:4-6 (one body, one Spirit, one hope, one Lord, one faith, one God and Father) should not be denied communion because they lack the one baptism, Kiffin replied that the seven foundations of unity are like seven links in a chain, not one of which can be taken away without destroying the whole.[221]

11. To the objection that love, not baptism, is the visible sign of Christian discipleship, Kiffin responded that love keeps Christ's commandments.[222]

Bunyan never responded to Kiffin. By the time *A Sober Discourse* appeared in print, Bunyan was engaged in a feverish season of writing and ministry. Greaves dates the composition of seven of Bunyan's works to 1682-1683.[223] Or perhaps political tensions arising from the various

218. Kiffin, *Sober Discourse*, 149.

219. Kiffin, *Sober Discourse*, 151-52.

220. Kiffin, *Sober Discourse*, 154. Kiffin did not explicitly affirm paedobaptist churches to be true churches; he simply denied that upholding Scriptural order is what "unchurches" them.

221. Kiffin, *Sober Discourse*, 154-60.

222. Kiffin, *Sober Discourse*, 160-63 (a printing error in the original has pp. 130-31 succeeding pp. 160-61).

223. *The Holy War* (March 1681-January 1682), *Of Antichrist, and His Ruine* (February-May 1682), *The Greatness of the Soul* (June-October 1682), *An Exposition of the First Ten Chapters of Genesis* (October/November 1682-June 1683), *A Holy Life, the Beauty of Christianity* (late June-August 1683), *A Case of Conscience Resolved* (September 1683), and *Seasonable Counsel: Or, Advice to Sufferers* (October 1683-January 1684). See Greaves, *Glimpses of Glory*, 639.

efforts to exclude the Catholic James II from succeeding Charles II, and the "Tory Backlash" that followed, kept Bunyan otherwise occupied.[224] Or maybe Bunyan simply felt he had said all that needed to be said on the matter. Whatever the reason, *A Sober Discourse* brought the communion controversy to a close.

Seven Degrees of Separation

The communion controversy spanned ten years and ten publications from six different authors.[225] Yet no resolution was reached; neither side proved successful in convincing the other of the error of their ways. How did these two groups, both in agreement that credobaptism by immersion was the only true baptism, arrive at such radically distinct positions on whether or not baptism was a term of communion in the church? Underneath the polemics and prooftexting, Bunyan and his Baptist opponents were separated by seven fundamentally irreconcilable ecclesiological convictions.

The Church as Binary or Ternary

Bunyan and the Baptists differed over the nature of the church as binary or ternary. This division comes to light in the way each side argued their case either for or against baptism as the initiating ordinance into the church. Bunyan viewed the church in binary terms, as either universal/invisible or particular/visible, and he reasoned that baptism could not be the initiating ordinance into either one. "*Baptism makes thee no member of the Church, neither particular nor universall: neither doth it make thee a visible Saint: It therefore gives thee neither right to, nor being of membership at all.*"[226] If baptism is the initiating ordinance into the universal/invisible

---

224. "Tory Backlash" is Greaves's phrase (Greaves, *Glimpses of Glory*, 479). Though Bunyan was not directly involved in such plots, Greaves outlines Bunyan's close relationships with various plotters (470–73, 489–91). On persecution during this period and its impact on Bunyan, see Greaves, *Glimpses of Glory*, 455–62.

225. From 1671–1681, with publications from Bunyan (*A Confession of My Faith; Differences in Judgment; Peaceable Principles and True*), Henry Jessey (essay appended to *Differences in Judgment*), Thomas Paul (*Some Serious Reflections* and his [no longer extant] response to *Differences in Judgment*), John Denne (*Truth Outweighing Error* and *Hypocrisies Detected* [no longer extant]), Henry Danvers (*A Treatise of Baptism*), and William Kiffin (*A Sober Discourse*).

226. Bunyan, *Confession of My Faith*, 4:164.

church, then only Baptists can belong to this church, for only Baptists are baptized. If baptism is the initiating ordinance into the particular/visible church, then not only must baptism be repeated each time a person joins a particular church, but the only true, visible church would be a Baptist church, for only a Baptist church practices true baptism. Bunyan knew most Baptists were unwilling to affirm either conclusion, that is, to either "unchristian" paedobaptist saints, or "unchurch" paedobaptist churches.[227] For Bunyan, one is made a member of the universal/invisible church by the baptism of the Spirit, and a member of a particular/visible church by "a discovery of the Faith and Holiness, and a Declaration of the willingness of a Person to subject himself to the Laws and the Government of Christ in his Church."[228] Bunyan's view of the church as either universal/invisible or particular/visible drove him to deny that baptism was the initiating ordinance into either one. Bunyan began with the nature of the church, and reasoned his baptismal theology from there.

The Baptists began with baptism and reasoned from there to the nature of the church. Driven by what they saw as clear scriptural precept and precedent, they were convinced that baptism is the initiating ordinance into the church. But which church? The universal or the particular? The invisible or the visible? Thomas Paul initially denied that baptism is the initiating ordinance into a particular/visible church, but later, under pressure from Danvers and others, clarified that baptism is the initiating ordinance into the *"universal, orderly, Church-visible."*[229] Denne affirmed, "For that which ought to be administered upon Conversion, before Church-membership, is an initiating Ordinance."[230] Danvers asserted that baptism is "the *Listing, Es-*

---

227. Bunyan, *Differences in Judgment*, 4:221–22; *Peaceable Principles and True*, 4:274. Kiffin denied this conclusion (Kiffin, *Sober Discourse*, 154). Denne was suspicious of the faith of the unbaptized (J. Denne, *Truth Outweighing Error*, 97–98). Bunyan thought Thomas Paul denied that paedobaptist churches were true churches: "Further, you count their communion among *themselves, unlawful,* and therefore *unwarrantable*; and have concluded, *they are joyned to Idols, and that they ought not to be shewed the pattern of the House of God, until they be ashamed of their sprinkling in their Infancy, and accept of and receive Baptism as you.* Yea, you count them as they stand, not the Churches of God; saying, *We have no custom, nor the churches of God"* (Bunyan, *Peaceable Principles and True*, 4:269).

228. Bunyan, *Differences in Judgment*, 4:199–200.

229. For Paul's denial, see Paul, *Some Serious Reflections*, 3–4. For Bunyan's astounded response, see Bunyan, *Differences in Judgment*, 4:198. For Paul's clarification, see Bunyan, *Peaceable Principles and True*, 4:273.

230. J. Denne, *Truth Outweighing Error*, 51.

pousing, Covenanting, Ingrafting, Implanting Ordinance," and the "*entrance and door* into the Visible Church."[231] Neither Denne nor Danvers addressed the questions that arise from linking baptism to the visible church. In his second work, Paul tried to evade the troubling implications of this view by positing that baptism is the initiating ordinance into the "*universal, orderly, Church-visible*," a claim Bunyan regarded as nonsensical.

> Now I would yet learn of this Brother where this church is; for if it be *Visible*, he can *tell* and also *shew* it. But, to be short, there is no such Church: The universal Church cannot be visible; a great part of that vast Body being already in Heaven, and a great part as yet (perhaps) unborn.
> But if he should mean by *Universal*, the whole of that part of this Church that is on Earth, then neither is it *visible* or *orderly*. 1. Not *Visible*; for the greatest part remains always to the best mans eye utterly invisible.
> 2. This Church is not *Orderly*; that is, hath not Harmony in its outward and visible parts of worship; some parts opposing and contradicting the other most *severely*. . . .
> So then by *Universal, Orderly, Visible Church*, this Brother must mean those of the Saints only, that have been, or are baptized as we; this is clear, because Baptism (saith he) maketh a Believer a member of *this Church*; his meaning then is, that there is an *Universal, Orderly, Visible Church*, and they *alone* are the *Baptists*; and that every one that is baptized, is by that made a member of the *Universal, Orderly, Visible Church of Baptists*, and that the whole number of the rest of the Saints are utterly excluded.[232]

It appears that Kiffin agreed with Paul, for he called baptism a "means of implanting men into Christ, or the body of Christ the Church, *Gal.* 3. 27. *Rom.* 6. 3. . . . not into this or that particular Church; but into that one Church of Christ, which is distributed into several parts and particular Societies."[233] It is doubtful that Kiffin regarded baptism as implanting one into the universal/invisible church, for this would mean that anyone who is unbaptized is cut off from the communion of saints, and Kiffin explicitly denied that paedobaptism is a damning error.[234] Therefore, he must

---

231. Danvers, *Treatise of Baptism* p.s. 44, 52.

232. Bunyan, *Peaceable Principles and True*, 4:273–74. Bunyan was quoting from Paul's reply to *Differences in Judgment*, which is no longer extant.

233. Kiffin, *Sober Discourse*, 137–38.

234. "And the Error [i.e., paedobaptism] being not so fundamental as to endanger their Eternal State, we esteem them Christian Brethren and Saints, for whose further illumination we dayly put up our Prayers" (Kiffin, *Sober Discourse*, 6).

have meant something similar to what Paul expressed, that there is in fact a third category of the church, visible but not particular, yet neither strictly universal.[235] Still, Kiffin used exclusive language: "not into this or that particular Church; but into that one Church of Christ."[236] The implication of this view seems to be that while there may be true paedobaptist saints, there are no true paedobaptist churches. Kiffin explicitly denied this insinuation, stating, "We censure none so rigidly as to take upon us to Unchristian or Unchurch them," yet it is the necessary implication of his position.[237] In order to affirm that a paedobaptist church is a true visible church, one must either deny that baptism is the initiating ordinance into the visible church, or else affirm that paedobaptism is a true yet imperfect form of baptism; Kiffin was unwilling to do either.[238] This left the Baptists with three forms of the church: (1) a universal/invisible church comprised of all the elect of all ages; (2) a non-particular/visible church of Baptists upon the earth or within a given region; and (3) a particular/visible Baptist church that is a local subset of (2). According to Kiffin, baptism is the initiating ordinance into the second of the three.

Baptism as Symbol or Sacrament

Bunyan and the Baptists also differed over the nature of baptism as symbol or sacrament. For Bunyan, baptism in water is the outward sign of the baptism of the Spirit, but there is no essential relationship between the two. Throughout the communion controversy, Bunyan only spoke of baptism in symbolic terms, never as a means of grace.[239] Not only can water baptism

---

235. Matthew Ward, commenting upon this quote from *A Sober Discourse*, notes, "Kiffin's vision clearly meant one great Baptist church in each city" (Ward, "Baptism as Worship," 30). Ward notes that Hanserd Knollys held a similar position, and cites Knollys, *World That Now Is*, 8, 44, 45.

236. Kiffin, *Sober Discourse*, 138.

237. Kiffin, *Sober Discourse*, 154. As Kiffin was reticent to "Unchurch" paedobaptists, he likely would have claimed that a paedobaptist church was a true, yet disorderly, church. Nevertheless, Bunyan thought the logic of Kiffin's argument denied such a conclusion.

238. "To obviate a Cavil, which may be made, the Reader may understand that under the term [Unbaptized] we comprehend all persons that either were never Baptized at all, or such as have been (as they call it) *Christned* or Baptized (more properly Sprinkled) in their Infancy" (Kiffin, *Sober Discourse*, 9).

239. Outside the polemics of controversy, however, Bunyan could speak of baptism as a means of grace. See Bunyan, *Holy Life*, 9:254; *Desire of the Righteous Granted*, 13:130.

and Spirit baptism be distinguished, they can be severed, such that one can and often does possess the substance without the shadow.

> For here you must note, I distinguish between the doctrin and the practise of Water-baptism; The Doctrin being that which by the outward sign is presented to us, or which by the outward circumstance of the act is preached to the believer: viz. *The death of Christ; My death with Christ; also his resurrection from the Dead, and mine with him to newness of life.* This is the doctrin which Baptism preacheth, or that which by the outward action is signified to the believing receiver. Now I say, he that believeth in Jesus Christ; that [hath] richer and better then that, *viz.* is dead to sin, and that lives to God by him, he hath the heart, power and doctrine of Baptism: all then he wanteth, is but the sign, the shadow, or the outward circumstance thereof. . . . The best of Baptisms he hath; he is Baptized by that one spirit; he hath the heart of Water-baptism, he wanteth only the outward shew, which if he had would not prove him a truly visible Saint; it would not tell me he had grace in his heart.[240]

A person can be baptized in the Spirit without being baptized in water; likewise, one can be baptized in water without being baptized in the Spirit. But if one has the "best of Baptisms," the baptism of the Spirit, yet lacks the baptism in water, he has that which is primary and substantial, and ought not be rejected for want of that which is secondary and "shadowish."

The Baptists vehemently disagreed. Though baptism in water can be distinguished from the baptism of the Spirit, the sign from the thing signified, they must never be severed such that the church accepts one who possesses the latter but neglects the former. For Thomas Paul, the doctrine of baptism was inseparable from the practice of baptism: "Is it enough to hold practical Doctrines, to know them so as to hold them, and yet not do them? You need never ask a believer whether he hold a practical Doctrine, his obedience to it will always speak for him."[241] What if an Old Testament believer had neglected the practice of the sacrifices and ceremonies of the old covenant, while professing faith in the Messiah to come, of whom those sacrifices and ceremonies were but types and shadows? Would God have approved of him?[242] Denne wrote, "We readily allow that, and oftentimes

---

240. Bunyan, *Confession of My Faith*, 4:172. See also Bunyan, *Differences in Judgment*, 4:211–16.

241. Paul, *Some Serious Reflections*, 15.

242. "Under the Law all the Sacrifices of that dispensation with their Sabaths and

find that many have the Doctrine (although not without light) without the Practice, whom it seems are such as *John Bunyan* is bold to have communion with." Nevertheless, Bunyan "hath no Scripture-warrant for it, and it is a great boldness to adventure in Church-Communion beyond what is written, yea, contrary to what is written."[243] In other words, though a thing may be possible, that does not make it permissible.

Though Paul and Denne were unwilling to sever the sign from the thing signified, their argument did not rest upon the efficacy of baptism, at least not explicitly so, but rather upon the necessity of obedience to God's revealed Word. William Kiffin, on the other hand, argued from the nature of baptism and its efficacy as a means of grace, employing explicitly sacramental language: "As the *Supper* is a Spiritual participation of the *Body* and *Blood* of Christ by Faith, and so (not meerly by the work done) is a means of Salvation; so *Baptism Signs* and *Seals* our Salvation to us which lies in *Justification* and discharge of sin, *&c*."[244] In fact, it is baptism's function as a sign and seal of the new covenant that renders paedobaptism meaningless:

> Christ looks for a Believer, which no Infant can at present be said to be, the want of which, makes the Baptism null, for if there be no Bond, no Covenant, no Obligation in it (as 'tis plain there is not, and they confess it) than there is no Sealing, for a Seal serves but to Ratifie and Confirm a Bond and Covenant, and as there is no Sealing, so there is no exhibition or conveyance of anything from Christ, for there are no Pipes to receive it, that is, as an Ordinance, there is no Reason in the use of it. . . . Infant Baptism is as much a nullity as the Marrying or Ordination of Infants.[245]

An infant cannot exercise faith; therefore, its "baptism" cannot function as a seal of the new covenant, for inclusion in the new covenant is conditioned upon faith. Paedobaptism is therefore a nullity. A paedobaptist believer must therefore be regarded as unbaptized; and lacking baptism,

---

other things, were Tipes of that Christ who was the substance of all those Ceremonies: If any of them then that professed Faith in the *Messiah* to come, should upon scruples, or want of pretended light, neglect the whole, or part of that Tipical Worship, why may not a man say of them, as this advocate says of the practice under debate? They had the richer and better Sacrifice, they had the substance and body of all the Tipes: So that this principle puts the whole of Gods instituted Worship, both under the Law and Gospel, to the highest uncertainties" (Paul, *Some Serious Reflections*, 16–17).

243. J. Denne, *Truth Outweighing Error*, 87.

244. Kiffin, *Sober Discourse*, 25–26.

245. Kiffin, *Sober Discourse*, 77–78.

the sign and seal of the new covenant, such a one has no ratification or confirmation of his covenant with God. Therefore, though God may accept him into fellowship with himself, the church may not. For the benefits of Christ through his church may be granted only to those bearing the sign and seal of the covenant.[246]

Baptism and the Regulative Principle

Bunyan and the Baptists further differed on their interpretation and application of the regulative principle. Both sides appealed to the regulative principle as the basis of their argument, and both sides accused the other of violating the principle in favor of human inventions. Bunyan repeatedly demanded of the Baptists "precept, precedent, or example" for making baptism the initiating ordinance of the church, as well as for excluding unbaptized saints from church communion. "Where have you one word of God, that forbiddeth a person, so qualified, as is signified in mine Argument, the best Communion of Saints for want of Water? There is not a syllable for this in all the Book of God."[247]

In reply, the Baptists continually pointed to dominical precept, apostolic precedent, and primitive church practice of those who believed the gospel first being baptized, and afterward brought into church communion. But these did not satisfy Bunyan. He readily affirmed that the pattern set forth in the primitive church was that of belief, then baptism, then belonging. But in the absence of an explicit command to exclude the unbaptized from church communion, he was unwilling to do so.

---

246. Under this heading, "sacramental" does not mean everything modern Baptist Sacramentalists mean by the term. For instance, it does not mean that Kiffin held baptism to be regenerative (cf. Cross, "Baptismal Regeneration," 149–74). Stanley Fowler acknowledges that early Baptist sacramental language was left somewhat vague: "Given the Puritan-Separatist roots of Baptist churches, it would appear that the Calvinistic concept of baptism as a 'seal' of union with Christ by faith continued to shape the way in which Baptists described the efficacy of the baptism of professed believers. However, this understanding was largely unelaborated, due to the necessity to focus their baptismal debates on the points at which they departed from their historical roots" (Fowler, *More Than a Symbol*, 20). It is best to understand Kiffin's sacramental language in a strictly covenantal (rather than regenerative) sense. Kiffin meant something similar to what Bobby Jamieson means when he refers to baptism as "the initiating oath-sign of the new covenant" and an "effective sign of church membership" (Jamieson, *Going Public*, 55–80, 137–57).

247. Bunyan, *Differences in Judgment*, 4:231. See also Bunyan, *Confession of My Faith*, 4:162, 169; *Differences in Judgment*, 4:235.

> At this I have called for your proofs; the which you have attempted to produce; but in conclusion, have shewed none other, but, *That the Primitive Churches had those they received baptized before so received.*
>
> I have told you, that this, though it were granted, cometh not up to the Question; *for we ask not, whether they were so baptized? But, whether you find a word in the Bible that justifieth your concluding that it is your Duty to exclude those of your holy Brethren that have not been SO baptized?*[248]

In the absence of an explicit command to exclude the unbaptized from church communion, Bunyan appealed to another explicit command: receive the weak in faith, and welcome them as Christ has welcomed you (Rom 14:1; 15:7). "*That there being no Precept, President nor Example in all the Scripture for our excluding our holy Brethren that differ in this point from us; therefore we ought not to dare to do it,* but contrariwise to receive them; because God hath given us sufficient proof that himself hath received them, whose example in this case he hath commanded us to follow, *Rom 14. 15.*"[249] Thus, Bunyan appealed to the regulative principle for his practice of open communion, and accused the Baptists of violating the principle by their strict communion.

Kiffin provided the most effective response to Bunyan, accusing Bunyan (without mentioning his name) of holding to the normative principle, that whatever is not expressly forbidden is permissible. In response to the demand for a "*Rule, or express Warrant of Scripture to Exclude Persons fearing God, from receiving the Lords Supper, who by vertue of their Faith have a Right to it,*" Kiffin wrote that this "supposes, That whatsoever is not forbidden in Scripture, is Lawful; and so the Receiving of Believers that are not baptized to the Supper, being not Prohibited, is therefore Lawful."[250] Kiffin

---

248. Bunyan, *Peaceable Principles and True*, 4:269–70. He earlier wrote in his *A Confession of My Faith*, "For herein lyes the mistake, To think that because in time past, Baptism was administered upon conversion, *that therefore it is the initiating, and entring ordinance* to Church-communion: when by the word no such thing is testifyed of it" (Bunyan, *Confession of My Faith*, 4:162). Also, "That Water-baptism hath formerly gone first is granted: But that it ought of necessity so to do, I never saw proof" (4:169). Kiffin claimed that 2 Thess 3:6 provided explicit warrant for the exclusion of the unbaptized (Kiffin, *Sober Discourse*, 17–18).

249. Bunyan, *Peaceable Principles and True*, 4:270 (see also 4:276). See Bunyan, *Confession of My Faith*, 4:172–74; *Differences in Judgment*, 4:216–19. This was also Jessey's argument in Jessey, "Appendix," in Bunyan, *Differences in Judgment*, 4:259–60, 263.

250. Kiffin, *Sober Discourse*, 118, 120.

demonstrated that the proper interpretation of the regulative principle includes both explicit command and necessary inference:

> That if by *Precept, President,* or *Example,* is meant such, in *express* words, *viz.* such Texts of Scripture as prohibit Practices by name and circumstance, then Popish Purgatory, and Monkery and ten thousand other things, as Doctor *Owen* well says, may be made Lawful by this Argument, there being not an express word in Scripture that prohibits those things by their very name, because not then in being. If it be meant what may be inferred by *direct and plain consequence* in the true *Logical* Notion of it, without Sophistry or Quibble, I am satisfied we can produce *Precept, President,* and *Example* that it is our Duty to withdraw from disorderly Walkers.[251]

Kiffin claimed precept, precedent, and example for his position. Could Bunyan show the same for his? "For what man dare go in a way which hath neither Precept nor Example to warrant it, from a Way that hath a full Current of both? yet they that will admit Members into the Visible Church without Baptism, do so."[252]

Baptism as a Matter of Conscience or Command

The most disputed text in the entire communion controversy was Romans 14–15. This text was employed to great effect by both Bunyan and Jessey. Bunyan insisted that Romans 14–15, with its command that the church at Rome receive those who are weak in faith despite differences of opinion in non-essential, outward, circumstantial matters of conscience, applied to the present question of baptism. For Bunyan, this argument was unanswerable, which his opponents "so *tenderly* touch as if it *burnt* your fingers."[253] The command is clear: receive all whom God receives, on the same basis upon which God receives them. "The *Rule* by which they are directed to do it [i.e., receive the weak in faith], is that by which we perceive *that Christ hath received them*: But Christ did not receive them by Baptism, but as given to him by the Father: Him therefore concerning whom we are convinced, that he by the Father is given to Christ, *Him should we receive.*"[254]

---

251. Kiffin, *Sober Discourse*, 3–4 (see also 28–31).
252. Kiffin, *Sober Discourse*, 92. This is a quotation from an unnamed, but "very noted and Learned Author now living" (91).
253. Bunyan, *Differences in Judgment*, 4:216.
254. Bunyan, *Differences in Judgment*, 4:217.

The Baptist response to the Romans 14–15 argument was to circumscribe the apostle's exhortation. First, the matters about which Paul wrote dealt with issues of Jewish law—eating and drinking, and holy days. Paul was not talking about gospel ordinances like baptism.[255] Second, Paul could not have been talking about receiving the unbaptized, because he was writing to a congregation of baptized believers. And third, the receiving of which Paul spoke could not refer to receiving into church communion, because those to whom he wrote already enjoyed such communion.[256]

Bunyan was unconvinced. "You may not, cannot, ought not to dare to limit the Exhortation to receiving of one another into each others affections only; and not also receiving Saints into Communion."[257] To reject one whom God has accepted is a very serious sin, surely more serious than the neglect of baptism. "I say again, To make Water-baptism a bar and division betwixt Saint and Saint, every-whit otherwise gracious and holy alike: This is *like fasting for strife, and debate, and to smite with the fist of wickedness*; and is not to be found within the whole Bible, but is wholly an order of your own devising."[258] "He erreth in a circumstance, thou errest in a substance."[259] For Bunyan, baptism was a matter of conscience, and therefore differences of opinion must be tolerated for the sake of unity. For the Baptists, baptism was a matter of command, admitting of no deviation from the Scriptural institution, even at the cost of division.

Baptismal Perspicuity and the Need for "Light"

Bunyan opened the controversy by claiming that paedobaptist saints have an acceptable—nay, "invincible"—excuse for their neglect of baptism: they have no light regarding credobaptism. It is God that gives light; to be

---

255. Paul, *Some Serious Reflections*, 21; J. Denne, *Truth Outweighing Error*, 92. "The weakness spoken of in the Text, hath Relation only to those mistakes that did attend some of them touching a liberty of eating, or not eating Meats, or the keeping or not keeping of days which were things in themselves of an indifferent Nature, the doing or not doing of which, was not Sin, as the Apostle in that chapter plainly shews; and hath no Relation to the Order of Worship prescribed by Christ, much less to the Practice or not Practice of Ordinances" (Kiffin, *Sober Discourse*, 130–31).

256. Paul, *Some Serious Reflections*, 20–21; J. Denne, *Truth Outweighing Error*, 89–90; Kiffin, *Sober Discourse*, 129–32. Bunyan disputed these last two points in Bunyan, *Differences in Judgment*, 4:204–5, 216–19, 243.

257. Bunyan, *Differences in Judgment*, 4:217.

258. Bunyan, *Differences in Judgment*, 4:219.

259. Bunyan, *Confession of My Faith*, 4:173.

baptized apart from light would be to sin against God, for "whatever is not of faith is sin."[260] Underneath this logic was a denial of the perspicuity of baptism. On the other hand, the Baptists insisted that baptism was a clear command of Christ, as clear as any ordinance of Scripture, "written as with a Sun beam, that he that runs may read."[261] Therefore, a refusal to submit to baptism is not due to a want of light, but is either the result of a failure to "seriously enquire after it," blatant disobedience, or worse, unbelief.[262] Kiffin wrote, "It deserves to be seriously considered, whether the neglect of the Ordinance of Baptism doth not more arise from the want of a heart to obey God therein, by reason of the contempt put upon it, then for want of Light. Is any Ordinance of Jesus Christ more plain and clear than this?"[263]

Bunyan did not agree. "Your supposition, That very few Professors will seriously enquire after Water-baptism, *is too rude*. What! must all the Children of God, that are not baptized for want of Light, be still stigmatized with want of serious inquiry after God's mind in it?"[264] Bunyan was prepared to give grace to those convictional paedobaptists who accepted the Zwinglian argument that baptism is the new covenant analog to circumcision in the covenant of grace, to be applied to the believer and his children. The Baptists had no category for the convictional paedobaptist, at least not in their writings produced during the communion controversy. Neither did they

---

260. "But why were they not circumcised [i.e., the Israelite generation who were uncircumcised for forty years in the wilderness]? Doubtless there was a reason; either they wanted time, or opportunity, or instruments, or something. But they could not render a bigger reason than this. *I have no light therein*: which is the cause at this day that many a faithful man denyeth to take up the ordinance of Baptism, But I say what ever the hindrance was, it mattereth not; our brethren have a manifest one, an invincible one, one that all the men on earth nor Angels in heaven cannot remove; *For it is God that createth light*; and for them to do it without light would but prove them unfaithfull to themselves, and make them sinners against God; *For whatever is not of faith is sin*" (Bunyan, *Confession of My Faith*, 4:170). For similar arguments, see Bunyan, *Confession of My Faith*, 4:174–75; *Differences in Judgment*, 4:202–4, 216, 220; *Peaceable Principles and True*, 4:277.

261. Paul, *Some Serious Reflections*, 55.

262. "And must Baptism be such a Rock of offence to professors, that very few will seriously enquire after it, or submit to it?" (Paul, *Some Serious Reflections*, 55). Denne attributed disobedience in baptism to unbelief: "What, is not obedience to Christ, to an holy Ordinance, to a Duty enjoyned, a character of a Saint, yea a visible character? is not the contrary a breach, some breach at least in a good and holy life? . . . What is Infidelity, is it not a horrid sin?" (J. Denne, *Truth Outweighing Error*, 71).

263. Kiffin, *Sober Discourse*, 159.

264. Bunyan, *Differences in Judgment*, 4:245.

accept Bunyan's argument about "want of light." Paul pointedly asked, "Is it a Persons light, that gives being to a Precept? is it not his sin, though he want light? . . . Suppose men plead want of light in other Commands, must they be excused?"[265] Danvers stated that ignorance does not absolve from sin, and that Bunyan's argument "not only justifies the *neglect* of the *true*, but the Exercise of *false* Worship; and not only bears out in *rejecting* of Christs, but the *embracing* of Antichrists appointments. . . . A Rule if observed, what corrupt Doctrine or Practice might not be introduced thereby?"[266] Denne justifiably noted that Bunyan made himself famous refuting the Quakers on this very point. "He hath often cryed out against others for saying, *The Light within is the Rule for Christians to walk by*; but now he himself confidently affirms it, yea, in opposition to positive Commands."[267] He then suggested that the "greatest part of men" would wish to have Bunyan as an advocate on the last day, that he might blame God for their disobedience for failing to provide them with sufficient light.[268]

The Membership Requirements of the Visible Church

The communion controversy revealed two fundamentally different standards for membership in the visible church. For Bunyan, the membership requirements of the particular/visible church must be identical to the membership requirements of the universal/invisible church. As baptism in water is not required for membership in the latter, it cannot be required for membership in the former. The only membership requirement for entrance into the universal/invisible church is faith, made visible not by baptism, but by a holiness defined as obedience to the "moral precept evangelized." "Faith and Holiness, must be the Essentials, or Basis, upon, and for the sake of which you receive them: Holiness (I say) yet not such as is circumstantial, but that which is such in the very heart of it."[269] This logic lay beneath Bun-

265. Paul, *Some Serious Reflections*, 7.
266. Danvers, *Treatise of Baptism* p.s. 48.
267. J. Denne, *Truth Outweighing Error*, 78.
268. J. Denne, *Truth Outweighing Error*, 79.
269. Bunyan, *Differences in Judgment*, 4:199. For Bunyan, it is holiness that makes the saint visible, and thereby qualified for membership in the visible church. Baptism cannot be the source of visible sainthood. "The person then that is baptized stands by that, a member of no Church at all, neither of the visible, nor yet of the invisible. A visible Saint he is, but not so by Baptism; for he must be a visible Saint before, else he ought not to be baptized" (Bunyan, *Confession of My Faith*, 4:164; *Peaceable Principles and True*, 4:274). Anyone can be baptized; baptism is no sure sign of saving faith. "Yes, it is evident,

yan's constant assertion that the particular/visible church must receive all whom God receives, on the same basis upon which God receives them. The particular/visible church has no right to make its membership any more or less stringent than God.[270] It is a great sin and offense to God to reject one whom God has accepted and thereby to deny such a one his birthright; so great is this sin, in fact, that doing so brought down God's judgment upon Nonconformists in the form of the Clarendon Code.[271] "Is it not a wickedness to make that a Wall of Division betwixt us, which God never commanded to be so?"[272] For Bunyan, the universal/invisible church is the pattern for the particular/visible church, and the membership of the latter must approximate as closely as possible that of the former.

For the Baptists, the pattern for the visible church (however it is understood, whether universal, particular, or something in between) is not the invisible church, but the apostolic church. Therefore, the requirements for membership in the visible church must be identical to the membership requirements established by Scripture. Though there was ambiguity among Baptists as to whether baptism functioned as the initiating ordinance into the particular/visible church or the *"universal, orderly, Church-visible,"* all Baptists agreed that in the New Testament none were received into church communion without baptism, and therefore in the present none ought to be received into church communion apart from the same. To usurp both Scriptural precept and apostolic precedent is to be "wise above what is Written," and to provoke God to judgment, whose rule regarding the ordinances of worship must be strictly followed.[273]

---

that a man may be desirous of Water, that a man may be baptized, and neither own the Doctrine of Repentance, nor know on whom he should believe" (Bunyan, *Differences in Judgment*, 4:247).

270. That the requirements of the particular/visible church must not be less stringent than those of the universal/invisible church was the basis of the first thesis in Bunyan's defense of his open-communion practice: "*I dare not have communion with them that profess not faith and holiness*; or that are not visible Saints by calling. . . . Now he that is visibly or openly prophane, cannot be then a visible Saint, for he that is a visible Saint must profess faith, and repentance, and consequently holyness of life: And with none else dare I communicate" (Bunyan, *Confession of My Faith*, 4:154).

271. "Shall I add, Is it not that which greatly prevailed to bring down these judgments, which at present we feel and groan under; I will dare to say, it was the cause thereof" (Bunyan, *Confession of My Faith*, 4:183).

272. Bunyan, *Differences in Judgment*, 4:233.

273. Kiffin in Paul, *Some Serious Reflections*, A5. "That the order of Christ's Commission, as well as the matter therein contained, to be observed, may easily be concluded

The Controlling Principle of Evangelical Unity or Ecclesiological Purity

Yet underneath all other differences lay a distinctive impulse that drove each side to their respective conclusions. Bunyan's conclusions were controlled by the fundamental desire for evangelical unity. "*Faith, and Holiness, are my professed principles*," he wrote in the prefatory epistle to *A Confession of My Faith*.[274] Evangelical faith and holiness was the lens through which Bunyan read Scripture, and the foundation upon which he constructed his ecclesiology. A visible saint is one who shares a common faith in the gospel of justification by the imputed righteousness of Christ, and a common experience of regeneration that gives birth to a life of obedience to Christ. Those not possessing faith and holiness are to be excluded from church communion, because they are cut off from God. "*I dare not have communion with them that profess not faith and holiness*; or that are not visible saints by calling."[275] On the other hand, those possessing faith and holiness are to be received into church communion, because God has received them. "Now him that God receiveth and holdeth communion with, him you should receive and hold communion with."[276] Bunyan could not conceive of excluding from the covenant community one whom God had included in the new covenant in Christ. To do so is to provoke God to judgment, and to deprive his children of their birthright, thus hindering the excluded saint's faith and holiness. "If we shall reject visible Saints by calling, Saints that have communion with God; that have received the Law, at the hand of Christ, that are of an holy conversation among men; they desiring to have communion with us, as much as in us lyeth, we take from them their very priviledge, and the blessings to which they were born of God."[277] To say Bunyan was unconcerned with ecclesiological purity would

---

from Gods severity toward them that sought him not according to due order; 1 *Chron.* 15.13. Was God so exact with his people then, that all things, to a pin, must be according to the pattern in the Mount? *Heb.* 7.16, and 9, 10. whose Worship then comparitvely, to the Gospels, was but after the Law of a carnal Commandment: and can it be supposed, he should be so indifferent, now to leave men to their own liberty, to time and place his appointments contrary to what he hath given an express rule for, in his word, as before shewed, *Ezekiel* 44.7, 9, 10. *It was the Priests Sin formerly to bring the Uncircumcised in heart and flesh into his house*" (Paul, *Some Serious Reflections*, 47–48).

274. Bunyan, *Confession of My Faith*, 4:135.
275. Bunyan, *Confession of My Faith*, 4:154.
276. Bunyan, *Confession of My Faith*, 4:173.
277. Bunyan, *Confession of My Faith*, 4:182. See also Bunyan, *Differences in Judgment*, 4:230–34.

be a slander.[278] This was the entire rationale behind his dissent from the established Church. But should the occasion arise when evangelical unity and ecclesiological purity come into conflict, ecclesiological purity must bow the knee to evangelical unity.[279] "I say again, To make Water-baptism a bar and division betwixt Saint and Saint, every-whit otherwise gracious and holy alike: This is *like fasting for strife, and debate, and to smite with the fist of wickedness*; and is not to be found within the whole Bible, but is wholly an order of your own devising."[280]

The Baptists, on the other hand, were driven by the fundamental desire for ecclesiological purity.[281] They agreed with Bunyan on the necessity of evangelical faith and holiness; in fact, they would have defined such terms in very similar ways, with the possible exception of Denne. But their ultimate ecclesiological concern was to maintain pure worship and church order according to the rule of Scripture. "We must abide by the rule of Christ," was their constant refrain. "And no less exact are Christians to be in the Administration of Gospel Ordinances; since to deviate from the express Rule, is branded with the odious Title of *Will-Worship* and *humane Tradition*."[282] "It is a superlative and desperate piece of audacity for men to presume to mend any thing in the Worship of God; for it supposes the All-wise Law giver capable of error, and the attempter wiser than his Maker."[283] Thus, should evangelical unity and ecclesiological purity come into conflict, evangelical unity must bow the knee to ecclesiological purity. As Thomas Paul stated, "That man that makes affection the rule of his walking, rather then Judgement, it is no wonder to me, if he go out of the way. . . . But must our love to these [unbaptized saints], indulge

---

278. "Thou must also keep close to Gospel-worship, publick and private: doing of those things that thou has warrant for from the Word, and leaving of that, or those things for others that will stick to them, that have no stamp of God upon them" (Bunyan, *Seasonable Counsel*, 10:28). Bunyan repeatedly denied that he denigrated baptism, or any of the ordinances of God. See Bunyan, *Confession of My Faith*, 4:160; *Differences in Judgment*, 4:193. "But, Sir, who have I pleaded for, in the denyal of any one Ordinance of God? Yea, or for their neglect of it either?" (4:203).

279. "Wherefore when that of God, that is great, is overweighed by that which is small; it is the wisdom of them that see it, to put load to the other end of the scale; untill the things thus abused, poise in their own place" (Bunyan, *Confession of My Faith*, 4:181).

280. Bunyan, *Differences in Judgment*, 4:219.

281. This is similar to the thesis of Matthew Ward in his monograph *Pure Worship*, wherein he argues that liturgical purity was the seventeenth-century Baptist distinctive.

282. Kiffin, *Sober Discourse*, 28.

283. Kiffin, *Sober Discourse*, B4.

them in any act of disobedience?"[284] The Baptists could not conceive of altering of the rule of Christ, who is the Lord of the church, not even for such a worthy cause as peace and unity.

> When the question shall be askt, *Who hath required this at your hands?* I doubt it will be no sufficient plea to say, That if we have erred in any Punctilio's of Divine Truth, it was for Peace and Unions sake, *&c.* For, *No motions of Peace are to be made or received with loss of Truth*: Nor may the Laws, Orders, and Prescriptions of Christ be altered, or varied, in any tittle, upon any pretense whatsoever, God having never given any such Prerogative to mankind, as to be Arbitrators how he may be best and most decently Worshiped.[285]

It may be objected that Bunyan did not consider baptism a part of church worship, and therefore to characterize this debate as one of evangelical unity versus ecclesiological purity is a false dichotomy, at least in Bunyan's case. "Water-baptism giveth neither being, nor well-being to a Church, neither is any part of that Instituted Worship of God, that the Church, as such, should be found in the Practice of."[286] But Bunyan's baptismal theology was formed by his concern for evangelical unity. Because Bunyan could not fit baptism within his paradigm of the church, whether particular/visible or universal/invisible, in such a way as to maintain evangelical unity, he severed baptism from the church, and read the Scriptures accordingly. Presuppositions exert a powerful influence upon conclusions.

"Brethren: Close; Close; Be One"

Bunyan concluded *A Confession of My Faith* with this irenic call to his separated brethren (the Baptists): "I return now to those that are visible Saints by Calling, that stand at a distance one from another, upon accounts before specifyed: Brethren: Close; Close; Be one as the Father and Christ is one."[287] But they could not close. The gap between them simply could not be bridged without either side conceding essential ecclesiological convictions regarding the nature of the church, the nature of baptism, and the relationship between the two. And if ecclesiological unity proved impossible, can Bunyan legitimately be termed a Baptist?

284. Paul, *Some Serious Reflections*, 29–30.
285. Kiffin, *Sober Discourse*, B6–B7.
286. Bunyan, *Differences in Judgment*, 4:221.
287. Bunyan, *Confession of My Faith*, 4:186.

Chapter 5

Strict Communion and Seventeenth-Century Baptist Identity

Baptisme is an ordinance of the new Testament, given by Christ, to be dispensed upon persons professing faith, or that are made Disciples; who upon profession of faith, ought to be baptized, and after to partake of the Lords Supper.[1]

Holding Fast to "That Good Old Principle"

BUNYAN PUBLISHED HIS FINAL offering in the communion controversy, *Peaceable Principles and True*, in 1674. In a December 1676 letter addressed to the Southwark congregation of which Henry Jessey was pastor until his death in 1663, the Bedford Church responded to a request from the Southwark Church to release Martha Cumberland into their membership.

> We receaved your letter and by it a signification of your readines to receave our sister Martha Cumberland, but before we can with such fredome as we desire, deliver hir up to you, we must take leave to propound to you, and to desire your faithfull answer therto, to witt whether that good old principle once professed by you in the time of our honored brother Jese, that communion, church communion of saints, not withstanding difference in judgment about water baptisme, be yet a church principle with you.[2]

---

1. *Confession of Faith of Seven Congregations* (1646) art. 39.
2. *Minutes*, 79.

The church complained that "we have heare to fore over and over offered to give hir up to that church walkeing with our honered brother Coken, brother Palmer or brother Owen, but none of these congregations would content hir."³ The reason the Bedford Church repeatedly suggested that Sister Cumberland join the London Congregationalist churches of George Cokayne, Anthony Palmer, and John Owen, was because several members of the Bedford Church "are receaved by and hold communion with them," and because "they being also of that Christian principle afore mentioned, to hold communion with saints as saints."⁴ The church reported that they took Sister Cumberland's refusal to join with these congregations "very ill," and interpreted her refusal as evidence of a "stoborne and selfe willed spirit," particularly because she had informed them that if they would not consent to her joining the Southwark congregation, "she would take hir leave to doe it."⁵ The church expressed a concern that perhaps Sister Cumberland refused their suggestions because "she is possesed with that opinyon of holding communion with non of the saints but such of them as have bine baptised after personall confesion of faith."⁶ The church left no doubt as to why they refused to grant the request of the Southwark Church. "These things being soe, should we commend this sister to you we should not only consent with hir to hir rejecting those churches at London, but countinance also hir trampleing upon us at home, esspecially hir trampleing upon that good and godlie principle stood to and mainetained by us and by you in former days."⁷ The first signature attached to the letter was that of John Bunyan. Three months later, in March 1677, the church gave Samuel Hensman over in membership to the congregation in Braintree precisely because of their open-communion position: "and this we the willinger doe because we are in formed conserneing you, beloved, you are not ridged in your principles, but are for communyan with saints by saints, and have bine taught by the word to receave the brotherhood because they are beloved and receaved of the Father and the Sone."⁸ Again, the first signature appended was Bunyan's.

In 1684, Bunyan published *The Pilgrim's Progress, Part Two*, containing a much-debated reference to the Interpreter's bath. *The Pilgrim's Progress*,

3. *Minutes*, 79.
4. *Minutes*, 79–80.
5. *Minutes*, 80.
6. *Minutes*, 80.
7. *Minutes*, 80.
8. *Minutes*, 82.

Part One, published in 1678 but written between 1666–1672 before the communion controversy, contained nothing resembling baptism. But in *The Pilgrim's Progress, Part Two*, as Christiana, Mercy, and the children prepare to depart the House of Interpreter, Interpreter instructs them to "tarry a while, for, said he, you must orderly go from hence."[9] He then orders Innocent, a "Damsel" of the house:

> Take them and have them into the Garden, to the *Bath*, and there wash them, and make them clean from the soil which they have gathered by travelling. Then *Innocent* the Damsel took them and had them into the Garden, and brought them to the *Bath*, so she told them that there they must wash and be clean, for so her Master would have the Women to do that called at his House as they were going on *Pilgrimage*. They then went in and washed, yea they and the Boys and all, and they came out of that *Bath* not only sweet, and clean; but also much enlivened and strengthened in their Joynts: So when they came in, they looked fairer a deal, then when they went out to the washing.
>
> When they returned out of the Garden from the *Bath*, the *Interpreter* took them and looked upon them and said unto them, *fair as the Moon*. Then he called for the *Seal* wherewith they used to be *Sealed* that were washed in his *Bath*. So the *Seal* was brought, and he set his Mark upon them, that they might be known in the Places whither they were yet to go.[10]

It is tempting to view this scene as a reference to baptism. It occurs immediately after both Christiana and Mercy provide their testimonies of conversion, and after the Interpreter provides Mercy with the assurance of salvation.[11] Likewise, the bath is administered in order that the pilgrims may "orderly go from hence," for so the "Master would have the Women to do that called at his House as they were going on pilgrimage."[12] The concern that the ordinances be "orderly" was often voiced by seventeenth-century Baptists. Finally, upon receiving the bath, the pilgrims are sealed by the

---

9. Bunyan, *Pilgrim's Progress*, 2:195. Roger Sharrock convincingly argues that *The Pilgrim's Progress, Part One*, was composed during the second half of Bunyan's first imprisonment, though not published until 1678 (Sharrock, *John Bunyan*, 70–73).

10. Bunyan, *Pilgrim's Progress*, 2:195.

11. Bunyan, *Pilgrim's Progress*, 2:194–95. "Now when *Mercie* was in Bed, she could not sleep for joy, for that now her doubts of missing at last, were removed further from her than ever they were before. So she lay blessing and Praising God who had had such favour for her" (2:195).

12. Bunyan, *Pilgrim's Progress*, 2:195.

Interpreter, "that they might be known in the Places whither they were yet to go."[13] The Baptists likewise spoke of baptism as the visible mark of a visible saint, the sign and seal of the new covenant. Hence, Roger Sharrock regarded the Interpreter's bath as "an addition to the house calculated to have a special appeal to Baptists—a Bath of Sanctification. There is no reference in the earlier version to the episode of the sacrament of baptism by immersion; however, though a concession is now made to a sectarian feeling, Bunyan does not give pride of place to the symbolic bath; he simply remarks that the pilgrims were strengthened as well as purified by it."[14]

But there are serious problems with understanding the Interpreter's bath as a reference to baptism. First, if Christiana and Mercy's bath refers to credobaptism, does the bath of Christiana's four boys refer to paedobaptism? The boys appear quite young at this stage of the narrative, they give no profession of faith in the House of Interpreter, and they are not catechized until their lengthy stay at the Palace Beautiful.[15] If this is indeed a "special appeal to the Baptists," it is a confusing one at best. Second, Bunyan glossed in the margin next to his description of the Interpreter's bath, "*The Bath* Sanctification."[16] The effect of this bath is that they came out "not only sweet, and clean; but also much enlivened and strengthened in their Joynts: So when they came in, they looked fairer a deal, then when they went out to the washing."[17] Not in the bath itself, but immediately following, the pilgrims receive the Interpreter's seal, which "greatly added to their Beauty," and also "added to their gravity, and made their Countenances more like them of Angels."[18] It is difficult to reconcile the efficacy of this "*Bath* [of] Sanctification" with Bunyan's contention a decade earlier that "Neither if I be baptized, am I the better? neither if I be not, am I the worse? not the better before God, not the worse before Men."[19] Nor is it easy to reconcile with the tenor of Bunyan's baptismal theology that elevated the baptism of the Spirit above baptism in water, and severed the sign from the thing signified. Finally, in the same year in which Bunyan published *The Pilgrim's Progress, Part Two* (1684), he published another

13. Bunyan, *Pilgrim's Progress*, 2:195.
14. Sharrock, *John Bunyan*, 144.
15. Bunyan, *Pilgrim's Progress*, 2:211–13, 217–18.
16. Bunyan, *Pilgrim's Progress*, 2:195.
17. Bunyan, *Pilgrim's Progress*, 2:195.
18. Bunyan, *Pilgrim's Progress*, 2:195–96.
19. Bunyan, *Differences in Judgment*, 4:220.

treatise, *A Holy Life, the Beauty of Christianity*, in which it is apparent that Bunyan still abhorred strict communion as a "sinful mixture of truth and iniquity together," by which he presumably meant the truth of credobaptism and the iniquity of strict communion.[20] Bunyan wrote,

> Here's a *Presbyter*, heres an *Independent*, an *Anabaptist*, so joyned each man to his own opinion, that they cannot have that communion one with another, as by the testament of the Lord Jesus they are commanded and injoyned. . . .
>
> I have often said in my heart, what is the reason that some of the brethren should be so shy of holding communion, with those every whit as good, if not better, than themselves? Is it because they think themselves unworthy of their holy fellowship? No verily: it is because they exalt themselves, they are leavened with some iniquity that hath mixed it self with some good opinions that they hold, and therefore it is that they say to others, *stand by thy self, come not near me, for I am holier than thou.*[21]

Bunyan's firm disavowal of strict communion in *A Holy Life, the Beauty of Christianity*, likewise published in 1684, mitigates against viewing the Interpreter's bath as evidence of a development in Bunyan's baptismal theology or an alteration in his open-communion convictions.[22]

On August 19, 1688, Bunyan preached to the congregation pastored by John Gammon in Boar's Head Yard in London.[23] As with Bunyan's other ecclesiastical associations, Gammon's was an open-membership congregation. On his way to London, Bunyan rode through a downpour, and according to the anonymous author of *A Continuation of Mr. Bunyan's Life*, which was attached to a later edition of *Grace Abounding*, Bunyan soon "fell sick of a violent fever."[24] Though his contemporaries attributed his illness to his exposure to the weather, Richard Greaves asserts that the "illness that claimed

---

20. Bunyan, *Holy Life*, 9:327.

21. Bunyan, *Holy Life*, 9:327–28. Again, "some good opinions" is probably a reference to credobaptism.

22. Richard Greaves likewise denies that the Interpreter's bath is a reference to baptism: "Moreover, his own marginal notation explains that the bath mandated by Innocent is sanctification, a process essential to the Christian life, unlike baptism" (Greaves, *Glimpses of Glory*, 509).

23. Greaves, *Glimpses of Glory*, 597. His text was John 1:13; an abridged version may be found in Bunyan, *Mr. John Bunyan's Last Sermon*, 12:87–94.

24. Anonymous, *Continuation of Mr. Bunyan's Life*, 1:64.

Bunyan was probably influenza, though pneumonia is also a possibility."[25] Bunyan died twelve days later, on August 31, 1688, at the home of John Strudwick, a grocer in Holborn Bridge and a member of George Cokayne's Congregationalist church.[26] He was buried on September 2 in Strudwick's vault in the Nonconformist cemetery in Bunhill Fields.[27] Bunyan preached his final sermon to an open-membership congregation, died in the home of a Congregationalist friend, whose Congregationalist pastor likely preached his funeral.[28] It would seem, then, that Bunyan went to his grave steadfast in his commitment to "that good old principle" of open communion.

Did Bunyan's Baptist opponents remain just as steadfast in their commitment to strict communion throughout the seventeenth century? This chapter expands beyond the communion controversy of the 1670s to examine the wider conversation among seventeenth-century credobaptists concerning the relationship between baptism, church membership, and the Lord's Supper.[29] It argues that strict communion was not simply the majority view held by the more rigid of the Baptist sect, but was in fact so dominant among seventeenth-century Baptists, and so integrated into their wider ecclesiology, that strict communion should be considered a seventeenth-century Baptist distinctive, and therefore open-communion credobaptists like Bunyan, the Bedford Church, and the network of open-communion churches of which it was a part, should be regarded as something other than Baptist. In defense of this thesis, this chapter demonstrates: first, that open communion was an isolated ecclesiological position, not sufficiently widespread or connected to the broader Baptist movement to qualify as a minority view within that movement; second, that strict communion was so dominant among seventeenth-century Baptists as to be considered universal; and third, that the omission of strict communion language in the

---

25. Greaves, *Glimpses of Glory*, 599. Two accounts of Bunyan's illness and death exist: Doe, *Struggler*, 3:766; Anonymous, *Continuation of Mr. Bunyan's Life*, 1:64. The two accounts disagree as to the date of Bunyan's death (*Continuation* states that Bunyan died on August 12, *Struggler* gives August 31 as the date), but they agree as to the general details.

26. Greaves, *Glimpses of Glory*, 599.

27. Greaves, *Glimpses of Glory*, 599.

28. Greaves writes, "Of his funeral service we know virtually nothing, although Cokayne, Strudwick's pastor, probably officiated" (Greaves, *Glimpses of Glory*, 599).

29. This chapter defines "credobaptist" in the general sense of one who personally affirms believer's baptism as the proper biblical administration of the ordinance, and "Baptist" in the specific sense of one who defines the church as an assembly of (credo-)baptized believers. This monograph asserts, therefore, that Jessey, Bunyan, Tombes, et al. were credobaptists, but not Baptists.

1677/1689 London Baptist Confession was driven by changing political circumstances rather than shifting biblical convictions, and therefore does not represent a new openness to open communion as a valid Baptist position. It is argued that the 1677/1689 London Baptist Confession is internally inconsistent in its doctrine of the church, and should therefore be understood as an anomaly in an otherwise coherent and consistent Baptist ecclesiology, an ecclesiology that demands strict communion.

Open Communion in the Seventeenth Century

In an influential 1972 article, the renowned Baptist historian B. R. White argues that Baptists, though traditionally divided into two classifications, General and Particular, should more accurately be divided into three:

> In the early years, that is, at least up to 1660 and probably, effectively to the close of the seventeenth century, there were *three*, not two, significant groups. The first, and earliest was the General Baptist community, this stemmed directly from John Smyth and the older Separatism. Their tradition in the matter of "open" and "closed" membership was simple and consistent: they all practiced "closed" communion and, hence, "closed" membership....
>
> The second group was that of the "closed" membership Particular Baptists who originally broke away from the Independent or Congregationalist tradition represented by the Jacob-Lathrop-Jessey church but whose closest ecclesiological links and sympathies were undoubtedly with the Separatists. The third group, a rather loosely linked company, tended to believe Calvinistic doctrines, to share an Independent churchmanship and also to argue for believer's baptism while not excluding from church fellowship those who held infant baptism to be valid. This group is represented by Henry Jessey, John Tombes, John Bunyan, Vavasor Powell in Wales and others such as the members of the congregation at Broadmead, Bristol. They could almost equally easily be represented as "open" membership Particular Baptists or as Independents who tolerated diversity of view in their congregations about the right and proper subjects of baptism.[30]

---

30. White, "Open and Closed Membership," 330–31. White's taxonomy of seventeenth-century Baptists is considered authoritative, and his article is nearly ubiquitous in the secondary literature. It is therefore noteworthy that the argument of this monograph (that open communionists like Bunyan ought to be classified as Independents rather than Baptists) is considered by White an "almost equally" viable position.

Among those included in this third group, this monograph has already examined the works of Bunyan. It remains to explore the writings of the other advocates of open communion whom White lists, in order to discern how widespread were open-communion credobaptists in the seventeenth century, and how connected they were to the Baptist movement.

Henry Jessey

In 1650, Henry Jessey published *A Storehouse of Provision*, a collection of Jessey's answers to various questions related to Christian faith and practice. While the topics addressed range far and wide, over a quarter of the work is dedicated to the question of "*the warrantablenesse of Communion together of Believers, that differ about Baptisme.*"[31] This section is comprised of two letters, and an addendum. The first letter was written by Jessey in 1647 in response to a question "Propounded from a *Church* in the Country," the "Saints in W. H. I."[32] This church, apparently a strict-communion congregation, had written to Jessey, asking, "*Upon what grounds we admit of Communion, of Beleevers, that are of different Judgements. Especially, whether* Baptisme *be so specially requisite to Communion, as that without union in that principlee there cannot be a walking together in Communion?*"[33] Jessey responded with five arguments in favor of open communion, then answered seven objections to the practice.[34] The second letter was written in 1649 to a church "on another Coast" in response to the question, "*Whether such as have been baptized since they have been [a] made Disciples; may lawfully admit to partake in the Lords Supper, such as are approved believers?*"[35] It would seem this letter likewise came from a strict-communion church, for to its question the church appended five arguments against open communion to which it invited Jessey's response: (1) it is disorderly; (2) it is idolatry; (3) the apostles received only baptized believers into the church; (4) the apostolic church admitted only baptized believers to the Lord's Supper; (5) there is neither precept nor precedent for the admittance of the unbaptized into membership or communion.[36] Jessey responded to these

31. Jessey, *Storehouse of Provision*, A8–A9.
32. Jessey, *Storehouse of Provision*, 93.
33. Jessey, *Storehouse of Provision*, 94.
34. For the first letter, see Jessey, *Storehouse of Provision*, 93–103.
35. Jessey, *Storehouse of Provision*, 104–5.
36. Jessey, *Storehouse of Provision*, 105. It is also conceivable that both churches simply listed the arguments presented to them against their open-communion practice

five arguments, then answered twelve objections to his practice.[37] Toward the end of *A Storehouse of Provision*, Jessey appended a section that should have been included with the previous two letters, in which he answered sixteen more objections to open communion.[38]

Jessey's arguments were echoed and expanded by Bunyan two decades later. Like Bunyan, Jessey appealed to a narrow application of the regulative principle. Though he admitted that in the apostolic church baptism ordinarily preceded church communion, without explicit precept or precedent for rejecting the unbaptized, the church must not set limits beyond what God has established.[39] Like Bunyan, Jessey argued from Romans 14–15 that baptism is a matter of conscience requiring "light," and that the church is commanded to receive those who are weak in faith.[40] Like Bunyan, Jessey denied that baptism is the form of a church.

> Where is *matter* and *forme*, there is a true Church; the *Matter* of a true Church, to be Saints visibly; the *Forme*, a gathering of these out from the world, and *joyning of them together* to worship the Lord in truth, so far as *know*, or shall know; and edifie themselves.
>
> The *Forme giveth the being*: the *being*, when it is lost, then the *Forme* is lost. Hence it appears that *Baptisme* is not the *Forme*; for else, when some are cast out, *Baptisme* is lost; and if they be received to have *being* in the Church again, they must be *baptized* again, which is absurd. Therefore I judge, that the Churches called *Independents*, or *Separates*, having both the *matter*, and *forme* of Churches, are *true Churches*.[41]

---

and were seeking Jessey's help in responding; however, it seems more likely that both congregations practiced strict-communion.

37. For the second letter, see Jessey, *Storehouse of Provision*, 104–[32]. Due to a printing error, pp. 129–32 are numbered pp. 119–22.

38. For the addendum, see Jessey, *Storehouse of Provision*, 174–203. The addendum is entitled, "Moe Objections Answered, about Communion Together By Believers that Differ about Baptime: Which should have bin put before the last line of page 128."

39. Jessey, *Storehouse of Provision*, 94–95, 98, 100, 113, 120, 123, 183.

40. Jessey, *Storehouse of Provision*, 98, 110–11, 119, 185, 190.

41. Jessey, *Storehouse of Provision*, 102. Jessey continued: "And that they are weak, and are more, then there are of those of late baptized, and these are offended at this distance, in denying Communion to such: And by that Ground, *Rom.* 15. 1. 2. our practice of Communion with such, as we doe, seemes more agreeable to the Rule, as tending more to take off offences. and so edifies the more" (102–3). Two points are worth noting: (1) Jessey undoubtedly felt compelled to make this argument because he believed the Baptist position denied that "Churches called *Independents*, or *Separates*," were true churches; (2) It appears that Jessey aligned himself neither with the "Independents, or

And like Bunyan, underneath Jessey's arguments lies the subjection of the principle of ecclesiological purity to the principle of evangelical unity.

> Mark well, what are the *Tearmes, or Grounds, or special Causes*, why any persons were, and are to be received by Saints into Communion? viz.
>
> 1. Such as we judge *God receives*, and rejects not, we should receive *Rom.* 14. 3.
>
> 2. Such as *have fellowship (we judge) with the Father, and the Sonne.* 1 *Joh.* 1. 3. 4.
>
> 3. Such as have that Spirit given to them and have their *hearts purified by faith*, God puts no difference betwixt them that are weakest about *Ordinances*, and others. *Acts* 15. 9. Then why should we?
>
> 4. Such as *God hath* evidently *given Repentance* unto life.
>
> Or 5ly. Such as we have ground to judge to *be Disciples. Act.* 9. 26. These things that are the maine, were, and are the *grounds of receiving*; and not consent about the *Forme*, or manner of Ordnance; nor should a difference herein be judged such *Idolatry*, as to cause a refusall of such, as are found in the maine.[42]

Though there is no evidence that Bunyan read *A Storehouse of Provision*, it may be assumed that he was familiar with Jessey's arguments due to the association of the Bedford Church with Jessey's Southwark congregation.[43]

Henry Jessey was undeniably an open-communion credobaptist, but was he a Baptist? Not only did the Particular Baptist movement emerge out of separation from Jessey's Southwark congregation over the issues of baptism and communion, but even when in 1645 Jessey received

---

Separates" (i.e., paedobaptist Congregationalists) nor with "those of late baptized" who distanced themselves from such (i.e., Baptists). Jessey seems to have identified himself as something else altogether. See also Jessey, *Storehouse of Provision*, 199–200.

42. Jessey, *Storehouse of Provision*, 108–9 (see also 102–3). Jessey was apparently responding to the Baptist position, which equated paedobaptism with idolatry.

43. For example, in December 1659, due to the "weakenes of our brother Burton, and the great burthen of preaching and caring for the Church that lyes upon him," the Bedford Church ordered that letters be sent "to Mr. Simson, Mr. Jesse and Mr, Cockin for their assistance and furtherance in our inquiring out such an able godly man as may be suitable for our help" (*Minutes*, 34). And in June 1674, the church ordered that a letter be sent to "that church of whom brother Jesse once was pastor, to know whether it be their church principle still to hold communion with saints as saint[s] though differing in judgment about watter baptizm" (77). Duesing discusses the connections between Jessey and the Bedford Church in Duesing, *Henry Jessey*, 219–21. See also Greaves, *Glimpses of Glory*, 61–62.

credobaptism, he kept his church from incorporating credobaptism into their ecclesiology and did not sign the 1646 London Baptist Confession with its explicit affirmation of strict communion. While Jessey maintained good relations with the Particular Baptists, it is doubtful that these relations were closer than those Jessey enjoyed with the larger Nonconformist community. The evidence suggests that the London Baptists did not regard Jessey as a Baptist, nor did Jessey consider himself among their number.

John Tombes

John Tombes's inclusion in White's list of representative open-communion Baptists is questionable at best. Michael Renihan persuasively argues that Tombes has been miscategorized as a Baptist, for despite his personal conviction regarding credobaptism, he remained a lifelong Anglican. Renihan suggests "Anglican Antipaedobaptist" as the proper denominator for Tombes.

> Tombes will be shown to be reformational, Calvinistic, baptistic as regards baptism and his view of the Covenant of Grace, a "divine" in the sense of one who attained great proficiency in divinity. However, he was not a Baptist in the common use of the term, then, or in the present. A belief that states that baptism is for believers exclusively is not enough to call someone a Baptist, just as this view alone was not enough to denominate one as an Anabaptist in the seventeenth century.... "Baptist" as a title entails more than a certain view of baptism.[44]

Renihan defines "Baptists" as those who "(1) believed in baptism for believers alone by immersion, and who (2) organized themselves into particular societies as churches of believers and baptised men and women."[45] Even if it were granted that open communion was a seventeenth-century Baptist position, John Tombes should not be considered a Baptist, for Tombes was not even a Nonconformist. Furthermore, Tombes knew what Baptists were

44. M. Renihan, *Antipaedobaptism*, 3-4. For M. Renihan's taxonomy of seventeenth-century antipaedobaptists (Anabaptists, Baptists, Abaptists, and Anglican Antipaedobaptists), see *Antipaedobaptism*, 19-31.

45. M. Renihan, *Antipaedobaptism*, 22. Renihan goes on to write, "Because Baptists of both sorts [General and Particular] held to and rigorously practiced the baptism of believers only (credobaptism) as essential to the proper ordering and constituting of particular churches, they should be understood as Baptists specifically under the general heading of Antipaedobaptists. The point being that the connotations of 'Baptist' are wider than baptismal practice alone. It assumes a certain ecclesiological outlook as well" (23).

and what they believed, and he did not consider himself among their number. In *An Apology for the Two Treatises* (1646), Tombes referred to article 33 of the First London Baptist Confession (1644):

> I confesse I have met with some writings which put Baptism into the definition of the Church, as necessary to the being of a visible Church, and the words in the *Confession of Faith and of the 7 Churches of Anabaptists about London* [*being baptized into that faith*] Artic. 33. are somewhat doubtfull, though they seem rather to import that Baptisme is necessary to the right order of a Christian Church, then to the being of a Church; and I confesse that they hold that members are added to the Church by Baptisme and not otherwise, and hold a nullity of Paedo baptisme, must needs say the Churches that have no other then Infant-Baptisme, are no true Churches; nor their members Church-members . . . and to voluntary separation necessary. But these points of the necessity of right Baptisme, not onely to the right order, but also to the being of a visible Church and Church-member, and to voluntary separation barely for the defect of it, I have ever disclaimed.[46]

Though Tombes was willing to give the London Baptists the benefit of the doubt, he admits that the internal logic of their confession indicated that credobaptism is of the essence of the church, a position Tombes thoroughly rejected. Yet despite the clear evidence that Tombes was not a Baptist, he continues to be cited as a proponent of the open-communion Baptist position.[47]

In 1645, Tombes wrote *An Examen of the Sermon of Mr. Stephen Marshal*, which exercised immense influence during the baptism debates of the 1640s. It was Tombes's *Examen* that proved decisive in Jessey's acceptance of credobaptism.[48] Tombes's *Examen* was not a defense of open communion, but of credobaptism. In fact, in the course of arguing against paedobaptism, Tombes actually laid the foundation for strict communion.

---

46. Tombes, *Apology or Plea*, 65–66.

47. M. Renihan writes, "It is the Baptist historians [like B. R. White] who have muddied the waters surrounding John Tombes. They have perceived him as one of their own standing against the establishment for his ideals. In actuality, Tombes was trying to bring greater reform to the established church. This is a needed distinction in order to understand the tension between his sacramental theology and his ecclesiology" (M. Renihan, *Antipaedobaptism*, 4).

48. Duesing, *Henry Jessey*, 190–91. Duesing notes that Tombes's influence upon Jessey was "in addition to the circumstances Jessey experienced as pastor of the JLJ church," which Duesing examines in *Henry Jessey*, 143–95.

Marshall had asserted that baptized infants *"being members of the Church of Christ, having their share in the communion of Saints, are remembered at the Throne of grace every day by those that pray for the welfare of the Church, and particularly, in those prayers which are made for his blessing upon his Ordinances."*[49] Tombes responded, "As for *being members of the Church*, if you mean the invisible Church, neither I nor you can affirm or deny; its in Gods bosome alone; if you mean the visible, you must make a new definition of the visible Church afore Infants baptized will be proved members."[50] Tombes further argued that paedobaptists were inconsistent in admitting infants to one ordinance (baptism), yet excluding them from the other (the Lord's Supper).

> This argument is good, *ad homines*, against the partie opposite, proceeding upon the Paedobaptists hypotheses or suppositions; to wit, 1. *That those to whom the Covenant belongs, to them the seale belongs*; 2. *That to the infants of believers, the Covenant belongs*; 3. *That the Lords Supper is a seale of the Covenant as well as Baptisme*. And these are your hypotheses. Now then if this be a good argument, children are to be baptized, because they are in the Covenant, and the seale belongs to those in Covenant, by the same reason they are to receive the Lords Supper, because they are in Covenant, and the seale belongs to those in Covenant. Now this argument is strengthened from other hypotheses, as that the Lords Supper succeeds Passeover, as Baptisme Circumcision, but children not of yeares of discretion had the Passeover, therefore they are to have the Lords Supper.[51]

In the first passage, Tombes tied baptism and membership in the visible church to faith: only believers may be baptized members of the visible church.[52] In the second passage, Tombes tied baptism and the Lord's Supper together, such that it is inconsistent to administer one seal of the covenant and yet withhold the other. It is one short step further to say that membership, baptism, and the Lord's Supper are bound together, all three requiring faith. One might respond to Tombes that if it is inconsistent to administer baptism but not the Lord's Supper, then it is likewise inconsistent to administer the Lord's Supper but not baptism, to which

49. Marshall quoted in Tombes, *Examen of the Sermon*, 166.
50. Tombes, *Examen of the Sermon*, 166–67.
51. Tombes, *Examen of the Sermon*, 167–68.
52. "It is not Baptisme of it selfe that will yeeld a plea of any force . . . but the promise of God, and the condition of faith in Christ" (Tombes, *Examen of the Sermon*, 167).

practice Tombes consented by affirming credobaptism yet communing in the Church of England.[53] Yet Tombes did not follow his own logic. For Tombes, ecclesiological purity bowed the knee, not to evangelical unity, as in the case of Bunyan and Jessey, but to ecclesiastical unity. Because baptism was not the form of the church, the Church of England was a true church, and therefore separation "may" amount to schism.[54]

In 1652, Tombes published another work, *An Addition to the Apology for the Two Treatises concerning Infant-Baptisme*, written in response to Robert Baillie's *Anabaptisme*.[55] Tombes felt that Baillie misrepresented his works, and sought the opportunity to vindicate himself. Among the charges Baillie laid upon Tombes was, "*That I am unwilling to join with any of the Anabaptists Churches, and they are unwilling to baptize non-members.*"[56] Tombes answered the first charge by explaining that while he was not willing to separate from the established Church, yet this should not be viewed as a rejection of the "Anabaptist" churches, which he yet regarded as true churches.[57] In response to the second charge (which Tombes could not answer himself, for he was not a Baptist), Tombes wrote a letter to

> an Elder of one of their Churches intreating him to consult with some others, and to give me resolution in these questions:

---

53. In *An Apology or Plea for the Two Treatises*, Tombes appeared to distance himself from those who "hold a nullity of Paedo baptisme," and disclaimed the "voluntary separation barely for the defect of it [baptism]" (Tombes, *Apology or Plea*, 65–66). Therefore, Tombes may have regarded paedobaptism to be a true yet defective form of baptism, in which case the Church of England did not administer the Lord's Supper to the unbaptized. Even so, one might argue that such a view is inconsistent with Tombes's affirmation of credobaptism. If paedobaptism is a defective yet true form of baptism, why annul it by receiving credobaptism?

54. Tombes wrote in *An Addition to the Apology for the Two Treatises Concerning Infant-Baptisme*, "For a man may be willing to joine himself as a Member to any of the Anabaptists Churches, *and yet not dare to gather a separated Church*, not every one who joins as a member with a separated Church being guilty of a schism, which a gatherer of a separated Church may be guilty of" (Tombes, *Addition to the Apology*, 20). Tombes proceeded to hint at his rationale for not separating, namely that he still held out hope for the reformation of the Church of England.

55. Baillie, *Anabaptism*.

56. Tombes, *Addition to the Apology*, 19. This is the fourteenth of twenty-one criminations that Tombes answered.

57. Tombes, *Addition to the Apology*, 20. It is unclear how "a gatherer of a separated Church may be guilty of" schism, and yet the church he gathered be a true church.

> 1. What joining in Communion do you require without which you will not baptize any?
>
> 2. Whether on my profession of repentance and faith in the Lord Jesus, and readiness to hold communion with all the Churches of Christ in the things of Christ, though I do not promise to be a fixed member in any of their Congregations, you would admit me to baptisme?[58]

To this letter, Tombes received "this following answer subscribed by three graduates in schooles, godly and learned men in these words":

> That which we require and without which we will not baptize any is a persons manifestation of himselfe to be a believer in Jesus Christ, and to desire baptisme according to the revealed will of Christ, and in obedience thereunto, we do not baptize any into this or that particular congregation: but only into that one body in general spoken of 1 Cor. 12. 13. As touching joining in communion, we in this case require no more, than a manifest readinesse to hold communion with all the Churches of Christ in the things of Christ, and accordingly to shew a real willingnesse to have communion with any particular Church of Christ according as the hand of God shall give opportunity, and true seasonablenesse of and for the same. Thus we judge and practice accordingly.[59]

This response was signed by Benjamin Coxe, Henry Jessey, and Hanserd Knollys. To this response, Knollys affixed an addendum:

> I do testifie the substance hereof to be the professed judgement of that congregation whereto I am joined, and also that congregation, where Mr. Kiffin, Patient, and Spilsbury are joined, who did affirm so much to be their own judgement also. The Scripture upon which we so practice is that Acts 8.37, 38.[60]

Duesing understands this response to indicate an openness to mixed communion on the part of the signatories. He writes, "So while Cox's 1646 Appendix indicates a clear closed membership position, the statement he makes to Tombes suggests a willingness to participate in mixed communion with, at the very least, a church such as Henry Jessey's."[61]

---

58. Tombes, *Addition to the Apology*, 20–21.
59. Tombes, *Addition to the Apology*, 21.
60. Tombes, *Addition to the Apology*, 21.
61. Duesing, *Henry Jessey*, 238.

But another explanation may make better sense of the evidence. By "a readinesse to hold communion with all the Churches of Christ in the things of Christ," the Baptists may have meant the *Baptist* Churches of Christ, in the things of Christ *as the Baptists understand them*. Coxe, Knollys, Kiffin, Patient, and Spilsbury were all signatories of the 1646 revision of the London Baptist Confession, which defined a church as "a company of visible Saints, called and separated from the world by the Word and Spirit of God, to the visible profession of the faith of the Gospel, being baptized into that faith, and joyned to the Lord, and to each other, by mutuall agreement in the practical enjoyment of the ordinances commanded by Christ their Head and King."[62] It then defined baptism as "an ordinance of the new Testament, given by Christ, to be dispensed upon persons professing faith, or that are made Disciples; who upon profession of faith, ought to be baptized, and after to partake of the Lords Supper."[63] Putting these two articles together, the 1646 London Baptist Confession defined a true church as a Baptist church. Though, as the previous chapter demonstrated, the Baptists were at times reticent to follow this logic to its conclusion, their commitment to credobaptism and strict communion seemed to many, including Bunyan, to necessitate such a conclusion. Matthew Ward, in a series of articles on Tombes's correspondence with the Baptists in *An Addition to the Apology*, dates the letter to Tombes sometime after the 1646 revision of the London Baptist Confession, yet before mid-1649, when Thomas Patient left London to pastor a church in Dublin.[64] It would be odd indeed if Coxe, Knollys, Kiffin, Patient, and Spilsbury all signed a strong statement of strict Baptist communion in August 1646, then in less than three years' time affirmed what amounted to a statement of open communion, which would be the case if "all the Churches of Christ" included the established Church of which Tombes was a member, and "the things of Christ" included paedobaptism.[65]

Underlying this response is the seventeenth-century Baptist conception of a *via media* between the universal/invisible church and the

---

62. *Confession of Faith of Seven Congregations* (1646) art. 33.

63. *Confession of Faith of Seven Congregations* (1646) art. 39.

64. Ward, "John Tombes's Answer, 1."

65. Ward draws the same conclusion: "To make a long story short, when Benjamin Cox wrote that Baptist churches baptized anyone who was willing to be in communion with all or any of the Churches of Christ, he very well may have meant only Baptist churches" (Ward, "John Tombes's Answer, 3").

particular/visible church—that of a non-particular/visible church.⁶⁶ According to the Baptists, it is into this third conception of the church that the believer is baptized. Hanserd Knollys would later write in 1681, "That there be but ONE Church in one City; and that all the Congregations of Saints in that City (called Churches) bear but one Name, to wit, the Church of God in that City, as in the Apostles daies, Act 15. 4. 22. 1 Cor. 1. 2."⁶⁷ Knollys's vision of "ONE Church in one City" included the careful observance of "Gospel-Order," which demands: "That the Order of the Gospel be carefully observed, and kept in the Administration of God's Sacred Ordinances, in the Admission of Members, in the Ordination of Church-Officers, and in withdrawing from every Brother that walketh *Disorderly*."⁶⁸ In other words, Knollys's "ONE Church in one City" was a Baptist church. This appears to be the meaning of the Baptists' response to Tombes's question about baptism and communion. Understood in this way, the Baptists' response contained three affirmations: (1) they baptize only upon a credible profession of faith and a desire for baptism; (2) they do not baptize into a particular congregation, but into the one, true (Baptist) non-particular/visible church; (3) in order to join into communion with this one, true (Baptist) non-particular/visible church, a baptized believer must demonstrate a readiness to hold communion with *all* the particular congregations of this one, true (Baptist) non-particular/visible church, by joining in communion with *any* of the particular congregations as God shall providentially give opportunity. It should be noted that their response did not specifically answer Tombes's question about whether they would baptize one who did not intend to become a member of any of their congregations. In fact, their response could be read as a denial.

Why Henry Jessey's name was attached to this response remains a mystery. There are two possibilities. It is possible that this response was written by

66. This ternary Baptist conception of the church in contrast to Bunyan's binary conception is examined in the previous two chapters. The Savoy Declaration likewise had a category for the non-particular/visible church, although it was adamant that this church did not administer the ordinances or have any offices: "The whole body of men throughout the world, professing the faith of the Gospel and obedience unto God by Christ according unto it, not destroying their own profession by any Errors everting the foundation, or unholinesse of conversation, are & may be called the visible Catholick Church of Christ, although it is not intrusted with the administration of any Ordinances, or have any offices to rule or govern in, or over the whole Body" (*Declaration of the Faith* [1658] art. 26.2).

67. Knollys, *World That Now Is*, 50, cited in Ward, "John Tombes's Answer, 3."

68. Knollys, *World That Now Is*, 52.

Coxe, then sent to Jessey and Knollys for approval as two prominent London credobaptists. Upon receipt, each read into the response his own definitions of the terms, which were left somewhat vague, and on that basis affirmed it. This may seem unlikely, as by 1646–1649, each party should have known what the other believed, particularly considering Jessey did not sign the 1646 revision of the London Baptist Confession with its explicit affirmation of strict communion. However, it seems even less likely that Coxe and Knollys (with Knollys also affixing the names of Kiffin, Patient, and Spilsbury) would have denied the principle of strict Baptist communion they held so firmly, not only at the time, but for the remainder of their lives. In any case, not only is Tombes not to be considered a Baptist, but his writings cannot be utilized in defense of open communion as it pertains to Baptist churches. Tombes and the Baptists were speaking a different language because they operated within a different ecclesiological construct.

Vavasor Powell

In addition to Bunyan, Jessey, and Tombes, White mentions Vavasor Powell and the Broadmead Church in Bristol as representatives of seventeenth-century open-communion Baptists. Vavasor Powell (1617–1670) was a Welsh Nonconformist and Fifth Monarchist, who spent significant time in London in the 1640s and 1650s, before enduring the last eleven years of his life in prison. Powell adopted credobaptism in 1655, but remained intimate enough with the Congregationalists to be invited to the Savoy Conference in 1658, an invitation he politely declined.[69] Prior to his arrest in February 1660, Powell was active in itinerant ministry in both Wales and England,

69. Stephen K. Roberts writes that after 1655, Powell existed "in an intermediate position between the Independents, who held with infant baptism, and the Strict Baptists of [John] Miles. Nevertheless, he was still considered enough of an Independent to be invited in 1658 to the assembly to devise a declaration of faith" (Roberts, "Vavasor Powell"). There may be a link between Bunyan and Powell via John Child in the mid-1650s, but the link is circumstantial at best (Greaves, *Glimpses of Glory*, 90–91). It is worth noting that Greaves refers to Powell as an "Independent," yet persists in referring to Bunyan as an "open-membership Baptist," though they purportedly held the same open-membership, credobaptistic principles. Both Powell and Bunyan published scathing attacks on the Common Prayer Book: Powell, *Common-Prayer-Book No Divine Service* (1660); Bunyan, *I Will Pray with the Spirit* (1662). Greaves suggests that Bunyan read Powell's book (Greaves, *Glimpses of Glory*, 156). Greaves also suggests that Bunyan may have contributed to the completion of Powell's *A New and Useful Concordance to the Holy Bible*, which Powell left unfinished at his death in 1670 (Greaves, *Glimpses of Glory*, 270–71).

but at no point were his ecclesiological affiliations strictly Baptist. Powell's views on baptism and church communion are known from a single source, *The Life and Death of Mr. Vavasor Powell* (1671), a largely first-person account of his life, ministry, and faith compiled by an anonymous editor and published after his death. This work contains a detailed confession of faith in which Powell specified his conviction regarding credobaptism:

> Though Baptism be not absolutely necessary to salvation, yet being commanded by Christ, it is the duty of all professing and visible Believers, and penitent persons: Men and Women, to be Baptized once, and that upon the first Believing and Conversion, and before they enter into a particular visible Church, or partake of the Lords Supper: *Acts* 2. 41, 42. Yet it is not Baptism, but an Interest in Christ, that gives any a Right to either: Neither is it the proper work of Baptism to conferr or work grace, but to seal, confirm and encrease it, 1 *Pet.* 3. 21. much less are all those that are Baptized true believers and saved, *John* 3, 3, 5. *Acts* 8.13, 23.[70]

This is a stronger statement of the duty of baptism than Bunyan ever produced.[71] While Powell denied that baptism "gives any a Right" to either membership or the Lord's Supper, he does make baptism a "duty" prior to entering into membership and partaking of the Lord's Supper. However, Powell's next statement seems more explicitly open-communion: "But in this of baptism, as in many other cases, difference in perswasion and practice may well consist with Brotherly love and Christian communion, see *Phil*, 3. 15. *Rom.* 14, &c."[72] However, a few pages later, in an appendix to Powell's confession of faith, there are twelve "brief Arguments concerning Beleivers Baptism, which were bles'd to the satisfaction of a Doubting friend (upon that subject) to whom he sent them."[73] The twelfth and final argument for credobaptism is, "Because it is previous and antecedaneous to

---

70. Powell, *Life and Death*, 35–36.

71. Powell later wrote, "And this [i.e., the Lord's Supper], together with Baptism are, and may be accounted (though not so called in Scripture) Gospel-signs and seals of the Covenant of Grace; as Circumcision and Passover were before unto the Jews, *Mat.* 26.26,27,28,29. 1 *Cor.* 10.16. & 11.23,24,25,26. *Rom.* 4.11. *Col*, 2.11,12" (Powell, *Life and Death*, 38).

72. Powell, *Life and Death*, 36.

73. Powell, *Life and Death*, 49. The pagination of this work is muddled. This "Appendix" is unnumbered, and falls between p. 48 of Powell's "Confession" and p. 33 of "Some gracious Experimental and very choyce Sayings, and Sentences, collected out of his Papers."

Church-communion and to the orderly partaking of the Lords-Supper, *Acts* 2. 41, 42. 9. 18, 26, 27, 28."[74] In light of this statement, it is possible his earlier reference to "Brotherly love and Christian communion" refers broadly to fellowship amongst Christians and churches rather than narrowly to membership and communion within a particular church. Whatever the case, Powell was neither an unambiguous proponent of open communion, nor an unambiguously affiliated Baptist; therefore, his writings provide little in the way of evidence of an open-communion Baptist position.

The Broadmead Church, Bristol

The Broadmead Church in Bristol formed in the 1640s as a dissenting paedobaptist congregation.[75] Debate over the proper subjects of baptism began in 1651:

> And in those Halcyon days of Prosperity, liberty, and Peace, it Pleased ye Lord to breake forth more primitive light and purity in Reformation of worship, to bring ye Church to a more Exact keepeing to ye Holy Scripture; so that some of ye Members began to Question what Rule they had for Sprinkleing of Children; and upon Examination finding noe bottome for it but men's Inventions and tradition. And many that were preachers of this latter age, knowing there was noe other ground but tradition for that practice, they endeavoured to finde out a way to hold it up by Arguments from ye Covenant made with Abraham.[76]

In 1652, one of Broadmead's members, Thomas Munday, "being convinced in ye year of our Lord 1652, he desired leave of ye congregation to goe and joyne himselfe to ye other Church in Bristoll that were all Baptized."[77] After failing to convince Munday to retain their paedobaptist convictions, the church dismissed him to join the Pithay Particular Baptist Church, a congregation with ties to William Kiffin's Devonshire Square congregation,

---

74. Powell, *Life and Death*, 50.

75. Information for the Broadmead Church in Bristol comes from *The Records of a Church of Christ in Bristol, 1640–1687*, edited by Roger Hayden. Hayden's helpful analysis is found on pp. 1–78. The records, whose first author was Edward Terrill (1634–1685), begin on p. 79. It should be noted that *Records of a Church* is not the official minutes of the church but rather the reflections and interpretations of individuals regarding events related to the church.

76. Hayden, *Records of a Church*, 103–4.

77. Hayden, *Records of a Church*, 105.

having associated with that church during their exile in London during the war.[78] In 1653, when another member, Timothy Cattle, became convinced of credobaptism and requested that the church administer such baptism to him, the Broadmead Church "agreed that if any were convinced of that ordinance, they might practice it; desireing that such persons soe convinced, and practicing that ordinance of Baptism in that Scripturall manner, would keepe their places in ye Church, and not leave their Communion notwithstanding."[79] The church sent Cattle to London to be baptized by Henry Jessey, "a gracious, holy, Baptized minister, in London."[80] After this, "divers others of ye Church were Baptized, according to Scripture Example, in a River," presumably by Cattle.[81] The following year, the Broadmead Church's pastor, Thomas Ewins, and ruling elder, Robert Purnell, traveled to London to be baptized by Jessey.[82] By 1672, believer's baptism was the dominant view of the Broadmead Church, and most members were received into communion following baptism.[83]

This trajectory towards full Baptist views continued over the next two decades. According to Roger Hayden, "It was in [George] Fownes' ministry that Broadmead moved to a Particular Baptist position. Undoubtedly the strain of intense persecution had its effect, as did the views of Edward Terrill, the ruling elder at this time. By 1689, Thomas Vaux, Fownes's successor in the pastorate, was able to sign the Particular Baptist Confession of Faith, on behalf of Broadmead, and as a member of the Western Baptist Association."[84] Though the 1689 London Baptist Confession does not take an explicit stance on the issue of strict communion, the Broadmead Church was no longer an open-communion church when it signed the confession. An examination of the *Records* reveals a church that bears little resemblance to the Bedford Church. For the Broadmead

---

78. Hayden, *Records of a Church*, 70.

79. Hayden, *Records of a Church*, 105.

80. Hayden, *Records of a Church*, 105. For Jessey's deep ties to Wales, see Duesing, *Henry Jessey*, 98n3, 128–29, 160–63.

81. Hayden, *Records of a Church*, 105.

82. Hayden, *Records of a Church*, 111. Hayden notes, "The reason for seeking baptism in London was [that] the mixed communion views of Purnell would not have been acceptable to the Particular Baptist congregation at the Pithay" (111n33).

83. Hayden, *Records of a Church*, 16.

84. Hayden, *Records of a Church*, 47. This is in spite of the fact that Fownes "had earlier shared a congregation with the Independent minster, Anthony Palmer, in London" (47).

Church in the seventeenth century, open communion was a way station on the congregation's journey from paedobaptism to strict Baptist communion. Conversely, open communion was a founding principle of the Bedford Church, a principle to which it remained steadfastly committed throughout the seventeenth century.[85]

Summary

The foregoing survey of seventeenth-century proponents of open communion has demonstrated that open communion was an isolated ecclesiological position, not sufficiently widespread or connected to the broader Baptist movement to qualify as a minority view within that movement. Of those B. R. White lists as representatives of "open-communion Baptists," John Tombes was never a Baptist, but remained a lifelong Anglican, and therefore his works cannot be adduced as an example of an open-communion Baptist position; Vavasor Powell scarcely addressed the subject at all, and what he did write was as ambiguous as his ecclesiological affiliations; and the Broadmead Church in Bristol was only briefly open communion before adopting strict Baptist principles. Outside of Bunyan, it appears the only substantive seventeenth-century defense of open-communion by a credobaptist came from the pen of Henry Jessey. Yet the London Baptist churches that produced the 1646 London Baptist Confession separated from Jessey's Southwark congregation for precisely this reason, and Jessey's own church adopted strict communion after his death. There is, therefore, little reason to consider Bunyan, the Bedford Church, and its small network of open-communion congregations "Baptist," or to view them as a minority voice within the larger Baptist movement. Rather, they represent a unique, self-contained denomination, separate from both the Congregationalists and Baptists of the latter half of the seventeenth century.

---

85. Though the Broadmead Church in Bristol is the most famous "open-communion Baptist church" outside of the Bedford Church, Richard Greaves writes, "Not unique to the Bedford church, the practice was followed by congregations at Bury St. Edmonds, Bristol, Cambridge, Nottingham, Hexham, Southwark, and Dublin" (Greaves, *Glimpses of Glory*, 273). Greaves cites Nuttall, *Visible Saints*, 119–20, as evidence. However, it has been demonstrated that the Bristol and Southwark congregations did not remain open communion throughout the seventeenth century, but became strict communion as the century progressed. And of the "Bury St. Edmonds, Bedford, Cambridge, Dublin, and Nottingham" churches, Nuttall states that these "continued predominantly paedobaptist" (*Visible Saints*, 119). Only the Hexham church could truly be called open communion.

Strict Communion in the Seventeenth Century

On the other hand, strict communion was so dominant among seventeenth-century Baptists as to be considered universal. This monograph has already examined the works of Thomas Paul, John Denne, Henry Danvers, and William Kiffin, Bunyan's opponents in the communion controversy. These men were not members of a fringe Baptist sect, nor were they on the periphery of the Baptist movement. Kiffin was a prominent figure in the Particular Baptist movement from its inception, the only man to sign both the 1644 and 1689 London Baptist Confessions. In the 1650s, Kiffin helped to spread the Particular Baptist faith throughout the British Isles. In 1672, he secured licenses for himself and other Particular Baptists under the Declaration of Indulgence. Throughout his life, he was involved in debates pertinent to Baptist life, from Quakerism to women's prayer meetings to congregational singing.[86] Thomas Paul was likely a member of Kiffin's Devonshire Square congregation. In addition to the communion controversy, he was also a participant in the debate between London Baptists and Quakers in the 1670s.[87] John Denne, the son of the Cambridgeshire General Baptist Henry Denne, was a prominent General Baptist in his own right, securing licenses in 1672 for himself and fourteen other General Baptists in Huntingdonshire and Cambridgeshire.[88] Henry Danvers was known more for his revolutionary activities than his religious ministry, but his *Treatise of Baptism* (1673) was popular enough to provoke responses from the Congregationalists Richard Blinman (*An Essay Tending to Issue the Controversie about Infant Baptism* [1674]) and Obediah Wills (*Infant-Baptism Asserted and Vindicated by Scripture and Antiquity* [1674]), the Presbyterian Richard Baxter (*More Proofs of Infants Church-Membership and Consequently Their Right to Baptism* [1675]), and Bunyan (*Peaceable Principles and True* [1674]).[89]

In addition to these four combatants in the communion controversy (Paul, Denne, Danvers, Kiffin), numerous other prominent seventeenth-century Baptists, both General and Particular, wrote explicitly in defense of strict communion.

---

86. White, "William Kiffin," 155–57. See also Haykin, "By the Compass of the Word," 367–79; *Kiffin, Knollys and Keach*, 42–52.

87. Underwood, "Thomas Paul," 13–14.

88. White, "John Denne," 224–25.

89. Greaves, "Henry Danvers [1982]," 210–11.

Thomas Helwys

In 1607, in order to escape persecution in England, the Gainsborough Separatist congregation led by John Smyth and the Scrooby Manor congregation led by John Robinson relocated to Amsterdam, where the "Ancient Church" led by Francis Johnson had lived and worshipped since 1597.[90] Even though Johnson had been Smyth's professor at Cambridge, Smyth refused to unite his congregation with the Ancient Church due to Smyth's evolving views on church polity and worship.[91] These evolving views caused a rift between the Gainsborough and Scrooby Manor congregations, and within six months, Robinson relocated his congregation to Leyden.[92] But the most revolutionary change of all was Smyth's adoption of credobaptism. Joe Early Jr. writes, "This nullified the baptism he had received by the Church of England and, in actuality, all infant baptism. Moreover, Smyth argued that the Church of England was not a true church; therefore, it could not dispense the true ordinances. For Smyth and Helwys, the true church was a local, visible church composed of two or three members bound by a confession of their personal faith followed by baptism."[93] According to William Estep, "Early in 1609 or late in 1608 Smyth and his congregation unchurched themselves and reconstituted the church upon the basis of believers' baptism instead of a church covenant."[94] But this new definition of a true church posed a problem for Smyth: it meant there was no true church in Amsterdam from which to receive true baptism. The solution was described by John Robinson in his 1614 *Of Religious Communion*:

---

90. Early, *Life and Writings of Thomas Helwys*, 18–19; Estep, *Anabaptist Story*, 287–88; Lee, *Theology of John Smyth*, 52–54. Early writes that prior to their immigration to Amsterdam, the Gainsborough and Scrooby Manor congregations "were in actuality a single church" (Early, *Life and Writings of Thomas Helwys*, 22).

91. Early lists three reasons why Smyth did not unite with the Ancient Church: (1) the Ancient Church's three-fold presbytery versus Smyth's uniform pastoral ministry; (2) Smyth's view of "spiritual worship" which prohibited the use of books; (3) Smyth's view of tithing as a New Testament ordinance (Early, *Life and Writings of Thomas Helwys*, 20–21). Smyth's *The Differences of the Churches of the Separation* (1608) lists six principal areas of disagreement, but they fit nicely into Early's three categories (Smyth, *Differences of the Churches*, A3). See also Lee, *Theology of John Smyth*, 52–59, who further distills the conflict into two broad areas of disagreement: the liturgy and the ministry of the church.

92. Early, *Life and Writings of Thomas Helwys*, 22–23.

93. Early, *Life and Writings of Thomas Helwys*, 23–24.

94. Estep, *Anabaptist Story*, 288.

> Lastly, if the Ch: be gathered by baptism, then will *Mr. Helw:* his Ch: appear to all men to be built vppon the sand, considering the bapt: it had, & hath: which was, as I have heard from themselves, on this manner. *Mr. Smith, Mr. Helw:* & the rest, haveing vtterly dissolved, & disclaymed their former Ch: state, & ministery, came together to erect a new Ch: by baptism: vnto which they also ascribed so great vertue, as that they would not so much as pray together, before they had it. And after some streyning of courtesy, who should begin, & that of *John Baptist*, Math: 3: 14. misalledged, *Mr. Smith* baptized first himself, & next *Mr. Helwys*, & so the rest, makeing their particular confessions.[95]

This "se-baptism" utterly confounded Robinson. Into what church was Smyth baptized? By what authority? And if Smyth's baptism was not valid (and Robinson was certain it was not), then the same must be true of the baptisms of Helwys and the rest.[96] Within a year, Smyth became convinced that he had erred, that the Dutch Mennonites were a true church practicing true baptism, and that he should have received baptism from them. At this realization, Smyth and thirty-two members of his congregation requested membership in the Waterlander Mennonite Church.[97]

Helwys, however, held firm to his conviction that the baptism he received at Smyth's hand was a true baptism, and his congregation of ten remaining members was a true church, a church whose communion was strictly fenced in by credobaptism. In 1610, Helwys wrote his *Confession of the Faith of the True English Church*, in which he stated, "That the Church is the assemblage of the faithful, baptized in the name of the Father, the Son and the Holy Spirit," specifying in the next article, "That baptism is the external sign of a remission of sins and mortification, and is a renovation of life and for that reason does not extend to children."[98] The following year, Helwys was even more explicit in his *A Declaration of Faith of English People Remaining at Amsterdam in Holland*, which is "recognized by the majority of Baptist scholars as the first true English Baptist confession of

---

95. Robinson, *Of Religious Commvnion*, 48.

96. "I demaund into what Ch: he entered by baptism? or entering by baptism into no Ch: how his baptism could be true, by their own doctrine? Or *Mr. Smithes* bapt: not being true, nor he by it entering into any Church, how *Mr. Helw:* his baptism could be true, or into what Ch: he entered by it?" (Robinson, *Of Religious Commvnion*, 48).

97. Early, *Life and Writings of Thomas Helwys*, 25; Estep, *Anabaptist Story*, 289–91; Lee, *Theology of John Smyth*, 83–95.

98. Articles 9 and 10 in Helwys, *Confession of the Faith* (1610), 62.

faith."[99] Article 13 stated, "That every Church is to receive in all their members by Baptism upon the Confession of their faith and sins wrought by the preaching of the Gospel, according to the primitive institution, Matthew 28. 19. And practice, Acts 2. 41. And therefore Churches constituted after any other manner, or of any other persons are not according to CHRIST'S Testament."[100] Clear and unambiguous, the first Baptist church and the first Baptist confession regarded strict communion as the only valid position for a true church of Christ. From Smyth's *The Differences of the Churches of the Separation* (1608), which started the congregation on the road to separation from their Separatist brethren, to Helwys's *A Declaration of Faith of English People Remaining at Amsterdam in Holland* (1611), which expounded the faith of this new Baptist church, Helwys's congregation was driven by its commitment to ecclesiological purity. Just as it would for Baptists sixty years later during the communion controversy, ecclesiological purity triumphed over evangelical unity.

Helwys and his colleague, John Murton, relocated the church back to England in 1612, where they organized the first Baptist church on English soil, just outside London in Spitalfields.[101] The question of General Baptist descent from the Spitalfields congregation is an open debate. Traditionally, church historians have traced the General Baptist movement to the Helwys/Murton congregation, and the Particular Baptist movement to those churches that emerged out of the "JLJ" Semi-Separatist church in London in the 1640s.[102] In his influential 2006 monograph *The Early English Baptists*, Stephen Wright challenged this traditional view, arguing that the Helwys/Murton congregation at Spitalfields faded into obscurity due to the imprisonment and isolationism of its leaders, and had essentially no influence upon the later Baptist movement. Wright contends that later General Baptists emerged in the 1640s out of Semi-Separatism, alongside

99. Early, *Life and Writings of Thomas Helwys*, 64.

100. Helwys, *Declaration of Faith* (1611), 71.

101. Early, *Life and Writings of Thomas Helwys*, 35.

102. For example, Estep writes, "This small congregation [i.e., the Helwys/Murton church] with such an unpromising beginning, established on English soil a church from which the General Baptists of England trace their beginning" (Estep, *Anabaptist Story*, 291). A. C. Underwood refers to John Smyth as "the fountain-head of consecutive Baptist history" and "the father and founder of the organized Baptists of England and of the General Baptists in particular" (Underwood, *History of the English Baptists*, 45, quoted in Garrett, *Baptist Theology*, 31). B. R. White states that "the first, and earliest was the General Baptist community, this stemmed directly from John Smyth and the older Separatism" (White, "Open and Closed Membership," 330).

the Particular Baptists.[103] This debate is often connected to the question of Anabaptist influence, and is beyond the scope of this monograph. What is pertinent is that strict communion was the immediate and dominant impulse of the earliest English Baptist church, the necessary implication of its foundational ecclesiology.

The Particular Baptists of 1640s London

Though historians debate the question of continuity between the Helwys/Murton congregation and the later General Baptist movement, all agree that 1640s London was the seedbed for the Particular Baptist movement. In particular, the "JLJ" Church in Southwark, London "spawned" several churches that rose to influence in 1640s London. As Duesing notes, "Often the genesis for the new churches centered around the growing differences over the issue of baptism.[104] The first such separation occurred in 1633, when Samuel Eaton and seven others received "a further Baptism."[105] Then, in 1638, six more members departed the JLJ Church and joined with John Spilsbury, again over the issue of baptism.[106] In 1640, the JLJ Church split, with half following Praisegod Barebone, and half remaining with Jessey. Once again,

---

103. Wright, *Early English Baptists*, 45–74, 99–102. Writes states, "It is unclear whether the pre-war Murton tradition survived in 1630s London" (72). "There is little reason to connect (or identify) the London churches of Edward Barber and Thomas Lambe (both known later as General Baptists) with the pre-war tradition of Helwys and Murton" (76).

104. Duesing, *Henry Jessey*, 144–45. "Spawned" in the previous sentence is Duesing's description of the causal relationship between the JLJ Church and the Particular Baptist churches.

105. The phrase "further Baptism" comes from Stinton, *Repository*, 1:7, quoted in Duesing, *Henry Jessey*, 148. The precise nature of this "further Baptism" is addressed in Duesing, *Henry Jessey*, 148–53, where Duesing discusses the opinions of B. R. White (believer's baptism in 1633), Murray Tolmie (Separatist baptism in 1633, with believer's baptism sometime after), and Stephen Wright (believer's baptism in 1638) (White, "Samuel Eaton," 10–21; Tolmie, *Triumph of the Saints*, 23, 192–93; Wright, *Early English Baptists*, 228–30). Duesing concludes, "When was Samuel Eaton baptized and was that believer's baptism by conviction? The evidence seems to confirm that sometime between 1633 and 1638 the believer's baptism Eaton received by John Spilsbury was of a convictional nature affirming that baptism was not for infants" (Duesing, *Henry Jessey*, 152–53).

106. Stinton no. 1 records that six church members "desireing to depart & not to be censured. . . . They haveing first forsaken Us & Joyned with Mr Spilsbury" (Stinton, *Repository*, 1:7, quoted in Duesing, *Henry Jessey*, 156). It is likely that Spilsbury had earlier split from another Separatist Church, for there is no indication that Spilsbury was associated with the JLJ Church (Duesing, *Henry Jessey*, 156; Wright, *Early English Baptists*, 229; Tolmie, *Triumph of the Saints*, 25).

baptism was at the center of the divide.[107] At this juncture, the credobaptism practiced by the Separatists was still by the mode of sprinkling; the first recorded immersion would not occur until early in 1642.[108] On January 9, 1642, Richard Blunt baptized Samuel Blacklock, Blacklock baptized Blunt, and then together the two baptized a host of others.[109] In all, fifty-three members separated from the JLJ Church and formed two, closely related congregations, one under the leadership of Blunt and the other under the leadership of Thomas Kilcop. They were soon joined by a third group, Spilsbury's congregation, who also adopted believer's baptism by immersion, then by a fourth, a congregation in Crutched Fryers led by John Green and John Spencer, then a fifth, Eaton's former congregation, now led by William Kiffin.[110] Within two years, there would be seven Particular Baptist churches in London to sign the 1644 London Baptist Confession.

Although some signatories had expressed their views on baptism and the church prior to the autumn of 1644, the London Baptist Confession was a watershed moment for the Particular Baptist movement.[111] According to

107. "The Church became two by mutall consent just half being with Mr P. Barenone [sic], and the other halfe with Mr H. Jessey" (Stinton, *Repository*, 2:10, quoted in Duesing, *Henry Jessey*, 165). Barebone desired to remain Semi-Separatist, while Jessey was moving toward a fully Separatist position; "Whereas Jessey would also continue to have church members who never abandoned their infant baptism, the additional difference between the two groups lies in the growing openness Jessey and his followers had to the arguments for both baptism by immersion and baptism for believers" (165–66).

108. This was after Richard Blunt's return from the Netherlands, to which he had been dispatched by the JLJ Church to learn about the Netherlanders's practice of immersion and views of baptismal succession (Duesing, *Henry Jessey*, 169–74). "Gathering together on 9 January 1641/1642, the two companies served to enact what would be known as the restoration of the practice of immersion for believer's baptism and, as some have maintained, the official start to the English Baptist movement" (173–74). For a discussion of the difficulty of dating this event, see Duesing, *Henry Jessey*, 173n92.

109. "It seems likely that Blunt first baptized Blacklock and then Blacklock must have baptised Blunt. No doubt after this they each baptized those whose names in the list followed their own" (White, "Baptist Beginnings," 37). Whether Blunt was baptized in the Netherlands, presumably by Jan Batten, or in London by Blacklock, is discussed in Wright, *Early English Baptists*, 85–89; Duesing, *Henry Jessey*, 175–76. The question of who baptized Richard Blunt has implications for early Particular Baptist views of baptismal succession and authority.

110. Belyea, "Origins of the Particular Baptists," 45; Haykin, *Kiffin, Knollys and Keach*, 30; Duesing, *Henry Jessey*, 178–79.

111. For example, Kilcop, *Short Treatise of Baptisme*; Spilsbury, *Treatise*. P. J. Anderson asserts, "At least thirty-four pamphlets addressing the issue of baptism were published between 1640 and June, 1645" (Anderson, "Letters of Henry Jessey," 39n14, quoted in Duesing, *Henry Jessey*, 166).

B. R. White, "This document has considerable significance for the early development of the Particular Baptist churches and for their doctrine of the Church: it provides, on the one hand, the first clear evidence of intercongregational co-operation among the Calvinistic Baptists and, on the other, the doctrinal standard for the first period of their expansion which closed with the Restoration of Charles II in 1660."[112] The confession contains fifty-two articles, fifteen dealing with the doctrine of the church (33–47). The 1644 London Baptist Confession clearly implies, though does not explicitly endorse, strict communion. Article 33 states:

> That Christ hath here on earth a spirituall Kingdome, which is the Church, which he hath purchased and redeemed to himselfe, as a peculiar inheritance: which Church, as it is visible to us, is a company of visible Saints, called & separated from the world, by the word and Spirit of God, to the visible profession of the faith of the Gospel, being baptized into that faith, and joyned to the Lord, and each other, by mutuall agreement, in the practical injoyment of the Ordinances, commanded by Christ their head and King.[113]

There are several relevant points worth noting in article 33.

- With regard to the nature of the church, the article affirms a global church militant, which is Christ's "spirituall Kingdome" on earth.[114] This global church militant is manifested as "a company of visible Saints," that is, a particular, visible church.

- This particular, visible church is comprised of "visible Saints," and none other; that is, the article confesses a regenerate church membership.

- These visible saints are those who have been "called & separated from the world, by the word and Spirit of God, to the visible profession of that faith of the Gospel, *being baptized into that faith*" (italics added). The plain reading of this statement is that baptism is the means by which faith is visibly professed. In other words, the article envisions a particular, visible, regenerate, baptized church.

---

112. White, "Doctrine of the Church," 570. For the background of the 1644 London Baptist Confession, see White, "Doctrine of the Church," 570–90; Wright, *Early English Baptists*, 121–42. Wright states, "The London Confession of 1644 was a union of seven churches, which replaced a loose association" (Wright, *Early English Baptists*, 136).

113. *Confession of Faith* (1644) art. 33.

114. This is the Baptist *tertium quid* examined in previous chapters, a non-particular/visible (i.e., earthly) church.

- The means by which these baptized saints are gathered into a particular, visible church ("joyned to the Lord, and each other") is by covenant—"by mutuall agreement." This covenanting together occurs subsequent to the baptizing ("being baptized into that faith, and joyned").

- The purpose of this particular, visible, regenerate, baptized, covenanted church is "the practical injoyment of the Ordinances, commanded by Christ their head and King." Clearly, one of the ordinances practiced and enjoyed by the particular, visible, regenerate, baptized, covenanted church is the Lord's Supper.

In other words, the logical flow of article 33 implies that baptism precedes and is necessary unto membership in the church and participation in the Lord's Supper.

The 1644 London Baptist Confession contains three articles on baptism. Baptism is to be "dispensed onely upon persons professing faith, or that are Disciples" (art. 39), by "dipping or plunging the whole body under water" (art. 40), and administered by a "preaching Disciple, it being no where tyed to a particular Church, Officer, or person extraordinarily sent, the Commission injoyning the administration, being given to them under no other consideration, but as considered Disciples" (art. 41).[115] It is intriguing that the 1644 London Baptist Confession contains no reference to the Lord's Supper, an oversight rectified in the 1646 revision. It did, however, establish an association of Baptist churches that excluded those that did not "walk by one and the same Rule": "And although the particular Congregations be distinct and severall Bodies, every one as a compact and knit Citie in it selfe; yet are they all to walk by one and the same Rule, and by all meanes convenient to have the counsell and help one of another in all needfull affaires of the Church, as members of one body in the common faith under Christ their onely head."[116]

Hanserd Knollys returned from New England in 1641 and joined the JLJ Church. It was his refusal to baptize his infant child that provoked a series

---

115. *Confession of Faith* (1644) arts. 39, 40, 41. In the 1646 revision, the comma between "particular Church, Officer" in article 41 was omitted, yielding instead "it [i.e., baptism] being no where tyed to a particular Church officer, or person extraordinarily sent," suggesting that the comma was in error (*Confession of Faith of Seven Congregations* [1646] art. 41). If such is the case, the 1644 London Baptist Confession does not deny that baptism is the initiating ordinance into the particular/visible church, a topic of much debate in the later communion controversy; see the discussion in chapter 4.

116. *Confession of Faith* (1644) art. 47.

of debates in early 1644 involving Knollys, Kiffin, and Jessey.[117] In 1645, Knollys departed from the JLJ Church to form his own congregation of baptized believers, along with a number of other members of the JLJ Church.[118] Soon thereafter, Jessey, being finally convinced of credobaptism by reading Tombes's *Examen*, received believer's baptism at the hand of Knollys on June 29, 1645.[119] But while Knollys continued his pilgrimage toward Baptist convictions regarding strict communion, becoming a signatory of the 1646 revision of the London Baptist Confession, Jessey adopted an open-communion stance, or what Duesing calls a "mixed ecclesiology."[120]

What was it that drove Knollys to strict Baptist communion? In 1645, the same year he departed from Jessey's church to form his own congregation of baptized believers, Knollys wrote *A Moderate Answer*, a response to John Bastwick's *Independency Not Gods Ordinance*. Bastwick had posed and answered two main questions: "There is a twofold question between us, they call the Presbyterians, and our Brethren they tearme Independents. The first is concerning the government of the Church, *viz.* whether it be Presbyterian Dependent, or Presbyterian Independent. The second question is, concerning the gathering of Churches."[121] The first question Bastwick answered with four propositions in favor of Presbyterian government, which Knollys quoted and rebutted point-by-point.[122]

---

117. Duesing, *Henry Jessey*, 179–84. A portion of these debates is recorded in Stinton, *Repository*, 4:25–26.

118. Duesing, *Henry Jessey*, 189.

119. Duesing, *Henry Jessey*, 189–95. Jessey became convinced of immersion in 1641/1642: "Jessey, from now on, *immersed* the children he baptized" (White, "Baptist Beginnings," 36).

120. Duesing prefers the term "mixed ecclesiology" rather than "open membership" or "open communion": "For Jessey, church membership can be mixed or comprised of believers with varying baptismal experiences. Often this position has been labeled 'open membership,' but as will be shown, this term is misleading; for Jessey, and those like him, did have restrictions on the requirements for membership. Therefore, logically following a mixed church membership is Jessey's view of a mixed participation in the Lord's Supper among both members and non-members without respect to baptism. This position has frequently been recognized as 'open communion,' but as will be shown, this term also has its limitations" (Duesing, *Henry Jessey*, 200–201).

121. Bastwick, *Independency Not Gods Ordinance*, 7.

122. Bastwick's four propositions were: (1) "That there were many Congregations and severall Assemblies of Beleevers in the Church of Ierusalem, in the which they enjoyed all acts of worship, and all the Ordinances amongst themselves, and did partake of all acts of Church-fellowship, especially of preaching, and in the administration of the Sacraments, and Prayer, and that before the Persecution we reade of, *Acts* 8 v. 2.";

The second question arose out of Bastwick's concern over what he considered the schismatical activity of the Independents. Bastwick queried, "Whether Ministers of the Gospell may out of already congregated Assemblies of beleevers, select and choose the most principle of them, into a Church-fellowship peculiar unto themselves, and admit of none into their society, but such as shall enter in by a private covenant, and are allowed by the consent and approbation of all the Congregation?"[123] From Bastwick's perspective, the Independents were siphoning members away from the (soon-to-be-Presbyterian) Church of England to form their own covenanted enclaves. Bastwick then provided his understanding of the biblical method of gathering churches: first, "That Christ having given a Commission to his Apostles to teach all Nations, and baptize them, . . . the Apostles practiced accordingly"; second, "That the condition or tearmes, which they were to propound unto all Nations and people upon which they were to be admitted into the church were Faith, Repentance, and Baptisme"; third, "that the Apostles and all succeeding Ministers of the Gospel should admit whosoever beleeved, and were baptized, to be Members of the Church, and teach them to observe no other things but what Christ commanded them, and for which they had his Word and warrant."[124] Knollys responded by stating his full agreement with Bastwick's words, and then asserted that this is precisely what "some Churches of God in this City" were, in fact, doing.[125] Though Knollys spoke in general terms of "some godly and learned men of approved guifts and abilities for the Ministerie" who "came to sojourn in this great City, and preached the Word of God," the context makes clear that he is speaking of the Baptist churches of London:

---

(2) "That all these Congregations and several Assemblies made but one Church"; (3) "That the Apostles and Elders governed, ordered, and ruled this Church, joyntly, and by a Common-counsell, and Presbytery"; (4) "That this Church of Ierusalem, and the government of the same, is to be a pattern for all severall congregations and assemblies in any City or vicinity to unite into one Church; and for the Officers of those congregations to governe that Church joyntly in a Colledge or Presbyterie" (Bastwick, *Independency Not Gods Ordinance*, 11–12). Knollys's rebuttals to these four propositions may be found in Knollys, *Moderate Answer*, 3–14. The foundation of Knollys's response is a denial that the church in Jerusalem was comprised of several particular congregations, and therefore that it was ruled by a common presbytery.

123. Bastwick, *Independency Not Gods Ordinance*, 98.

124. This is Knollys's summary of Bastwick's three points (Knollys, *Moderate Answer*, 18–19). They are originally found in Bastwick, *Independency Not Gods Ordinance*, 100.

125. Knollys, *Moderate Answer*, 19.

> And the condition which those Preachers both publikely and privately propounded to the people, unto whom they Preached, upon which they were to be admitted into the Church was Faith, Repentance, and Baptism; and none other. And whosoever (poor as well as rich, bond as well as free, servants as well as Masters) did make a profession of their Faith in Christ Jesus, and would be baptized with water into the Name of the Father, Sonne, and Holy Spirit, were admitted Members of the Church; but such as did not beleeve, and would not be baptized they would not admit into Church-communion.[126]

Given Knollys's new convictions, and the fact that the Congregationalists did not baptize those who joined them from the Church of England, Knollys must be speaking of credobaptism and of Baptist churches.[127] What drove Knollys to this position? The commitment to adhere to "the practice of the Apostles rule, and practice of the primitive Churches, both in gathering, and admitting Members."[128] Four decades later, Knollys would argue for "ONE Church in one City" comprised of "all the Congregations of Saints in that City (called Churches)," and that "this one Church, and all the Congregations of Saints, that are Members thereof, walk by one and the same Rule *of the written Word of God,*" and that "the Order of the Gospel be carefully observed, and kept in the Administration of God's Sacred Ordinances, in the Admission of Members, in the Ordination of Church-Officers, and in withdrawing from every Brother that walketh *Disorderly.*"[129] Knollys was driven to strict Baptist communion by his preeminent commitment to ecclesiological purity—a church formed according to the "Rule of the written Word of God"—even at the expense of evangelical unity.

---

126. Knollys, *Moderate Answer*, 19–20.

127. It must be admitted that Knollys did not explicitly spell out credobaptism or specify that he was speaking of the Particular Baptist churches of London. Rather, he argued in favor of general Independency against Presbyterianism. But four lines of evidence suggest that by "baptism" Knollys intended credobaptism, and by "churches" he intended Baptist churches: (1) Knollys had been of credobaptistic convictions for at least three years at the time of writing; (2) earlier in 1645, Knollys felt strongly enough about strict Baptist communion that he separated from the JLJ Church to form his own congregation; (3) Knollys signed his name to the 1646 revision of the London Baptist Confession, which specified strict Baptist communion; (4) paedobaptist Independents did not baptize converts from the Church of England.

128. Knollys, *Moderate Answer*, 20.

129. Knollys, *World That Now Is*, 50–52.

Jessey, on the other hand, was driven to a different conclusion by a different commitment, remaining firmly open-communion throughout his life and ministry. Duesing explains:

> Jessey's reception of believer's baptism was the product of a change in his personal beliefs, but it was not a change he felt he should mandate for his church. The semi-separatist heritage Jessey received from the Jacob-Lathrop congregation, combined with Jessey's desire to maintain ties with the Independent and other movements of similar nature prevented him from aligning his church concretely with the Particular Baptists in London. These convictions and circumstances left Jessey with a flexible ecclesiology.[130]

Though personally convinced of credobaptism, the desire to maintain relationships with the other evangelicals in London proved determinative. In other words, evangelical unity superseded ecclesiological purity. Jessey would not exclude an evangelical believer from membership, or exclude an evangelical church from association, over an errant view of baptism. As was demonstrated in the previous chapter, though the Baptists repeatedly denied that their strict-communion stance implied that unbaptized evangelicals were not true Christians or that their churches were not true churches, open-communionists like Bunyan and Jessey regarded this as the necessary implication of their view.[131]

Did Jessey's open-communion stance alienate him from the Particular Baptists of London? Duesing says no, quoting B. R. White, who says, "No high walls grew between the mother church and her rigorist daughters," and Steven Wright, who states that Jessey became "perhaps the most influential of all Baptists during the Commonwealth and the Protectorate."[132] But White's full statement points to a different conclusion:

> It is equally noteworthy that no high walls grew between the mother church and her rigorist daughters during the years from 1633 until sometime after the publication of the 1644 *Confession*: in 1638 Samuel Eaton was arrested at worship with Jessey's congregation, in 1640 Richard Blunt was discussing the mode of baptism within it and, later still, William Kiffin, who may never

---

130. Duesing, *Henry Jessey*, 197–98.

131. See Bunyan, *Differences in Judgment*, 4:221–22; *Peaceable Principles and True*, 4:274.

132. Duesing, *Henry Jessey*, 195; White, "Doctrine of the Church," 586–87; Wright, *Early English Baptists*, 75.

have been a member of the Jacob-Lathrop-Jessey Church, shared the internal debate about believer's baptism. Hence there were, in 1644, several factors encouraging the first London Particular Baptist congregations toward close co-operation.[133]

White specifically restricts the period in question to 1633–1644, and implies that "high walls" then grew between "the mother church and her rigorist daughters" as a result of the publication of the 1644 London Baptist Confession. Furthermore, White's point is that the association among Particular Baptist congregations *after* 1644 was informed by the associationalism of the JLJ Church *prior to* 1644, not that the Particular Baptist churches were associated with the JLJ Church after 1644: "It was noted earlier that five of the signatories in 1644 had had experience of the family of congregations which developed around that founded by Henry Jacob. It is this background in English Independency from experience of which it seems likely that the Particular Baptist associations were to grow."[134] Furthermore, Wright's statement says nothing of Jessey's relationship with the Particular Baptists, but rather speaks of Jessey's prominence as a "Trier" from 1654 on.[135] In fact, Wright is explicit in stating that

> the practice here [in Murray Tolmie's *Triumph of the Saints*] of referring to Jessey as a 'Particular Baptist' is highly misleading. The Particular Baptists were linked in a communion closed to all but believers' Baptists. Jessey, Simpson, and two or three other such persons who may figure on the lists, were members of Calvinistic churches open to Baptists and Independents. They were friendly with the Particular Baptist leaders and shared with them ideas about theology, but sought to build their own group of churches on their own terms.[136]

This is not to suggest that Jessey was cut off from the London Particular Baptists after the publication of the 1644 London Baptist Confession. The letter to Tombes examined above suggests a continued relationship with Knollys and Benjamin Coxe, and Wright asserts, "The Particular Baptists maintained

---

133. White, "Doctrine of the Church," 586–87.

134. White, "Doctrine of the Church," 586.

135. "During the 1630s, the London church founded by Henry Jacob, and led by his successors John Lathrop and Henry Jessey, was home to several who later became believers' Baptists. These included Jessey himself, perhaps the most influential of all Baptists during the Commonwealth and the Protectorate, which he served as a 'Trier' from 1654" (Wright, *Early English Baptists*, 75).

136. Wright, *Early English Baptists*, 173n98.

a close friendship with Henry Jessey," citing Jessey's attendance with Knollys in late-1646 "for the restoring of an old blind woman to her sight, by anointing her with oyle in the name of the Lord," and an event in the summer of 1647 in which Jessey and Kiffin rented a room together at London House.[137] According to Wright, "Jessey's record made it hard to attack him and was probably important in winning the cooperation of those who remembered with affection the days of the anti-episcopal common front, before the atmosphere was soured by factional resentment."[138] In other words, Jessey's continued relationship and cooperation with the London Baptists was due to their shared history and the personal respect he commanded. But Jessey was the exception to the rule. Bunyan had no shared history with the London Baptists, and they certainly did not respect the Tinker. This explains the vast difference in the way the two were treated by the Baptists; the former as a friend, the latter as a foe. But that the London Baptists viewed Jessey as a fellow Baptist goes beyond the evidence.

By 1645, Benjamin Coxe had emerged as a leader of the nascent Particular Baptist movement, such that in late 1645, he participated with Kiffin and Knollys in a debate with the Presbyterians over baptism.[139] On January 26, 1646, Coxe, along with Samuel Richardson, presented a revised confession of faith to the House of Commons.[140] This revision included several significant changes from the 1644 London Baptist Confession, due in part to criticism from Daniel Featley's *The Dippers Dip't*. Changes from the 1644 London Baptist Confession include article 31 with the addition of a statement on the private ownership of property, article 36 with the omission of "Pastors, Teachers" from the list of church officers alongside elders and deacons, article 38 with the deletion of "and not by constraint to be compelled from the people by a forced Law" in reference to the maintenance of church officers, and article 41 with an alteration in who is qualified to baptize from "a preaching Disciple" to simply a "Disciple," though this is qualified at the end of the article by "men able to preach the Gospel."[141] Additionally, the

---

137. Wright, *Early English Baptists*, 169–70. Wright cites Edwards, *Gangraena*, 3:19, for the Knollys/Jessey incident.

138. Wright, *Early English Baptists*, 169. Wright goes on to state that "social, ideological and historical ties bound the Particular Baptist leaders to the Independents" (170).

139. Wright, *Early English Baptists*, 147. Wright states that Coxe was "an ordained clergyman and an Oxford MA."

140. Wright, *Early English Baptists*, 148. For the background on the 1646 revision, see Wright, *Early English Baptists*, 143–48.

141. These changes from the 1644 London Baptist Confession are noted in Lumpkin, *Baptist Confessions of Faith*, 165–67.

1646 revision included a strong statement of liberty of conscience (marginal note to art. 48), an expanded treatment of the magistracy (arts. 48–51), and a statement on the resurrection of the dead (art. 52).[142] But for the purposes of this monograph, the most significant change in the 1646 revision is the addition of an explicit statement on strict Baptist communion. In the 1646 revision, article 39 reads: "Baptisme is an ordinance of the new Testament, given by Christ, to be dispensed upon persons professing faith, or that are made Disciples; who upon profession of faith, ought to be baptized, and after to partake of the Lord's Supper."[143] The same year, Coxe published *An Appendix to a Confession of Faith*, in which he hoped to clarify concerns that the 1646 revision had raised among some at the Westminster Assembly.[144] Regarding baptism, Coxe asserted that while not absolutely necessary for salvation, yet it is essential to Christian obedience:

> Although a true beleever, whether baptized, or unbaptized, be in the state of salvation, and shal certainly be saved: yet in obedience to the Command of *Christ* every beleever ought to desire Baptism, and to yeeld himself to be baptized according to the rule of *Christ* in his Word: And where this obedience is in faith performed, there *Christ* makes this his Ordinance a means of unspeakable benefit to the beleeving soul, *Acts* 2. 38. *Acts* 22. 16. *Rom.* 6. 3, 4. 1 *Pet.* 3. 21. And a true beleever that here sees the command of *Christ* lying upon him, cannot allow himself in disobedience thereunto, *Acts* 24. 16.[145]

Coxe further defined a church as "a company of baptized beleevers": "Beleevers baptized ought to agree and joyn together in constant profession of the same doctrine of the Gospel, and in professed obedience thereunto, and also in fellowship, and in breaking of bread, and in prayers, *Acts* 2. 42. And a company of baptized beleevers so agreeing and joyning

---

142. *Confession of Faith of Seven Congregations* (1646) arts. 48–52.

143. *Confession of Faith of Seven Congregations* (1646) art. 39.

144. "And if our judgement touching some particulars, wherein we seem, or are supposed, to dissent from some others, do not appear cleerly enough in that confession, I hope the same shall somewhat more cleerly appear in this ensuing Appendix" (Coxe, *Appendix to a Confession of Faith*, 3). The title page stated that the *Appendix* was "published for the further clearing of Truth, and discovery of their mistake who have imagined a dissent in fundamentals where there is none" (1).

145. Coxe, *Appendix to a Confession of Faith*, 9–10.

together, are a Church or Congregation of Christ, *Acts* 2. 47."[146] Regarding admission to the Lord's Supper, Coxe wrote:

> Though a beleevers right to the use of the Lords Supper doe immediately flow from Jesus Christ apprehended and received by faith; yet so as much as all things ought to be done not onely decently, but also in order; 1 *Cor.* 14. 40. and the word holds forth this order, that disciples should be baptized, *Matth.* 28. 19, *Acts* 2. 38—and then be taught to observe all things (that is to say, all other things) that Christ commanded the Apostles, *Matth.* 28. 20. and accordingly the Apostles first baptized disciples, and then admitted them to the use of the Supper, *Acts* 2. 41, 42. we therefore doe not admit any to the use of the Supper, nor communicate with any in the use of this ordinance, but disciples baptized, lest we should have fellowship with them in their doing contrary to order.[147]

Coxe's *Appendix* was the clearest statement of strict communion to come from the Particular Baptists of London in the 1640s, and contained many of the same arguments used by Paul, Denne, and Danvers in the 1670s, and Kiffin in 1681. The Baptists could not admit the unbaptized to communion, lest they transgress the rule of Christ. Again, ecclesiological purity superseded evangelical unity. Thus, in 1640s London, the seedbed of the Particular Baptist movement, there existed a clear and consistent ecclesiology requiring strict Baptist communion. Indeed, strict communion was the *raison d'être* of the Particular Baptist movement.

The General Baptists of the Seventeenth Century

According to B. R. White, the General Baptists had a simple way of handling debate over strict communion: there was none. "Their [i.e., the General Baptist] tradition in the matter of 'open' and 'closed' membership was simple and consistent: they all practised 'closed' communion and, hence, 'closed membership.' . . . The practice of 'closed membership' continued with the foundation of the New Connexion of General Baptists in 1770. . . . This continued to be their policy and their practice down to 1891 when they joined the Baptist Union."[148] White's assessment is confirmed by a survey of seventeenth-century General Baptist confessions, by the writings that emerged from the pens of General Baptists in a communion controversy

---

146. Coxe, *Appendix to a Confession of Faith*, 10.
147. Coxe, *Appendix to a Confession of Faith*, 11.
148. White, "Open and Closed Membership," 330.

Strict Communion and Seventeenth-Century Baptist Identity

with the Independent John Goodwin, and by the writings of the preeminent seventeenth-century General Baptist theologian, Thomas Grantham.

During the seventeenth century, General Baptists in England "composed and adopted four noteworthy confessions of faith."[149] In 1651, thirty General Baptist churches from the Midlands gathered at Leicester to adopt a confession called *The Faith and Practice of Thirty Congregations, Gathered According to the Primitive Pattern*.[150] According to William Lumpkin, "The Confession is important because it is the first General Baptist statement representing the views of more than one church, rather than because of the prominence of its author or signatories. It shows essential agreement with the first General Baptist Confession (1611)."[151] It also contains the first General Baptist reference to immersion as the proper mode of baptism.[152] Articles 47–50 deal with the subject of baptism: baptism must follow conscious repentance (art. 47), baptism must be by immersion (art. 48), and to refuse baptism is to "reject the counsel of God against themselves" (art. 49).[153] Article 50 states, "That those which received the word of God preached by the Ministrie of the Gospel,

---

149. Garrett, *Baptist Theology*, 35. Lumpkin writes, "The Baptist confessions of faith which appeared during the period of the Commonwealth (1650–1659) were closely connected with the association movement, and they often served as its unifying instruments" (Lumpkin, *Baptist Confessions of Faith*, 171–72). In other words, these confessions of faith reflect the common beliefs of wide swaths of the seventeenth-century General Baptist tradition.

150. Lumpkin, *Baptist Confessions of Faith*, 172.

151. Lumpkin, *Baptist Confessions of Faith*, 173. Intriguingly, Lumpkin writes, "No consistently Arminian system is revealed; rather, some traditional emphases of Calvinism are set forth" (173).

152. Though the term "immersion" is not used, it seems to be implied. Article 48 states, "That the way and manner of baptising, both before the death of Christ, and since his resurrection and ascension, was to go into the water, and to be baptized" (*Faith and Practice of Thirty Congregations* [1651] art. 48 [182]). Garrett writes, "Article 48 seems to prescribe immersion as the form of baptism, thus reflecting the influence of the Particular Baptists, who had adopted immersion, on the General Baptists" (Garrett, *Baptist Theology*, 35).

153. Article 47: "That the Baptisme which the Lord Jesus commanded his disciples to teach ought to be known by every one, before they submit themselves, or obey it; *Acts* 2. 38, 41." Article 48: "That the way and manner of baptising, both before the death of Christ, and since his resurrection and ascension, was to go into the water, and to be baptised; *Math.* 3. 6. *Math.* 1. 5. and 8. 9." Article 49: "That when Baptisme is made known, or any other Action of obedience, then for men to refuse it, they are said to reject the counsel of God against themselves; *Luk.* 7. 30" (*Faith and Practice of Thirty Congregations* arts. 47–49 [182]).

and were Baptized according to the Counsel of God, at the same time or day they were of the visible Church of God, Acts 2. 41."[154] Article 52 then connects baptism, the church, and its ordinances:

> That the chief or only ends of a people baptised according to the counsel of God, when they meet together as the congregation or fellowship of Christ, are, or ought to be, for to walk sutably; or to give up themselves unto a holy conformity to all the Laws or Ordinances of Jesus Christ, answerable to the gifts and graces received, improving them for the glory of God, and the edification of each other in love, Eph. 4. 15, 16.[155]

Article 53 then specifies that one of these ordinances given to the church is the Lord's Supper.[156] Though the General Baptist churches of the Midlands did not adopt a statement of strict communion as explicit as the 1646 London Baptist Confession, there exists a clear line of continuity between articles 47–53: only those who repent should be baptized (47), by immersion (48); to refuse to be baptized is to reject the counsel of God (49); only baptized believers are of the visible church (50), which church is founded upon the apostolic doctrine as its only foundation (51); those baptized according to the counsel of God are gathered into a congregation of Christ in order to give themselves to the ordinances of Christ (52), including the Lord's Supper (53).

In 1654, General Baptist leaders in London assembled to counter the Quaker threat. They did so from both the positive and negative angles. Negatively, John Griffith wrote a pamphlet critique entitled *A Voice from the Word of the Lord to Those Grand Imposters Called Quakers*. Positively, they published a confession of faith. Not having time to compose an original confession, the assembly adopted *en toto* a confession written a few years earlier by Thomas Lover, about whom little else is known.[157]

---

154. *Faith and Practice of Thirty Congregations* art. 50 (182).

155. *Faith and Practice of Thirty Congregations* art. 52 (183).

156. "That Jesus Christ took Bread, and the juice of the Vine, and brake, and gave to his Disciples, to eat and drink with thanksgiving; which practice is left upon record as a memorial of his suffering, to continue in the Church until he come again; *1 Cor. 11. 23, 24, 25, 26*" (*Faith and Practice of Thirty Congregations* art. 53 [183]).

157. "Apparently time did not permit the working out of an original doctrinal statement. Someone remembered that Thomas Lover (deceased) had a few years previously prepared a Confession which bore the title, 'The True Gospel-Faith Witnessed by the Prophets and Apostles, and Collected into Thirty Articles, Presented to the World as the Present Faith and Practice of the Church of Christ.' This Confession may have been

This confession became known as *The True Gospel-Faith Witnessed by the Prophets and Apostles, and Collected into Thirty Articles* (1654). Article 11 asserts, "That they that believe the things so preached ought to be dipped in water."[158] Article 13 declares, "That every believer dipped is to be joyned with believers dipped, which is the Church of *Christ*."[159] And article 16 states that this same congregation of baptized believers "ought to meet together to break bread."[160] Again, though strict communion is not explicitly prescribed, it is strongly implied.

In March 1660, just prior to the Restoration, General Baptists gathered for a general assembly in London, where they produced what became known as the Standard Confession. According to Lumpkin, "The forty men who signed the Confession of 1660 were a fairly representative group in that they represented the chief General Baptist districts."[161] The primary author was William Jeffery, with contributions from Thomas Monck and Matthew Caffyn.[162] The confession was presented to Charles II on July 26, 1660, was affirmed (in slightly revised form) by a larger general assembly in 1663, was edited and supplemented by Thomas Grantham in 1678, and was approved again at a general assembly in 1691.[163] According to Lumpkin, it is so named because "it is regarded as the 'Standard' Confession of General

---

a private one, or it may originally have been adopted by one or more churches. Nothing is known of Thomas Lover or his church, though Lover must have been an early leader among General Baptists. His Confession was taken over as the official statement of faith of the represented congregations. It appears that no changes were made in it, and full credit for its authorship was given to Lover" (Lumpkin, *Baptist Confessions of Faith*, 189–90).

158. *True Gospel-Faith* art. 11.

159. *True Gospel-Faith* art. 13.

160. *True Gospel-Faith* art. 16.

161. Lumpkin, *Baptist Confessions of Faith*, 220.

162. "William Jeffery, also of Kent, though a young man, was author of the remarkable doctrinal work, *The Whole Faith of Man*, which by 1660 was already a 'standard work of reference and appeal' for General Baptists. It seems reasonable to suppose that Jeffery had very much responsibility in connection with the preparation of the Confession of 1660. Certainly McGlothlin was in error in supposing that Thomas Grantham composed the Confession. Grantham did not even sign the Confession in 1660 and he did not become prominent until some years later. Thomas Monck of Hertfordshire and Matthew Caffyn of Sussex and Kent may have made some contribution to the Confession" (Lumpkin, *Baptist Confessions of Faith*, 221).

163. Lumpkin, *Baptist Confessions of Faith*, 223.

Baptists."[164] The Standard Confession is explicit and uncompromising in its stance on strict communion. Article 11 states:

> That the right and only way of gathering Churches, (according to Christs appointment, *Mat.* 28. 19, 20.) is first to teach, or preach the Gospel, *Mark* 16. 16. to the Sons and Daughters of men; and then to *Baptise* (that is in English to *Dip*) in the name of the Father, Son, and holy Spirit, or in the name of the Lord Jesus Christ; such only of them, as profess *repentance towards God, and faith towards our Lord Jesus Christ*, Acts 2. 38. Acts 8. 12. Acts 18. 8. And as for all such who preach not this Doctrine, but instead thereof, that Scriptureless thing of Sprinkling of Infants (*falsly called Baptisme*) whereby the pure *word of God is made of no effect*, and the new Testament-way of bringing in Members, into the Church by regeneration, cast out; when as the bond-woman & her son, that is to say, that old Testament-way of bringing in Children into the Church by generation, is cast out, as saith the Scripture, *Gal.* 4. 30, 22, 23, 24. *Mat.* 3. 8, 9. all such we utterly deny, forasmuch as we are commanded to *have no fellowship with the unfruitful works of darkness, but rather to reprove them*, Ephes. 5. 11.[165]

Article 13 goes on to say, "That it is the duty of such who are constituted as aforesaid, to *continue stedfastly in Christs and the Apostles Doctrine, and assembling together, in fellowship, in breaking of Bread, and Prayers,* Acts 2. 42."[166]

Finally, in 1678, the General Baptists of the Midlands, including the counties of Bedfordshire, Buckinghamshire, and Hertfordshire, where the Bedford Church and its surrounding network of open-communion churches were firmly established, published *An Orthodox Creed*. The creed was primarily the work of Thomas Monck, a messenger from Buckinghamshire.[167] The purpose of *An Orthodox Creed* was two-fold. First, it was an attempt to demonstrate the essential Protestant orthodoxy of the General Baptists by adopting a slightly revised version of the Presbyterian Westminster Confession of Faith (1646), as the Congregationalists (the Savoy Declaration of 1658) and the Particular Baptists (the London Baptist

---

164. Lumpkin, *Baptist Confessions of Faith*, 223.

165. *Brief Confession or Declaration of Faith* [*The Standard Confession*] (1660) art. 11.

166. *Brief Confession or Declaration of Faith* [*The Standard Confession*] art. 13. Article 14 likewise speaks of "the primitive way, and order of constituting Churches" (refer to art. 11 quoted above).

167. Lumpkin, *Baptist Confessions of Faith*, 295.

Confession of Faith of 1677) had already done.[168] This is evident from the title page, which defines *An Orthodox Creed* as "A Protestant Confession of faith, BEING An ESSAY to Unite, and Confirm all true Protestants in the Fundamental Articles of the Christian Religion, against the Errors and Heresies of the Church of ROME." According to Lumpkin, "Theologically, in keeping with its unionistic purpose, the Confession approaches Calvinism more closely than any other General Baptist confession."[169] Second, it was a rejection of Matthew Caffyn's Hoffmannite Christology; Lumpkin writes, "The first eight articles are devoted entirely to the Trinity, those on the Incarnation and the Union of the Two Natures in Christ being especially full."[170] Despite its theme of focusing upon Protestant consensus, *An Orthodox Creed* contains a full-throated affirmation of strict Baptist communion. Article 28 specifies:

> Baptism is an Ordinance of the New Testament, ordained by Jesus Christ, to be unto the Party Baptized, or Dipped, a Sign of our entrance into the Covenant of Grace, and Ingrafting into Christ, and into the Body of Christ, which is his Church; And of Remission of Sin in the Blood of Christ, and of our Fellowship with Christ, in his Death and Resurrection, and of our living, or rising to newness of Life. And orderly none ought to be admitted into the Visible Church of Christ, without being first Baptized, and those which do really profess Repentance towards God, and Faith in and obedience to our Lord Jesus Christ are the only *proper Subjects*

---

168. "But as for their Faith in most, or all of the main Fundamentals of the Christian Religion, they do agree; as may appear to every Impartial Reader, that shall consider the Thirty Nine Articles of the Church of England, and Mr. Beza's Confession of Faith, and the Confession of Faith signed and published by the Assembly of Divines, and many others by the Baptists in England. Now if these several Confessions of Faith, be compared with this our Confession now published, it will appear we have endeavoured to unite with other Protestants aforesaid, in the main Fundamental Articles of the Christian Faith" (*Orthodox Creed* [1679], A4).

169. Lumpkin, *Baptist Confessions of Faith*, 296. Lumpkin notes that this Calvinistic "disposition is particularly evident in the articles on 'Predestination and Election' (article 9), 'The Covenants' (article 16), 'Original Sin' (article 15), 'Perseverance' (article 36), and 'The Invisible Church' (article 29)" (296). The prefatory epistle states, "*We have also in this our Confession of Faith, laboured to avoid the dangerous Rocks of* Pelagianism, Antinomianism, Arminianism, *and the* Remonstrants. *As also, (as well as we may) we have endeavoured to avoid the extreams of the* Superlapsarians, *and* Sublapsarians, *and others*" (*Orthodox Creed*, A5).

170. Lumpkin, *Baptist Confessions of Faith*, 296. The prefatory epistle states, "We are sure that the denying of Baptism is a less evil, than to deny the Divinity or Humanity of the Son of God" (*Orthodox Creed*, A6 [margin]).

of this Ordinance, according to our Lord's holy Institution, and Primitive Practice; and ought by the Minister, or Administrator, to be done in a solemn manner, in the Name of the Father, Son, and Holy Ghost, by *Immersion* or Dipping of the Person in the Element of Water; this being necessary to the due Administration of this holy Sacrament, as holy Scripture sheweth, and the first and best Antiquity witnesseth for some *Centuries of Years*.[171]

Article 30 states:

> Nevertheless, we believe the Visible Church of Christ on Earth, is made up of several distinct Congregations, which make up that one Catholick Church, or Mystical Body of Christ. And the Marks by which She is known to be the true Spouse of Christ, are these, *viz.* Where the Word of God is rightly Preached, and the Sacraments truly Administered, according to Christ's Institution, and the Practice of the Primitive Church; having Discipline and Government duly Executed, by Ministers or Pastours of God's Appointing, and the Church's Election, that is a true constituted Church: to which Church (and not elsewhere) all Persons that seek for Eternal Life, should gladly joyn themselves. And although there may be many Errors in such a Visible Church, or Congregations, they being not Infallible, yet those Errors being not Fundamental, and the Church in the *major*, or Governing part, being not Guilty, she is not thereby unchurched; nevertheless She ought to detect those Errors, and to Reform, according to God's holy Word, and from such Visible Church, or Congregations, no Man ought by any pretence whatever, schismatically to separate.[172]

Article 28 is explicit that "orderly none ought to be admitted into the Visible Church of Christ, without being first Baptized," and that only those who repent, believe, and obey Christ "are the only *proper Subjects* of this Ordinance, according to our Lord's holy Institution, and Primitive Practice." Therefore, when article 30 states that the second mark of a true visible church is that "the Sacraments [are] truly Administered, according to Christ's Institution, and the Practice of the Primitive Church," it is difficult to escape the implication that the only true visible church is a Baptist church. Where the remainder of article 30 appears to affirm that even those congregations with "many Errors" in non-foundational matters are

---

171. *Orthodox Creed* art. 28. Article 28 goes on to refute the "Popish Doctrine" of baptism.

172. *Orthodox Creed* art. 30.

not "unchurched," provided they are not guilty of errors in the *"major, or Governing part,"* it would appear that the signatories of *An Orthodox Creed* regarded baptism as a major error in the governance of a church, for the article is adamant that "no Man ought by any pretence whatever, schismatically to separate" from a true (though fallible) church. Yet there is no evidence that General Baptist churches refused to admit into membership those who separated from otherwise orthodox paedobaptist Nonconformist churches, which they surely would have done had they regarded such defectors as guilty of schism. And if General Baptist churches did not regard such separation as schism, then by their own definition, they did not consider paedobaptist churches to be true churches.

General Baptists were involved in a communion controversy of their own in the early 1650s when Thomas Lambe and William Allen engaged in a published debate with the Independent paedobaptist John Goodwin.[173] Lambe and Allen were originally members of Goodwin's Coleman Street congregation in London. In 1653, Allen was persuaded of credobaptism by the General Baptist evangelist Samuel Fisher. Allen in turn persuaded Lambe. Together, they led about twenty members out of Goodwin's church and founded their own General Baptist congregation at Lothbury. Goodwin responded to this secession by publishing *Philadelphia: or, XL. Queries* (1653), in which he propounded *"Whether Persons Baptized (as themselves call Baptism) after a profession of Faith, may, or may not, lawfully, and with a good Conscience, hold Communion with such Churches, who judg themselves truly Baptized, though in Infancy, and before such a Profession?"*[174] Goodwin argued against strict Baptist communion by making many of the same points Bunyan would make two decades later. For example, Goodwin questioned whether there is "any Precept, or Example

---

173. William Allen and Thomas Lambe (or Lamb) are frequently confused with other seventeenth-century Nonconformists of the same names. For this William Allen, see Keeble, "William Allen." This Thomas Lambe is not the Thomas Lambe (the "soap-boiler") who was an influential General Baptist pastor in 1640s London, who espoused a general atonement in *The Fountain of Free Grace Opened* (1645), and whose son Isaac signed the Particular Baptist *Confession of Faith* in 1689. Stephen Wright comments that this Thomas Lambe, "linen draper and philanthropist, was for many years confused with a namesake, a soap-boiler by trade: remarkably, both men were prominent General Baptists. The overwhelming evidence that they were not the same individual includes a petition subscribed in 1656 by two London Baptist congregations, each in fellowship with a different Thomas Lamb. The soap-boiler was to stay with the Baptists for the rest of his life, but the linen draper soon abandoned them" (Wright, "Thomas Lamb").

174. Goodwin, *Philadelphia*, title page.

in the Gospel, of any person, how duly soever baptized, who disclaimed *Christian* Communion, either in Church fellowship, or in any [of] the Ordinances of the Gospel, with those, whom he judged true Beleevers, upon an account only of their not having been baptized, especially after such a manner as he judged necessary for them to have been?"[175] Goodwin likewise questioned "Whether may persons, who are weak in the Faith, be rejected by a Church from communion with them, in case they desire it, only because they question, or dissent from, the sense of the generality of this Church, in some one point *of doubtful disputation?*"[176] Goodwin charged the Baptists with magnifying "the ceremony or external rite of Baptism to such an height, as to estimate *Christianity* by it, or to judg them no true or sound *Christians*, who are without it," and thereby they "stumble at the same stone of danger and peril of the Soul, at which the Jews stumbled, when they practiced and urged Circumcision as necessary for Justification."[177] Goodwin clearly understood the Baptist position to be a repudiation of all non-Baptist churches. In Query 19, Goodwin asked,

> Whether it is reasonable or *Christian*, that a company of true Believers, who have met together in the simplicity of their hearts in the fear of God, in the Name of *Jesus Christ*, mutually engaging themselves, as in the presence of God, to walk together in all the Ordinances of the Gospel, as far as they shall from time to time be revealed unto them, and walking accordingly, should be infamously stigmatized as no Church, no true Church of *Christ*, and consequently esteemed but as a rabble rout of the world only pretending Churchship.[178]

William Allen offered the first response to Goodwin with *An Answer to Mr. J. G. his XL. Queries* (1653), a point-for-point rejoinder to each of Goodwin's queries. When asked for precept or example for excluding the unbaptized (as the Baptists perceived paedobaptists to be) from church communion, Allen pointed to both dominical command and apostolic practice

---

175. Goodwin, *Philadelphia*, 3.
176. Goodwin, *Philadelphia*, 11.
177. Goodwin, *Philadelphia*, 17.
178. Goodwin, *Philadelphia*, 16. Goodwin continued, "And this by some one, or a few persons, only because they cannot see with their eyes, or practice that as necessary whereof, after much and earnest prayer unto God, after much enquiry and search, and this with all diligence and impartialness, in order to their conviction and satisfaction, doth no ways to them appear?" (16). This is essentially the same argument Bunyan (and Jessey) made about those who lack "light" in the matter of baptism.

of baptizing upon profession of faith.[179] To the objection that neither dominical command nor apostolic precept specifically demands the exclusion of the unbaptized from church communion, Allen responded that neither does the Scripture specifically command the baptizing of infants:

> For those that plead the Precept of circumcising Infants under the Law, as virtually requiring the baptizing of Infants under the Gospel, me thinks this should be satisfactory as to them, and so to the Querist himself, as touching the Case in hand, *viz.* where God requires Circumcision under pain of being excluded communion with the Church, [i.e., "cut off from his people"] . . .
>
> And therefore, if it be good reasoning from circumcision to Baptism, (which if it be not, let the Pedobaptists bid adieu to their cause of Infant Baptism, which is built and bottomed thereupon), then it follows undeniably by way of Analogie, that as uncircumcision by the command of God, did deprive persons of communion with the people of God in Church-fellowship, then, so non-Baptism does debar persons of Church-communion now.[180]

Allen employed an interesting argument for the necessity of strict Baptist communion:

> Baptism must needs precede the enjoyment of Church priviledge, in Church fellowship, in the Apostles dayes, because it was then, as it ought still to be, a means of planting men into Christ, or into the body of Christ the Church. Hence they were said to be *Baptized into Christ, Galathians 3. vers. 27. and to be baptized into his death, Romans 6. v. 3. and to be planted together into the likeness of his death, upon that accompt, ver. 5. of the same chapter.* And what does a planting and a planting together import, but the first puting together of Christians, in order to their growing together in Christ? and yet all this is done by Baptism. And may you not therefore, as well suppose trees to grow together, before they are planted together, as to suppose Christians to grow together before they are planted together, and yet planted together they are by Baptism: not into this or that particular Church, but into that one Church of Christ, which is distributed into severall parts and particular Societies.[181]

---

179. Allen, *Answer to Mr. J. G.*, 13–14.
180. Allen, *Answer to Mr. J. G.*, 11–12.
181. Allen, *Answer to Mr. J. G.*, 14.

The church is an orchard, and trees are planted in that orchard by baptism. A tree may be a tree without baptism, but it cannot be a part of the orchard. As with other Baptists surveyed in this monograph, Allen suggested that men are neither implanted into the universal/invisible church (lest baptism become necessary to salvation) nor into the particular/visible church (lest baptism be repeated every time one joins a new church).[182] Rather, men are implanted by baptism into the non-particular/visible church, which necessarily implies that the only true visible churches are Baptist churches. Goodwin understood this implication, and Allen did not deny it. Churches are constituted by baptism; belief must precede baptism; therefore, a gathering of unbaptized men, notwithstanding their otherwise godly lives, is not a true, visible church.[183] Allen wrote, "To this I say, that, what ever else a company of true Believers have done, yet if they have not done that which is necessary upon Scripture account to render themselves a true Church according to the Gospel order, then it is not unreasonable for a Christian to deny them to be such a Church."[184] This does not call into question their profession of faith; indeed, Allen asserted, "it is because we judge the Querist and others true Believers, that we do perswade them to be baptised."[185] The foundation of Allen's argumentation was the preeminent Baptist concern for ecclesiological purity:

> But if such an action be not only void of particular precept or example, yea and of generall precept too, but is also contrary to, and a transgression of a generall rule and precept, and a swerving from particular example stamp with Divine approbation; then I hope it is not lawfull, but unlawfull, which yet cleerly is the case of Baptized persons holding communion with unbaptized, in as much as it crosses that holy order of the Gospell, commission of Christ, and constant practice of primitive beleevers, Recorded in Scripture for

---

182. Allen denied that baptism justifies: "but what then, will it follow, that because these externall rites, baptism and the like, do not avail unto mens Justification when they are observed, that therefore they are not necessary unto Church-communion?" (Allen, *Answer to Mr. J. G.*, 19).

183. "It hath already been proved (as I conceive) in the answer to the first query, by some *text or passage of Scripture, either directly, or by some tolerable consequence*, or rather both directly, and also by clear and pregnant consequence, that Christian Churches were in the Apostles daies constituted, if not by baptism, yet not without baptism, and consequently that none were admitted into Church-fellowship but such as were baptized" (Allen, *An Answer to Mr. J. G.*, 22).

184. Allen, *Answer to Mr. J. G.*, 51.

185. Allen, *Answer to Mr. J. G.*, 53.

> our learning, which is to be observed and kept inviolably by all those servants of Christ, who are not willing to exchange Christs owne Order and Method, for that which is but of Man; and who are not willing to give way to Antichristian obtrusions, to justle out ways sanctified by the Lord Jesus for the feet of his Saints.[186]

Goodwin immediately responded to Allen with *Water-Dipping No Firm Footing for Church-Communion* (1653). The first half of this treatise is comprised of twenty-three considerations,

> Proving it not simply lawful, but necessary also in point of Duty, for persons Baptized after the new mode of Dipping, to continue in Communion with those Churches, or imbodied Societies of Saints, of which they were Members before the said Dipping or Baptizing; and that to betray their Trust, or Faith given unto Jesus Christ to serve him in the relation and capacity, whether of Officers, or other Members in these Churches respectively, by deserting these Churches, is a sin highly provoking in the sight of God.[187]

Once again, Goodwin offered many of the same arguments against strict Baptist communion that Bunyan would make in the 1670s. External rites and ceremonies may be set aside if they undermine the greater command to love and unity: "For, as our Saviour of the *Sabbath*, so say I of Baptism: Baptism was made for man, not man for Baptism."[188] Those who are truly saints by calling are baptized with the greater baptism of the Spirit, whether or not they are baptized in water.[189] Those whom God has accepted through faith in his Son must not be rejected for want of water.[190] Baptism neither constitutes a true church, nor gives the right of membership into the church.[191] Additionally, Goodwin offered a number of arguments Bunyan never made. For instance, Goodwin argued from the authority of the church over the individual: "No Authority can discharge, or disoblige, but that which is either greater then, or at least, equal unto that which bindeth. . . . I fear the sin of Church-breaking, yea and Church-deserting

---

186. Allen, *Answer to Mr. J. G.*, 41 (see also 42, 49).
187. Goodwin, *Water-Dipping No Firm Footing*, 5.
188. Goodwin, *Water-Dipping No Firm Footing*, 7.
189. Goodwin, *Water-Dipping No Firm Footing*, 8–9.
190. "Or can either a thing, or person, be made, or called common, in a more disgraceful, or reproachful way, then when men shall separate from them as unclean, or defective in Holiness?" (Goodwin, *Water-Dipping No Firm Footing*, 9 [see also 10–11]).
191. Goodwin, *Water-Dipping No Firm Footing*, 23–24, 43–49.

without the leave and consent of the Church deserted, will not be understood or duly considered by men, until the punishment of it come to be suffered, and then it will be too late."[192] Goodwin's underlying concern, and the foundation of his argument, was that strict Baptist communion destroys evangelical unity. It amounts to schism, a rending of the body of Christ. "In consideration whereof some of the ancient Fathers judged a schismatical rending and dividing of the Church, to proceed only from a diabolical spirit, and to be a sin of very near affinity with that which is unpardonable."[193] Withdrawing from visible saints over a disagreement regarding the subject and mode of baptism is tantamount to excommunication of those saints. Goodwin complained,

> The main, if not the only, ground and reason why our new-baptizing and baptized Brethren, reject the Baptism, so esteemed and practiced among us, is, because they suppose it to be a meer nullity, and to have nothing in it of the Baptism appointed by *Christ*. Upon this their supposition they proceed with the utmost severity against us, they excommunicate us, and deliver us up to *Satan*, that we may learn rightly to baptize.[194]

In the last half of the treatise, Goodwin responded to Allen's own responses to Goodwin's original *XL. Queries*, and provided a brief "Anatomy of Ana-Baptism," in which he organized the arguments for credobaptism into three categories: (1) those arguments which are "True, but not pertinent"; (2) those arguments which are "Fals, and therefore not pertinent"; and (3) those arguments which are "Conjecturall onely, and therefore very little pertinent."[195]

This second work of Goodwin's provoked two responses. The first was Allen's *Some Baptismal Abuses Briefly Discovered* (1653). Allen's work is divided into three sections. The first is an attempt to "disprove the Lawfulness of Infant Baptism." The second is an attempt to "prove it necessary

---

192. Goodwin, *Water-Dipping No Firm Footing*, 12–13. Several of Goodwin's "Considerations" are arguments rooted in the efficacy (as opposed to the nullity) of paedobaptism. See Goodwin, *Water-Dipping No Firm Footing*, 11–12, 14, 24–27, 36–43. Obviously, Bunyan never argued in like manner.

193. Goodwin, *Water-Dipping No Firm Footing*, 14–15 (see also 32–33).

194. Goodwin, *Water-Dipping No Firm Footing*, 24. "Now then I cannot but greatly wonder, that our Brethren should esteem it a matter of such high impiety in us, and deserving no less censure or punishment, then excommunication it self" (21).

195. For Goodwin's rejoinders to Allen's response, see Goodwin, *Water-Dipping No Firm Footing*, 52–86. For "Anatomy of Ana-Baptism," see Goodwin, *Water-Dipping No Firm Footing*, 87–90.

for persons to be Baptized after they believe, their Infant Baptism, or any pre-profession of the Gospel notwithstanding." The third is a "Discovering [of] the disorder and irregularity that is in mixt Communion of persons baptized, with such as are unbaptized, in Church fellowship."[196] In this third section, Allen stated that although his heart would "rejoycingly, without the least demur," continue in church communion with those unbaptized saints with whom he once had fellowship, "my reason and judgment carry it against my affection."[197] Allen then offered six reasons why his conscience was bound to strict Baptist communion:

1. Baptism is a foundational doctrine of a rightly-constituted church. Those who would "erect and constitute a Church unto Christ, [must] do what ever they do there in as much as in them lies, according to the Original Pattern given by God, and that in building they leave out no part of his foundation."[198]

2. The practice of the primitive, apostolic church was to "first be baptized, and then associate themselves in Church Bodies."[199]

3. Only those who are "regularly visible members of the universal *Church*" are in a "due and regular capacity of holding *Church-Communion* with a particular *Church*," and "Baptism is the Ordinance of visible initiation or admission into the universal *Church of Christ*."[200]

---

196. The previous quotations are from the title page of Allen, *Some Baptismal Abuses Briefly Discovered*. The prologue to the treatise also includes a dedicatory epistle to "His much Honoured and Dearly Beloved, Mr JOHN GOODWIN, and the Brethren of His Society," and a "Premonition to the Reader, touching the evil and dangerous effects of Infant Baptism." For Allen's arguments against paedobaptism, see *Some Baptismal Abuses*, 1–49. For Allen's arguments for the necessity of credobaptism, see *Some Baptismal Abuses*, 50–98.

197. Allen, *Some Baptismal Abuses*, 98–99.

198. Allen, *Some Baptismal Abuses*, 99–100.

199. Allen, *Some Baptismal Abuses*, 101.

200. Allen, *Some Baptismal Abuses*, 103. Allen insisted this was a "thing which generally hath been acknowledged, and is by Pedobaptists themselves constantly asserted" (103). Allen proceeded to write, "If then none are to be esteemed as visible members of the universal *Church*, but only such as are baptized, then none but such as are baptized may be admitted as members of a particular *Church*. For it is altogether irregular, indeed absurd, to admit any into particular *Church-Fellowship*, who are not first visible members of the Universal; because particular *Churches*, and so particular Church-members, receive their right of being such, of and from the Universal Church, and from that precedent standing they had there as branches and members of it" (104–5).

4. "This being Gods method, order, and way of bringing men into the enjoyment of *Church-communion*, and *Church* priviledges, *viz.* through the door of Baptism (as hath been already observed) this very method, and order of his, ought to be very sacred unto us, and inviolably observed by us."[201]

5. None were admitted to the Passover without first being circumcised; therefore, none ought to be admitted to the Lord's Supper without first being baptized.[202]

6. The Scriptures being so clear and full of light in this matter, to reject its counsel is to choose "a way that is more dubious and dark."[203]

Allen concluded by responding to three common objections to strict Baptist communion, including the oft-cited argument from Romans 14–15 that the church must welcome the weak in faith. Allen responded that since baptism is God's appointed means of receiving men into church communion (Allen calls baptism the "Bridge" and "Gate" into the church), baptism must not be included in those matters of indifference to which Romans 14–15 pertains.[204] Underneath Allen's arguments lie two dominant convictions. First, Allen was adamant that ecclesiological purity is of greater concern than evangelical unity. The church is God's house, and its order must accord with God's rule. Second, Allen insisted that baptism is the visible means of ingrafting a believer into the universal church, and is therefore the door, bridge, and gate into the particular church.

> Baptism then being so much of the general nature of the *Churches* visible being, as that no man can according to Scripture-rule, esteem any one duly and regularly a member thereof without it; those particular *Churches*, or *Church-members* then, that partake

---

201. Allen, *Some Baptismal Abuses*, 105–6.

202. Allen, *Some Baptismal Abuses*, 109. Allen admitted that this argument depended upon "Baptism bear[ing] the like relation to the Supper of the Lord, as circumcision did to Passover," yet he insisted that this "is a thing generally acknowledged by all" (109).

203. Allen, *Some Baptismal Abuses*, 109.

204. Allen, *Some Baptismal Abuses*, 116–18. The other two objections Allen answered were: (1) that Gal 3:27 and Rom 6:3 imply that not all members of the churches of Galatia or Rome were baptized; and (2) Rom 1:7 and Col 1:2 state that those who repent, believe, and are sanctified are fit members of the church, and as there are persons unbaptized (as the Baptists regard them) who have repented, believed, and been sanctified, baptism must not be a prerequisite to church fellowship. Allen handled these objections in ways typical of the other seventeenth-century Baptists surveyed in this monograph.

> not hereof, cannot in due form of Evangelical Law, nor according to the principles of reason, be esteemed particular *Churches*, or *Church-members* of the universal, but either of some other kind, or at the best of an un-evangelical form and constitution.[205]

Though Allen stopped short of an explicit denial that paedobaptist churches are true churches or that paedobaptist believers are true saints, the inescapable conclusion is that Allen regarded both as irregular and unevangelical.

The second response to Goodwin's *Water-Dipping No Firm Footing for Church-Communion* was Thomas Lambe's *Truth Prevailing Against the Fiercest Opposition* (1653). Lambe's work is a point-for-point rebuttal of Goodwin's twenty-three considerations. Lambe made several arguments that were repeatedly raised by strict-communion Baptists. For example, Lambe rejected Goodwin's assertion that since men become sons of God by faith and not by baptism, that the same should be accepted into church communion by faith and not by baptism. Lambe wrote, "That men become the Sons of God by faith in Christ Jesus, is plain in the Scriptures, as you say, but that any ones faith would have pass'd with the Churches in the primitive times for the faith of Gods elect, that should have been found sticking at obedience to any of the commands of Christ, appeareth not in Scripture, but much to the contrary."[206] In other words, only an obedient faith ought to be recognized by the church as authentic. Even if Lambe were willing to grant that the faith of the paedobaptist is sincere, yet he denied that they should on that account be granted communion in the church: "The reason [is] this, because Jesus Christ himself, who is the God of Order, hath appointed the Communion of the Disciples to be orderly, so that though persons be Disciples by faith, and so have a remote right to all priviledges of Church Communion, yet have not an immediate right thereto, till they desire it in that way which Christ hath appointed."[207] Lambe then marshalled six arguments proving that mixed communion is disorderly:

1. "If Baptism was the next thing immediately to be done by the order of Christ after being discipled, then to sit down with the Church in full communion before it, is a disorderly practise."[208]

---

205. Allen, *Some Baptismal Abuses*, 105.
206. Lambe, *Truth Prevailing*, 8.
207. Lambe, *Truth Prevailing*, 11.
208. Lambe, *Truth Prevailing*, 12.

2. "If the Scripture maketh Baptisme the gate or entrance into the visible Church or Body of Christ. Then is it a most disorderly practise for persons to sit down in Church-society without it."[209]

3. "That practise which bringeth down the esteem of Baptisme, and maketh it slighted, is against the Order of Christ. But for Disciples that are baptised, to walk together in a Church body with unbaptized, bringeth down the esteem of Baptisme, and maketh it sleighted."[210]

4. "That practise which consulteth the loss and spiritual damage of the Disciples, can never be an orderly practise. But for baptised Disciples to admit of unbaptized into full communion, is to consult their losse, and spiritual damage."[211]

5. "But for persons that are baptised, to sit down in Church bodies with unbaptized, in all reason will breed jarrs." Lambe earlier defined "jarrs" as "discentions and discords in the Church."[212]

6. "That practise which in the worship of God is not onely beside the custome of the first Churches, which was settled by the Apostles, but directly contrary, can never be an orderly practise."[213]

Lambe's arguments are grounded in the demand that the church be constructed according to the rule, or pattern, of Christ "with ALL POSSIBLE EXACTNESSE."[214] Another familiar argument is Lambe's insistence that the open-communion argument from Romans 14–15 is null and void, because those to whom Paul wrote were already baptized church members.[215] Less familiar is Lambe's argument that Baptist separation is not schism, because schism is defined as separation from a rightly-ordered church, of which paedobaptist churches are not; and Lambe's assertion that open communion "tendeth to the destruction of all Religion" by severing "that which is external, standing in the exercise of externall Ordinances"

---

209. Lambe, *Truth Prevailing*, 17. Lambe argued that "Baptisme is the Sacrament of entrance into the visible Church of Christ, all the Professors of Christian Religion hath met in it as one man" (17).

210. Lambe, *Truth Prevailing*, 26.

211. Lambe, *Truth Prevailing*, 27.

212. Lambe, *Truth Prevailing*, 27.

213. Lambe, *Truth Prevailing*, 29.

214. Lambe, *Truth Prevailing*, 30. For similar statements regarding precise obedience to the "order" or "rule" established by Christ, see *Truth Prevailing*, 47–48, 49–51, 71.

215. Lambe, *Truth Prevailing*, 32–34.

from "that which is internal, standing in a holy frame of heart and life."[216] Finally, Lambe exposited eight Scriptures in support of strict Baptist communion (Acts 2:41; Matt 28:19; 1 Cor 12:13; Acts 8:27; Gal 4:1–3; 1 Cor 11:24–26; Gal 5:6; Gal 3:27).[217]

From Lambe's contribution to the debate, three notes are of preeminent importance. First, Lambe insisted that while a paedobaptist may have true faith, the Church has no authority to formally recognize it as such apart from obedience to the ordinance of baptism. Second, though a society of paedobaptists may be a congregation of true believers, as it is not a rightly ordered church it cannot be a true church. And finally, it is apparent that Lambe was driven by a concern for ecclesiological purity that superseded his concern for evangelical unity. Lambe rejected paedobaptism, in part, because, "Infant-Baptisme disagreeth to the spiritual state of the Church under the new Testament, because Baptisme being the initiating Ordinance into the Church, it letteth in a sort of members which the new Testament knoweth not, namely, such as cannot worship God in Spirit, whereas the Scripture saith, *John* 4 23."[218] Lambe defended his alleged "Church-breaking" as demanded by the truth of Scripture: "it became me, as a friend to Truth, and for the honour of Jesus Christ, not onely to obey Christ by submitting to the Ordinance myself, but to strive the restoring it to its primitive puritity."[219] While his heart longed for evangelical unity, his preeminent commitment was to ecclesiological purity as defined by the Word of God. Describing his reluctance to publish his work, Lambe wrote,

> Had not the truth been dearer to me than any man, I had rather chose to loose my right hand, then set it to a book that frowneth on him, whose credit alwayes was, and still, is, right dear and pretious in my sight, so unhappy a thing it is for good men to be yoked with error in the things of Christ, that it maketh the most intimate friends, by opposition, look like bitter adversaries for the truth sake.[220]

---

216. Lambe, *Truth Prevailing*, 43–45, 72.

217. Lambe, *Truth Prevailing*, 98–125.

218. Lambe, *Truth Prevailing*, sixth page (unnumbered) of the dedicatory epistle to Goodwin's church.

219. Lambe, *Truth Prevailing*, ninth page (unnumbered) of the dedicatory epistle to Goodwin's church.

220. Lambe, *Truth Prevailing*, second page (unnumbered) of the dedicatory epistle to John Goodwin.

Goodwin responded to Allen with *Cata-Baptism* (1655), and John Price, a member of Goodwin's congregation, responded to Lambe with *The Anabaptists Meribah* (1656). The former is a lengthy defense of paedobaptism, and bears little direct relevance to the issue of church communion. The sole exception is where Goodwin refuted Allen's assertion that baptism is what makes one a visible saint. How can baptism make one a visible saint, if, as the Baptists insist, only saints ought to be baptized? Surely their visibility comes before baptism, and is ascertained on better grounds (Goodwin suggests love—John 13:35).[221] Bunyan made precisely the same argument.[222]

Price's response to Lambe is likewise primarily a defense of paedobaptism, and therefore only indirectly relevant to the present discussion. There are, however, two passages worth noting. First, Price refuted Lambe's assertion that baptism is the initiating ordinance into the church. Price responded, "I suppose you mean, not *the Church* generall, but *de jure*, it is the initiating Ordinance into particular *Churches*. If that be your meaning, this then is such a conclusion, as you can hardly make good, no not by any *ifs, may-bee's, and why-nots*, gatherable from any place, or places in the Holy Scriptures; that is to say, that baptism did make any person *ipso facto*, a member of any particular Church."[223] The interesting note is that Price assumed Lambe could not have meant that one was baptized into the universal church; therefore, he must have meant that one was baptized into particular churches. Like Bunyan, Price was operating with a binary conception of the church, while his opponents conceived of a *tertium quid*, a non-particular/visible church. This was a consistent point of departure between open and strict communionists in the seventeenth century. A second note of interest is Price's response to Lambe's accusation that Goodwin's open-communion position meant that anyone could join the church: "Upon this ground godly *Presbyterians, Episcopal, Popish, nay heathenish persons may be received.*"[224] Price's response would likewise find an echo in Bunyan two decades later:

---

221. John Goodwin, *Cata-Baptism*, 272–77.

222. "A visible Saint he is, but not made so by Baptism; for he must be a visible Saint before, else he ought not to be baptized" (Bunyan, *Confession of My Faith*, 4:164); "His visibility is already; he is already a visible Member of the Body of Christ, and after that baptized. His Baptism then neither makes him a Member, nor a Visible Member, of the Body of Jesus Christ" (Bunyan, *Peaceable Principles and True*, 4:274).

223. Price, *Anabaptists Meribah*, 49.

224. Quoted in Price, *Anabaptists Meribah*, 63.

I reply: If a Presbyterian, a prelaticall man, a Papist, nay a heathen can give a visible testimony of *his communion and fellowship with God*, and that *God hath accepted him*, though he should scruple the manner of baptism, and severall circumstances therein, and should make his application unto us, giving sufficient testimony *that God hath accepted* him, and he promising to walk as a visible believer, in all the good wayes of God, (what ever your principle is) I am not ashamed to tell you that my opinion is, that he should be *received* into Church-fellowship with us, and make no scruple of entertaining those that have received the Holy Ghost, as well as we.[225]

The General Baptist communion controversy of 1653–1655 was famous in its time. In his postscript response to Bunyan's *Differences in Judgment*, Henry Danvers cited Allen's *Some Baptismal Abuses Briefly Discovered* and Lambe's *Truth Prevailing Against the Fiercest Opposition*, which Danvers said "are done with the *Judgment, Strength of Argument*, and *Authority of Scripture*, that notwithstanding they have both of them personally declined those Truths, so *zealously* and *understandingly* pleaded for by them."[226] But it failed to have the lasting influence as did the communion controversy in which Bunyan was engaged in the 1670s, and that for two reasons. First, unlike the controversy of the 1670s, the controversy of the 1650s was not among credobaptists only, but between credobaptists and paedobaptists, and was therefore frequently sidetracked by debate over the proper subjects of baptism. As debate over the relationship of baptism to church communion is, by the nature of the case, more relevant to credobaptists than to paedobaptists, the controversy of the 1670s likewise proved more relevant.[227] It is noteworthy, however, that Bunyan echoed many of Goodwin's arguments; the same arguments that worked for Goodwin's Independent ecclesiology worked for Bunyan's. Second, as Danvers noted, despite their thoughtful arguments and forceful rhetoric, both Lambe and Allen eventually conformed to the Church of England. This undercut their credibility among Nonconformists of every stripe, as Bunyan's words testify: "I shall not bestow Paper and Ink upon *Him* [John Denne], nor yet upon

225. Price, *Anabaptists Meribah*, 63. To the objection that open communion means that "you may have communion with the members of Antichrist," Bunyan replied, "If there be a visible Saint yet remaining in that Church; let him come to us, and we will have communion with him" (Bunyan, *Confession of My Faith*, 4:184).

226. Danvers, *Treatise of Baptism* p.s. 53.

227. All paedobaptists regard credobaptists as baptized, but few credobaptists regard paedobaptists as baptized. Thus, debates over the terms of communion are more relevant in credobaptist circles than in paedobaptist circles.

Mr. *Lamb*; the one already, *having given his profession the lye*, and the other perhaps they that know his Life, will see little of Conscience in the whole of his Religion, and conclude him not worth taking notice of."[228]

While General Baptists disavowed Lambe and Allen after their departure from the Baptist faith, and would therefore be loath to permit them to speak for the General Baptist position, the same could not be said of Thomas Grantham, widely considered the preeminent General Baptist theologian of the seventeenth century.[229] Grantham's massive six-hundred-page *Christianismus Primitivus* "was the first General Baptist systematic theology."[230] Book 2 of *Christianismus Primitivus* addresses the topic of ecclesiology. Grantham stated his underlying ecclesiological principle at the beginning:

> As the Internal Part of Christian Religion is carefully to be preserved, even so a necessity lieth upon the Servants of God to preserve and maintain (as Instruments in his hand) the External Part of the Christian Religion also, lest at any time they be deceived by specious pretense to the Power, the better to subvert the form of Godliness, or the form of Doctrine which was delivered to the Primitive Churches.[231]

The utmost ecclesiological concern of the servants of God must be to preserve the primitive purity of the worship of God. To the standard Protestant definition of the true church as existing "*Where the Word of God is sincerely taught, and the Sacraments rightly administered,*" Grantham added that "the Church of Christ [is] now obliged by Gospel rules, to worship God according to his will, declared in the Holy Scriptures, which are strictly to be observed."[232] In other words, the sacraments are rightly administered only where they are administered in exact accordance with God's ordinance. And God ordained that believers only should be admitted

---

228. Bunyan, *Peaceable Principles and True*, 4:288.

229. Garrett calls Grantham "the leading General Baptist theologian during the last half of the seventeenth century" (Garrett, *Baptist Theology*, 42). Clint Bass calls Grantham "the most prolific writer of the General Baptists in the latter seventeenth century" (Bass, *Thomas Grantham*, 1). Bass cites statements to the same effect from Leon McBeth, A. C. Underwood, and William Brackney.

230. Bass, *Thomas Grantham*, 1.

231. Grantham, *Christianismus Primitivus* 2.2.1. The doctrine of the church is addressed in "The Second Part of the Second Treatise," where the pagination begins anew at page 1. References will thus be cited 2.2.1 (book, part, page).

232. Grantham, *Christianismus Primitivus* 2.2.2–3.

to his sacraments, a point which Grantham argued at length.²³³ Therefore, only a Baptist church can be a true visible church, for baptism is essential to a rightly-constituted church.²³⁴ And only the baptized can be members of a true visible church: "And we do teach, as a most Infallible Doctrine, *That without profession of Faith, manifestation of Repentance, and being baptized with Water in the Name of Jesus Christ, &c. no Person can be orderly admitted into the Church or Kingdom of God on Earth*."²³⁵ Though Grantham was eager to maintain unity with non-Baptist believers, he could not grant them assurance of their eternal state: "How they shall be acquitted from, or punished for this Error of Opinion at the last, the Judg of all only knoweth. Mean while we must stand to sound Principles, and look for Salvation in the way wherein God holds it forth to Men. Mark 16. 16. *He that Believeth, and is Baptized, shall be saved*."²³⁶ Likewise, in Grantham's *St. Paul's Catechism*, Grantham argued clearly and succinctly that no man may be a member and enjoy the privileges of a church without baptism, and that no true church may be constituted without baptism. Again, the principle driving Grantham to this conclusion is the "Rule of God's Word."²³⁷

---

233. Grantham, *Christianismus Primitivus* 2.2.6-15.

234. Grantham argued that credobaptism is essential to the constitution of a true church in Grantham, *Christianismus Primitivus* 2.2.17-23. Bass writes, "Grantham considered the church to be divided into two categories: the visible and the invisible church. Members of the visible church could be identified by their likeness to the primitive church. Only those who followed the teachings of the Apostles could rightfully be called the visible, or true, church. Grantham made baptism the determining factor of church constitution. Baptism itself was the covenant through which believers entered the visible church. As it was restricted to believers only, membership in the visible church was limited to the spiritually regenerate. According to Grantham, Baptists made up the visible church, while the invisible church consisted of those who possessed saving faith" (Bass, *Thomas Grantham*, 42). It is noteworthy that Bass writes, "Grantham's belief that Baptists were the visible church and that the invisible church consisted of a mixture of Baptists and pedobaptists appears to have been held by the majority of Baptists in the seventeenth century" (45). This assertion is validated by the evidence presented in this chapter.

235. Grantham, *Christianismus Primitivus* 4.2.41.

236. Grantham, *Christianismus Primitivus* 3.5.31. Bass writes that "Grantham's conclusion on this matter would have brought little comfort to the non-Baptists" (Bass, *Thomas Grantham*, 43).

237. "No true church can be formed by Man's device. There must be the Rule of God's Word to direct us, or nothing is done well in the forming a Church. Christ hath given express Order to form his Church by Repentance, Faith, and Baptism, as we have shewed. If he has also given order to form Churches without Baptism, then he must needs be the Author of Confusion, which he is not" (Grantham, *St. Paul's Catechism*, 300).

The foregoing survey of seventeenth-century General Baptist confessions, the communion controversy of the 1650s, and the ecclesiological position of their preeminent theologian demonstrate not only that strict communion was a seventeenth-century General Baptist distinctive, but that they arrived at this position because they were driven by the same foundational impulse that drove their Particular Baptist brethren, namely, ecclesiological purity—a church properly ordered according to the rule of Scripture.

The Particular Baptists of the Seventeenth Century

It remains to demonstrate that Particular Baptists outside of 1640s London were just as committed to the principle of strict communion. The views of Thomas Paul (*Some Serious Reflections on that Part of Mr. Bunion's Confession of Faith* [1673]), William Kiffin (*A Sober Discourse of Right to Church Communion* [1681]), and Hanserd Knollys (*The World That Now Is* [1681]), all of whom were influential Particular Baptists during the latter half of the seventeenth century, have already been examined. One influential voice that has not yet been heard is that of Benjamin Keach. Keach's influence upon late-century Particular Baptists can hardly be overstated. Baptist historian Michael A. G. Haykin reports, "In a recently published history of religion in Britain Michael Mullett has identified Benjamin Keach as the leading Baptist theologian of his era, similar in importance for his denomination as Richard Baxter was for the English Presbyterians, John Owen for the Congregationalists and Robert Barclay (1648–1690) for the Quakers."[238] Keach wrote extensively on the doctrine of the church, including what Haykin called "the first Calvinistic Baptist treatise specifically devoted to ecclesiastical polity," *The Glory of a True Church, and Its Discipline Display'd* (1697).[239] In this work, Keach defined a "True and Orderly Gospel-Church":

> A Church of Christ, according to the Gospel-Institution, is a Congregation of Godly Christians who as a Stated-Assembly (being first baptized upon the Profession of Faith) do by mutual agreement and consent give themselves up to the Lord, and one another, according to the Will of God; and do ordinarily meet together in one Place, for the Publick Service and Worship of

---

238. Haykin, *Kiffin, Knollys and Keach*, 84.

239. Haykin, *Kiffin, Knollys and Keach*, 83; Keach, *Glory of a True Church*. Additionally, Keach penned eight treatises defending believer's baptism (Garrett, *Baptist Theology*, 84). The most famous of these treatises is Keach, *Gold Refin'd*.

God; among whom the Word of God and Sacraments are duly administered, according to Christ's institution.[240]

Thus, a true church is a Baptist church.[241] Yet, though baptism is a prerequisite to membership, it is not the form of the church. The form of the church is the solemn and mutual covenant, "to walk in the Fellowship of that particular Congregation, and submit themselves to the Care and Discipline thereof, and to walk faithfully with God in all his Holy Ordinances, and there to be fed and have Communion, and worship God there, when the Church meets (if possible) and give themselves up to the watch and charge of the Pastor and Ministry thereof."[242] Keach's commitment to closed communion went beyond even his contemporaries Kiffin and Knollys, for he required not only believer's baptism but the laying on of hands as well.[243]

Not only did every influential Particular Baptist pastor-theologian of the seventeenth century ascribe to strict Baptist communion (assuming, as this monograph suggests, that Bunyan and Jessey ought not to be considered seventeenth-century Baptists), but strict communion is codified in every Particular Baptist confession of the seventeenth century, with one very significant exception. The 1644 London Baptist Confession and its 1646 revision have already been examined. In 1655, the Midland

---

240. Keach, *Glory of a True Church*, 5–6.

241. This is not to suggest that Keach (or a number of other Baptist pastor-theologians surveyed in this chapter) was always consistent in following this definition to its logical implication. Few Baptists wished to deny that a paedobaptist church was a true church. In his *Exposition of the Parables Series Two*, Keach discussed the six fundamentals set forth in Heb 6:1–2. Keach wrote, "These six principles therefore, as here laid down, are fundamentals of a gospel church; . . . True, a church may be materially a true church, and formally true, too, (i.e., they may give themselves up to the Lord, and to one another, as a congregation, to walk together in the fellowship of the gospel) who may not be baptized, nor own laying on of hands; but then they must be considered, not a complete gospel church, but in some things defective, in respect to its constitution and regular gospel form, or as wanting a pillar, &c. A house may be a real house, though it may want a principal post it stands on; it may be pretty firm, and may stand though one be missing, however, it is not so safe, to want one principle of the doctrine of Christ" (Keach, *Exposition of the Parables Series Two*, 32, quoted in J. Renihan, *Edification and Beauty*, 45).

242. Keach, *Glory of a True Church*, 7. The next paragraph begins, "A Church thus constituted," implying that the church is constituted by the mutual covenant of baptized believers (7).

243. "In respect to close communion Keach agreed with but went beyond Kiffin by insisting that not only believer's baptism by immersion but also laying on of hands be prerequisite to receiving the Lord's Supper" (Garrett, *Baptist Theology*, 85). See Copeland, *Benjamin Keach*, 56–60.

Association of Particular Baptists published a brief, sixteen-article confession. Though strict communion is not explicitly demanded, it is affirmed by necessary implication. Article 13 states that only believers should be baptized. Article 14 asserts that true baptism is by immersion only. Article 15 then states, "That persons so baptized ought, by free consent, to walk together, as God shall give opportunity in distinct churches, or assemblies of Zion, continuing in the Apostles' doctrine and fellowship, breaking of bread and prayers, as fellow-men caring for one another, according to the will of God. All these ordinances are enjoined in His Church, to be observed till His Second Coming, which we all ought diligently to wait for."[244] "Distinct" (i.e., particular/visible) churches are comprised solely of "persons so baptized" (i.e., credobaptism by immersion).

The following year (1656), the Somerset Association likewise adopted a confession of faith. Lumpkin maintains that the confession is largely the work of Thomas Collier.[245] Article 24 states:

> That it is the duty of every man and woman, that have repented from dead works, and have faith towards God, to be baptized [Acts 2:38; 8:12, 37, 38], that is dipped or buried under the water [Rom 6:3, 4; Col 2:12]. in the name of our Lord Jesus [Acts 8:16]. Or in the name of the Father, Son and holy Spirit [Matt 28:19]; therein to signify and represent a washing away of sin [Acts 22:16], and their death burial and resurrection with Christ [Rom 6:5; Col 2:12]. and being thus planted in the visible church or body of Christ [1 Cor 12:3]. Who are a company of men and women separated out of the world by the preaching of the gospel [Acts 2:41; 2 Cor 6:17], do walk together in communion, in all the commandements, of Jesus [Acts 2:42]. wherein God is glorified, and their souls comforted [2 Thes 1:11, 12; 2 Cor 1:4].[246]

---

244. *Sixteen Articles of Faith and Order* [*Midland Confession*] art. 15.

245. "It was evidently the work of Collier" (Lumpkin, *Baptist Confessions of Faith*, 200). "The Confession bears the mark of careful preparation, and the impress of Collier can be seen at various points" (201). Lumpkin states that the Somerset Confession is "notable on two accounts: first, it represents the earliest important effort at bringing Particular and General Baptists into agreement and union; and second, it clearly enunciates three distinctively Baptist principles,—the duty of a church to receive only those who give evidence of having been regenerated, the right of a church to call out and ordain its own ministers, and the obligation of the church to send representatives to preach the gospel to the world" (202). On the first of these notes (the alleged blending of Particular and General Baptist doctrines), Garrett advises caution, stating that such an assertion "must be balanced by the absence of major Arminian doctrines" (Garrett, *Baptist Theology*, 61).

246. *Confession of Faith of Several Churches of Christ* [*Somerset Confession*] (1656) art. 24. In the original text, the verses are written out in full.

Strict Communion and Seventeenth-Century Baptist Identity

Thus, the Somerset Confession explicitly enjoins strict communion: believers are "planted in the visible church or body of Christ" by credobaptism. The necessary implication of such a statement is that only Baptist churches are true visible churches, for only the baptized are implanted into such a church.

In 1677, a general meeting of Particular Baptists was held in London for the purpose of producing a new confession of faith. Four considerations prompted the calling of the assembly and the ratification of the new confession. First, copies of the 1644 London Baptist Confession (or its 1646 revision) had grown scarce.[247] Second, the Baptist faith had experienced much growth over the intervening decades, calling for a confession ratified by more than seven churches.[248] Third, there was a need for greater clarity and order of doctrines than was to be found in the 1644 Confession.[249] Fourth, seventeen years of persecution had produced a desire among Particular Baptists to draw near to the Presbyterians and Congregationalists in order to present a united front among Calvinistic Nonconformists.[250] The general assembly determined the best way to ac-

---

247. "And forasmuch, as that *Confession* [the 1644 London Baptist Confession] is not now commonly to be had" (*Confession of Faith* [1677], 2).

248. "And also that many others have since embraced the same truth which is owned therein; it was judged necessary by us to joyn together in giving a testimony to the world; of our firm adhering to those wholesome Principles, by the publication of this which is now in your hand" (*Confession of Faith* [1677], 2).

249. "And therefore we did conclude it necessary to express ourselves the more fully, and distinctly; and also to fix on such a method as might be most comprehensive of those things which we designed to explain our sense, and belief of" (*Confession of Faith* [1677], 3).

250. "We have no itch to clogge Religion with new words, but to readily acquiesce in that form of sound words, which hath been, in consent with the holy Scriptures, used by others before us; hereby declaring before God, Angels, & Men, our hearty agreement with them [Presbyterians and Congregationalists], in that wholesome Protestant Doctrine, which with so clear evidence of Scriptures they have asserted [in the Westminster Confession and Savoy Declaration]" (*Confession of Faith* [1677], 4–5 [see also 109]). Lumpkin writes, "The renewal of persecution [after the withdrawal of the 1672 Declaration of Indulgence] brought dissenting groups nearer to one another and especially brought Baptists and Congregationalists nearer to Presbyterians. Defiance of the Conventicle Act by the large Presbyterian party, which had been the dominant ecclesiastical group under the Commonwealth, made enforcement of that Act all but impossible. Observing the success of the Presbyterians, other Dissenters were emboldened. Moreover, it was important that Dissenters form a united front, which might be demonstrated by a show of doctrinal agreement among themselves. The very document which would be best proof of this agreement on essential matters was at hand, the Westminster Confession"

complish these aims was to adopt a "baptized" version of the Westminster Confession of Faith (1646), as the Congregationalists had earlier revised the Westminster Confession in the Savoy Declaration (1658).[251]

According to Lumpkin, "A circular letter was sent to the Particular Baptist churches in England and Wales asking that representatives be sent to a general meeting in 1677. By the time this meeting was held, it appears that Elder William Collins of the Petty France Church in London had worked over the Westminster document, altering it as he saw fit."[252] However, Haykin claims that the 1677 London Baptist Confession was the product of both William Collins and Nehemiah Coxe, who were co-pastors of the Petty France Church.[253] Regardless, the Confession was approved by the gathered representatives and published anonymously, but "Put forth by the ELDERS and BRETHREN of many CONGREGATIONS of Christians (baptized upon Profession of their Faith) in *London* and the Country."[254] In September 1689, following the accession of William and Mary and the Act of Toleration, one hundred and seven churches sent messengers to London for a general assembly, which approved and republished the 1677 Confession.[255]

(Lumpkin, *Baptist Confessions of Faith*, 236). Haykin writes, "The furnace of common affliction only served to reinforce in the minds of many Calvinistic Baptists just how much they shared with fellow Calvinists who were either Presbyterians or Congregationalists, the latter being then known as Independents. Moreover, there was at hand a document which could concretely demonstrate the essential doctrinal unity between these three groups, namely, the *Westminster Confession of Faith*" (Haykin, *Kiffin, Knollys and Keach*, 63). Haykin lists four contextual factors that prompted the 1677 general assembly and the new confession: (1) the threat of persecution; (2) the threat of Hyper-Calvinism; (3) the threat from Quakers; (4) the "doctrinal defection" of Thomas Collier (62–69).

251. "And finding no defect, in this regard, in that fixed on by the assembly, and after them by those of the Congregational way, we did readily conclude it best to retain the same *order* in our present confession" (*Confession of Faith* [1677], 3–4). For a description of the "numerous and marked differences between this Confession and that of 1644," see Lumpkin, *Baptist Confessions of Faith*, 237, and for a list of differences between the *Second London Baptist Confession* (1689) and the *Westminster Confession*, see Lumpkin, *Baptist Confessions of Faith*, 237–38.

252. Lumpkin, *Baptist Confessions of Faith*, 236.

253. Haykin, *Kiffin, Knollys and Keach*, 49.

254. *Confession of Faith* (1677), title page.

255. Lumpkin, *Baptist Confessions of Faith*, 238. The general assembly met in response to a circular letter sent by seven London Particular Baptist pastors: William Kiffin, Hanserd Knollys, John Harris, George Barrett, Benjamin Keach, Edward Man, and Richard Adams (Lumpkin, *Baptist Confessions of Faith*, 238). A second edition of the 1677 London Baptist Confession had been reissued in 1688 by William Collins and

Among the many differences between the Second London Baptist Confession (1677/1689) and the First London Baptist Confession (1644/1646) is its apparent shift on the issue of strict Baptist communion. Article 39 in the 1646 Confession explicitly states, "Baptisme is an ordinance of the new Testament, given by Christ, to be dispensed upon persons professing faith, or that are made Disciples; who upon profession of faith, ought to be baptized, and after to partake of the Lords Supper."[256] But the 1677 Confession contains no such statement. No longer is a visible church defined as

> a company of visible Saints, called and separated from the world by the Word and Spirit of God, to the visible profession of the faith of the Gospel, being baptized into that faith, and joyned to the Lord, and to each other, by mutuall agreement in the practical enjoyment of the ordinances commanded by Christ their Head and King.[257]

The 1677 Confession omits any explicit reference to baptism in its definition of the visible church:

> The Members of these Churches are Saints by calling, visibly manifesting and evidencing (in and by their profession and walking) their obedience unto that call of Christ; and do willingly consent to walk together according to the appointment of Christ, giving up themselves, to the Lord & one to another by the will of God, in professed subjection to the Ordinances of the Gospel.[258]

On the one hand, one should not read too much into the absence of explicit strict communion language, for if one defines the proper subjects of the "Ordinances of the Gospel" as the Confession itself does, namely, as "Those who do actually profess repentance towards *God*, faith in, and obedience, to our Lord Jesus," then "subjection to the Ordinances of the Gospel" requires credobaptism, and thus, strict communion.[259] On the other hand, there is a reason explicit references to strict communion were removed. That reason

---

Benjamin Keach. Keach then condensed the Confession and reissued it again in 1697 on behalf of his church (Lumpkin, *Baptist Confessions of Faith*, 239).

256. *Confession of Faith* (1646) art. 39.

257. *Confession of Faith* (1646) art. 33.

258. *Confession of Faith* (1677) 26.6.

259. *Confession of Faith* (1677) states, "Those who do actually profess repentance towards *God*, faith in, and obedience, to our Lord Jesus, are the only proper subjects of this ordinance [baptism]" (29.2).

is found in the appendix to the 1677 Confession, the majority of which is an irenic refutation of paedobaptism.

> We are not insensible that as to the order of Gods house, and entire communion therein there are some things where we (as well as others) are not at a full accord among our selves, as for instance; the known principle, and state of the consciences of diverse of us, that have agreed in this Confession is such; that we cannot hold Church-communion, with any other then Baptized-believers, and Churches constituted of such; yet some others of us have a greater liberty and freedom in our spirits that way; and therefore we have purposely omitted the mention of things of that nature, that we might concurre, in giving this evidence of our agreement, both among our selves, and with other good Christians, in those important articles of the Christian Religion, mainly insisted on by us: and this notwithstanding we all esteem it our chief concern, both among our selves, and all others that in every place call upon the name of the Lord Jesus Christ our Lord, both theirs and ours, and love him in sincerity, to endeavour to keep the unity of the Spirit, in the bond of peace, and in order thereunto, to exercise all lowliness and meekness, with long-suffering, forbearing one another in love.
>
> And we are perswaded if the same method were introduced into frequent practise between us and our Christian friends who agree with us in all the fundamental articles of the Christian faith (though they do not so in the subject and administration of baptism) it would soon beget a better understanding, and brotherly affection between us.[260]

The general assembly of Particular Baptists gathered in London desired unity with the Calvinistic, paedobaptist Nonconformists (i.e., the Presbyterians and Congregationalists). But such an olive branch would be the highest hypocrisy did not the Baptists likewise open their arms to their closer cousins, the open-communion credobaptist churches. Therefore, they extended liberty of conscience to the latter, in hope of receiving the same from the former. It was the desire for evangelical unity, prompted by the common experience of persecution, that drove the 1677 general assembly to expand its ecclesiological fences.

The 1689 general assembly did not meet in secret under the shadow of persecution; the accession of William and Mary and the Act of Toleration brought a new era of freedom to English Baptists. The assembly passed a

---

260. *Confession of Faith* (1677), 137–39.

resolution stating, "In those things wherein one church differs from another church in their principles or practices, in point of communion, . . . we cannot, shall not impose upon any particular church therein, but leave every church to their own liberty to walk together as they have received from the Lord."[261] Gone is the stated concern for evangelical unity, replaced by a concern for ecclesiastical liberty. While the context of persecution provoked a desire to unite with other evangelicals against a common threat, the context of toleration provoked a desire to protect the autonomy of the local church and the liberty of the individual conscience. In both 1677 and 1689, contextual factors drove the omission of strict communion language from the Second London Baptist Confession.

Some historians have suggested another contributing factor to the shift away from strict Baptist communion reflected in the 1677 London Baptist Confession: the influence of John Bunyan upon the Petty France Church in London, of which William Collins and Nehemiah Coxe were copastors. Michael Haykin, who suggests that Coxe was a coauthor of the Confession along with Collins, writes,

> One of the reasons for this difference between the two confessions is that Nehemiah Coxe, who was intimately involved in drawing up the *Second London Confession*, had been called to the ministry in 1672 by the open communion, open membership church in Bedford which John Bunyan (1628–1688) pastored from 1672 till his death sixteen years later. Moreover, Petty France Church in London, which Coxe later pastored, regularly received into its membership believers from open communion Calvinistic Baptist churches.[262]

Haykin's suggestion is intriguing, but assumes that Coxe still shared Bunyan's open-communion convictions, or at least remained sympathetic to

---

261. Quoted in Haykin, *Kiffin, Knollys and Keach*, 50. Haykin cites Ivimey, *History of the English Baptists*, 1:490. Interestingly, Haykin notes that, "A. C. Underwood and Joshua Thompson, both twentieth-century Baptist historians, have understood this resolution to mean that while fellowship and recognition was to be extended to open communion churches with closed membership, it was not to be extended to those churches which, like Bunyan's, held to both open communion and open membership" (Haykin, *Kiffin, Knollys and Keach*, 50).

262. Haykin, *Kiffin, Knollys and Keach*, 49–50. For the claim that the Petty France Church received members from open communion Calvinistic Baptist churches, Haykin cites Dowley, "London Congregation," 233–34. However, in that article, the only open-communion church Dowley cites as evidence is the Broadmead Church, Bristol, which, as demonstrated above, was only moderately and temporarily open-communion.

them. But in 1674, Coxe was censured by the Bedford Church for having a "tendencie to make rents and devisions in the congregation."²⁶³ It was suggested in chapter 2 of this monograph that the root of these "rents and devisions" was Coxe's views on baptism and membership, and that these views contributed to his departure for London and the Petty France Church. In other words, it is just as likely that Coxe was an advocate of strict communion at the time he helped draft the 1677 Confession as that he was sympathetic to open communion.

Bunyan scholar Anne Dunan-Page goes far beyond Haykin in her 2006 article, "John Bunyan's *A Confession of My Faith* and Restoration Anabaptism."²⁶⁴ Dunan-Page attempts to draw several lines of influence from Bunyan, through the Petty France Church, to the 1677 London Baptist Confession. She writes, "The Petty France congregation is rarely mentioned in connection with Bunyan, although there are indications that he may indeed have been well acquainted with some of its members."²⁶⁵ As examples, she cites Nehemiah Coxe, Edward Harrison, John Gammon (in whose church in Boar's Head Bunyan preached his final sermon in August 1688), and the erstwhile John Child (who had once been a member of the Bedford Church).²⁶⁶ Furthermore, she states of the Petty France Church, "There is no evidence that it insisted on baptizing believers who came to it after rejecting baptism in their original congregation, making it de facto an open-communion church, although it insisted upon baptizing its own members."²⁶⁷ Dunan-Page concludes, "Given this network of associations, it is tempting to conclude that Petty France might have provided Bunyan with a Baptist London circle where his views were heeded, despite the vehemence of the published criticisms that have survived."²⁶⁸ Through

263. *Minutes*, 77.
264. Dunan-Page, "John Bunyan," 19–40.
265. Dunan-Page, "John Bunyan," 26.
266. Dunan-Page, "John Bunyan," 26–27, 30.
267. Dunan-Page, "John Bunyan," 26. Dunan-Page cites the same Dowley article that Haykin cited (see above).
268. Dunan-Page, "John Bunyan," 27. She even suggests Bunyan stayed in the homes of Petty France members during his 1676 exile from Bedford: "In 1676, at a time when the government renewed its attacks on dissenters, Bunyan disappeared for a few months from Bedford. Richard Greaves has suggested that he accepted the hospitality of prominent Congregationalists [Greaves, *Glimpses of Glory*, 315, 338–39]. . . . But it is equally plausible that we should look for him in the house of one of the Londoners he knew best, his old friend Nehemiah Cox and in a congregation that had gained a reputation for welcoming provincial Baptists in the capital" (Dunan-Page, "John Bunyan," 34).

the Petty France Church, Dunan-Page credits Bunyan with influencing the shift on strict-communion represented in the 1677 London Baptist Confession.[269] While intriguing, Dunan-Page's evidence is circumstantial. Furthermore, if the 1677 London Baptist Confession was intended to be an olive branch from the Baptists to Bunyan and the Bedford Church, there is no evidence Bunyan received it as such. He nowhere mentions the Confession, the Petty France Church, William Collins, or Nehemiah Coxe after his departure from Bedford.

The best solution to the question of why the 1677 and 1689 general assemblies omitted all explicit references to strict communion is that contextual factors (persecution in 1677, toleration in 1689) provoked the Baptists in those historical moments to elevate evangelical unity (1677) and ecclesiastical liberty (1689) over ecclesiological purity. But does this softening towards open communion reflected in the 1677/1689 London Baptist Confession represent an ecclesiological change significant enough to alter seventeenth-century Baptist identity? Should open communion be considered a valid seventeenth-century Baptist position? Four considerations suggest not.

First, the internal logic of the 1677/1689 London Baptist Confession still demands strict communion. Its definition of the visible church as "Saints by calling" who "consent to walk together according to the appointment of Christ . . . in professed subjection to the Ordinances of the Gospel," and its definition of baptism as properly administered only to "Those who do actually profess repentance towards *God*, faith in, and obedience, to our Lord Jesus," logically necessitates strict communion.[270] A true shift in the seventeenth-century Baptist position would demand a corresponding shift in either its definition of the visible church or its position regarding the proper subjects of baptism. The statement in the 1677 Appendix regarding the removal of any explicit reference to strict communion represents an inconsistency driven by external circumstance rather than a change in ecclesiological conviction.

---

269. "If William Collins is indeed to be credited with the redrafting of the Westminster Confession that appeared in 1677, whose terms must have been opposed by the likes of John Child, I suggest he cannot have failed to be influenced in his choice of words and names by the arguments of the open communionists who gravitated around Petty France: John Gammon, 'the ingenious Mr. Tull' [Samuel Tull?] and the refugee Bunyan" (Dunan-Page, "John Bunyan," 34).

270. *Confession of Faith* (1677) 26.6; 29.2.

Second, in light of the preponderance of evidence presented in this chapter from the spectrum of seventeenth-century Baptist thought, the omission of strict communion language in the 1677/1689 London Baptist Confession represents an anomaly in an otherwise consistent and coherent Baptist ecclesiology, an anomaly driven not by Scriptural conviction but by historical context. The stated explanation for the omission in the 1677 Confession was the desire for evangelical unity in the face of the common threat of persecution. It is noteworthy that in the Appendix to the 1677 Confession, in which the assembly expressed its desire for unity and its willingness to "imbrace and own" those churches that disagreed over baptism, there is no scriptural argument given in support of its decision.[271] There is no reference, for instance, to Romans 14–15, the key passage to which Jessey and Bunyan repeatedly made reference. Furthermore, "imbrace and own" does not mean "embrace and own as a Baptist church," but rather "embrace and own as a true church," as the rest of the passage makes clear:

> So may it be now as to many things relating to the service of God, which do retain the names proper to them in their first institution [i.e., baptism], but yet through inadvertency (where there is no sinister design) may vary in their circumstances, from their first institution. And if by means of any antient defection, or of that general corruption of the service of God, and interruption of his true worship, and persecution of his servants by the Antichristian Bishop of *Rome*, for many generations; those who do consult the Word of God, cannot yet arrive at a full and mutual satisfaction among themselves, what was the practice of the primitive Christian Church, in some points relating to the *Worship* of God: yet inasmuch as these things are not of the essence of Christianity, but that we agree in the fundamental doctrines thereof, we do apprehend, there is sufficient ground to lay aside all bitterness and prejudice, and in the spirit of love and meekness to imbrace and own each other therein; leaving each other at liberty to perform such other services (wherein we cannot concur) apart unto God, according to the best of our understanding.[272]

---

271. *Confession of Faith* (1677), 141–42. The entire Appendix may be found in *Confession of Faith* (1677), 109–42.

272. *Confession of Faith* (1677), 141–42.

In other words, the 1677 London Baptist Confession did not so much expand the definition of a Baptist church, as it expanded the definition of a true church and a sincere Christian.[273]

Third, the dominant and representative voices of seventeenth-century Particular Baptist thought continued as staunch defenders of strict communion, even after the publication of the 1677 London Baptist Confession. William Kiffin wrote *A Sober Discourse of Right to Church Communion* in 1681. Hanserd Knollys published *The World That Now Is* the same year. Benjamin Keach wrote *The Glory of a True Church, and Its Discipline Display'd* in 1697, eight years after the publication of the 1689 London Baptist Confession. While it cannot be proven that these three men participated in the 1677 general assembly, as the 1677 Confession was published anonymously, all three men were signatories of the circular letter that called for the general assembly.[274] And it is a fact that all three signed the 1689 Confession.[275] For these Particular Baptist leaders, the omission of strict communion from the 1677/1689 London Baptist Confession did not reflect a change of heart as to what it means to be Baptist, only a more generous understanding of what it means to be evangelical.

Fourth, although the representatives who attended the general assembly of 1677 remain anonymous, of the "upwards of, one hundred BAPTISED CHURCHES" attending the 1689 assembly, only three churches are reputed to have been open-communion: the Broadmead Church of Bristol (pastored by Thomas Vaux), the Plymouth Church of Devon (represented by Samuel Buttall, who became its pastor the following year), and the Stevington Church of Bedfordshire (represented by John Carter).[276] However, as

---

273. Hence, they agreed with both the Westminster Confession of Faith (25.5) and the Savoy Declaration (26.3) that, "The purest Churches under heaven are subject to mixture, and error" (*Confession of Faith* [1677] 26.3). As discussed above, these were affirmations many Baptists had been unwilling to make in the previous decades.

274. Lumpkin, *Baptist Confessions of Faith*, 238.

275. Lumpkin, *Baptist Confessions of Faith*, 239.

276. J. Renihan, *1677/1689*, 70. Renihan writes, "At the London Assemblies, the majority of churches would have been closed membership, but open membership churches were present as well" (J. Renihan, *Edification and Beauty*, 47). In a footnote on this sentence, Renihan writes, "Broadmead, Bristol was indisputably open-membership. In addition, Plymouth and Stevington were most likely the same. The Plymouth church unanimously called a paedobaptist, Robert Brown, as minister in 1687. This could not happen in a closed membership church. In addition, the presence of Samuel Buttall, a former member of the open-membership London church previously under the ministry of Henry Jessey points to open-membership practices. See Plymouth Church Manuscript

demonstrated above, the Broadmead Church was only moderately and temporarily open-communion, and by 1689 was, in fact, a strict-communion church. For the other two churches, Plymouth and Stevington, the evidence for their open-communion position is limited. The Plymouth Church was in the midst of much turmoil in the years surrounding the 1689 assembly, calling three pastors in three years, one a paedobaptist (Robert Brown). The Stevington Church became strict-communion perhaps as early as 1688, and definitely by the early-1690s.[277] Therefore, one of the primary arguments often cited by Baptist historians for the inclusion of open-communion churches within the seventeenth-century Baptist fold is less than convincing.[278] Of the three reputedly open-communion congregations present, two were already strict-communion by the time of the 1689 assembly (or soon to become so), and the third was in a state of ecclesiological turmoil.

In light of the evidence, it is therefore best to regard the omission of explicit strict communion language from the 1677/1689 London Baptist Confession as an anomaly in seventeenth-century Baptist thought driven by historical-contextual factors, rather than as signaling a sudden reversal of a century of consistent Baptist identity. While the omission may signal a softening of the definition of a true church, it does not signal an alteration in the definition of what it means to be Baptist. While "the exception that proves the rule" is a phrase often used to explain away contradictory evidence, in this case it seems to apply.[279] It was a concern

---

Copy Extracts from Church Book 1648–1776, 13, 26. The Stevington church endured a division when they 'altered their judgments about the practice of baptisme,' apparently in the early 1690s (though it may have been as early as 1688). They adopted a closed-membership stance. See Tibbutt, *Some Early Nonconformist Church Books*, 36, 37, 59" (J. Renihan, *Edification and Beauty*, 47n34). See Renihan's notes in J. Renihan, *1677/1689*, 142 (for Buttall), 143 (for Carter), 171 (for Vaux).

277. J. Renihan, *Edification and Beauty*, 47n34.

278. This argument can be traced back to B. R. White's 1972 article, "Open and Closed Membership," examined above. Haykin, for example, writes, "Yet, as White has pointed out, there was at least one open membership church which sent a representative to this Calvinistic Baptist Assembly in 1689, namely, Broadmead Church in Bristol. Believer's baptism and a personal profession of faith before the church were the normal requirements for admission to membership in this church, but on occasion some were received into membership solely on the basis of a personal testimony" (Haykin, *Kiffin, Knollys and Keach*, 50). However, the last record of someone being received into membership without being baptized was Sister Hollister in 1681 (Hayden, *Records*, 53n40; cf. 225).

279. Peter Naylor asserts that the omission of explicit strict communion language from the 1677 London Baptist Confession was the result of the "disinclination of the Calvinistic Baptists to publicize their disagreements on this issue," and that this "was

for evangelical unity that drove the general assembly of 1677 to drop the language of strict communion from its confession, the same principle the drove Bunyan to open communion, thus demonstrating the thesis of this monograph. Where the concern for ecclesiological purity remained preeminent, English Baptists held to strict communion. Where the need for evangelical unity or political expediency superseded this principle, strict communion proved dispensable.

Bunyan and Baptist Identity

This chapter has argued that strict communion should be considered a seventeenth-century Baptist distinctive, for strict communion is the necessary implication of the Baptist definition of a true visible church. Although they vary in the precise wording, every Baptist theologian surveyed in this chapter defined a true visible church as an assembly of baptized believers, as does every Baptist confession of faith, with one very notable exception, the 1677/1689 London Baptist Confession, examined above. A commitment to strict communion is the *raison d'être* of the Baptist movement. Without strict communion, there is no Baptist church.

On the other hand, open communion was an isolated phenomenon, not sufficiently widespread or connected to the wider Baptist movement to be considered a minority position within that movement. Of the prominent representatives of "open-communion Baptists" listed by B. R. White, John Tombes was a lifelong Anglican who refused to separate from the established Church because he continued to affirm its legitimacy. Henry Jessey managed to maintain close relationships with London Baptists because of their shared history within London Nonconformity. It is telling, however, that for his Southwark congregation, like the Broadmead Church in Bristol, open communion was merely a way station on the road to strict Baptist communion. Vavasor Powell's writings on the relationship between baptism and the church were as ambiguous as his ecclesiological affiliations. Bunyan and the Bedford Church flatly refused to associate with the Baptists.

---

certainly a manoeuvre, and may even be interpreted as an exception that gives some endorsement to the prevailing rule" (Naylor, *Calvinism, Communion*, 87). Likewise, concerning the omission from the 1689 London Baptist Confession, "This was not a compromise born of uncertainty but a reflex in the context of the accession of William III in 1688 and the Toleration Act a year later. All concerned needed to show that their house was in order" (88). Naylor later explains the 1689 omission as "to a greater or lesser extent a needed political ploy" (238).

The only thing these two groups shared in common was credobaptism, but credobaptism is not enough to make one Baptist. To be Baptist in the seventeenth century was to gather a church of baptized believers according to the "primitive pattern," the "Scriptural order," the inviolable rule of the Word of God. This created an irreconcilable tension between a concern for ecclesiological purity and evangelical unity. If a true church is an assembly of baptized believers, and paedobaptism is not true baptism, then a paedobaptist is not truly baptized, and a paedobaptist church is not a true church. These implications were clearly destructive of evangelical unity. Yet during the seventeenth century (the 1677/1689 London Baptist Confession excepted), evangelical unity was the price Baptists were willing to pay for ecclesiological purity. But in the context of seventeenth-century England, one or the other of these two principles must gain the upper hand. For the Baptists, ecclesiological purity triumphed over evangelical unity. For Bunyan and the Bedford Church, evangelical unity triumphed over ecclesiological purity. This tension proved the dividing line among seventeenth-century credobaptists, and Bunyan and the Baptists fell on opposite sides.

Chapter 6

Evangelical Independent: A Reevaluation of Bunyan's Ecclesiological Identity

> I must tell you (avoiding your *slovenly* Language) I know none to whom that Title [Baptist] is so proper as *to the Disciples of* John. And since you would know by what Name I would be distinguished from others; I tell you, I would be, and hope I am, *a Christian*; and chuse, if God should count me worthy, *to be called a Christian, a Believer* or other such Name which is approved by the Holy Ghost. And for those Factious Titles of *Anabaptists, Independents, Presbyterians*, or the like, I conclude that they came neither from *Jerusalem*, nor *Antioch*, but rather from *Hell* and *Babylon*; for they naturally tend to divisions, *you may know them by their fruits.*[1]

ECCLESIOLOGICAL IDENTITY IS NOT an exact science, particularly in the free church tradition. Baptist identity is ideological, not institutional, which means that the definition of "Baptist" is to some degree relative and historically fluid, determined more by consensus than by confessional adherence. What passes for "Baptist" in one era may not in another. Furthermore, there always exists a gap between theology and practice, between orthodoxy and orthopraxy; even the best theologians fail at times to act in ways consistent with their convictions. The omission of explicit strict communion

---

1. Bunyan, *Peaceable Principles and True*, 4:270.

language from the 1677/1689 London Baptist Confession is a case in point. Therefore, the question, "Was Bunyan a Baptist?" is too imprecise to be adequately answered. But a response can be offered to the question, "What is the best historical-ecclesiological categorization for John Bunyan and the network of open-communion churches that flourished in and around Bedfordshire in the latter-half of the seventeenth century?" As the quotation above attests, Bunyan resisted such categorization, contending that they were "Factious Titles" that "naturally tend to divisions." While that may be true in one's own time, theological and ecclesiological categories are necessary to the historian's task of understanding the convictions, relationships, and influence of those who have gone before. This chapter will therefore examine the various historical, theological, and ecclesiological labels that are most often applied to Bunyan in the secondary literature, before suggesting a new label that more accurately describes his theological and ecclesiological convictions and differentiates him from his contemporaries who held to significantly different, even contradictory, views.[2]

Puritan

Bunyan is often classified as a Puritan.[3] "Puritan" is a notoriously slippery term to define and must be understood in its historical, theological,

---

2. Not every label examined in this chapter is mutually exclusive. For example, "Puritan" and "Evangelical" tend to be used primarily in an historical-theological sense to describe one's broader theological commitments within a particular historical timeframe, while "Congregationalist" and "Baptist" tend to be used in a denominational sense to describe one's distinctive ecclesiological convictions. Bunyan is therefore regarded by some as both a Puritan and a Congregationalist, or as a Puritan and a Baptist, or as an Evangelical and a Baptist. Yet there is no scholarly consensus regarding the historical timeframes of theological movements, and even ecclesiological labels are historically situated. Therefore, history, theology, and ecclesiology must be taken into account.

3. For example, Beeke and Pederson include Bunyan in their compendium of influential Puritans (Beeke and Pederson, *Meet the Puritans*, 101–12). Likewise, Beeke and Jones, while admitting the historical difficulty of describing Bunyan as a Puritan, nevertheless regard him as an exemplar of Puritan theology and ethos, particularly what they refer to as the "pilgrim mentality," which they describe as a diamond with six facets: it is biblical, pietist, churchly, warfaring, methodical, and two-worldly (Beeke and Jones, *Puritan Theology*, 2, 215–16, 426–27, 428, 459, 509, 511, 513–15, 562, 613, 616–17, 708, 717–24, 821, 830, 832, 836, 843–44, 853, 863, 892, 925, 931, 963). See esp. their chapter on "Puritan Theology Shaped by a Pilgrim Mentality" (843–58). David Hall regards Bunyan as an example of the Puritan "practical divinity" (Hall, *Puritans*, 109–43, 316). D. Martyn Lloyd-Jones includes Bunyan in his addresses on Puritanism (Lloyd-Jones,

and ecclesiological senses.⁴ Historically and ecclesiologically, Puritanism may be understood as a reform movement within the Church of England, beginning with the Elizabethan Settlement in 1558/1559 and ending with the Act of Uniformity in 1662.⁵ Theologically, however, Puritanism refers to a broad movement of Reformed orthodoxy in England.⁶ In this theological sense, Puritanism transcends its historical and ecclesiological bounds. Joel Beeke and Mark Jones define Puritanism in its theological sense as a "vigorous Calvinism" marked by four characteristics: (1) "Experientially, it was warm and contagious"; (2) "evangelistically, it was aggressive, yet tender"; (3) "ecclesiastically, it sought to practice the headship of Christ over the faith, worship, and order of His body, the church"; (4)

Puritans, 390–411). Finally, Brian Najapfour points to the Puritan nature of Bunyan's conversion, sermons, writings, and especially his "experiential pneumatology" (Najapfour, "John Bunyan," 142–59). These works represent just a sampling of the prevalent tendency to identify Bunyan as a Puritan in the broader, theological sense of the term.

4. "One of the most difficult tasks for the church historian is to define Puritanism" (Beeke and Jones, *Puritan Theology*, 1). The literature on the history and theology of Puritanism is vast, but David Hall's recent work, *The Puritans: A Transatlantic History*, is exceptional for its depth and breadth, narrating the quest for a "thorough reformation" of the church in England, Scotland, and the New England colonies. Also noteworthy is Joel R. Beeke and Mark Jones's magisterial *A Puritan Theology*, which is an historical and systematic theology of Puritanism. Other authoritative works on Puritanism and Separatism include Knappen, *Tudor Puritanism*; Burrage, *Early English Dissenters*; White, *English Separatist Tradition*; *English Puritan Tradition*; Brachlow, *Communion of Saints*; Collinson, *Elizabethan Puritan Movement*; Coffey and Lim, *Cambridge Companion to Puritanism*.

5. "In 1662, with the passing of the Act of Uniformity, those within the Church of England who wished for a more thorough reformation of its practices, and who found themselves unable to accept what they regarded as popish aspects of the Book of Common Prayer, were forced to make a difficult choice: either they should conform and give up their deeply-held beliefs about the church; or they should leave the church in protest. Nearly two-thousand chose the latter option and thus Puritanism made the transition to nonconformity" (Trueman, "Puritan Theology as Historical Event," 253, quoted in Beeke and Jones, *Puritan Theology*, 3). Norman Sykes, on the other hand, regards the 1689 Act of Toleration as the terminus of historical Puritanism (Sykes, *English Religious Tradition*, 66, cited in Beeke and Jones, *Puritan Theology*, 4). Beeke and Jones summarize: "Whatever the year, Puritanism has special reference to issues of church and state, theology and worship in the sixteenth and seventeenth centuries" (*Puritan Theology*, 4).

6. "The vast majority of Puritans were part of the larger theological movement called Reformed orthodoxy" (Beeke and Jones, *Puritan Theology*, 2). Coffey and Lim write, "Puritanism was a variety of Reformed Protestantism, aligned with the continental Calvinistic churches rather than with the Lutherans" (Coffey and Lim, "Introduction," 2, quoted in Beeke and Jones, *Puritan Theology*, 2).

"politically, it was active, balanced, and bound by conscience toward God, in the relations of king, Parliament, and subjects."[7]

Judging by the foregoing rubrics, Bunyan may be considered a Puritan in its theological sense only. Historically, the vast majority of Bunyan's ministry and influence occurred after 1662. Ecclesiologically, Separatists like Bunyan were not strictly Puritans.[8] Theologically, however, Bunyan hits all the marks. His "practical divinity" was experientially warm and contagious, as *Grace Abounding to the Chief of Sinners*, *The Pilgrim's Progress*, and his numerous "experimental" works abundantly testify.[9] He was evangelistically aggressive, yet tender. His treatises explode with passionate appeals to the unconverted to close with Christ, and his gifts as an evangelist and

---

7. Beeke and Jones, *Puritan Theology*, 5.

8. "[Bunyan] was, first of all, a sectary and not a Puritan. Traditionally Puritans had preferred the possibility of reforming the existing state church rather than separating from it, as did the sectaries" (Greaves, *John Bunyan*, 23). In a 2011 article, however, Brian Najapfour argued that "the undeniable truth that Bunyan belonged to the sectarian world does not imply that Bunyan cannot be considered a Puritan" (Najapfour, "John Bunyan," 148). On the contrary, Najapfour argues that "Bunyan uniquely possessed the spirit of both sectarianism and Puritanism" (143). Najapfour defends this claim by pointing to the essentially Puritan nature of Bunyan's conversion, sermons, writings, and especially his "experiential pneumatology" (152–59). In the end, Najapfour concludes that it is best to classify Bunyan as a "sectarian Puritan" (159).

9. For the Puritan "practical divinity," see Hall, *Puritans*, 109–43. Hall defines "practical divinity" as the Puritan way of translating doctrine into a personal faith that was "experimentall" and "inward" (109). He then identifies five overlapping themes of the practical divinity: covenant theology, the "golden chain" of salvation, law, providence, and predestination (115–18). The Puritan practical divinity was concerned with the process of conversion, with pursuing assurance of salvation, and with living in "watchfulness" through a host of devotional practices which were the "beating heart of the practical divinity," those "routines of moral and spiritual duties" that "marked the pilgrim's pathway to heaven" (120, 122). The devotional practices were both private and communal, inward and outward, and included such disciplines as self-examination, listening to sermons, partaking of the sacraments, learning the catechism, and family worship. Hall notes that while many in the mid-seventeenth century began to deviate from the Puritan practical divinity, "To tens of thousands of others, however, this bundle continued to shape their understanding of the 'pathway' to salvation. . . . Of the many witnesses to the persistence of this model, the most interesting may be John Bunyan" (316). After discussing Bunyan's quest for assurance as detailed in *Grace Abounding to the Chief of Sinners*, Hall continues, "Bunyan's may seem an unusually prolonged quest. Yet it becomes less extreme if we remember that the makers of the practical divinity regarded conversion as lifelong. A 'first conversion' was merely the starting point for a process of self-examination and attending to the 'means of grace'" (316). "Experimental" is Offor's word to describe Bunyan's works dealing with the soul, as opposed to his "doctrinal," "practical," and "allegorical, figurative, and symbolical" works (Offor, *Works of John Bunyan*).

preacher were renowned among his contemporaries. John Brown reported that when Charles II asked John Owen, why he, the immensely educated Oxford scholar, would go to sit under the preaching of an uneducated country pastor, Owen replied, "I would willingly exchange my learning for the Tinker's power of touching men's hearts."[10] Ecclesiastically, Bunyan was committed to the rule of Christ over the church's faith, worship, and order. As was demonstrated in chapter 4, the difference between Bunyan and his Baptist opponents was not that the Baptists held to the regulative principle while Bunyan did not. Both sides strenuously appealed to the regulative principle as the basis for their respective positions. Finally, Bunyan was "politically ... active, balanced, and bound by conscience toward God, in the relations of king, Parliament, and subjects," Beeke and Jones's fourth characteristic of Puritanism. He addressed church/state relations numerous times in his writings, and his thought reflects the Puritan tension between freedom of conscience and submission to the magistrate.[11] In addition, Bunyan's theology bears the hallmarks of Puritan influence. Bunyan was loath to admit his indebtedness to sources outside of Scripture, and thus mentioned only five Puritan works in all of his written corpus: Lewis Bayly's *The Practise of Pietie* (1613), Arthur Dent's *The Plaine Mans Pathway to Heaven* (1601), Samuel Clarke's *A Mirrour or Looking-Glass Both for Saints and Sinners* (1646), John Dod's *A Plaine and Familiar Exposition of the Tenne Commandements* (1605), and his beloved *The Actes and Monuments* (1563) by John Foxe.[12] Yet despite his reticence, Bunyan scholars

---

10. Brown, *John Bunyan*, 382. Whether this anecdote is fact or myth, Bunyan's homiletical gifts are well-attested. Michael Haykin calls Bunyan "one of the great evangelists of the Puritan era," who "could have described his passion for the lost in terms that Whitefield or Wesley would gladly have owned" (Haykin, "Evangelicalism and the Enlightenment," 52).

11. For example, see Bunyan, *Holy City*, 3:96; *Confession of My Faith*, 4:136, 153; *Discourse of the House*, 7:128, 153, 172; *Seasonable Counsel*, 10:48, 99–104; *Exposition of the First Ten Chapters*, 12:122–23, 144–45, 162–64, 173, 267–68; *Paul's Departure and Crown*, 12:358; *Of Antichrist*, 13:421–29, 439–41. See also Galen Johnson's article on the tension between Bunyan's concern for religious liberty and his political conservatism in Johnson, "Conflicted Puritan Inheritance," 103–15.

12. For Bunyan's professions of theological independence, see Bunyan, *Solomon's Temple Spiritualiz'd*, 7:9; *Light for Them*, 8:51; *Of Antichrist*, 13:475–76; *Grace Abounding*, 80. For Bayly and Dent, see Bunyan, *Grace Abounding*, 8. For Clarke, see Bunyan, *Life and Death of Mr. Badman*, 56, 134, 146. For Dod, see Bunyan, *Doctrine of the Law*, 2:35. For Foxe, see Bunyan, *Few Sighs from Hell*, 1:358; *I Will Pray with the Spirit*, 2:239, 247; *Discourse on the House*, 7:159–63; *Come & Welcome*, 8:383–84; *Seasonable Counsel*, 10:22, 55, 64, 69, 102; *Of Antichrist*, 13:497–98; *Grace Abounding*, 76–77; *Relation of the*

have detected decisive Puritan influence, in particular that of William Perkins (preaching and soteriology) and John Owen (covenant theology).[13] However, because he was not a Puritan in the historical and ecclesiological sense, "Puritan" is not the most accurate ecclesiological label for John Bunyan, though it remains a helpful descriptor of his theological heritage in the "vigorous Calvinism" of English Reformed orthodoxy.

Evangelical

In his seminal 1989 work *Evangelicalism in Modern Britain*, David Bebbington argues that Evangelicalism emerged as a distinct movement in Britain in the 1730s, was the result of the Enlightenment assumptions of John Locke, Isaac Newton, Thomas Reid, and others, and is marked by four characteristics, collectively known as "Bebbington's Quadrilateral": "*conversionism*, the belief that lives need to be changed; *activism*, the expression of the gospel in effort; *biblicism*, a particular regard for the Bible; and . . . *crucicentrism*, a stress on the sacrifice of Christ on the cross."[14] Bebbington asserts that Evangelicalism "represents a sharp discontinuity in the Protestant tradition."[15] The new Evangelical movement was driven by a new approach to assurance of salvation, which Bebbington argues is far more certain and robust than its Puritan ancestor. "The fulcrum of change was the doctrine of assurance. Those who knew their sins forgiven

---

Imprisonment, 114; *Pilgrim's Progress*, 2:243. Richard Greaves compiled an extensive list of books that Bunyan either definitely or likely read in Greaves, *Glimpses of Glory*, 603–6. See also Campbell, "Fishing in Other Men's Waters," 137–51; Pooley, "Bunyan's Reading," 101–16.

13. For Perkins's influence upon Bunyan's preaching and soteriology, through Perkins's *The Arte of Prophecying* and *A Golden Chaine*, see Greaves, *Glimpses of Glory*, 173, 212, 605; Owens, "Bunyan's Posthumously Published Works," 349; Sharrock, *John Bunyan*, 20–22, 96; Pooley, "Bunyan's Reading," 110; Wallace, "Bunyan's Theology," 77. For Owen's influence on Bunyan's covenant theology, see Wallace, "Bunyan's Theology," 71; Greaves, *Glimpses of Glory*, 226, 297, 301, 315, 329, 344–47, 353, 360, 619, 373n; *John Bunyan*, 41–44, 57–59, 62, 73, 77, 79, 88–89, 105, 107–8, 117, 128, 147, 156–57, 159.

14. Bebbington, *Evangelicalism in Modern Britain*, 2–3.

15. Bebbington, *Evangelicalism in Modern Britain*, 74. It should be noted that Bebbington does not deny that some continuity exists with earlier Protestantism; rather, he asserts that the discontinuities are greater and therefore sufficient to classify Evangelicalism as a distinct movement originating in 1730s Britain. See Bebbington, *Evangelicalism in Modern Britain*, 34–35; "Response," 417–32.

were freed from the debilitating anxieties for Christian mission."[16] Bebbington's thesis has won widespread scholarly acceptance. According to Timothy Larson, "Indeed, Bebbington's definition is now receiving the ultimate compliment of being cited without acknowledgement, as if it is not one scholar's opinion but simply the truth we all know."[17] Nevertheless, Bebbington's work has provoked a number of responses from scholars who see more continuity between Evangelicalism and its Protestant predecessors than Bebbington allows.[18]

In a 2016 article, Peter Morden tests Bebbington's thesis on the case of John Bunyan, whose *Pilgrim's Progress* was "highly prized by a wide range of eighteenth and nineteenth-century evangelicals. Indeed, by the beginning of the nineteenth century it had become a 'key evangelical document,' regarded by many as second only to the Bible in importance. As such, it had a significant shaping effect on evangelical spirituality."[19] According to Morden, Bunyan provides the perfect test-case: "If even Bunyan, an iconic figure in modern evangelicalism, was qualitatively different from the later movement in important ways, then perhaps a major shift did indeed take place at the beginning of the eighteenth century."[20] Evaluating Bunyan by the rubric of Bebbington's Quadrilateral, Morden finds significant

---

16. Bebbington, *Evangelicals in Modern Britain*, 74. Bebbington goes on to write, "The activism of the Evangelical movement sprang from its strong teaching on assurance. That, in turn, was a product of the confidence of the new age about the validity of experience. The Evangelical version of Protestantism was created by the Enlightenment" (74).

17. Larson, "Reception Given *Evangelicalism*," 29. Haykin writes, "This 'functional definition of evangelicalism' has found widespread scholarly approval and employment" (Haykin, "Evangelicalism and the Enlightenment," 49). Haykin provides a long list of scholars who accept Bebbington's thesis (49n61).

18. Many of these scholars contributed essays to Haykin and Stewart, *Emergence of Evangelicalism*. The essays in this volume argue for continuity between eighteenth-century Evangelicalism and sixteenth- and seventeenth-century Reformed and Protestant traditions. The arguments follow three main lines: regional continuity (in Scotland, Wales, England, New England, and Holland), chronological continuity (particularly with the Magisterial Reformers and the Puritans), and doctrinal continuity (in the doctrines of conversion/assurance, eschatology, and inspiration/inerrancy). See also Stewart, "Did Evangelicalism Predate the Eighteenth Century?"; Williams, "Was Evangelicalism Created by the Enlightenment?"

19. Morden, "John Bunyan," 80. Morden cites Hannah Marshman and Charles Spurgeon as examples of Bunyan's influence (79–81). In the quotation above, Morden is citing Hofmeyr, *Portable Bunyan*, 1. He also cites Ivimey, *History of the English Baptists*, 2:42.

20. Morden, "John Bunyan," 82.

continuities in the areas of biblicism, crucicentrism, and conversionism.[21] Morden even adds one further area of continuity, Bunyan's "catholicity," or ecumenism.[22] But Morden also finds significant discontinuity in two areas. First, he finds Bunyan's prolonged and tortuous quest for assurance of salvation inconsistent with the "confident" doctrine of assurance and the "clear" and "linear" conversion narratives found in later Evangelicalism.[23] When it comes to the doctrine of assurance, Morden sees Bunyan as far more Puritan than Evangelical: "Bunyan's Puritan casuistry diverged from the approach typical of later 'enlightened' evangelicalism."[24] Second, Morden finds discontinuity is regard to "eschatology, activism and mission."[25] According to Morden, Bunyan's eschatology was "ambivalent," not like the "robust" and "optimistic" postmillennialism of Evangelicals like Jonathan Edwards.[26] And although Morden admits that Bunyan was extraordinarily active by any objective standard, yet his activism was different than that of later Evangelicals in both its nature and its scope. Evangelical activism was "confident, grounded . . . on full assurance of salvation and driven by an optimistic postmillennial hope."[27] It was also "pragmatic," leading them to "eschew doctrinal speculation and aim for theological simplicity which

---

21. On Bunyan's biblicism: "Bunyan shared the basic evangelical commitment to live out of the text of Scripture; indeed, he was perceived as exemplifying this and providing a standard to aim at" (Morden, "John Bunyan," 84). On Bunyan's crucicentrism: "Bunyan's work also exhibits a thoroughgoing commitment to the cross of Christ. . . . He insists that the cross is the place where sin is dealt with. Those who received salvation did so only through the sacrifice of Christ; they were justified only by his blood and reconciled to God only by his death" (84). On Bunyan's conversionism: "Conversionism such as [Bunyan's] was characteristic of eighteenth and nineteenth-century evangelicalism. Indeed, Bunyan's approach was influential in helping some later figures adopt invitational evangelistic preaching for themselves" (86). Morden cites Andrew Fuller as especially influenced by Bunyan's conversionism.

22. "Another parallel can be adduced, for Bunyan also evinced a certain irenic spirit, a 'catholicity' which led him, for example, to espouse open communion principles: both credobaptists and dissenting paedobaptists were welcome to the Lord's Table in Bedford" (Morden, "John Bunyan," 87).

23. Morden, "John Bunyan," 91.

24. Morden, "John Bunyan," 94.

25. Morden, "John Bunyan," 94.

26. "In short, it is far from certain that Bunyan was postmillennial in the way that later generations would understand the term. Overall, his eschatology was ambivalent" (Morden, "John Bunyan," 94–95).

27. Morden, "John Bunyan," 97.

Evangelical Independent

cleared away all obstacles to passionate, invitational gospel preaching."[28] Furthermore, Bunyan's activism was largely confined to Bedfordshire and London, while Evangelicals like Wesley and Whitefield, Edwards, Fuller, and Carey exercised a global reach.

It is not the purpose of this section to debate or defend Bebbington's thesis, but rather to evaluate whether "Evangelical" is an accurate and helpful historical-theological label for Bunyan ("Evangelical" is not usually employed in an ecclesiological sense). According to Morden, though Bunyan exemplifies the Evangelical characteristics of biblicism, crucicentrism, and conversionism, he fails to match Evangelicalism's activism and diverged from Evangelicalism's foundational doctrine of assurance. But Morden has overstated these discontinuities. Many later Evangelicals endured prolonged conversion travails that bear similarities to Bunyan's experience narrated in *Grace Abounding to the Chief of Sinners* and Christian's experience in *The Pilgrim's Progress*. Three of the "Fathers" of modern Evangelicalism—Jonathan Edwards, George Whitefield, and John Wesley—all embarked upon long and difficult quests for conversion and assurance.[29] In a 2008 essay, Michael Haykin asserts that Bebbington erred in making Jonathan Edwards the father of the new, confident Evangelical doctrine of assurance, for Bebbington failed to note that Edwards's view of assurance changed following the 1734–1735 and the 1740–1742 Northampton revivals, as Edwards became increasingly disturbed over the apparent false conversions that occurred during the revivals.[30] Edwards's *The Distinguishing*

---

28. Morden, "John Bunyan," 97.

29. George Marsden describes Edwards's long and excruciating quest for true conversion and full assurance in chapters 2–3 of his magisterial biography of Edwards, the third chapter aptly titled, "The Pilgrim's Progress" (Marsden, *Jonathan Edwards*, 25–58). In Thomas Kidd's opinion, "In Whitefield's world, conversion to faith in Christ was no polite, simple affair. You did not just walk an aisle and ask Jesus to come into your heart. It was a titanic spiritual struggle—the defining struggle of one's life—to find out whether God or the devil would ultimately command your soul's allegiance" (Kidd, *George Whitefield*, 20). Kidd then describes Whitefield's quest for true conversion and assurance (20–37). Wesley's disastrous ministry in Georgia, his fateful transatlantic conversations with the Moravians, and his eventual "heart-warming" experience at Aldersgate are detailed in Woods, *Burning Heart*, 49–69.

30. Haykin, "Evangelicalism and the Enlightenment," 55–56. See Haykin's discussion of Edwards's doctrine of assurance in reference to Bebbington's thesis (55–59). Haykin notes that Edwards "rethought his view of assurance" as a result of the "fanaticism of some and the false professions of others" during the 1734–1735 and 1740–1742 revivals (56). Haykin cites Edwards's 1751 letter to Thomas Gillespie as evidence of Edwards's doubts concerning the authenticity of many of the conversions during the revivals (56).

Marks of a Work of the Spirit of God (1741), through which Bebbington claims "others in the Reformed tradition learned how to hearten new believers rather than throw them back into painful introspection," and by which "Edwards created an Evangelical framework for interpreting Christian experience," does not represent Edwards's final word on assurance, but was followed up by his *A Treatise Concerning Religious Affections* (1746), which was written to guard against false assurance more than excessive doubt.[31] Haykin demonstrates that it was this cautious rather than "bold" and "robust" doctrine of assurance that Edwards passed on to succeeding generations of Calvinistic Evangelicals like John Ryland Jr., Andrew Fuller, and John Sutcliffe.[32] Not only was Bunyan's experience of conversion similar to the reputed pillars of Evangelicalism, but one should not read *Grace Abounding to the Chief of Sinners* as though it were Bunyan's final word on assurance. Bunyan had much to say upon the subject, and his pastoral counsel to those anxious about the state of their soul and his answer to the question of how true faith may be discerned is in alignment with the mature thought of Edwards expressed in his *A Treatise Concerning Religious Affections*.[33]

---

31. Bebbington, *Evangelicalism in Modern Britain*, 47. For the background of Edwards's thought expressed in *On the Religious Affections*, see Marsden, *Jonathan Edwards*, 284–90, 304–5. Marsden writes, "Rather, unlike his earlier two awakening works, which were first of all designed to show critics that ecstatic phenomena did not prove anything one way or the other, *Affections* was directed first of all toward the misguided emphases of the extreme New Lights who had led many people into arrogant self-delusion" (285). Further, "During 1745, when he was writing *Religious Affections*, it [the fact that 'many communicant members were not showing proper evidence of a regenerate life'] was much on his mind as he described signs that should distinguish true believers from hypocrites" (304).

32. Haykin, "Evangelicalism and the Enlightenment," 55–59. For Bebbington's reference to the Evangelical doctrine of assurance as "robust," see Bebbington, *Evangelicalism in Modern Britain*, 45. For Edwards's doctrine of assurance as "bold," see Bebbington, *Evangelicalism in Modern Britain*, 47.

33. For example, Bunyan, *Doctrine of the Law*, 2:16–17, 210–26; *Come & Welcome*, 8:259–73, 299–301, 353–57, 362–64; *Jerusalem Sinner Saved*, 11:85–92. Haykin also cites Edwards's *Treatise Concerning the Religious Affections* (1746) as "the classic work on spirituality in the period of the Great Awakening, . . . which must also be regarded as the fruit of many years of reflection on the nature of genuine piety. . . . The theological vision and spirituality of Edwards's *Religious Affections* had a profound influence on eighteenth-century evangelicalism, which would have helped to disseminate Edwards's mature reflections on the doctrine of assurance" (Haykin, "Evangelicalism and the Enlightenment," 57). See also Sharon Lei's PhD dissertation on Bunyan's doctrine of assurance (Lei, "To 'Make a Travailer of Thee'"). Lei interacts with R. T. Kendall and David

Evangelical Independent

Neither was Bunyan's eschatology as "ambivalent" or pessimistic as Morden assumes. Although in *A Vindication of . . . Some Gospel Truths Opened* (1657) Bunyan asserted a premillennial return of Christ, by *The Holy City* (1665) Bunyan appears to posit thoroughly postmillennial and remained so to the end of his life.[34] Bunyan believed the millennium would be inaugurated by Antichrist's fall; but even before that event, he was optimistic about the future of the church and the spread of the gospel, particularly since the age of "Altar-work" (the Reformers who recovered the gospel) had given way to the age of "Temple-work" (the Nonconformists who recovered the believers' church). The last phase would be the age of "City-work," the inauguration of the millennium, upon completion of which "the Church of Christ [will] hath obtained a compleat conquest and victory over the world, and hath got her enemies and them that hate her, *to lye at her feet, and to lick the dust of the soles thereof.*"[35] Morden cites Jonathan Edwards as an example of the "optimistic" Evangelical postmillennialism, but it is unclear how Edwards's postmillennialism was more optimistic than Bunyan's.[36] Morden also asserts that Evangelical activism differed from Bunyan's in its nature and scope. According to Morden, Evangelical activism was marked by "remarkable energy, praying, preaching, visiting, itinerating, writing, publishing, networking, engaging in social action and generally working unstintingly. . . . By contrast a significant amount of Bunyan's activity, when viewed in the round, was directed to introspective soul-searching and questions of church order and discipline."[37] This is a remarkable mischaracterization of Bunyan's life, ministry, and writings;

Bebbington on pp. 274–80. John Knott calls the later Bunyan "a formidable preacher of assurance" (Knott, "Bunyan and the Holy Community," 201).

34. See Bunyan, *Vindication*, 1:205; *Holy City*, 3:82, 90, 128, 155, 158, 174, 177; *Solomon's Temple Spirituali'zd*, 7:19; *Discourse of the House*, 7:172–73; *Christ a Compleat Saviour*, 13:329; *Of Antichrist*, 13:434–35. See also Greaves, *John Bunyan and English Nonconformity*, 49–50; Greaves, *Glimpses of Glory*, 177, 181, 184–88. Greaves argues that *The Holy War* is constructed upon a postmillennial framework (*Glimpses of Glory*, 426–28). See also Ross, "Paradise Regained," 73–89. Morden only interacts with Bunyan's *Exposition of the First Ten Chapters of Genesis* and only cites Crawford Gribben's *Puritan Millennium* for his conclusion that Bunyan's eschatology was "ambivalent" (Morden, "John Bunyan," 94).

35. Bunyan, *Holy City*, 3:135. See also Greaves, *Glimpses of Glory*, 182–84.

36. Morden writes, "Whilst there is a measure of continuity between Bunyan and Edwards, important dimensions of their respective eschatologies and their practical outworkings stand in sharp contrast" (Morden, "John Bunyan," 95).

37. Morden, "John Bunyan," 97.

the list of activities Morden provides as characteristic of Evangelicals all describe Bunyan, with the possible exception of "engaging in social action," if by that one means the kind of orphanage and prison ministry engaged in by Whitefield and the Wesleys. Even then, is it not possible that political and economic factors had more to do with the difference in the nature and scope of activism than a difference in eschatology?

But perhaps the area of greatest continuity between Bunyan and the Evangelicals lies in his evangelical ecumenism, or what Morden calls his "catholicity."[38] Bunyan detested denominational labels, calling them "Factious Titles" that "tend to divisions."[39] He cared only for a unity grounded in a shared evangelical faith and holiness.

> Here is one runs a *Quaking*, another a *Ranting*; one again runs after the *Baptism*, and another after the *Independency*. Here's one for *Free-will*, and another for *Presbytery*; and yet possibly most of all these Sects run quite the wrong way, and yet every one is for his Life, his Soul, either for Heaven or Hell.
>
> If thou now say, which is the way? I tell thee it is CHRIST THE SON OF MARY, THE SON OF GOD. . . . So then thy business is, (if thou wouldest have Salvation) to see *if Christ be thine*, with all his Benefits: Whether *he hath covered thee with his Righteousness*, whether he hath shewed thee that *thy Sins are washed away with his Heart-Blood*, whether thou art *planted* into *him*, and whether thou have *Faith* in *him*, so as to make a *Life* out of *him*, and *Conform* thee to *him*. . . . And for the Lords sake take heed, and do not deceive thy self, and think thou art in the *way*, upon too slight grounds; for if thou miss of the *way*, thou wilt miss of the Prize, and if thou miss of that, I am sure thou wilt lose thy Soul, even that Soul which is worth more than the whole World.[40]

In this evangelical ecumenism, Bunyan shared with later Evangelicals a heartfelt concern for evangelical unity that superseded ecclesiological purity and denominational loyalty.

Nevertheless, as Bebbington's thesis has achieved widespread scholarly acceptance, "Evangelical" as a proper noun is not the most helpful label to apply to Bunyan, for it immediately raises the specter of anachronism. Yet it is important to highlight the numerous and underappreciated continuities

---

38. Morden, "John Bunyan," 87.
39. Bunyan, *Peaceable Principles and True*, 4:270.
40. Bunyan, *Heavenly Foot-Man*, 5:152-53.

that exist between Bunyan and the eighteenth- and nineteenth-century Evangelicals who revered him.

The previous sections have examined two potential historical-theological labels for Bunyan, concluding that while significant theological continuities exist, yet according to widely-accepted historical definitions, Bunyan is too late to be a Puritan and too early to be an Evangelical. Though both labels remain theologically accurate, on their own they result in historical confusion, having the appearance of anachronism that detracts from the argument of this monograph. What is needed is an historical label that highlights these theological continuities, yet also fits within the ecclesiological context of the second half of the seventeenth century. The following sections will examine specifically ecclesiological labels that could plausibly be applied to Bunyan.

Baptist

A survey of the secondary literature reveals that most scholars regard Bunyan as a Baptist; the same appears to be true of popular opinion.[41] The reason is simple: Bunyan was a credobaptist. However, the burden of this monograph has been to show that though this is the case, it is inaccurate and unhelpful to classify Bunyan as a Baptist, for it clouds the picture of what both Bunyan and the Baptists believed. The case against Bunyan's Baptist identity is comprised of two main arguments: associational and ecclesiological.

The associational argument was made in chapter 2, where it was demonstrated that while Bunyan and the Bedford Church were vitally connected to a network of open-communion churches in and around Bedfordshire, and enjoyed close relationships with Congregationalist churches in London, they refused to associate with strict-communion Baptist churches. This rejection of Baptist identity was manifested in three primary ways:

1. The Bedford Church repeatedly refused to recommend or transfer members to strict-communion Baptist churches, instead recommending them to paedobaptist Congregationalist churches.

2. In 1672, Bunyan applied for a license under the Declaration of Indulgence for himself and twenty-five others, part of a plan to establish a network of churches throughout Bedfordshire and surrounding

41. See chapter 1 for the survey of secondary literature.

counties. Though he could have applied for these licenses as a Baptist, every one of the licenses is filed as "Congregationall."

3. In 1692, four years after Bunyan's death, the Bedford Church called Ebenezer Chandler, a paedobaptist, as its pastor, demonstrating a willingness not only to receive paedobaptist members, but also to permit the practice of paedobaptism by those so convinced.

The ecclesiological argument was made in chapters 4 and 5. Chapter 4 examined the communion controversy of the 1670s, and demonstrated that Bunyan and the Baptists diverged over seven foundational ecclesiological convictions:

1. *The church as binary or ternary.* Bunyan viewed the church in binary categories, as either universal/invisible or particular/visible, and determined that baptism could not be the initiating ordinance into either one. To regard baptism as the initiating ordinance into the former would be to "unchristian" paedobaptists, and to regard baptism as the initiating ordinance into the latter would be to "unchurch" paedobaptist churches. The Baptists viewed the church in three forms: (1) the universal/invisible church comprised of all the elect of all ages; (2) the non-particular/visible church of Baptists upon the earth or within a given region; (3) a particular/visible church comprised of baptized believers bound together by covenant. According to most Baptists, baptism was the initiating ordinance into the second of the three. The necessary implication of the Baptist view is that while there may be true paedobaptist saints, there can be no true paedobaptist churches.

2. *Baptism as symbol or sacrament.* For Bunyan, baptism in water was the outward sign of the baptism of the Spirit, but there was no essential relationship between the two. Throughout the communion controversy, Bunyan only spoke of baptism in symbolic terms, never as a means of grace. Not only could water baptism and Spirit baptism be distinguished, they could be severed, such that one could and often did possess the substance without the shadow. The Baptists were unwilling to sever the sign from the thing signified. Though water baptism could be distinguished from the baptism of the Spirit, they must never be divorced such that the church accepts one who possesses the first but neglects the second. In other words, though such a thing may be possible, that does not make it permissible. William Kiffin explicitly spoke of baptism as a means of grace, the sign and seal of salvation.

If there is no sign, there is no seal. This spiritualist strain in Bunyan further separated him from the Baptists.

3. *Baptism and the regulative principle.* Both sides appealed to the regulative principle as the basis of their argument, and both sides accused the other of violating that principle in favor of human invention. Bunyan repeatedly demanded of the Baptists "precept, precedent, or example" for making baptism the initiating ordinance of the church, as well as for excluding unbaptized saints from church communion. The Baptists continually pointed to dominical precept, apostolic precedent, and primitive church pattern of those who believed the gospel receiving baptism, and only then being welcomed into church communion. Kiffin, especially, argued from the definition of the regulative principle as including both explicit command and necessary inference.

4. *Baptism as a matter of conscience or command.* Much of the communion debate revolved around the interpretation of Romans 14–15. Bunyan insisted that this text, with its instruction that the church at Rome receive those who are weak in faith despite differences of opinion in non-essential, outward, circumstantial matters of conscience, applied to the present question of baptism. For Bunyan, Romans 14–15 established a clear and undeniable paradigm: the church must receive all whom God has received, on the same basis upon which God has received them. The Baptists responded that baptism is not a matter of conscience but of command, allowing no deviation from the Scriptural institution. Furthermore, they repeatedly denied that Romans 14–15 applied to baptism, since the "weak in faith" in Rome were already baptized members of the church.

5. *Baptismal perspicuity and the need for "light."* Bunyan had a category for the convictional paedobaptist, arguing that they refused believer's baptism because they lacked sufficient "light"—i.e., the illumination of the Holy Spirit to understand the biblical administration of the ordinance. Therefore, since "whatever is not of faith is sin," paedobaptism was no breach of obedience nor smear upon the sincerity of their faith, and should not exclude them from church communion. The Baptists had no category for the convictional paedobaptist, insisting that baptism was as clear as any ordinance of Scripture, "written as with a Sun beam, that he that runs may read." Therefore, a refusal to submit to baptism was not due to a want of light, but was

either the result of a failure to "seriously enquire after it," blatant disobedience, or worse, unbelief.

6. *The membership requirements of the visible church.* For Bunyan, the membership requirements of the particular/visible church must be identical to the membership requirements of the universal/invisible church. As baptism in water is not required for membership in the latter, it must not be required for membership in the former. The only requirement for membership in the universal/invisible church is evangelical faith, made visible not by baptism, but by evangelical holiness. For the Baptists, the pattern for the visible church is not the invisible church, but the apostolic church. Therefore, the requirements for membership in the visible church must be identical to the membership requirements established in Scripture.

7. *The controlling principle of evangelical unity or ecclesiological purity.* Bunyan's conclusions were controlled by the fundamental concern for evangelical unity. A visible saint is one who possesses evangelical faith and holiness, and as such is a member of the invisible church and cannot be excluded from the visible church without provoking God to judgment by rejecting one whom He has received. The Baptists were driven by the fundamental concern for ecclesiological purity. The truth must never be sacrificed for the sake of unity. The visible church must be ordered according to the rule of Scripture. This is not to suggest that the Baptists were unconcerned about evangelical unity, or that Bunyan was unconcerned about ecclesiological purity. But when those two principles came into conflict, a choice had to be made, and Bunyan and the Baptists found themselves standing on opposite sides.

Chapter 5 examined the writings of representative seventeenth-century Baptist theologians and every significant seventeenth-century Baptist confession of faith in order to demonstrate that strict communion was not simply the majority view held by the more rigid of the Baptist sect, but was so dominant among seventeenth-century Baptists, and so integrated into their wider ecclesiology, that strict communion should be considered a seventeenth-century Baptist distinctive. On the other hand, seventeenth-century open-communion credobaptists like Bunyan were so small and isolated from the wider Baptist movement, that they should be classified as something other than Baptist.

Evangelical Independent

It has sometimes been argued that Bunyan identified himself as a Baptist, on the basis of a comment made in *The Heavenly Foot-Man*, in which Bunyan counseled his readers to "keep Company with the soundest Christians, that have most Experience of Christ, and be sure thou have a care of *Quakers, Ranters, Free-willers*: Also do not have too much Company with some *Anabaptists*, though I go under that name my self."[42] However, it ought to be noted that Greaves dates this work to 1667–1668, four years before the commencement of the communion controversy.[43] It is possible that the distance that separated Bunyan from the Baptists was not as evident to him before the controversy as it would be after. It is also possible that Bunyan was using "Anabaptist" as a synonym for "credobaptist," rather than as an ecclesiological label synonymous with "Baptist." Regardless, though Bunyan's self-identity must be taken into account, it does not outweigh the preponderance of evidence from the entirety of the seventeenth century that suggests that strict communion was a Baptist distinctive.

In summary, the only Baptist distinctive that Bunyan shared with seventeenth-century Baptists was credobaptism, but as this monograph has demonstrated, credobaptism was not sufficient to qualify one as a seventeenth-century Baptist.[44] A Baptist in the seventeenth century (and arguably still today) is, as Michael Renihan argues, one who "(1) believed in baptism for believers alone by immersion, and who (2) organized themselves into particular societies as churches of believers and baptised men and women."[45] Bunyan fits the former qualification, but repudiated the second. Therefore, Bunyan cannot be identified as a seventeenth-century Baptist. And though it is admitted that Baptist identity is ideological rather than institutional, and therefore somewhat subjective and historically fluid, it may be that the fields of Baptist history and Baptist ecclesiology would benefit from a more precise definition of what it means to be "Baptist." Then as now, the term implies more than credobaptism.

---

42. Bunyan, *Heavenly Foot-Man*, 5:153.

43. Greaves, *Glimpses of Glory*, 638.

44. Bunyan also shared with the Baptists a commitment to congregational polity and regenerate church membership, but these were not strictly seventeenth-century Baptist distinctives, as they were also held by the Congregationalists. Religious liberty, if considered a seventeenth-century Baptist distinctive, might be an exception to the statement above, for both Bunyan and the Baptists adhered to the principle. For Bunyan's views on religious liberty, see Greaves, *John Bunyan and English Nonconformity*, 51–70.

45. M. Renihan, *Antipaedobaptism*, 22.

Congregationalist

If Bunyan was not a Baptist, then what was he? It is tempting to classify Bunyan as a Congregationalist. Certainly, his closest affiliations outside of his own network of open-communion churches were with Congregationalists like John Owen, Anthony Palmer, George Griffith, and George Cokayne. And when he applied for licenses under the Declaration of Indulgence in 1672, he registered as "Congregationall." Yet "Congregationalist" is not the best term to apply to Bunyan because it demands too much historical and ecclesiological (baptismal) qualification. Prior to the Savoy Declaration in 1658, Matthew Bingham's suggestion of "baptistic congregationalist" may have been an adequate descriptor for Bunyan.[46] But with the Savoy Declaration, Congregationalism increasingly became a distinct and identifiable denomination descriptive of paedobaptist Nonconformist churches holding to congregational polity. Therefore, to describe Bunyan as a Congregationalist carries the wrong baptismal and ecclesiological connotation. Furthermore, "baptistic congregationalist" fails to adequately identify the Bedford Church, as not every member was baptized.

Evangelical Independent

This monograph suggests "Evangelical Independent" as the most accurate ecclesiological label to describe John Bunyan, the Bedford Church, and the network of open-communion churches of which it was the central hub. "Independent" distinguishes Bunyan from both Congregationalists and Baptists, and "Evangelical" acknowledges the foundational principle of Bunyan's ecclesiology—evangelical unity founded upon evangelical faith and holiness. It should be noted that this ecclesiological label employs "Evangelical" as an adjective and not as a proper noun. It is acknowledged that to do so may invite some confusion with the term as defined by Bebbington. In response, three points may be asserted. First, no other adjective adequately captures the foundational principle of Bunyan's ecclesiology, the controlling principle that determined his ecclesiological conclusions. Second, the use of the term "evangelical" to describe those committed to the principles of Reformed orthodoxy clearly predates the Evangelical

---

46. Bingham, *Orthodox Radicals*, 3–10, 40–41, 117. Numerous other scholars have likewise maintained that denominational lines were blurred in mid-century Nonconformity (see chapter 1).

Awakening of 1730s Britain. Whether or not "Evangelicalism" is to be identified as a distinct movement growing out of the Evangelical Awakening, "evangelical" as an adjective was in parlance long before the eighteenth century. Third, if it does invite historical confusion, perhaps this is an indication of greater continuity between "Evangelicals" and their Protestant ancestors than Bebbington acknowledges, and that the line of demarcation is not as clear as he assumes. As demonstrated above, there is tremendous unity between Bunyan and later Evangelicals, such that they may be regarded as the heirs of Bunyan's evangelical, ecumenical ethos.

"Independent" already has some traction in the world of Bunyan scholarship. For instance, Christopher Hill writes in his biographical study of Bunyan:

> Bunyan himself rejected the label "Baptist," no doubt in part because of his unhappiness about the rigidity of "closed-communion" Baptists.... When the Bedford church took out its license in 1672 it was as "congregational"; not "Baptist." Other churches which historians pigeon-hole as Baptist did the same. Sectarian lines were not yet fully drawn. Many churches traditionally called "congregationalist" sheltered under the name "Presbyterian" in 1672. As late as 1766 the Bedford church still thought of itself as "Independent."[47]

B. R. White writes in an influential 1972 article describing the three kinds of seventeenth-century Baptists,

> The third group, a rather loosely linked company, tended to believe Calvinistic doctrines, to share an Independent churchmanship and also to argue for believer's baptism while not excluding from church fellowship those who held infant baptism to be valid. This group is represented by Henry Jessey, John Tombes, John Bunyan, Vavasor Powell in Wales and others such as the members of the congregation at Broadmead, Bristol. They could almost equally easily be represented as "open" membership Particular Baptists or as Independents who tolerated diversity of view in their congregations about the right and proper subjects of baptism.[48]

Dewey Wallace argues that "Bunyan's specific loyalty was to a congregation on the borderline between Independent and Baptist."[49] Bunyan scholars have

---

47. Hill, *Tinker and a Poor Man*, 293–94.

48. White, "Open and Closed Membership," 330–31.

49. Wallace, "John Bunyan," 22. David Calhoun similarly labels Bunyan as "a Baptist or Independent" (Calhoun, *Grace Abounding*, 182).

long acknowledged the difficulty of labelling Bunyan a Baptist, affirming that Bunyan and the Bedford Church sat atop the proverbial wall between Baptist identity and Independency. Through the force of evidence and argument, this monograph has attempted to move Bunyan off that wall and set him firmly on the side of seventeenth-century Independency.

But "Independent," without any qualification, likewise invites confusion, for it fails to distinguish open-communion Independent churches from paedobaptist Congregationalist churches. As "Independent" and "Congregationalist" are often used synonymously to describe all non-Baptist, non-Presbyterian Nonconformists of the seventeenth century, an adjective is needed to distinguish a church like John Bunyan's from a church like John Owen's. Murray Tolmie's suggestion of "Baptistic Independent" is a tempting candidate, but again, not all members of such churches were baptized according to the credobaptist definition; furthermore, some "Baptistic Independent" churches allowed the practice of paedobaptism (e.g., the Bedford Church under Ebenezer Chandler's pastorate).[50] "Open-communion Independent" is another tempting candidate, but does not adequately describe the fundamental convictions of such churches, which were not open-communion for the sake of being open-communion, but were open-communion for the sake of evangelical unity. Thus, this monograph suggests "Evangelical" to function in this adjectival role, for no other term adequately describes the foundational principle that defined Bunyan,

---

50. "The majority of [Jessey's] congregation refused to follow his example in undergoing believer's baptism, and his church became a mixed communion congregation including Baptists and non-Baptists, based upon church covenant. Eventually most members were rebaptized, but at Jessey's death there were still some who had not adopted Baptist practices. Jessey scrupulously refused to impose uniformity in the congregation and he skillfully avoided further disputes or schisms during the rest of his pastorate. This was a considerable personal achievement, and its results were important: for 'Baptized Independent' congregations were eventually organized on Jessey's principles in various parts of England, including the Broadmead Church at Bristol and John Bunyan's church at Bedford" (Tolmie, *Triumph of the Saints*, 59–60). Tolmie earlier writes that "the parent church under Jessey's pastorate also came to practice believer's baptism on a latitudinarian basis; but the Jessey church could with equal justification be grouped as a normal example with the Independent gathered churches" (50). In fact, in a later table containing all the separate churches of London in 1646, Tolmie includes Jessey's church with the "Independent gathered churches" rather than with the Particular Baptist churches (122). Mark Bell's suggestion of "Independent Baptist" suffers from the same deficiency: "Nevertheless, the best way to characterize Jessey and other open communion Baptists like him is as an Independent Baptist.... The most famous Independent Baptist congregation was that of John Bunyan" (Bell, *Apocalypse How?*, 67–68).

the Bedford Church, and the small network of churches with which it was so intimately associated.

Bunyan wrote in his preface to *A Confession of My Faith*, "*Faith and Holiness, are my professed principles, with an endeavour, so far as in me lyeth, to be at peace with all men.*"[51] Bunyan's evangelical faith made him a Separatist. Ironically, however, his commitment to evangelical unity prevented him from being a Baptist. Were it not for his conviction regarding credobaptism, he may have been a Congregationalist. No existing ecclesiological label quite fits Bunyan; a new one is needed. Bunyan was an Evangelical Independent, as were the churches in and around Bedfordshire over which he presided as their *de facto* bishop.[52] But this label is not only crucial to understanding Bunyan, it is essential to understanding what it means to be Baptist. The fundamental issues that separated Bunyan from the Baptists in the seventeenth century remain in play today, and this monograph has sought to identify and clarify those issues. Credobaptist churches must decide which principle will take precedence: ecclesiological purity or evangelical unity. Elevating the former will make them Baptist; elevating the latter will make them like Bunyan.

---

51. Bunyan, *Confession of My Faith*, 4:135–36.

52. "[Bunyan] quickly became the organizing bishop of the whole district" (Brown, *John Bunyan*, 232). David Calhoun comments, "John Bunyan became a recognized leader among the dissenting churches of his part of England. Some, though most often in a jeering manner, called him 'Bishop Bunyan.' Bunyan ministered to his own congregation in Bedford and to other churches in Bedfordshire, Hertfordshire, Cambridgeshire, Surrey, and London, so far as it was possible in the intermittent persecution of those years" (Calhoun, *Grace Abounding*, 33).

Bibliography

Ahenakaa, Anjov. "Justification and the Christian Life in John Bunyan: A Vindication of Bunyan from the Charge of Antinomianism." PhD diss., Westminster Theological Seminary, 1997.

Alblas, Jacques B. H. "The Reception of *The Pilgrim's Progress* in Holland During the Eighteenth and Nineteenth Centuries." In *Bunyan in England and Abroad: Papers Delivered at the John Bunyan Tercentenary Symposium, Vrije Universiteit, Amsterdam 1988*, edited by M. van Os and G. J. Schutte, 121-32. Amsterdam: Vrije Universiteit Press, 1990.

Allen, William. *An Answer to Mr. J. G. His XL. Queries*. London: Printed for the Author, 1653.

———. *Some Baptismal Abuses Briefly Discovered*. London: Printed for Henry Cripps and Ledowick Lloyd, 1653.

Allison, Greg R. *Sojourners and Strangers: The Doctrine of the Church*. Foundations of Evangelical Theology. Wheaton: Crossway, 2012.

Anderson, P. J. "Letters of Henry Jessey and John Tombes to the Churches of New England, 1645." *Baptist Quarterly* 28.1 (1979) 30-40.

Anonymous. *A Continuation of Mr. Bunyan's Life*. In vol. 1 of *The Works of John Bunyan*, edited by George Offor, 62-65. London: 1854. Reprint, Edinburgh: Banner of Truth, 1991.

Archer, Robert. "Like Flowers in the Garden: John Bunyan and His Concept of the Church." *Baptist Quarterly* 36.6 (1996) 280-93.

Armitage, Thomas. *A History of the Baptists*. New York: Bryan, Taylor, and Co., 1887.

Asty, John. "Memoirs of the Life of John Owen, DD." In *A Complete Collection of the Sermons of the Reverend and Learned John Owen, DD*, edited by John Asty. London: Printed for John Clark, 1721.

Baillie, Robert. *Anabaptism, the True Fountain of Independency, Antinomy, Brownisme, Familisme, and the Most of the Other Errours, Which for the Time Doe Trouble the Church of England, Unsealed*. London: Printed for Samuel Gellibrand, 1647.

Bakewell, Thomas. *A Confutation of the Anabaptists, and All Others Who Affect Not Civill Government*. London: Printed for T. Bankes, 1644.

Bibliography

Ban, Joseph D. "Was John Bunyan a Baptist? A Case-Study in Historiography." *Baptist Quarterly* 30.8 (1984) 367–76.

Bass, Clint C. *Thomas Grantham (1633–1692) and General Baptist Theology*. Centre for Baptist Studies in Oxford. Oxford: Regent's Park College, 2019.

Bastwick, John. *Independency Not Gods Ordinance*. London: Printed for Michael Spark, 1645.

Baxter, Richard. *More Proofs of Infants Church-Membership and Consequently Their Right to Baptism*. London: Printed for N. Simmons, 1675.

Bayly, Lewis. *The Practise of Pietie*. London: Printed for John Hodgets, 1613.

Bebbington, David. *Evangelicalism in Modern Britain: A History from the 1730s to the 1980s*. London: Unwin Hyman/Routledge, 1989. Reprint, New York: Routledge, 1993.

———. "Response." In *The Emergence of Evangelicalism*, edited by Michael A. G. Haykin and Kenneth J. Stewart, 417–32. Nottingham: APOLLOS, 2008.

Beeke, Joel R. "John Bunyan on Justification." *Puritan Reformed Journal* 5.2 (2013) 107–30.

Beeke, Joel R., and Mark Jones. *A Puritan Theology: Doctrine for Life*. Grand Rapids: Reformation Heritage, 2012.

Beeke, Joel R., and Randall J. Pederson. *Meet the Puritans: With a Guide to Modern Reprints*. Grand Rapids: Reformation Heritage, 2006.

Bell, Mark R. *Apocalypse How? Baptist Movements During the English Revolution*. Macon: Mercer University Press, 2000.

Belyea, Gordon L. "Origins of the Particular Baptists." *Themelios* 32.3 (2007) 40–67.

Bingham, Matthew C. *Orthodox Radicals: Baptist Identity in the English Revolution*. Oxford Studies in Historical Theology. Oxford: Oxford University Press, 2019.

Birch, Ian. *"To Follow the Lambe Wheresoever He Goeth:" The Ecclesial Polity of the English Calvinistic Baptists 1640–1660*. Monographs in Baptist History. Eugene: Pickwick, 2017.

Blinman, Richard. *An Essay Tending to Issue the Controversie about Infant Baptism*. London: Printed for Richard Chiswell, 1674.

Booth, Abraham. *Apology for the Baptists*. 1778. Reprint, Boston: Manning and Loring, 1808.

Brachlow, Stephen. *The Communion of Saints: Radical Puritans and Separatist Ecclesiology, 1570–1625*. Oxford: Oxford University Press, 1988.

A Brief Confession or Declaration of Faith: Set Forth by Many of Us, Who Are (Falsely) Called Ana-Baptists [*The Standard Confession*]. London: Printed for F. Smith, 1660.

Brown, John. *The House of God Opened and His Table Free for Baptists and Paedobaptists*. London: Printed for the Author, 1777.

Brown, John. *John Bunyan: His Life, Times, and Work*. London: Wm. Isbister, 1886. Reprint, Delhi: Facsimile, 2020.

Brown, Sylvia. "Bunyan and Empire." In *The Oxford Handbook of John Bunyan*, edited by Michael Davies and W. R. Owens, 665–81. Oxford: Oxford University Press, 2018.

Bulkley, Stephen. *A Short History of the Anabaptists of High and Low Germany*. York: N.p., 1643.

Bunyan, John. *The Acceptable Sacrifice: Or, the Excellency of a Broken Heart*. In vol. 12 of *The Miscellaneous Works of John Bunyan*, edited by W. R. Owens, 1–82. Oxford: Clarendon, 1994.

———. *The Advocateship of Jesus Christ*. In vol. 11 of *The Miscellaneous Works of John Bunyan*, edited by Richard L. Greaves, 93–216. Oxford: Clarendon, 1985.

Bibliography

———. *The Barren Fig-Tree*. In vol. 5 of *The Miscellaneous Works of John Bunyan*, edited by Graham Midgeley, 1–64. Oxford: Clarendon, 1986.

———. *A Book for Boys and Girls*. In vol. 6 of *The Miscellaneous Works of John Bunyan*, edited by Graham Midgeley, 183–270. Oxford: Clarendon, 1980.

———. *A Case of Conscience Resolved*. In vol. 4 of *The Miscellaneous Works of John Bunyan*, edited by T. L. Underwood, 291–330. Oxford: Clarendon, 1990.

———. *A Caution to Stir Up to Watch Against Sin*. In vol. 6 of *The Miscellaneous Works of John Bunyan*, edited by Graham Midgeley, 175–82. Oxford: Clarendon, 1980.

———. *Christ a Compleat Saviour*. In vol. 13 of *The Miscellaneous Works of John Bunyan*, edited by W. R. Owens, 253–334. Oxford: Clarendon, 1994.

———. *Christian Behaviour*. In vol. 3 of *The Miscellaneous Works of John Bunyan*, edited by J. Sears McGee, 1–62. Oxford: Clarendon, 1987.

———. *Come & Welcome to Jesus Christ*. In vol. 8 of *The Miscellaneous Works of John Bunyan*, edited by Richard L. Greaves, 229–392. Oxford: Clarendon, 1979.

———. *A Confession of My Faith, and a Reason of My Practice*. In vol. 4 of *The Miscellaneous Works of John Bunyan*, edited by T. L. Underwood, 131–88. Oxford: Clarendon, 1990.

———. *A Defence of the Doctrine of Justification by Faith in Jesus Christ*. In vol. 4 of *The Miscellaneous Works of John Bunyan*, edited by T. L. Underwood, 1–130. Oxford: Clarendon, 1990.

———. *The Desire of the Righteous Granted*. In vol. 13 of *The Miscellaneous Works of John Bunyan*, edited by W. R. Owens, 97–160. Oxford: Clarendon, 1994.

———. *Differences in Judgment About Water-Baptism, No Bar to Communion*. In vol. 4 of *The Miscellaneous Works of John Bunyan*, edited by T. L. Underwood, 189–264. Oxford: Clarendon, 1990.

———. *A Discourse of the Building, Nature, Excellency, and Government of the House of God*. In vol. 6 of *The Miscellaneous Works of John Bunyan*, edited by Graham Midgeley, 271–317. Oxford: Clarendon, 1980.

———. *A Discourse of the House of the Forest of Lebanon*. In vol. 7 of *The Miscellaneous Works of John Bunyan*, edited by Graham Midgeley, 117–74. Oxford: Clarendon, 1989.

———. *A Discourse upon the Pharisee and the Publicane*. In vol. 10 of *The Miscellaneous Works of John Bunyan*, edited by Owen C. Watkins, 105–236. Oxford: Clarendon, 1988.

———. *The Doctrine of the Law and Grace Unfolded*. In vol. 2 of *The Miscellaneous Works of John Bunyan*, edited by Richard L. Greaves, 1–226. Oxford: Clarendon, 1975.

———. *Ebal and Gerazim*. In vol. 6 of *The Miscellaneous Works of John Bunyan*, edited by Graham Midgeley, 103–28. Oxford: Clarendon, 1980.

———. *An Exhortation to Peace and Unity* [Apocryphal]. In vol. 2 of *The Works of John Bunyan*, edited by George Offor, 742–54. London: 1854. Reprint, Edinburgh: Banner of Truth, 1991.

———. *An Exposition of the First Ten Chapters of Genesis, and Part of the Eleventh*. In vol. 12 of *The Miscellaneous Works of John Bunyan*, edited by W. R. Owens, 95–278. Oxford: Clarendon, 1994.

———. *A Few Sighs from Hell*. In vol. 1 of *The Miscellaneous Works of John Bunyan*, edited by T. L. Underwood and Roger Sharrock, 221–383. Oxford: Clarendon, 1980.

———. *Grace Abounding to the Chief of Sinners*. In *Grace Abounding with Other Spiritual Autobiographies*, edited by John Stachniewski and Anita Pacheco. Oxford: Oxford University Press, 2008.

Bibliography

———. *The Greatness of the Soul, and the Unspeakableness of the Loss Thereof*. In vol. 9 of *The Miscellaneous Works of John Bunyan*, edited by Richard L. Greaves, 133–246. Oxford: Clarendon, 1981.

———. *The Heavenly Foot-Man*. In vol. 5 of *The Miscellaneous Works of John Bunyan*, edited by Graham Midgeley, 131–78. Oxford: Clarendon, 1986.

———. *The Holy City*. In vol. 3 of *The Miscellaneous Works of John Bunyan*, edited by J. Sears McGee, 63–196. Oxford: Clarendon, 1987.

———. *A Holy Life the Beauty of Christianity*. In vol. 9 of *The Miscellaneous Works of John Bunyan*, edited by Richard L. Greaves, 247–352. Oxford: Clarendon, 1981.

———. *The Holy War*. Edited by Roger Sharrock and James F. Forrest. Oxford: Clarendon, 1980.

———. *I Will Pray with the Spirit and with the Understanding Also*. In vol. 2 of *The Miscellaneous Works of John Bunyan*, edited by Richard L. Greaves, 227–86. Oxford: Clarendon, 1975.

———. *Instruction for the Ignorant*. In vol. 8 of *The Miscellaneous Works of John Bunyan*, edited by Richard L. Greaves, 1–44. Oxford: Clarendon, 1979.

———. *Israel's Hope Encouraged*. In vol. 13 of *The Miscellaneous Works of John Bunyan*, edited by W. R. Owens, 1–96. Oxford: Clarendon, 1994.

———. *The Jerusalem Sinner Saved: Or, Good News for the Vilest of Men*. In vol. 11 of *The Miscellaneous Works of John Bunyan*, edited by Richard L. Greaves, 1–92. Oxford: Clarendon, 1985.

———. *The Life and Death of Mr. Badman*. Edited by James F. Forrest and Roger Sharrock. Oxford: Clarendon, 1988.

———. *Light for Them that Sit in Darkness*. In vol. 8 of *The Miscellaneous Works of John Bunyan*, edited by Richard L. Greaves, 45–160. Oxford: Clarendon, 1979.

———. *A Mapp Shewing the Order and Causes of Salvation and Damnation*. In vol. 12 of *The Miscellaneous Works of John Bunyan*, edited by W. R. Owens, 415–24. Oxford: Clarendon, 1994.

———. *Mr. John Bunyan's Last Sermon*. In vol. 12 of *The Miscellaneous Works of John Bunyan*, edited by W. R. Owens, 83–94. Oxford: Clarendon, 1994.

———. *Of Antichrist, and His Ruine*. In vol. 13 of *The Miscellaneous Works of John Bunyan*, edited by W. R. Owens, 417–504. Oxford: Clarendon, 1994.

———. *Of Justification by an Imputed Righteousness*. In vol. 12 of *The Miscellaneous Works of John Bunyan*, edited by W. R. Owens, 279–352. Oxford: Clarendon, 1994.

———. *Of the Law and a Christian*. In vol. 12 of *The Miscellaneous Works of John Bunyan*, edited by W. R. Owens, 407–14. Oxford: Clarendon, 1994.

———. *Of the Trinity and a Christian*. In vol. 12 of *The Miscellaneous Works of John Bunyan*, edited by W. R. Owens, 399–406. Oxford: Clarendon, 1994.

———. *On the Love of Christ*. In vol. 6 of *The Miscellaneous Works of John Bunyan*, edited by Graham Midgeley, 129–32. Oxford: Clarendon, 1980.

———. *One Thing Is Needful*. In vol. 6 of *The Miscellaneous Works of John Bunyan*, edited by Graham Midgeley, 53–102. Oxford: Clarendon, 1980.

———. *Paul's Departure and Crown*. In vol. 12 of *The Miscellaneous Works of John Bunyan*, edited by W. R. Owens, 353–98. Oxford: Clarendon, 1994.

———. *Peaceable Principles and True*. In vol. 4 of *The Miscellaneous Works of John Bunyan*, edited by T. L. Underwood, 265–90. Oxford: Clarendon, 1990.

———. *The Pilgrim's Progress*. Edited by W. R. Owens. Oxford: Oxford University Press, 2003.

BIBLIOGRAPHY

———. *Prison Meditations.* In vol. 6 of *The Miscellaneous Works of John Bunyan*, edited by Graham Midgeley, 37–52. Oxford: Clarendon, 1980.

———. *Profitable Meditations.* In vol. 6 of *The Miscellaneous Works of John Bunyan*, edited by Graham Midgeley, 1–36. Oxford: Clarendon, 1980.

———. *Questions about the Nature and Perpetuity of the Seventh-Day-Sabbath.* In vol. 4 of *The Miscellaneous Works of John Bunyan*, edited by T. L. Underwood, 331–90. Oxford: Clarendon, 1990.

———. *A Relation of the Imprisonment of Mr. John Bunyan.* In *Grace Abounding with Other Spiritual Autobiographies*, edited by John Stachniewski and Anita Pacheco, 95–122. Oxford: Oxford University Press, 2008.

———. *Reprobation Asserted.* In vol. 2 of *The Works of John Bunyan*, edited by George Offor, 335–58. London: 1854. Reprint, Edinburgh: Banner of Truth, 1991.

———. *The Resurrection of the Dead, and Eternal Judgment.* In vol. 3 of *The Miscellaneous Works of John Bunyan*, edited by J. Sears McGee, 197–292. Oxford: Clarendon, 1987.

———. *The Saints Knowledge of Christ's Love.* In vol. 13 of *The Miscellaneous Works of John Bunyan*, edited by W. R. Owens, 335–416. Oxford: Clarendon, 1994.

———. *Saved by Grace.* In vol. 8 of *The Miscellaneous Works of John Bunyan*, edited by Richard L. Greaves, 161–228. Oxford: Clarendon, 1979.

———. *Scriptural Poems.* In vol. 2 of *The Works of John Bunyan*, edited by George Offor, 389–412. London: 1854. Reprint, Edinburgh: Banner of Truth, 1991.

———. *Seasonable Counsel: Or, Advice to Sufferers.* In vol. 10 of *The Miscellaneous Works of John Bunyan*, edited by Owen C. Watkins, 1–104. Oxford: Clarendon, 1988.

———. *Solomon's Temple Spiritualiz'd.* In vol. 7 of *The Miscellaneous Works of John Bunyan*, edited by Graham Midgeley, 1–116. Oxford: Clarendon, 1989.

———. *Some Gospel-Truths Opened According to the Scriptures.* In vol. 1 of *The Miscellaneous Works of John Bunyan*, edited by T. L. Underwood and Roger Sharrock, 1–116. Oxford: Clarendon, 1980.

———. *The Strait Gate.* In vol. 5 of *The Miscellaneous Works of John Bunyan*, edited by Graham Midgeley, 65–130. Oxford: Clarendon, 1986.

———. *A Treatise on the Fear of God.* In vol. 9 of *The Miscellaneous Works of John Bunyan*, edited by Richard L. Greaves, 1–132. Oxford: Clarendon, 1981.

———. *A Vindication of the Book Called, Some Gospel-Truths Opened.* In vol. 1 of *The Miscellaneous Works of John Bunyan*, edited by T. L. Underwood and Roger Sharrock, 117–220. Oxford: Clarendon, 1980.

———. *The Water of Life.* In vol. 7 of *The Miscellaneous Works of John Bunyan*, edited by Graham Midgeley, 175–220. Oxford: Clarendon, 1989.

———. *The Works of John Bunyan.* Edited by George Offor. 3 vols. London: 1854. Reprint, Edinburgh: Banner of Truth, 1991.

Burrage, Champlin. *The Early English Dissenters in the Light of Recent Research (1550–1641).* 2 vols. New York: Russell & Russell, 1966.

Burrough, Edward. *The True Faith of the Gospel of Peace Contended For, in the Spirit of Meekness: And the Mystery of Salvation (Christ Within, the Hope of Glory) Vindicated in the Spirit of Love against the Secret Opposition of John Bunyan, A Professed Minister in Bedfordshire.* London: Printed for Giles Calvert, 1656.

Buttfield, William. *Free Communion an Innovation, Or, An Answer to Mr. John Brown's Pamphlet, Entitled, The House of God Opened and His Table Free, &c.* London: Printed for G. Keith, 1778.

BIBLIOGRAPHY

Calhoun, David B. *Grace Abounding: The Life, Books & Influence of John Bunyan.* Geanies House, Fearn: Christian Focus, 2005.

Campbell, Gordon. "'Fishing in Other Men's Waters: Bunyan and the Theologians." In *Conventicle and Parnassus, Tercentenary Essays,* edited by N. H. Keeble, 137–51. Oxford: Oxford University Press, 1988.

Church Book of Bunyan Meeting, 1650–1821. Edited by G. B. Harrison. London: J. M. Dent & Sons, 1928.

Clarke, Anthony. "A Feast for All? Reflecting on Open Communion for the Contemporary Church." In *Baptist Sacramentalism 2,* edited by Anthony R. Cross and Philip E. Thompson, 92–116. Milton Keynes: Paternoster, 2008.

Clarke, Samuel. *A Mirrour or Looking-Glass Both for Saints and Sinners.* London: Printed for John Bellamy, 1646.

Coffey, John, and Paul C. H. Lim, eds. *The Cambridge Companion to Puritanism.* Cambridge: Cambridge University Press, 2008.

Coleridge, Samuel Taylor. *The Literary Remains of Samuel Taylor Coleridge.* Edited by Henry Nelson Coleridge. Vol. 3. London: William Pickering, 1838.

———. *Marginalia: Part 2.* Edited by George Whalley. Vol. 12 of *The Collected Works of Samuel Taylor Coleridge.* Princeton: Princeton University Press, 1985.

Collinson, Patrick. *The Elizabethan Puritan Movement.* Oxford: Oxford University Press, 1990.

Collmer, Robert G., ed. *Bunyan in Our Time.* Kent: Kent State University Press, 1989.

A Confession of Faith of Seven Congregations or Churches of Christ in London, Which Are Commonly (but Unjustly) Called Anabaptists. London: Printed for John Hancock, 1646.

A Confession of Faith of Several Churches of Christ, in the County of Somerset, and of Some Churches in the Counties Neer Adjacent. London: Printed for Thomas Brewster, 1656.

The Confession of Faith, of Those Churches Which Are Commonly (Though Falsly) Called Anabaptists. London: N.p., 1644.

A Confession of Faith, Put Forth by the Elders and Brethren of Many Congregations of Christians (Baptized upon Profession of Their Faith) in London and the Country. London: N.p., 1677.

Copeland, David A. *Benjamin Keach and the Development of Baptist Traditions in Seventeenth-Century England.* Lampeter: Edwin Mellen, 2001.

Cox, Francis A. *A Letter on Free Communion from a Pastor to the People of His Charge.* London: N.p., 1818.

Coxe, Benjamin. *An Appendix to the Confession of Faith.* London: N.p., 1646.

Cross, Anthony R. "Baptismal Regeneration: Rehabilitating a Lost Dimension of New Testament Baptism." In *Baptist Sacramentalism 2,* edited by Anthony R. Cross and Philip E. Thompson, 149–74. Milton Keynes: Paternoster, 2008.

Cross, Anthony R., and Philip E. Thompson, eds. *Baptist Sacramentalism 2.* Studies in Baptist History and Thought. Milton Keynes: Paternoster, 2008.

Dagg, John L. *An Essay in Defense of Strict Communion.* Penfield: Benjamin Bradley, 1845.

———. *A Treatise on Church Order.* Charleston: Southern Baptist, 1858. Reprint, Paris: Baptist Standard Bearer, 2006.

Danvers, Henry. *A Treatise of Baptism.* London: Printed for Francis Smith, 1673.

Davies, Michael. "*Grace Abounding to the Chief of Sinners*: John Bunyan and Spiritual Autobiography." In *The Cambridge Companion to Bunyan,* edited by Anne Dunan-Page, 67–79. Cambridge: Cambridge University Press, 2010.

———. *Graceful Reading: Theology and Narrative in the Works of John Bunyan*. Oxford: Oxford University Press, 2002.

———. "Spirit in the Letters: John Bunyan's Congregational Epistles." *Seventeenth Century* 24.2 (2009) 323–60.

Davies, Michael, and W. R. Owens, eds. *The Oxford Handbook of John Bunyan*. Oxford: Oxford University Press, 2018.

A Declaration of the Faith and Order Owned and Practiced in the Congregational Churches of England. London: N.p., 1659.

Denne, Henry. *The Quaker No Papist, in Answer to The Quaker Disarm'd*. London: Printed for Francis Smith, 1659.

Denne, John. *Truth Outweighing Error*. London: Printed for Francis Smith, 1673.

Dent, Arthur. *The Plaine Mans Path-Way to Heaven*. London: Printed for Robert Dexter, 1601.

Desiring God. "Are Paedobaptists Unrepentant?" *Desiring God* (blog), August 17, 2007. https://www.desiringgod.org/articles/are-paedobaptists-unrepentant.

Dever, Mark E. "The Spiritual Church: 'Let Us Not Divide'—John Bunyan and Baptism." *Bibliotheca Sacra* 172 (2015) 131–38.

Dod, John, and Robert Cleaver. *A Plaine and Familiar Exposition of the Tenne Commandements*. London: Printed for Thomas Man, 1605.

Doe, Charles. *The Struggler*. In vol. 3 of *The Works of John Bunyan*, edited by George Offor, 763–68. London: 1854. Reprint, Edinburgh: Banner of Truth, 1991.

Dowley, T. E. "A London Congregation during the Great Persecution: Petty France Particular Baptist Church, 1641–1688." *Baptist Quarterly* 27 (1977–1978) 233–39.

Duesing, Jason G. *Henry Jessey: Puritan Chaplain, Independent and Baptist Pastor, Millenarian Politician and Prophet*. Mountain Home: BorderStone: 2014.

Dunan-Page, Anne. "John Bunyan's *A Confession of My Faith* and Restoration Anabaptism." *Prose Studies* 28.1 (2006) 19–40.

Dunan-Page, Anne, ed. *The Cambridge Companion to Bunyan*. Cambridge: Cambridge University Press, 2010.

Early, Joe. *The Life and Writings of Thomas Helwys*, Early English Baptist Texts. Macon: Mercer University Press, 2009.

Edwards, Jonathan. *The Distinguishing Marks of a Work of the Spirit of God*. In vol. 2 of *The Works of Jonathan Edwards*, 257–77. Peabody: Hendrickson, 2003.

———. *A Treatise Concerning the Religious Affections*. In vol. 1 of *The Works of Jonathan Edwards*, 234–343. Peabody: Hendrickson, 2003.

Edwards, Thomas. *Gangraena: Or a Catalogue and Discovery of Many of the Errours, Blaphemies and Pernicious Practices of the Sectaries in This Time*. London: Printed for Ralph Smith, 1646.

Estep, William R. *The Anabaptist Story: An Introduction to Sixteenth-Century Anabaptism*. 3rd ed. Grand Rapids: Eerdmans, 1996.

Everitt, Alan. *The Community of Kent and the Great Rebellion 1640–1660*. Leicester: Leicester University Press, 1966.

The Faith and Practice of Thirty Congregations, Gathered According to the Primitive Pattern. In *Baptist Confessions of Faith*, edited by William Lumpkin, 174–88. Rev. ed. Valley Forge: Judson, 1969.

Featley, Daniel. *The Dippers Dip't*. 1645. 7th ed. London: Printed for Richard Royston, 1660.

Bibliography

———. "A Warning for England Especially for London in the Famous History of the Frantick Anabaptists Their Wild Preachings & Practices in Germany." In *The Dippers Dip't*, 217–58. 7th ed. London: Printed for Richard Royston, 1660.

Fiddes, Paul S. "Baptists and 1662: The Effect of the Act of Uniformity on Baptists and its Ecumenical Significance for Baptists Today." *Ecclesiology* 9 (2013) 183–204.

———. "Covenant and the Inheritance of Separatism." In *The Fourth Strand of the Reformation: The Covenant Ecclesiology of Anabaptists, English Separatists, and Early General Baptists*, edited by Paul S. Fiddes, 63–91. Centre for Baptist History and Heritage Studies. Oxford: Regent's Park College, 2018.

———. "Introduction: The Fourth Strand?" In *The Fourth Strand of the Reformation: The Covenant Ecclesiology of Anabaptists, English Separatists, and Early General Baptists*, edited by Paul S. Fiddes, 1–14. Centre for Baptist History and Heritage Studies. Oxford: Regent's Park College, 2018.

Fiddes, Paul S., ed. *The Fourth Strand of the Reformation: The Covenant Ecclesiology of Anabaptists, English Separatists, and Early General Baptists*. Centre for Baptist History and Heritage Studies. Oxford: Regent's Park College, 2018.

Finn, Nathan A. "Baptism as a Prerequisite to the Lord's Supper." White Paper 9, Center for Theological Research, 2006.

Forrest, James F. "Allegory as Sacred Sport: Manipulation of the Reader in Spenser and Bunyan." In *Bunyan in Our Time*, edited by Robert G. Collmer, 93–112. Kent: Kent State University Press, 1989.

Fowler, Edward. *The Design of Christianity*. London: Printed for R. Royston, 1671.

Fowler, Stanley. *More Than a Symbol: The British Baptist Recovery of Baptist Sacramentalism*. Studies in Baptist History and Thought. Carlisle: Paternoster, 2002.

Foxe, John. *The Acts and Monuments of John Foxe: A New and Complete Edition*. Edited by George Townsend and Stephen Reed Cattley. 8 vols. London: R. B. Seeley and W. Burnside, 1837–1841.

Fuller, Andrew. *The Admission of Unbaptized Persons to the Lord's Supper Inconsistent with the New Testament*. In *The Complete Works of Andrew Fuller, With a Memoir of His Life*, 855–59. London: G. and J. Dyer, Paternoster Row, 1846.

———. *The Gospel Worthy of All Acceptation; or, The Duty of Sinners to Believe in Jesus Christ*. 1784. Reprint, Boston: American Doctrinal Tract Society, 1837.

———. *Strict Communion in the Mission Church at Serampore*. In *The Complete Works of Andrew Fuller, With a Memoir of His Life*, 855. London: G. and J. Dyer, Paternoster Row, 1846.

———. *Strictures on the Rev. John Carter's "Thoughts on Baptism and Mixed Communion, in Three Letters to a Friend; in Which Some Animadversions Are Made on the Rev. Abraham Booth's Apology."* In *The Complete Works of Andrew Fuller, With a Memoir of His Life*, 853–54. London: G. and J. Dyer, Paternoster Row, 1846.

———. *Thoughts on Open Communion, in a Letter to the Rev. W. Ward, Missionary at Serampore*. In *The Complete Works of Andrew Fuller, With a Memoir of His Life*, 854–55. London: G. and J. Dyer, Paternoster Row, 1846.

Furlong, Monica. *Puritan's Progress: A Study of John Bunyan*. London: Hodder & Stoughton, 1975.

Garrett, James Leo. *Baptist Theology: A Four-Century Study*. Macon: Mercer University Press, 2009.

———. "Restitution and Dissent Among Early English Baptists: Part 1." *Baptist History and Heritage* 12.4 (1977) 198–210.

Bibliography

Gay, David, et al., eds. *Awakening Words: John Bunyan and the Language of Community.* Newark: University of Delaware Press, 2000.

George, Timothy, and David S. Dockery, eds. *Baptist Theologians.* Nashville: Broadman, 1990.

Goodwin, John. *Cata-Baptism: Or New Baptism, Waxing Old, and Ready to Vanish Away.* London: Printed for H. Cripps and L. Lloyd, 1655.

———. *Philadelphia: Or, XL. Queries.* London: Printed for Henry Cripps and Lodowick Lloyd, 1653.

———. *Water-Dipping No Firm Footing for Church-Communion.* London: Printed for Henry Cripps and Lodowick Lloyd, 1653.

Grantham, Thomas. *Christianismus Primitivus: Or, the Ancient Christian Religion.* London: Printed for Francis Smith, 1678.

———. *St. Paul's Catechism.* London: Printed for J. Darby, 1693.

Greaves, Richard L. *Glimpses of Glory: John Bunyan and English Dissent.* Stanford: Stanford University Press, 2002.

———. "Henry Danvers." In vol. 1 of *Biographical Dictionary of British Radicals,* edited by Richard L. Greaves and Robert Zaller, 210–11. Brighton: Harvester, 1982.

———. "Henry Danvers." *Oxford Dictionary of National Biography,* January 3, 2008. https://doi.org/10.1093/ref:odnb/7134.

———. *John Bunyan.* Courtenay Studies in Reformation Theology. Grand Rapids: Eerdmans, 1969.

———. "John Bunyan and the Authorship of Reprobation Asserted." *Baptist Quarterly* 21.3 (1965) 126–31.

———. *John Bunyan and English Nonconformity.* London: Hambledon, 1992.

———. "John Bunyan's 'Holy War' and London Nonconformity." *Baptist Quarterly* 26.4 (1975) 158–68.

———. "The Organizational Response of Nonconformity to Repression and Indulgence: The Case of Bedfordshire." *Church History* 44 (1975) 1–13.

———. *Saints and Rebels: Seven Nonconformists in Stuart England.* Macon: Mercer University Press, 1985.

Greaves, Richard L., and Robert Zaller, eds. *Biographical Dictionary of British Radicals in the Seventeenth Century.* 3 vols. Brighton: Harvester, 1982–1984.

Gribben, Crawford. *The Puritan Millennium: Literature and Theology, 1550–1682.* Studies in Christian History and Thought. Rev. ed. Eugene: Wipf & Stock, 2008.

Griffith, John. *A Voice from the Word of the Lord to Those Grand Impostors Called Quakers.* London: Printed for Francis Smith, 1654.

Grudem, Wayne. *Systematic Theology: An Introduction to Bible Doctrine.* Grand Rapids: Zondervan, 1994.

———. *Systematic Theology: An Introduction to Bible Doctrine.* Rev. ed. Grand Rapids: Zondervan, 2007.

Hall, David D. *The Puritans: A Transatlantic History.* Princeton: Princeton University Press, 2019.

Hall, Robert. *On Terms of Communion, with a Particular View to the Case of the Baptists and Paedobaptists.* Boston: Wells and Lilly, 1816.

———. *A Reply to the Rev. Joseph Kinghorn.* Leicester: Thomas Combe, 1818.

Hammett, John S. *Biblical Foundations for Baptist Churches: A Contemporary Ecclesiology.* 2nd ed. Grand Rapids: Kregel Academic & Professional, 2019.

Bibliography

———. "Church Membership, Church Discipline, and the Nature of the Church." In *Those Who Must Give an Account: A Study of Church Membership and Church Discipline*, edited by John S. Hammett and Benjamin L. Merkle, 7–28. Nashville: B&H Academic, 2012.

———. *40 Questions About Baptism and the Lord's Supper*. Grand Rapids: Kregel Academic, 2015.

———. "Regenerate Church Membership." In *Restoring Integrity in Baptist Churches*, edited by Thomas White et al., 21–43. Grand Rapids: Kregel, 2008.

Hammett, John S., and Benjamin L. Merkle, eds. *Those Who Must Give an Account: A Study of Church Membership and Church Discipline*. Nashville: B&H Academic, 2012.

Hammond, Mary. "*The Pilgrim's Progress* and its Nineteenth-Century Publishers." In *Reception, Appropriation, Recollection: Bunyan's Pilgrim's Progress*, edited by W. R. Owens and Stuart Sim, 99–118. Oxford: Peter Lang, 2007.

Harding, Esther. *Journey into Self*. Boston: Sigo, 1993.

Hayden, Roger, ed. *The Records of a Church of Christ in Bristol, 1640-1687*. Bristol: Bristol Record Society, 1974.

Haykin, Michael A. G. "Evangelicalism and the Enlightenment: A Reassessment." In *The Emergence of Evangelicalism*, edited by Michael A. G. Haykin and Kenneth J. Stewart, 37–60. Nottingham: APOLLOS, 2008.

———. *Kiffin, Knollys and Keach: Rediscovering our English Baptist Heritage*. Leeds: Reformation Today, 1996.

Haykin, Michael A. G., and Kenneth J. Stewart, eds. *The Emergence of Evangelicalism: Exploring Historical Continuities*. Nottingham: APOLLOS, 2008.

Helm, Paul. "John Bunyan and 'Reprobation Asserted.'" *Baptist Quarterly* 28.2 (1979) 87–93.

Helwys, Thomas. *Confession of the Faith of the True English Church*. In *The Life and Writings of Thomas Helwys*, edited by Joe Early, 60–63. Early English Baptist Texts. Macon: Mercer University Press, 2009.

———. *A Declaration of Faith of English People Remaining at Amsterdam in Holland*. In *The Life and Writings of Thomas Helwys*, edited by Joe Early, 64–73. Early English Baptist Texts. Macon: Mercer University Press, 2009.

Hill, Christopher. "Bunyan's Contemporary Reputation." In *John Bunyan and His England, 1628-88*, edited by Anne Laurence et al., 3–15. London: Hambledon, 1990.

———. *A Tinker and a Poor Man: John Bunyan and His Church, 1628-1688*. New York: Alfred A. Knopf, 1989.

Hindmarsh, D. Bruce. *The Evangelical Conversion Narrative: Spiritual Autobiography in Early Modern England*. Oxford: Oxford University Press, 2005.

Hofmeyr, Isabel. *The Portable Bunyan: A Transnational History of the Pilgrim's Progress*. Princeton: Princeton University Press, 2004.

Howell, Robert Boyte C. *The Terms of Communion at the Lord's Table*. Philadelphia: American Baptist, 1846.

Ivimey, Joseph. *Baptism, the Scriptural and Indispensable Qualification for Communion*. London: N.p., 1824.

———. *The History of the English Baptists*. 4 vols. London: Printed for the Author, 1811–1830.

Jamieson, Bobby. *Going Public: Why Baptism Is Required for Church Membership*. Nashville: B&H Academic, 2015.

Bibliography

Jessey, Henry. "Appendix" to *Differences in Judgment About Water Baptism, No Bar to Communion*. In vol. 4 of *The Miscellaneous Works of John Bunyan*, edited by T. L. Underwood, 252–64. Oxford: Oxford University Press, 1990.

———. *A Storehouse of Provision, to Further Resolution in Severall Cases of Conscience*. London: Printed for T. Brewster, 1650.

Jeter, Jeremiah B. *Baptist Principles Reset*. Edited by R. H. Pitt. Richmond: Religious Herald, 1902.

Johnson, Galen. "'Be Not Extream': The Limits of Theory in Reading John Bunyan." *Christianity and Literature* 49.4 (2000) 447–64.

———. "The Conflicted Puritan Inheritance of John Bunyan's Political Writings." *Baptist History and Heritage* 38.2 (2003) 103–15.

———. *Prisoner of Conscience: John Bunyan on Self, Community, and Christian Faith*. Studies in Christian History and Thought. Milton Keynes: Paternoster, 2003. Reprint, Eugene: Wipf & Stock, 2005.

Jones, Marvin. *The Beginning of Baptist Ecclesiology: The Foundational Contributions of Thomas Helwys*. Monographs in Baptist History. Eugene: Pickwick, 2017.

Keach, Benjamin. *The Articles of Faith of the Church of Christ, or, Congregation Meeting at Horsley-Down*. London: N.p., 1697.

———. *The Axe Is Laid to the Root*. London: Printed for John Harris, 1693.

———. *Exposition of the Parables Series Two*. 1858. Reprint, Grand Rapids: Kregel, 1991.

———. *The Glory of a True Church, and Its Discipline Display'd*. London: N.p., 1693.

———. *Gold Refin'd: or Baptism in Its Primitive Purity*. London: Printed for the Author, to be sold by Nathaniel Crouch, 1689.

Keeble, N. H., ed. *John Bunyan: Conventicle and Parnassus, Tercentenary Essays*. Oxford: Oxford University Press, 1988.

———. "'Of Him Thousands Daily Sing and Talk': Bunyan and His Reputation." In *Conventicle and Parnassus, Tercentenary Essays*, edited by N. H. Keeble, 241–63. Oxford: Oxford University Press, 1988.

———. "William Allen." *Oxford Dictionary of National Biography*, January 3, 2008. https://doi.org/10.1093/ref:odnb/66999.

Kidd, Thomas S. *George Whitefield: America's Spiritual Founding Father*. New Haven: Yale University Press, 2014.

Kiffin, William. *A Sober Discourse of Right to Church Communion*. London: Printed for Enoch Prosser, 1681.

Kilcop, Thomas. *A Short Treatise of Baptisme*. London: N.p., 1642.

Kinghorn, Joseph. *Baptism, A Term of Communion at the Lord's Supper*. Norwich: Bacon, Kinnebrook, and Co., 1816.

———. *A Defence of "Baptism a Term of Communion." In Answer to the Rev. Robert Hall's Reply*. Norwich: Wilkin and Youngman, 1820.

Kipling, Rudyard. "The Holy War." In *The Complete Verse*, 234–35. London: Kyle Cathie, 1990.

Kishlansky, Mark. *A Monarchy Transformed: Britain 1603–1714*. New York: Penguin, 1996.

Knappen, M. M. *Tudor Puritanism: A Chapter in the History of Idealism*. Gloucester: Peter Smith, 1963.

Knollys, Hanserd. *A Moderate Answer unto Dr. Bastwicks Book; Called, Independency not Gods Ordinance*. London: Printed by Jane Coe, 1645.

———. *The World That Now Is, and the World That Is to Come*. London: Printed by Tho. Snowden, 1681.

Bibliography

Knott, John R. "Bunyan and the Holy Community." *Studies in Philology* 80.2 (1983) 200–25.
Lambe, Thomas [The "Soapboiler"]. *A Confutation of Infants Baptisme*. London: N.p., 1643.
———. *The Fountain of Free Grace Opened*. London: N.p., 1645.
Lambe, Thomas. *Truth Prevailing Against the Fiercest Opposition*. London: Printed for Francis Smith, 1653.
Larson, Timothy. "The Reception Given *Evangelicalism in Modern Britain*." In *The Emergence of Evangelicalism*, edited by Michael A. G. Haykin and Kenneth J. Stewart, 21–36. Nottingham: APOLLOS, 2008.
Laurence, Anne. "Bunyan and the Parliamentary Army." In *John Bunyan and His England, 1628–88*, edited by Anne Laurence et al., 17–29. London: Hambledon, 1990.
Laurence, Anne, et al., eds. *John Bunyan and His England, 1628–88*. London: Hambledon, 1990.
Lee, Jason K. "Baptism and Covenant." In *Restoring Integrity in Baptist Churches*, edited by Thomas White et al., 119–36. Grand Rapids: Kregel Academic, 2008.
———. *The Theology of John Smyth: Puritan, Separatist, Baptist, Mennonite*. Macon: Mercer University Press, 2003.
Leeman, Jonathan. "Baptist Sacramentology and the Concern with Donatism." *Mere Orthodoxy* (blog), January 8, 2019. https://mereorthodoxy.com/baptist-sacramentology-donatism-criticism.
———. "Church Membership and the Definition of Baptism." *Mere Orthodoxy* (blog), January 4, 2019. https://mereorthodoxy.com/church-membership-definition-baptism.
Lei, Sharon. "'To Make a Travailer of Thee': A Study of John Bunyan's Pastoral Theology with Particular Focus on Assurance." PhD diss., Trinity Evangelical Divinity School, 2014.
Lloyd-Jones, D. M. *The Puritans: Their Origins and Successors*. Edinburgh: Banner of Truth, 1987.
Luke, Samuel. *The Letter Books 1644–1645 of Sir Samuel Luke: Parliamentary Governor of Newport Pagnell*. Edited by H. G. Tibbutt. London: Her Majesty's Stationery Office, 1963.
Lumpkin, William. *Baptist Confessions of Faith*. Rev. ed. Valley Forge: Judson, 1969.
Luther, Martin. *Commentary on Galatians*. Translated by Erasmus Middleton. Grand Rapids: Kregel Classics, 1979.
Marsden, George M. *Jonathan Edwards: A Life*. New Haven: Yale University Press, 2003.
Mathis, David. "A Happy Baptist, Happy to Welcome Others: Strengthening Church Membership." *Gospel Coalition* (blog), March 6, 2012. https://www.thegospelcoalition.org/article/a-happy-baptist-happy-to-welcome-others.
Middleditch, Robert T. *A Baptist Church, the Christian's Home*. Charleston: Southern Baptist, 1854.
The Minutes of the First Independent Church (Now Bunyan Meeting) at Bedford 1656–1766. Edited by H. G. Tibbutt. Bedfordshire: Bedfordshire Historical Record Society, 1976.
Morden, Peter J. "John Bunyan: A Seventeenth-Century Evangelical?" *International Congregational Journal* 15.2 (2016) 79–100.
Mullett, Michael A. *John Bunyan in Context*. Keele: Keele University Press, 1996.
Mullins, E. Y. *The Axioms of Religion: A New Interpretation of the Baptist Faith*. Philadelphia: Griffith & Rowland, 1908.

Bibliography

Najapfour, Brian G. "John Bunyan: A Sectary or a Puritan or Both? A Historical Evaluation of His Religious Identity." *Puritan Reformed Journal* 3.2 (2011) 142–59.

Naylor, Peter. *Calvinism, Communion and the Baptists: A Study of English Calvinistic Baptists from the Late 1600s to the Early 1800s.* Studies in Baptist History and Thought. Milton Keynes: Paternoster, 2003. Reprint, Eugene: Wipf & Stock, 2006.

Newey, Vincent. "Bunyan's Afterlives: Case Studies." In *Reception, Appropriation, Recollection: Bunyan's Pilgrim's Progress*, edited by W. R. Owens and Stuart Sim, 25–48. Oxford: Peter Lang, 2007.

———. "Bunyan and the Confines of the Mind." In *The Pilgrim's Progress: Critical and Historical Views*, edited by Vincent Newey, 21–48. Totowa: Barnes & Noble, 1980.

———. "Bunyan and the Victorians." In *The Oxford Handbook of John Bunyan*, edited by Michael Davies and W. R. Owens, 573–89. Oxford: Oxford University Press, 2018.

Newey, Vincent, ed. *The Pilgrim's Progress: Critical and Historical Views.* Totowa: Barnes & Noble, 1980.

Newman, William. *Baptism: An Indispensable Pre-Requisite to Communion at the Lord's Table.* London: N.p., 1805.

———. *Moral and Ritual Precepts Compared, in a Pastoral Letter to the Baptist Church, at Bow, Middlesex, including Some Remarks on the Rev. Robert Hall's "Terms of Communion."* London: N.p., 1819.

Norman, R. Stanton. *The Baptist Way: Distinctives of a Baptist Church.* Nashville: Broadman & Holman, 2005.

Nuttall, Geoffrey F. "Church Life in Bunyan's Bedfordshire." *Baptist Quarterly* 26.7 (1976) 305–13.

———. *Visible Saints: The Congregational Way, 1640–1660.* Oxford: Blackwell, 1957.

Offor, George. "Memoir of John Bunyan." In vol. 1 of *The Works of John Bunyan*, edited by George Offor, i–lxxix. London: 1854. Reprint, Edinburgh: Banner of Truth, 1991.

Oliver, Robert W. *History of the English Calvinistic Baptists, 1771–1892: From John Gill to C. H. Spurgeon.* Edinburgh: Banner of Truth, 2006.

———. "John Collett Ryland, Daniel Turner and Robert Robinson and the Communion Controversy, 1772–1781." *Baptist Quarterly* 29 (1981) 77–79.

An Orthodox Creed: Or, A Protestant Confession of Faith. London: N.p., 1679.

Ortlund, Gavin. "Can We Reject Paedobaptism and Still Receive Paedobaptists?" *Mere Orthodoxy* (blog), January 3, 2019. https://mereorthodoxy.com/baptism-church-membership.

———. "There Is One Baptism, but Not One View of Baptism." *Mere Orthodoxy* (blog), January 7, 2019. https://mereorthodoxy.com/one-baptism-not-one-baptist-view-baptism.

Os, M. van, and G. J. Shutte, eds. *Bunyan in England and Abroad: Papers Delivered at the John Bunyan Tercentenary Symposium, Vrije Universiteit, Amsterdam 1988.* Amsterdam: Vrije Universiteit Press, 1990.

Owen, John. *A Complete Collection of the Sermons of the Reverend and Learned John Owen, DD.* Edited by John Asty. London: Printed for John Clark, 1721.

Owens, W. R. "Bunyan's Posthumously Published Works." In *The Oxford Handbook of John Bunyan*, edited by Michael Davies and W. R. Owens, 343–58. Oxford: Oxford University Press, 2018.

———. "John Bunyan and English Millenarianism." In *Awakening Words: John Bunyan and the Language of Community*, edited by David Gay et al., 81–96. Newark: University of Delaware Press, 2000.

Bibliography

———. "The Reception of *The Pilgrim's Progress* in England." In *Bunyan in England and Abroad: Papers Delivered at the John Bunyan Tercentenary Symposium, Vrije Universiteit, Amsterdam 1988*, edited by M. van Os and G. J. Schutte, 91–104. Amsterdam: Vrije Universiteit Press, 1990.

Owens, W. R., and Stuart Sim, eds. *Reception, Appropriation, Recollection: Bunyan's Pilgrim's Progress*. Oxford: Peter Lang, 2007.

Paul, Thomas. *Some Serious Reflections on That Part of Mr. Bunion's Confession of Faith*. London: Printed for Francis Smith, 1673.

Peel, Albert. *A Hundred Eminent Congregationalists, 1530–1924*. London: Independent, 1927.

Pfatteicher, Philip H. "Walking Home Together: John Bunyan and the Pilgrim Church." *Pro Ecclesia* 25.1 (2016) 90–104.

Piper, John. "Can You Update Us on the Baptism and Church Membership Issue from 2005?" *Desiring God* (blog), December 4, 2006. https://www.desiringgod.org/interviews/can-you-update-us-on-the-baptism-and-church-membership-issue-from-2005.

———. "Response to Grudem on Baptism and Church Membership." *Desiring God* (blog), August 9, 2007. https://www.desiringgod.org/articles/response-to-grudem-on-baptism-and-church-membership.

Piper, John, et al. "Baptism and Church Membership at Bethlehem Baptist Church: Eight Recommendations for Constitutional Revision." August 9, 2005. https://cdn.desiringgod.org/pdf/baptism_and_membership.pdf.

Poe, Harry L. "John Bunyan." In *Baptist Theologians*, edited by Timothy George and David S. Dockery, 26–48. Nashville: Broadman, 1990.

———. "John Bunyan's Controversy with the Baptists." *Baptist History and Heritage* 23.2 (1988) 25–35.

Pooley, Roger. "Bunyan's Reading." In *The Oxford Handbook of John Bunyan*, edited by Michael Davies and W. R. Owens, 101–16. Oxford: Oxford University Press, 2018.

———. "*Grace Abounding* and the New Sense of Self." In *John Bunyan and His England, 1628–88*, edited by Anne Laurence et al., 105–14. London: Hambledon, 1990.

———. "*The Pilgrim's Progress* and the Line of Allegory." In *The Cambridge Companion to Bunyan*, edited by Anne Dunan-Page, 80–94. Cambridge: Cambridge University Press, 2010.

Powell, Vavasor. *Common-Prayer-Book No Divine Service*. London: Printed for Livewell Chapman, 1660.

———. *The Life and Death of Mr. Vavasor Powell, that Faithful Minister and Confessor of Jesus Christ*. Edited anonymously and published posthumously. London: N.p., 1671.

———. *A New and Useful Concordance to the Holy Bible*. London: Printed for Eleanor Smith, 1671.

Price, John. *The Anabaptists Meribah; Or, Waters of Strife*. London: Printed for Henry Eversden, 1655.

Rasmussen, Joel D. S. "Bunyan and America." In *The Oxford Handbook of John Bunyan*, edited by Michael Davies and W. R. Owens, 590–607. Oxford: Oxford University Press, 2018.

Renihan, James M. *Edification and Beauty: The Practical Ecclesiology of the English Particular Baptists, 1675–1705*. Studies in Baptist History and Thought. Milton Keynes: Paternoster, 2008. Reprint, Eugene: Wipf & Stock, 2009.

Bibliography

Renihan, James M., ed. *The 1677/1689 London Baptist Confession of Faith*. Reprint, Grand Rapids: Christian Classics Ethereal Library, 1994–1999.

Renihan, Michael T. *Antipaedobaptism in the Thought of John Tombes*. Auburn: B&R, 2001.

Rigney, Joe. "Do Infant Baptisms Count? Reconsidering Open Membership." *Desiring God* (blog), July 27, 2022. https://www.desiringgod.org/articles/do-infant-baptisms-count.

Rivers, Isabel. "*The Pilgrim's Progress* in the Evangelical Revival." In *The Oxford Handbook of John Bunyan*, edited by Michael Davies and W. R. Owens, 537–54. Oxford: Oxford University Press, 2018.

Roberts, Stephen K. "Vavasor Powell." *Oxford Dictionary of National Biography*, October 3, 2013. https://doi.org/10.1093/ref:odnb/22662.

Robinson, John. *Of Religious Commvnion Private, & Publique*. N.p., 1614.

———. *The Works of John Robinson, Pastor of the Pilgrim Fathers with a Memoir of Annotations by Robert Ashton, Secretary of the Congregational Board, London*. Boston: Doctrinal Tract, 1851.

Robinson, Robert. *The General Doctrine of Toleration Applied to the Particular Case of Free Communion*. Cambridge: Printed by Francis Hodson, 1781.

Ross, Aileen. "Paradise Regained: The Development of John Bunyan's Millenarianism." In *Bunyan in England and Abroad: Papers Delivered at the John Bunyan Tercentenary Symposium, Vrije Universiteit, Amsterdam 1988*, edited by M. van Os and G. J. Schutte, 73–89. Amsterdam: Vrije Universiteit Press, 1990.

Ryland, John Collett. *A Modest Plea for Free Communion at the Lord's Table; Between True Believers of All Denominations*. London: Printed for J. Johnson, 1772.

Searle, Alison. "Bunyan and the Word." In *The Oxford Handbook of John Bunyan*, edited by Michael Davies and W. R. Owens, 86–100. Oxford: Oxford University Press, 2018.

Sharrock, Roger. "Bunyan Studies Today: An Evaluation." In *Bunyan in England and Abroad: Papers Delivered at the John Bunyan Tercentenary Symposium, Vrije Universiteit, Amsterdam 1988*, edited by M. van Os and G. J. Schutte, 45–59. Amsterdam: Vrije Universiteit Press, 1990.

———. *John Bunyan*. London: Hutchinson, 1954. Reprint, New York: St. Martin's, 1968.

———. "Spiritual Autobiography: Bunyan's *Grace Abounding*." In *John Bunyan and His England, 1628–88*, edited by Anne Laurence et al., 97–104. London: Hambledon, 1990.

———. "'When at the First I Took My Pen in Hand': Bunyan and the Book." In *John Bunyan: Conventicle and Parnassus: Tercentenary Essays*, edited by N. H. Keeble, 71–90. Oxford: Clarendon, 1988.

Shaw, George Bernard. "Better than Shakespeare." In *Dramatic Opinions and Essays*, 114–17. New York: Brentano's, 1922.

Shears, Jonathon. "Bunyan and the Romantics." In *The Oxford Handbook of John Bunyan*, edited by Michael Davies and W. R. Owens, 555–72. Oxford: Oxford University Press, 2018.

Sim, Stuart. "Bunyan and His Fundamentalist Readers." In *Reception, Appropriation, Recollection: Bunyan's Pilgrim's Progress*, edited by W. R. Owens and Stuart Sim, 213–28. Oxford: Peter Lang, 2007.

Simpson, Ken. "'The Desired Countrey': Bunyan's Writings on the Church in the 1670s." In *The Oxford Handbook of John Bunyan*, edited by Michael Davies and W. R. Owens, 220–40. Oxford: Oxford University Press, 2018.

BIBLIOGRAPHY

Sixteen Articles of Faith and Order [*The Midland Confession*]. In *Baptist Confessions of Faith*, edited by William Lumpkin, 198–200. Rev. ed. Valley Forge: Judson, 1969.

Smyth, John. *The Differences of the Churches of the Separation*. N.p., 1608.

Spilsbury, John. *A Treatise Concerning the Lawfull Subject of Baptisme*. London: N.p., 1643.

Spufford, Margaret. *Contrasting Communities: English Villagers in the Sixteenth and Seventeenth Centuries*. Cambridge: Cambridge University Press, 1974.

Spurgeon, Charles H. "The Wicked Man's Life, Funeral, and Epitaph [June 13, 1858]." In vol. 4 of *The New Park Street Pulpit*, 443. London: Passmore & Alabaster, 1858. https://www.spurgeon.org/resource-library/sermons/the-wicked-mans-life-funeral-and-epitaph/#flipbook/7.

Stewart, Kenneth J. "Did Evangelicalism Predate the Eighteenth Century? An Examination of David Bebbington's Thesis." *Evangelical Quarterly* 67.2 (2005) 135–53.

Stinton, Benjamin. *A Repository of Divers Historical Matters Relating to the English Antipedobaptists*. 1712. Unpublished manuscript held by the Angus Library, Regent's Park College, Oxford.

Straub, Jeffrey Paul. *The Making of a Battle Royal: The Rise of Liberalism in Northern Baptist Life, 1870–1920*. Monographs in Baptist History. Eugene: Pickwick, 2018.

Strong, Augustus Hopkins. *Systematic Theology*. Old Tappan: Fleming H. Revell, 1907.

Sykes, Norman. *The English Religious Tradition: Sketches of Its Influence on Church, State, and Society*. London: SCM, 1953.

Talon, Henri. *John Bunyan: The Man and His Works*. Translated by Barbara Wall. London: Rockliff, 1951.

Tibbutt, H. G., ed. *Some Early Nonconformist Church Books*. Bedfordshire: Bedfordshire Historical Society, 1972.

Tindall, William York. *John Bunyan: Mechanick Preacher*. New York: Columbia University Press, 1934. Reprint, New York: Russell & Russell, 1964.

Tolmie, Murray. *Triumph of the Saints: Separate Churches of London, 1616–1649*. Cambridge: Cambridge University Press, 1977.

Tombes, John. *An Addition to the Apology to the Two Treatises Concerning Infant-Baptism*. London: Printed for Hen. Cripps and Lodowick Lloyd, 1652.

———. *An Apology or Plea for the Two Treatises*. London: Printed for Giles Calvert, 1646.

———. *An Examen of the Sermon of Mr. Stephen Marshall About Infant Baptisme, in a Letter Sent to Him*. London: Printed for George Whitington, 1645.

The True Gospel-Faith Witnessed by the Prophets and Apostles, and Collected into Thirty Articles. London: Printed for Francis Smith, 1654.

Trueman, Carl R. "Puritan Theology as Historical Event: A Linguistic Approach to the Ecumenical Context." In *Reformation and Scholasticism: An Ecumenical Enterprise*, edited by Willem J. van Asselt and Eef Dekker, 253–75. Grand Rapids: Baker, 2001.

Turner, Daniel. *A Modest Plea for Free Communion at the Lord's Table; Particularly between the Baptists and the Paedobaptists. In a Letter to a Friend*. London: Printed for J. Johnson, 1772.

Tyler, John R. *Baptism: We've Got It Right . . . and Wrong: What Baptists Must Keep, and What We Must Change*. Macon: Smyth & Helwys, 2003.

Underwood, A. C. *A History of the English Baptists*. London: Carey Kingsgate, 1947.

Underwood, T. L. "Thomas Paul." In vol. 3 of *Biographical Dictionary of British Radicals*, edited by Richard L. Greaves and Robert Zaller, 13–14. Brighton: Harvester, 1984.

Bibliography

Urban, Josef. "John Bunyan's Experiential Exposition of the Doctrine of Justification." *Puritan Reformed Journal* 11.2 (2019) 129–58.

Vandiver, Dallas Wayne. *Who Can Take the Lord's Supper? A Biblical-Theological Argument for Close Communion*. Monographs in Baptist History. Eugene: Pickwick, 2021.

Vries, Pieter de. "John Bunyan and His Relevance for Today." *Puritan Reformed Journal* 2.1 (2010) 67–74.

———. *John Bunyan on the Order of Salvation*. Translated by C. van Haaften. New York: Peter Lang, 1994.

Waddington, John. *Congregational History 1567–1700*. London: Longmans, Green, and Co., 1874.

Wakefield, Gordon. *Bunyan the Christian*. London: HarperCollinsReligious, 1992.

Walker, David. "Bunyan's Reception in the Romantic Period." In *Reception, Appropriation, Recollection: Bunyan's Pilgrim's Progress*, edited by W. R. Owens and Stuart Sim, 49–67. Oxford: Peter Lang, 2007.

Wall, Cynthia. "Bunyan and the Early Novel." In *The Oxford Handbook of John Bunyan*, edited by Michael Davies and W. R. Owens, 521–36. Oxford: Oxford University Press, 2018.

Wallace, Dewey D. "Bunyan's Theology and Religious Context." In *The Oxford Handbook of John Bunyan*, edited by Michael Davies and W. R. Owens, 69–85. Oxford: Oxford University Press, 2018.

———. "John Bunyan: Tercentenary Publications and A Critical Edition of His Miscellaneous Writings." *Religious Studies Review* 19 (1993) 19–24.

Ward, Matthew. "Baptism as Worship: Revisiting the Kiffin/Bunyan Open-Communion Debate." *Artistic Theologian* 4 (2016) 17–31.

———. "John Tombes's Answer, 1: The Context." *Matt Ward, '97* (blog), September 29, 2014. http://mattward97.weebly.com/articles/john-tombess-answer-1-the-context.

———. "John Tombes's Answer, 2: The Relationships." *Matt Ward, '97* (blog), September 30, 2014. http://mattward97.weebly.com/articles/john-tombess-answer-2-the-relationships.

———. "John Tombes's Answer, 3: What Is Baptism?" *Matt Ward, '97* (blog), October 22, 2014. http://mattward97.weebly.com/articles/john-tombess-answer-3-what-is-baptism.

———. "John Tombes's Answer, 4: Implications." *Matt Ward, '97* (blog), October 29, 2014. http://mattward97.weebly.com/articles/john-tombess-answer-4-implications.

———. *Pure Worship: The Early English Baptist Distinctive*. Monographs in Baptist History. Eugene: Pickwick, 2014.

Watson, Jonathan D. *In the Name of Our Lord: Four Models of the Relationship between Baptism, Catechesis, & Communion*. Studies in Historical and Systematic Theology. Bellingham: Lexham, 2021.

Watts, Michael. *The Dissenters: From the Reformation to the French Revolution*. Oxford: Clarendon, 1978.

White, B. R. "Baptist Beginnings and the Kiffin Manuscript." *Baptist History and Heritage* 2.1 (1967) 27–37.

———. "The Doctrine of the Church in the Particular Baptist Confession of 1644." *Journal of Theological Studies* 19.2 (1968) 570–90.

———. *The English Puritan Tradition*. Nashville: Broadman, 1980.

———. *The English Separatist Tradition: From the Marian Martyrs to the Pilgrim Fathers*. Oxford: Oxford University Press, 1971.

Bibliography

———. "The Fellowship of Believers: Bunyan and Puritanism." In *Conventicle and Parnassus, Tercentenary Essays*, edited by N. H. Keeble, 1–19. Oxford: Oxford University Press, 1988.

———. "The Frontiers of Fellowship Between English Baptists, 1609–1660." *Foundations* 11.3 (1968) 244–56.

———. "John Denne." In vol. 1 of *Biographical Dictionary of British Radicals*, edited by Richard L. Greaves and Robert Zaller, 224–25. Brighton: Harvester, 1982.

———. "Open and Closed Membership among English and Welsh Baptists." *Baptist Quarterly* 24.7 (1972) 330–34.

———. "Samuel Eaton, Particular Baptist Pioneer." *Baptist Quarterly* 24.1 (1971) 10–21.

———. "William Kiffin." In vol. 2 of *Biographical Dictionary of British Radicals*, edited by Richard L. Greaves and Robert Zaller, 155–57. Brighton: Harvester, 1983.

White, Thomas, et al., eds. *Restoring Integrity in Baptist Churches*. Grand Rapids: Kregel Academic, 2008.

Whitley, W. T. "The Bunyan Christening." *Transactions of the Baptist Historical Society* (1911) 255–63.

Whitsitt, W. H. *A Question of Baptist History: Whether the Anabaptists in England Practiced Immersion before the Year 1641?* Louisville: C. T. Dearing, 1896.

Williams, Garry J. "Was Evangelicalism Created by the Enlightenment?" *Tyndale Bulletin* 53.2 (2002) 283–312.

Wills, Gregory A. "Sounds from Baptist History." In *The Lord's Supper: Remembering and Proclaiming Christ Until He Comes*, edited by Thomas R. Schreiner and Matthew R. Crawford, 285–312. NAS Studies in Bible & Theology. Nashville: B&H Academic, 2010.

Wills, Obediah. *Infant-Baptism Asserted and Vindicated by Scripture and Antiquity*. London: Printed for Jonathan Robinson, 1674.

Woods, A. Skevington. *The Burning Heart: John Wesley: Evangelist*. Milton Keynes: Paternoster, 1967.

Wright, Stephen. *The Early English Baptists, 1603–1649*. Woodbridge: Boydell, 2006.

———. "Thomas Lamb." *Oxford Dictionary of National Biography*, May 24, 2008. https://doi.org/10.1093/ref:odnb/15928.

Author Index

Ahenakaa, Anjov, 8n15
Alblas, Jacques B. H., 2n3
Allen, William, 158n76, 249–57, 260–62
Allison, Gregg R., 36n118
Anderson, P. J., 232n111
Archer, Robert, 8nn16–17, 139n270
Armitage, Thomas, 10n22
Asty, John, 75n17

Baillie, Robert, 218
Bakewell, Thomas, 25n75
Ban, Joseph D., 10n22, 12, 17n43, 21n59
Bass, Clint C., 262nn229–30, 263n234, 263n236
Bastwick, John, 235–36
Baxter, Richard, 10n22, 227
Bayly, Lewis, 48, 52, 283
Bebbington, David, 41, 284–91, 296–97
Beeke, Joel R., 8n15, 48nn19–20, 280n3, 281–83
Bell, Mark R., 5n8, 14, 18n45, 298n50
Belyea, Gordon L., 232n110
Bernard, Richard, 2n2
Bingham, Matthew C., 23–25, 296
Birch, Ian, 22
Blinman, Richard, 227
Booth, Abraham, 16–17, 26–28, 31n99, 39
Brachlow, Stephen, 281n4
Brontë, Charlotte, 3n5
Brown, John [18th century], 28

Brown, John [19th century], 7n14, 8n17, 10n22, 11n23, 44nn4–6, 45n8, 47n17, 48nn19–20, 58n59, 60, 63nn82–83, 67, 68n106, 72nn2–3, 75n17, 111n143, 112n146, 142n5, 144n11, 145n15, 283, 299n52
Brown, Sylvia, 2n3
Browning, Robert, 3n5
Bulkley, Stephen, 25n75
Bunyan, John, *passim. See also* Subject Index
Burrage, Champlin, 281n4
Burrough, Edward, 56n50, 173n143
Burton, John, 113n151
Buttfield, William, 28

Calhoun, David B., 3, 297n49, 299n52
Campbell, Gordon, 284n12
Clarke, Anthony, 36n118
Clarke, Samuel, 283
Coffey, John, 281n4, 281n6
Coleridge, Samuel Taylor, 3n5, 6, 57n52
Collinson, Patrick, 281n4
Collmer, Robert G., 6n9
Copeland, David A., 19n48, 265n243
Cox, Francis A., 30
Coxe, Benjamin, 219–22, 239–42
Cross, Anthony R., 195n246

Dagg, John L., 33–34

Author Index

Danvers, Henry, 28n87, 34, 77n21, 175–77, 181, 189n225, 190–91, 200, 227, 242, 261
Davies, Michael, 3n6, 6n9, 6n11, 7n13, 8n17, 43–44, 142n4
Defoe, Daniel, 3n5
Denne, Henry, 113n151, 171
Denne, John, 28n87, 34, 146n18, 160n80, 171–75, 177, 181, 183n192, 189n225, 190–91, 193–94, 198nn255–56, 199n262, 200, 203, 227, 242, 261
Dent, Arthur, 48, 52, 283
Dickens, Charles, 3n5
Dod, John, 283
Doe, Charles, 8n18, 58n59, 76n21, 210n25
Dowley, T. E., 271n262, 272n267
Duesing, Jason G., xi–xiii, 21–22, 214n43, 216n48, 219, 225n80, 231, 232nn107–11, 235, 238
Dunan-Page, Anne, 6n9, 8nn16–17, 10n21, 272–73

Early, Joe, 228, 229n97, 230n99, 230n101
Edwards, Jonathan, 287–89
Edwards, Thomas, 240n137
Eliot, George, 3n5
Estep, William R., 228, 229n97, 230n102
Everitt, Alan, 60n70

Featley, Daniel, 25n75, 240
Fiddes, Paul S., 62n80, 68n103, 78
Finn, Nathan A., 31n101, 36n118
Forrest, James F., 2n2
Fowler, Edward, 87–88, 142nn5–6
Fowler, Stanley, 36n118, 195n246
Foxe, John, 149n32, 283
Fuller, Andrew, 28, 30
Furlong, Monica, 7n12

Garrett, James Leo, 5n8, 230n102, 243n149, 243n152, 262n229, 264n239, 265n243, 266n245
Gibbs, John, 113n151
Gifford, John, 63–65, 89, 90, 108, 119, 124n206, 126n214, 144

Goodwin, John, 158n76, 243, 249–50, 252, 253–54, 257, 260–61
Grantham, Thomas, 243, 245, 262–63
Greaves, Richard L., 2n3, 7nn14–15, 8nn16–18, 9n21, 10n22, 11n24, 43n2, 44n6, 45n11, 46nn12–15, 47nn16–17, 49, 53n40, 56n48, 57n52, 58n59, 59n63, 60n68, 60n70, 61n77, 63n82, 67n101, 68n105, 70n110, 72n3, 75nn14–17, 76n18, 76n21, 85n53, 86n56, 112n147, 113n151, 128n219, 142nn5–6, 145n15, 146n17, 151n39, 160n80, 169n128, 170n129, 171nn134–35, 175n156, 177nn165–66, 181n185, 188, 189n224, 209–10, 214n43, 222n69, 226n85, 227n89, 272n268, 282n8, 284nn12–13, 289nn34–35, 295
Gribben, Crawford, 289n34
Griffith, John, 244
Grudem, Wayne, 35–36, 39n128

Hall, David D., 59n62, 280n3, 281n4, 282n9
Hall, Robert, 28–33
Hammett, John S., 5n8, 36n118
Hammond, Mary, 2n3
Harding, Esther, 7n12
Hayden, Roger, 224nn75–77, 225, 276n278
Haykin, Michael A. G., 227n86, 232n110, 264, 268, 271–72, 276n278, 283n10, 285nn17–18, 287–88
Helm, Paul, 76n21
Helwys, Thomas, 22–23, 228–30
Hill, Christopher, 2–3, 7n14, 13n31, 46n14, 47n16, 56n48, 297
Hindmarsh, D. Bruce, 4n6
Hofmeyr, Isabel, 2n3, 3, 285n19
Howell, Robert Boyte C., 31–34

Ivimey, Joseph, 30, 83n47, 271n261, 285n19

Author Index

Jamieson, Bobby, 36n117, 37–39, 195n246
Jessey, Henry, 78n25, 169–71, 189n225, 196n249, 197, 212–15, 218–22, 226, 250n178, 274
Jeter, Jeremiah B., 5n8
Johnson, Galen, 6n11, 7nn12–13, 283n11
Johnson, Samuel, 3n5
Jones, Mark, 280n3, 281–83
Jones, Marvin, 22–23

Keach, Benjamin, 264–65, 268n255, 275
Keeble, N. H., 2n3, 6nn9–10
Kendall, R. T., 288n33
Kidd, Thomas S., 287n29
Kiffin, William, 4, 27, 28n87, 30, 34, 81n35, 117, 151, 171n133, 177, 181–89, 190n227, 191–92, 194–97, 198nn255–56, 199, 201, 203–4, 227, 242, 264, 265n243, 275, 292–93
Kilcop, Thomas, 232n111
Kinghorn, Joseph, 28, 30–31
Kipling, Rudyard, 3n5
Kishlansky, Mark, 59n62, 67n101, 75n14
Knappen, M. M., 281n4
Knollys, Hanserd, 81n35, 192n235, 219–22, 235–37, 264, 268n255, 275
Knott, John R., 7n13, 289n33

Lambe, Thomas, 158n76, 177, 249, 257–61
Lambe, Thomas [The "Soapboiler"], 249n173
Larson, Timothy, 285
Laurence, Anne, 46n11
Lee, Jason K., 78n26, 228nn90–91, 229n97
Leeman, Jonathan, 36n118
Lei, Sharon, 288n33
Lewis, C. S., 3n5
Lim, Paul C. H., 281n4, 281n6
Lloyd-Jones, D. M., 280n3
Luke, Samuel, 46–47
Lumpkin, William, 25n75, 240n141, 243, 244n157, 245–47, 266, 267n250, 268, 275nn274–75

Luther, Martin, 56–58, 70

Marsden, George M., 287n29, 288n31
Marshall, Stephen, 216–17
Mathis, David, 36n117
Melville, Herman, 3n5
Middleditch, Robert T., 5n8
Morden, Peter J., 285–87, 289–90
Mullett, Michael A., 7n14, 8n16, 9n21, 10n22, 264
Mullins, E. Y., 5n8

Najapfour, Brian G., 281n3, 282n8
Naylor, Peter, 16–17, 26n80, 28n87, 28nn89–90, 30n98, 38n127, 277n279
Newey, Vincent, 2n3, 7n12
Newman, William, 30
Norman, R. Stanton, 5n8
Nuttall, Geoffrey F., 10n22, 67n101, 226n85

Offor, George, 2n2, 45n11, 49n25, 50n27, 67n101, 77n21, 83n47, 125n209, 282n9
Oliver, Robert W., 26nn80–81, 28, 29, 30n99
Ortlund, Gavin, 36n118
Overton, Richard, 2n2
Owen, John, 178, 197
Owens, W. R., 1n1, 2n3, 6n9, 86n56, 284n13

Pacheco, Anita, 1n1, 45n10, 75n16
Paul, Thomas, 9, 27, 28n87, 30, 34, 79–80, 150n36, 151–69, 171–81, 189n225, 190–94, 198nn255–56, 199–200, 201n273, 203–4, 227, 242, 264
Pederson, Randall J., 48nn19–20, 280n3
Peel, Albert, 10n22
Perkins, William, 284
Pfatteicher, Philip H., 7n13
Piper, John, 34–36, 39, 166n108
Poe, Harry L., 12–13
Pooley, Roger, 2n2, 7n12, 70n110, 149n32, 284nn12–13

Author Index

Powell, Vavasor, 222–24, 226, 278
Price, John, 260–61

Rasmussen, Joel D. S., 2n3
Renihan, James M., 18–20, 21n57, 68n104, 265n241, 275n276, 276n277
Renihan, Michael T., 15–16, 215, 216n47, 295
Rigney, Joe, 36n117
Rivers, Isabel, 2n3
Roberts, Stephen K., 222n69
Robinson, John, 228–29
Robinson, Robert, 26–28
Ross, Aileen, 86n56, 289n34
Ryland, John Collett, 26–28

Scott, Walter, 3n5
Searle, Alison, 70n110
Sharrock, Roger, 1n1, 4n6, 7n12, 7n14, 8n17, 44n6, 207n9, 208, 284n13
Shaw, George Bernard, 3n5
Shears, Jonathan, 2n3, 57n52
Sim, Stuart, 2n3
Simpson, Ken, 8n16
Smyth, John, 230
Spenser, Edmund, 2n2
Spilsbury, John, 78n25, 232n111
Spufford, Margaret, 177n166
Spurgeon, Charles H., xi–xii
Stachniewski, John, 1n1, 45n10, 75n16
Stevenson, Robert Louis, 3n5
Stewart, Kenneth J., 285n18
Stinton, Benjamin, 231nn105–6, 232n107, 235n117
Straub, Jeffrey Paul, 34n110
Strong, Augustus Hopkins, 34n110
Swift, Jonathan, 3n5
Sykes, Norman, 281n5

Talon, Henri, 7n14, 8n17, 57n52
Thackery, William Makepeace, 3n5
Tibbutt, H. G., 11n25, 109n135, 142n5, 276n276

Tindall, William York, 7n14, 8n17
Tolmie, Murray, 231nn105–6, 239, 298
Tombes, John, 215–22, 226, 235, 277
Trueman, Carl R., 281n5
Turner, Daniel, 26–28
Tyler, John R., 36n118

Underwood, A. C., 12n28, 230n102, 262n229, 271n261
Underwood, T. L., 12n27, 13n31, 146n17, 160n80, 227n87
Urban, Josef, 8n15

Vandiver, Dallas Wayne, 36n118
Vries, Pieter de, 7n15

Waddington, John, 10n22
Wakefield, Gordon, 7n14, 8nn16–17, 9n21, 57n53
Walker, David, 2n3
Wall, Cynthia, 2n3
Wallace, Dewey D., 8n16, 57n53, 85n53, 284n13, 297
Ward, Matthew, 4n7, 5n8, 20–21, 39n130, 78n25, 81n35, 192n235, 203n281, 220, 221n67
Watson, Jonathan D., 36n118
Watts, Michael, 59n62, 67n101, 75n14
White, B. R., 8n17, 9n21, 138–39, 211–12, 215, 216n47, 222, 226, 227n86, 227n88, 230n102, 231n105, 232n109, 233, 235n119, 238–39, 242, 276n278, 277, 281n4, 297
Whitley, W. T., 10n22
Whitman, Walt, 3n5
Whitsitt, W. H., 5n8
Williams, Garry J., 285n18
Wills, Gregory A., 31, 34
Wills, Obediah, 227
Woods, A. Skevington, 287n29
Wright, Stephen, 18, 230–31, 232n109, 233n112, 238–40, 249n173

Subject Index

Abaptist, 15n36, 215n44
Act of Toleration (1689), 21n59, 268, 270, 277n279, 281n5
Act of Uniformity (1662), 281. *See also* Clarendon Code (1661–65), Conventical Act (1664)
Adams, Richard, 268n255
Allen, William, 158n76, 249–57, 260–62
Anabaptist [Anabaptism]:
Continental, 9n19, 15, 18n45, 25, 215, 231
term for Baptist [or credobaptist], 9, 10n22, 13, 17n43, 88, 89n62, 90, 178, 209, 216, 218, 260, 279, 295
Ancient Church, Amsterdam, 228
Anglican [Anglicanism], 15, 49, 123, 124n202, 137n265, 146, 169, 215, 226, 277. *See also*
Church of England, Episcopalian, *and* Prelate
"Anglican Antipaedobaptist," 15, 215
Antichrist, 20, 80, 85, 90, 100, 105–6, 186, 200, 261n225, 274, 289
Antinomian [Antinomianism], 8n15, 47n16, 247n169
Antipaedobaptist, 15–16, 215
Arminian [or "Free-willer"], 8, 17n43, 243, 247n169, 266, 290, 295
Ashwell Church, Hertfordshire, 112n147

Baillie, Robert, 218
"Baptistic congregationalist," 23–25
Baptist ecclesiology, 26–39, 62n80, 144, 151–58, 171–77, 181–201, 203, 210–78, 292–94
Baptist identity, 4–5, 13–26, 65–69, 210–80, 295, 298–99
Baptist sacramentalism, 36n118, 195n246
"Baptistic Independent," 20n55, 298
Barber, Edward, 18n46, 231n103
Barebone [Barbone, Barbon], Praisegod, 20, 231, 232n107
Barclay, Robert, 264
Barrett, George, 268n255
Bastwick, John, 235–36
Batten, Jan, 232n109
Baxter, Richard, 4, 10n22, 60n68, 227, 264
Bayly, Lewis, 48, 52, 283
Beaumont, Richard, 47
Bebbington's Quadrilateral, 41, 284–91, 296–97
Bedford Church:
association with Congregationalists/Independents, 11, 21–22, 65–69, 158n77, 169n128, 205–6, 214, 291
congregational singing, 68–69, 110, 125
discipline, 68, 135–37, 143, 272

Subject Index

Bedford Church *(continued)*
  ecclesiological identity, 10n22, 11–15, 20–21, 23, 26, 41, 65–68, 112, 210, 226, 278, 296–99
  edification of members, 102–3
  foundational principles, 26, 62–65, 70, 72n2, 77–79, 104, 144, 226
  influence upon/relationship with Bunyan, 40, 43–44, 47–48, 51–52, 54–55, 57–59, 70, 72–73, 76, 99, 111, 120, 132–33, 139, 141–42, 271
  membership requirements, 64, 97–98, 298
  network of churches, 26, 67–70, 108–12, 144, 210, 214, 226, 291–92, 296, 298–99
  officers, 61–62, 72n4, 76, 110, 111n144, 113n149, 114n152, 115, 119–20, 141–42, 298–99
  origin, 59–62
  post-Bunyan, 11–12, 68–69, 110–12, 125, 292, 298
  refusal to associate with Baptists, 11, 20–21, 26, 65–67, 112, 205–6, 273, 278, 291
Bethlehem Baptist Church, Minneapolis, 35, 36n117
Beza, Theodore, 247
Bisbie, Elizabeth, 137n265
Blacklock, Samuel, 232
Blakely, Mr., 65
Blunham Church, Bedfordshire, 112n147
Blunt, Richard, 232, 238
Boar's Head Church, London, 209, 272
Bolton, Robert [Parliamentary Army Officer], 46n11
Bolton, Robert [Puritan], 61
Book of Common Prayer, 49, 122–24, 222n69, 281n5
Book of Sports (1618), 49n25
Booth, Abraham, 16–17, 26–28, 31n99, 39
Bonner, Edmund, 118n172
Bosworth, Sister, 62n77
Braintree Church, Essex, 67n100, 206

Breeden, William, 67n100
Broadmead Church, Bristol, 10n22, 19, 211, 222, 224–26, 271n262, 275–77, 297, 298n50
Brown, John [18th century], 28
Brown, Robert, 275n276, 276
Browne, Julian, 79n27
Bunhill Fields, xi–xii, 210
Bunyan, Elizabeth [Bunyan's second wife], 72n3
Bunyan, Elizabeth (b. 1654), 72n3
Bunyan, John:
  Anglican influence, 48–51, 69
  as Baptist, 8–10, 13–17, 19–22, 42, 112, 178, 183n193, 204, 226, 277–78, 280, 291–95
  as Congregationalist, 10–13, 42, 296
  as Evangelical, 41, 284–91
  as Independent, 12–13, 20n50, 23, 42, 297–98
  as Puritan, 41, 280–84, 291
  assurance, 53–58, 73–74, 286–88
  baptism, 44, 58, 72
  baptismal theology, 79, 129–32, 147–50, 159–69, 177–81, 189–90, 192–93, 195–204, 206–9, 291–95
  birth, 44
  burial, xi–xii, 210
  call to preach, 72–73, 114n152, 119–20
  childhood, 44–45
  children, 10n22, 47n17, 72n3
  conversion, 51–58
  covenant theology, 57n53, 77, 85–86, 95n79, 131, 174n147, 263n234, 284
  death, 70, 209–10
  ecclesiology, 4–5, 7–8, 40, 71–140
    discipline of the church, 134–39
    membership of the church [regenerate membership, membership requirements, congregational examination], 91–99, 139, 145–50, 159–69, 179, 189–90, 195–98, 200–3, 294

Subject Index

nature of the church [categories, form/matter, types, images, history/perpetuity], 77–86, 139, 179, 189–90, 200–1, 221, 292
officers of the church [elders/ pastors, deacons, gospel minister], 112–21, 139
ordinances of the church [baptism, Lord's Supper, terms of communion], 129–34, 139, 147–50, 159–69, 177–81, 189–90, 192–93, 195–204, 209–10, 292–94, 299
polity of the church [congregationalism, church/ state relations, congregational ministry, associationalism], 87n58, 95–98, 104–112, 139, 145
purpose of the church [evangelism, edification], 99–104, 139, 145–46, 283, 295
unity of the church [ecclesiastical separation, evangelical unity], 5, 26, 42, 86–92, 139, 146–47, 202–4, 278, 290, 294, 296–99
worship of the church [means of grace, preaching, prayer, psalm-singing, regulative principle, Lord's Day], 121–29, 139, 148, 166, 195–96, 283
ecclesiological identity, 4–5, 8–26, 41–42, 112, 204, 210, 226, 265, 277–78, 279–99
education, 44n6
eschatology, 86n56, 90, 286, 289–90
historical-critical studies of, 7
historical–theological studies of, 7–8
literary-critical analysis of, 5–7
literary legacy, 1–3
Lutheran influence, 56–58, 70
magistracy: loyalty to and limits of, 87n58, 105–7, 145–46, 283, 295
marriages, 47, 72n3
membership in Bedford Church, 58, 70, 72

mental health, 53n40
military service, 43n2, 45–47
ordained as pastor, 76, 111, 120, 141–42
parents, 44–45
preaching ministry, 72–75, 113n151
Presbyterian influence, 46, 52, 69
Puritan influence, 46–49, 52, 57n53, 69–70, 138, 283–84
religious radical influence, 46–47, 56, 69
soteriology, 4, 7, 87–88, 172, 284
theological independence, 70n110, 146n16
theological legacy, 3–4, 76
tinker, 2, 3n5, 44, 47, 51, 99, 179, 240, 283
trial and imprisonment, 43n2, 44, 53n40, 67, 75–76, 87n58, 122, 141–42, 145, 207n9
Bunyan, John (b. 1655), 72n3
Bunyan, Joseph (b. 1672), 10n22, 72n3
Bunyan, Margaret, 44n5
Bunyan, Mary (b. 1650), 47n17, 72n3
Bunyan, Sarah (b. 1666), 72n3
Bunyan, Thomas (b. 1656), 72n3
Bunyan, Thomas [Bunyan's father], 44n5
Burrough, Edward, 56n50, 173n143
Burton, John, 63n82, 108–9, 113n151, 214n43
Buttall, Samuel, 275, 276n276
Buttfield, William, 28

Caffyn, Matthew, 245, 247
Cardington Church, Bedfordshire, 112n147
Carey, William, 286
Carpenter, Richard, 46n15
Carter, John, 275, 276n276
Cattle, Timothy, 225
Chamberlaine, Sister, 97n88
Chandler, Ebenezer, 11n27, 68–69, 110–12, 125n208, 292, 298
Charles I, 45n11
Charles II, 75, 189, 233, 245, 283
Child, John, 109, 111, 137n265, 222n69, 272, 273n269

325

Subject Index

Church of England, xi, 10n22, 17, 23, 44n6, 48–51, 69, 75n17, 87–88, 91, 137, 218, 228, 236–37, 247n168, 261, 277, 281. *See also* Anglican, Episcopalian, *and* Prelate
Clarendon Code (1661–65), 201. *See also* Act of Uniformity (1662), Conventical Act (1664)
Clarke, Samuel, 283
Cokayne, George, 11, 66–67, 206, 209, 210n28, 296
Cokayne, Richard, 45n11
Coleman Street Church, London, 249
Collier, Thomas, 266, 268n250
Collins, William, 268, 271, 273
Commonwealth, 238, 239n135, 243n149, 267n250
communion controversies:
  17th century, 4–5, 8n16, 9, 10n21, 12, 16, 21–22, 39n130, 40–41, 76nn20–21, 78n25, 80–81, 89–90, 98–99, 126–27, 140, 142–205, 207, 210, 227, 230, 234n115, 249–64, 292–95
  18th century, 26–28
  19th century, 28–34
  20th century, 34
  21st century, 34–39
Congregationalist [Congregationalism], 5, 9n21, 10–13, 17n43, 21n59, 24, 42, 61, 65–67, 111n143, 112, 144, 146n16, 206, 210–11, 214n41, 222, 226–27, 237, 246, 264, 267–68, 270, 272n268, 280n2, 291–92, 296–99. *See also* Dissenter, Independent, Nonconformist, *and* Separatist
controlling ecclesiological principle:
  ecclesiological purity vs. ecclesiastical liberty, 271, 273, 277
  ecclesiological purity vs. ecclesiastical unity, 86–88, 91–93, 98, 145–47, 218
  evangelical unity vs. ecclesiological purity, 5, 19–21, 26, 88–91, 140, 144, 202–4, 213, 218, 230, 237–38, 242, 254, 256, 259, 262, 264, 270, 273–78, 290, 294, 298–99
Conventical Act (1664), 267n250. *See also* Act of Uniformity (1662), Clarendon Code (1661–65)
Cooper, Sister(s), 61n75, 72n3, 97n88, 104n115, 137n265
Cooper, Thomas, 67n101
Cotton End Church, Bedfordshire, 110
Coventon, Edward, 72n4, 79n27, 104n114, 137n265
Coventon, Joane, 62n77
Cox, Francis, 30
Coxe, Benjamin, 24n69, 60, 68, 219–22, 239–42
Coxe, Nehemiah, 20n50, 67n101, 68, 137n265, 268, 271–73
Cranfield Church, Bedfordshire, 112n147
Creake, Sister, 104n115
Croker, John, 135
Crompe, Roger, 97n88, 143
Cromwell, Oliver, 2, 63n82
Crutched Fryers Church, London, 232
Cumberland, Martha, 11, 66–67, 205–6

Dagg, John L., 33–34
Danvers, Henry, 28n87, 34, 77n21, 80, 160n80, 175–77, 179, 181, 189n225, 190–91, 200, 227, 242, 261
Deane, Richard, 135–37
Declaration of Breda (1660), 75
Declaration of Faith of English People Remaining at Amsterdam in Holland (1611), 229–30
Declaration of Indulgence (1672), 10–11, 67–68, 112n147, 142, 227, 267n250, 291, 296
Dell, William, 60
Denne, Henry, 113n151, 171, 227
Denne, John, 28n87, 34, 146n18, 160, 171–75, 177, 181, 183n192, 189n225, 190–91, 193–94, 198nn255–56, 199n262, 200, 203, 227, 242, 261
Dent, Arthur, 48, 52, 283
Dent, Edward, 137n265

326

Subject Index

Desiring God, 35, 36n117
Devonshire Square Church, London, 20–21, 151, 160n80, 224, 227
Dicks, Oliver, 137n265
Directory of Public Worship (1644), 49
Dissenter [Dissent], xi, 14, 17, 57n53, 85n53, 86–87, 91, 108, 144, 146, 171n133, 181, 183, 203, 224, 267n250, 272n268, 286n22, 299n52. *See also* Nonconformist, Independent, *and* Separatist
Dod, John, 283
Donne, John, 67n101, 108
Dyke, Daniel, 160n80

Eaton, Samuel, xi, 231–32, 238
Edwards, Jonathan, 286–89
Edworth Church, Bedfordshire, 110, 112n147
Elizabethan Settlement (1558/59), 281
Elstow Parish Church, Bedfordshire 44, 48–50
English Revolution/Civil Wars, 23, 45–47
Episcopalian [Episcopalianism], 10n22, 60, 104, 113, 120n185, 159n77, 169n126, 240, 260. *See also* Anglican *and* Church of England
Erbery, William, 46n15
Eston, John, 59, 62n77
Evangelical [Evangelicalism], 35–36, 38n124, 41–42, 280n2, 284–91, 296–99
Evangelical ["Great"] Awakening, 120, 288n33, 296–97
"Evangelical Independent," 5, 40, 42, 296–99
Ewins, Thomas, 225

Fairfax, Thomas, 47
Faith and Practice of Thirty Congregations (1651), 243–44
Featley, Daniel, 240
Fenne, John, 67n101, 72n4, 109, 119, 136
Fenne, Samuel, 67n101, 109n135, 135, 137
Fenne, Sister, 62n77
Fifth Monarchist, 222

Fisher, Samuel, 249
Ford, Thomas, 46, 52
form of the church:
    baptism, 15–16, 19n49, 20–23, 39n130, 164n100, 179, 188n220, 190–92, 213, 216, 220, 228–30, 238, 248–50, 252–53, 257, 259, 262–65, 278, 292
    baptism as covenant, 23, 37–38, 195n246, 263n234
    covenant, 23, 40n130, 62–65, 70, 77–79, 86, 95, 98, 104, 139, 189–90, 228, 234, 236, 265, 298n50
Fosket, Mary, 137n265
Fowler, Edward, 87–88, 142nn5–6
Fownes, George, 225
Fox, George, 39n129
Foxe, John, 149n32, 283
Foxe, Sister, 67n100, 103n108
Fryer, Sister, 67n100
Fuller, Andrew, 28, 30, 31n99, 286n21, 287–88

Gainsborough Church, Lincolnshire, 228
Gamlingay Church, Cambridgeshire, 68–69, 109–12
Gammon, John, 209, 272, 273n269
General Baptist defense of strict communion, 171–77, 228–31, 242–64
Gibbs, John, 46n15, 108, 109n135, 113n151
Gifford, John, 12, 44, 48, 55–58, 60–65, 70, 89–90, 99, 108, 115, 119, 124n206, 126n214, 144
Gillespie, Thomas, 287n30
Goldington Church, Bedfordshire, 112n147
Goodwin, John, 158n76, 243, 249–50, 252–54, 255n196, 257, 259nn218–20, 260–61
Gospel Coalition, 36n117
Grantham, Thomas, 243, 245, 262–63
Green, John, 232
Grew, John, 59, 61n77, 104n114, 108–9
Grew, Martha, 61n77, 66, 67n100
Griffith, George, 11, 66, 296

327

Subject Index

Griffith, John, 244
Grudem, Wayne, 35, 39n128

Hall, Christopher, 49
Hall, Robert, 28–33
Haynes church, 110–11, 112n147
Harper, Friend, 97n89
Harrington, Anthony, 59, 61, 62n77, 97, 103n108, 108–9
Harrington, Sister, 62n77
Harris, John, 268n255
Harrison, Edward, 272
Hauthorn, Sister, 137n265
Hayes, William, 63n82
Helwys, Thomas, 18, 22–23, 228–31
Hensman, Samuel, 67n100, 206
Hobson, Paul, 46n15, 47
Hocrafft, Samuel, 67n100
Hodell, Sister, 97n88
Hollister, Sister, 276n278
Honour, Sister, 79n27
Howell, Robert Boyte C., 31–34
Hustwhat, Katharine, 67n100, 103n108
Hyper-Calvinism, 16, 28, 268n250

Independent [Independency], xi, 5, 9nn20–21, 10n22, 12, 13n31, 14, 19, 20n50, 20n55, 24n69, 40, 42, 44, 67–68, 70, 81, 88, 89n62, 90, 138, 159n77, 169, 176n159, 178–80, 209, 211, 213, 222n69, 225n84, 235–36, 237n127, 238–39, 240n138, 243, 249, 261, 268n250, 279, 296–99. *See also* Congregationalist, Dissenter, Nonconformist, *and* Separatist
"Independent Baptist," 14, 298n50
Interregnum, 23–24, 44
Ivimey, Joseph, 30, 83n47, 271n261, 285n19

Jacob, Henry, 211, 238–39
James II, 189
Jamieson, Bobby, 36n117, 37–39, 195n246
Jeffery, William, 245

Jessey, Henry, xi, 10n22, 15, 18, 20–22, 39n129, 66, 78n25, 169–71, 189n225, 196n249, 197, 205, 210n29, 211–16, 218–19, 221–22, 225–26, 231, 232n107, 235, 238–40, 250n178, 265, 274, 275n276, 277, 297, 298n50
JLJ Church, London, 18, 22, 78n25, 169n128, 211, 216n48, 230–32, 234–35, 237n127, 238–39, 275n276, 298n50. *See also* Southwark Church, London
Johnson, Francis, 228

Keach, Benjamin, 19n48, 264–65, 268n255, 275
Keeling, John, 122
Kempston Church, Bedfordshire, 110, 112n147
Kettering Church, Northamptonshire, 28n87
Keysoe Church, Bedfordshire, 112n147
Kiffin, William, xi, 4, 24n69, 25, 27, 28n87, 30, 34, 81n35, 117, 151, 160n80, 171n133, 177, 181–88, 189n225, 190n227, 191–92, 194, 195n246, 196–97, 198nn255–56, 199, 201n273, 203nn282–83, 204n285, 219–20, 222, 224, 227, 232, 235, 238, 240, 242, 264–65, 268n255, 275, 292–93
Kilcop, Thomas, 232
Kinghorn, Joseph, 28, 30
Knollys, Hanserd, xi, 15n39, 24n69, 81n35, 192n235, 219–22, 234–37, 239–40, 264, 265, 268n255, 275

Lambe, Isaac, 249n173
Lambe, Thomas, 158n76, 177, 249, 257–62
Lambe, Thomas [The "Soapboiler"], 18n47, 231n103, 249n173
Lathrop, John, 211, 238–39
Laud, William, 18n47, 49n25, 59–60
Laying on of hands, 19n48, 64, 76n21, 89, 265

Subject Index

Latitudinarianism, 28, 87–88, 298n50
Limercy Church, Bedfordshire, 110
Linford, Sister, 143
Locke, John, 284
London Baptist Confession (1644/46), xi, 9n19, 25, 47, 60n68, 151n39, 159n79, 186n210, 205, 215–16, 220, 222, 226–27, 232–36, 237n127, 238–41, 244, 265, 267, 268n251, 269
London Baptist Confession (1677/89), xi, 16n39, 17–19, 26, 41, 146n16, 151n39, 186n210, 211, 225, 227, 249n173, 267–78, 280
Lothbury Church, London, 249
Lover, Thomas, 244, 245n157
Luke, Samuel, 46–47, 52
Luther, Martin, 56–58, 70

Man, Edward, 268n255
Man, William, 133n250
Marshall, Stephen, 216–17
Marshman, Hannah, 285n19
Mary II, 268, 270
Maulden church, 110, 111n143, 112n147
Maxey, Elizabeth, 137n265
Mead, Matthew, 67n100
Merrill, Humphrey, 97n88, 104n115, 112n145, 137n265
Merrill, Sister, 97n88, 104n115
Midland Confession (1655), 265–66
Millenarianism, 14
Monck, Thomas, 245–46
Munday, Thomas, 224
Munnes, Elizabeth, 62n77, 72n3
Murton, John, 18, 230–31

nature of the church (binary vs. ternary), 77–81, 86, 112, 179, 189–92, 201, 220–21
Nelson, Robert, 112n145, 137n265
New Model Army, 46–47
Newman, William, 30, 31n99
Newport Pagnell Church, Buckinghamshire, 112n147
Newton, Isaac, 284

Nonconformist [Nonconformity], xi, 4, 6n11, 11n24, 13–14, 24, 26, 40, 56, 59–60, 68, 70, 76, 83, 89, 91–92, 116, 141, 142n5, 145–47, 178–79, 201, 210, 215, 222, 249, 261, 267, 270, 277, 281n5, 289, 296, 298. *See also* Dissenter, Independent, *and* Separatist
Northern Baptist Convention, 34
Norton, Sister, 62n77

O'Hara, Charles, 46n11
Oakley Church, Buckinghamshire, 112n147
Orthodox Creed (1678), 246–49
Owen, John, 4, 11, 66–67, 75n17, 178, 197, 206, 264, 283–84, 296, 298

Palmer, Anthony, 11, 66–67, 206, 225n84, 296
Parliamentary Army, 43n2, 45–47
Particular Baptists defense of strict communion, 26–28, 30–34, 37–38, 151–58, 181–89, 231–42, 264–77, 292–94
Patient, Thomas, 219–20, 222
Paul, Thomas, 9, 27, 28n87, 30, 34, 79n29, 80, 150n36, 151–69, 171–82, 189n225, 190–94, 198–200, 201n273, 203–4, 227, 242, 264
Pelagianism, 25, 247n169
Perkins, William, 284
Petty France Church, London, 68, 268, 271–73
Piper, John, 34–36, 39, 166n108
Pithay Church, Bristol 224, 225n82
Plymouth Church, Devon, 275–76
Pope [Popish], 49n25, 123n197, 183, 197, 248n171, 260–61, 281n5. *See also* Roman Catholic
Powell, Vavasor, 211, 222–24, 226, 278, 297
Prelate, 59, 90, 123n197, 261. *See also* Anglican, Church of England, *and* Episcopalian

Subject Index

Presbyterian [Presbyterianism], 9n20, 10n22, 12, 13n31, 46, 52, 60, 69, 81, 88, 89n62, 90, 104, 159n77, 169, 178, 180, 209, 227, 235–36, 237n127, 240, 246, 260–61, 264, 267, 268n250, 270, 279, 290, 297–98
Price, John, 260–61
Protectorate, 238, 239n135
Puritan [Puritanism], 3, 18, 23, 41, 47–49, 52, 57n53, 59, 61, 69–70, 85n53, 195n246, 235, 280–84, 285n18, 286, 291
Purnell, Robert, 225

Quaker [Quakerism], 8, 17n43, 39n129, 56, 69, 90, 142n5, 173n143, 200, 227, 244, 264, 268n250, 290, 295

Radwell, Martha, 137n265
Ranter, 8, 17n43, 51n32, 56, 69, 290, 295
Reformed orthodoxy, 8n15, 281, 284, 296–97
Reformed tradition, 285n18, 288
Reid, Thomas, 284
Remonstrants 247n169
Restoration (1660), 4, 9n21, 21n59, 22, 24, 75, 141, 233, 245
Richardson, Samuel, 240
Robinson, John, 228–29
Robinson, Robert, 26–28
Rockefeller, John D., 34n110
Roman Catholic, 22n64, 123n197, 189, 247, 274, 281n5. *See also* Pope [Popish]
royalist, 60–61, 75
Royalist Army, 45
Rush, Elizabeth, 72n3
Ryland, John, 288
Ryland, John Collett, 26–28

Sabbatarian Baptists, 127–29
Savoy Declaration (1658), 146n16, 221n66, 222, 246, 267n250, 268, 275n273, 296
Scrooby Manor Church, Nottinghamshire, 228

Self-Denying Ordinance (1645), 46
Semi-Separatism, 59, 60n68, 61, 211, 230, 232n107, 238
Separatist [Separatism], xi, 18, 22–23, 59, 62, 78n26, 86–88, 91–92, 146–47, 195n246, 211, 213, 218n57, 228, 230, 231nn105–6, 232, 235, 240n138, 267, 277, 281n4, 282, 299. *See also* Dissenter, Independent, *and* Nonconformist
Sewster, Mr., 133n250
Simpson, John, 67n100, 239
Skelton, Brother, 97n89
Smith, Francis, 170n129
Smith, Thomas, 113n151, 120n185, 171
Smyth, John, 211, 228–30
Solemn League and Covenant (1643), 46
Somerset Confession (1656), 266–67
Southern Baptist Convention, 34
Southwark Church, London, 10n22, 66–67, 169n128, 205–6, 214, 226, 275n276, 277–78, 298n50. *See also* JLJ Church, London
Spencer, John, 232
Spencer, Sister, 62n77
Spensely, Richard, 72n4
Spilsbury, John, 78n25, 219–20, 222, 231–32
Spitalfields Church, London, 230
Spurgeon, Charles, xi–xiii, 285n19
St. John's Parish Church, Bedford, 63nn82–83, 75
Stagsden Church, Bedfordshire 112n147
Standard Confession (1660), 245–46
Stanton, John, 137n265
Sternhold and Hopkins, 125
Stevington Church, Bedfordshire, 112n147, 275–76
Strudwick, John, 210
Strong, Augustus H., 34n110
Sutcliffe, John, 288

Taylor, Richard, 68
Terrill, Edward, 224n75, 225
Thirty-Nine Articles (1662), 17, 146
Tilney, Sister, 65–66
Toft Church, Cambridgeshire, 112n147

Subject Index

Tombes, John, 15–16, 20, 22, 210n29, 211, 215–22, 226, 235, 239, 277, 297
True Gospel Faith (1654), 244–45
Tull, Mr. [Samuel?], 273n269
Turner, Daniel, 26–28

Vaux, Thomas, 225, 275, 276n276

Waite, Brother, 137
Waller, Mrs., 97
Wallis, Robert, 72n4, 104n114
Warner, Sister, 137n265
Waterlander Mennonite Church, Amsterdam, 229
Wells, Sister, 97n89
Westminster Assembly, 46, 60, 69, 146n16, 241, 247n168
Westminster Confession of Faith (1646), 146n16, 246, 247n168, 267n250, 268, 273n269, 275n273

Wesley, Charles, 290
Wesley, John, 283n10, 287, 290
Wheeler, William, 108, 109n135
Wildeman, John, 137n265
Whitebread, William, 109, 113n149, 137n265
Whitefield, George, 283n10, 287, 290
Whiteman, John, 104n114, 108–9, 136
Wilkins, John, 170n129
William III, 17, 268, 270, 277n279
Wilson, John, 103n108
Wingate, Francis, 75
Wills, Obadiah, 227
Witt, Sister, 97n88, 137n265
Wollaston Church, Northamptonshire, 108, 111n143
Wright, John, 67n101

Yorke, Elizabeth, 72n3

www.ingramcontent.com/pod-product-compliance
Lightning Source LLC
Chambersburg PA
CBHW070013010526
44117CB00011B/1541